Civic Engagement

Civic Engagement

Social Science and Progressive-Era Reform in New York City

JOHN LOUIS RECCHIUTI

PENN

University of Pennsylvania Press

Philadelphia

10   9   8   7   6   5   4   3   2   1

Published by
University of Pennsylvania Press
Philadelphia, Pennsylvania 19104-4112

Library of Congress Cataloging-in-Publication Data

Recchiuti, John Louis.
   Civic engagement : social science and progressive-era reform in New York City /
John Louis Recchiuti.
      p.   cm.
   ISBN-13: 978-0-8122-3957-7 (alk. paper)
   ISBN-11: 0-8122-3957-1 (alk. paper)
   Includes bibliographical references and index.
      1. Social problems—New York (State)—New York—History.   2. Social scientists in
government—New York (State)—New York—History.   3. Progressivism (United States
politics)—History—Case studies.   I. Title.
HN80.N5 R43   2006
303.48′409747109041—dc22   2006042156

For Amy, Jack, and Elizabeth

Contents

Illustrations

. . . this is the hour for experiment; and New York is the place, because it is the greatest social science laboratory in the world.

—Proposal for an Independent School of Social Science for Men and Women, 1918

The city is the natural laboratory of Social Science

—"Report on a Department of Social Science at Columbia College," 1894

Our modern cities are so many great laboratories for the social scientist

—William Howe Tolman, The City Vigilant, *1894*

New York presents the greatest laboratory in the Western hemisphere. . . . There is not a condition or problem of modern social life which is not represented here.

—Charles A. Beard, "New York City as a Political Science Laboratory," 1914

. . . a teeming Sociological Laboratory

—Samuel McCune Lindsay, "New York as a Sociological Laboratory," 1914

. . . for more grounding in the social sciences, I found my way into the great social laboratory of New York City.

—George Edmund Haynes, memoir, 1960

Introduction
"The Greatest Social Science Laboratory in the World"

This is a book about a small group of men and women who, captivated by the possibilities of a science of the social, built an expansive network of reform organizations in Progressive Era New York City and by their efforts changed a city, and beyond it a generation, and, to a considerable extent, a nation as well. In the late nineteenth and early twentieth centuries, New York City, the nation's leading metropolis, fed by streams of thought from Europe and America, became a hub—a vibrant, innovative center—of social science ideas and organization, an incubator for social science and progressive reform. Social science scholar-activists headed reform associations, bureaus, committees, and leagues; founded settlement houses; took on the challenge of scientific racism; launched urban and industrial surveys along with class uplift projects, child labor advocacy efforts, and good-government municipal commissions; battled for legislative change at local, state, and federal levels; and, in a flurry of activism, helped found a political party—the Progressive Party of 1912—to advance their reform views.

Most, though not all, of the men and women in these pages held advanced degrees in the social sciences, but all were passionate in their research and political advocacy. Nor did they always agree. Moderates favored middle-way reform, radicals fundamental (often socialistic) restructuring. Yet moderate and radical alike often worked in concert, through common organizations they had cooperated to build. The reform coalition in which they played a pivotal part—a coalition that included labor leaders, social gospelers, middle-class reformers, and women's reform organizations—captured the name *political progressive* for itself, and they and their allies meant by it a brand of politics that sought an expanded use of government.

The government social science scholar-activists sought was activist government, one that, through its laws, would shield the weak from exploitation by the strong, regulate the nation's new industrial economy, and advance racial equality. They saw the governed and the governors, guided or led by social scientists like themselves, as forging solutions to the issues of the day. They shared the view that the state need not restrict its agency to mere laissez faire rule-setting to ensure competitive markets. Unlike conservative social scientists, they believed that government might properly become a powerful regulatory force and a public service provider for the American people. The men and women of the social science network were not the primary holders of power, none financial barons or generals or industrial giants or elected officials, but through their research and public advocacy they shaped the decisions and actions of the powerful and not-so-powerful. High-brow and middle-brow intellects (intellectuals and intelligentsia), they were, in a common parlance, public intellectuals, civically engaged. Initially activists and advocates working inside the private centers of power in universities, settlement houses, and private agencies, over time they increasingly moved into policy-making positions of public power employed for humanitarian ends, even seeking to affect elections.

Modern American social science began with the opening of the nation's first social science graduate programs in the final quarter of the nineteenth century. In those first graduate schools of New York City, Chicago, Cambridge, and elsewhere, scholars with competing visions of the public weal and the ideal social order fought over high-stakes issues that they helped frame. Outside the academy, they sometimes found themselves at odds with others—politicians, capitalists, labor leaders, and directors of private foundations among them. But, with established institutions unwilling to take up controversial political or social issues, they launched associations, bureaus, and settlement houses of reform and contributed to the making or remaking of others, including universities and modern philanthropic foundations. Within a generation, social science, especially politically progressive social science, was a thriving force in policy-making and in the shaping of culture in the city and the nation. Social scientists, like the priestly, ministerial, and rabbinical class before them, used their beliefs as instruments for scholarship and action, as well as for their own social, cultural, and political empowerment.

Science occupied a central place in the culture in the late nineteenth and early twentieth centuries, but in the celebration of science was an undercurrent of uncertainty about just what science is. Science does not ground belief in an embrace of ages-old traditions or wish-fulfillments; it is skeptical and grounded in observation and evidence. In New York there was an uncommon excitement about the possibilities of a social science, a social science by which thoughtful men and women might master their world. Columbia sociologist Franklin Giddings wrote: "We need men not afraid to work; who will get busy with the adding machine and logarithms, and give us *exact studies,* such as we get from the psychological laboratories, not to speak of the biological and physical laboratories. Sociology can be made an exact quantitative science." Henry Rawie, an independent political economist, said: "If political economy is ever to discover its laws, it must find them in the relation the facts sustain to their cause, and it will find that such laws must be laws of force identical with the laws now made clear in the physical world." Rawie continued: "There is one royal road in science, and only one, the road leading from cause to effect." As social economist Edward Thomas Devine wrote in 1896: "The future of economic science in American universities is bright with promise of scholarly and useful work." "The attitude of the university world and of the public toward what is after all a new science, is all that could be desired." Envisioning themselves as scientists of human affairs, social scientists established social and economic "laboratories," practiced quantitative statistical analyses, and offered prescriptions for change.[1]

"The city is the natural laboratory of Social Science," declared an 1894 "Report on a Department of Social Science at Columbia College." The 1918 founders of the New School for Social Research—political scientist and historian Charles Beard a principal figure among them—in their *Proposal for an Independent School of Social Science for Men and Women* heralded New York City as "the greatest social science laboratory in the world."[2]

New York City was the national capital of finance, industry, shipping and trade, publishing, the arts, and immigration, a magnet that drew to it much of the best and most avant-garde in art and literature, and also a magnet for reform. With a population of 3,437,202 in 1900, by 1910 New York's population of 4,766,883 was more than twice that of Chicago, the nation's second-ranked city, three times as large as third-ranked Philadelphia, and six to nine times as large as St. Louis, Boston, Baltimore, and Cleveland, all cities that would contribute to Progressive Era American social science.[3] It was in New York City that the majority of the nation's principal organizations of reform on the most decisive and divisive issues in an industrializing economy were headquartered in the great era of social reform: the nation's leading organization to help the impoverished unemployed poor, the Charity Organization Society; America's first social settlement houses, University Settlement and College Settlement; the three premier organizations for legislation for workers' rights and social insurance, the National Consumers' League, the National Child Labor Committee, and the American Association for Labor Legislation; the most active group of inquiry into corrupt practices of government, the Bureau of Municipal Research; the new national organizations for civil rights for American blacks, the NAACP and the National Urban League. Social science scholar-activists were central in creating and leading each of these organizations. In the National Consumers' League, the Bureau of Municipal Research, and the American Association for Labor Legislation, they played *the* principal roles.

At the academic center of New York's dynamic social science activist network was Columbia University, the fifth oldest institution of higher education in the U.S., by 1910 the largest university in the country, and by the autumn of 1914, the *New York Times* reported, the largest university in the world.[4] Columbia's School of Political Science, founded in 1880 as the city's first social science graduate program, was one of the earliest, biggest, and most influential social science graduate programs in the U.S. In the four decades from 1880 to 1920 social science programs opened also at New York University, the College of the City of New York, the New York School of Philanthropy, the Rand School for Social Science, and the New School for Social Research. The academy was a central redoubt for professional social scientists, a training ground for the next generation of social scientists, and a battlefield for contested ideas (when the academy set limits on dissent, beyond which social scientists would venture at their peril).

The network of remarkable individuals were drawn to New York from across the country, many from the Midwest, a number from New England, a few from Europe. Among the leaders was Mary Kingsbury Simkhovitch who, after studying sociology and economics in graduate school at Radcliffe, the University of Berlin, and Columbia University (she became an adjunct lecturer in Barnard College's department of sociology), founded and led the Greenwich House social settlement. Florence Kelley, after helping found a social science club as an undergraduate at Cornell and undertaking graduate study at the University of Zurich and a law degree from Northwestern University, served as general secretary of the National Consumers' League. Frances Perkins, who studied economics and sociology in graduate programs at the University of Pennsylvania and at Columbia University, was executive secretary of the New York Consumers' League and later the first woman head of the U.S. Department of Labor. Edward T. Devine, Columbia professor of social economy, was executive secretary of the New York Charity Organization Society. Samuel McCune Lindsay, Columbia sociologist and professor of social legislation, was head of the National Child Labor Committee and the New York School of Philanthropy, secretary of the New York Bureau of Municipal Research, and an important figure in the

American Association for Labor Legislation. The Columbia economist Henry Rogers Seager, John B. Andrews (economics Ph.D., University of Wisconsin), Irene Osgood Andrews (graduate studies in political economy, University of Wisconsin), Crystal Eastman (masters degree in sociology, Columbia University; law degree, NYU), and Isaac M. Rubinow (economics Ph.D., Columbia; medical degree, NYU) were leading figures in the American Association for Labor Legislation. Columbia professors of political science Frank J. Goodnow and Charles Beard, and the directors of the New York Bureau of Municipal Research, NYU economist Frederick Cleveland, William Allen (political science Ph.D., University of Pennsylvania), and Henry Bruère (educated at University of Chicago and Harvard Law School), challenged the municipal corruption of Tammany Hall. Black intellectuals W. E. B. Du Bois (history Ph.D., Harvard University) and George Edmund Haynes (sociology master's, Yale; social economy Ph.D., Columbia) and white social scientists Franz Boas (anthropology), Edwin R. A. Seligman (economics), Francis A. Kellor (sociology), Henry Moskowitz (graduate study in economics at Columbia; doctorate, Erlangen, Germany), and Mary White Ovington (economic studies at the Harvard Annex) championed the fight for civil rights and against bigotry. At a time in American history when fewer than 3 percent of eighteen- to twenty-four-year olds went to college or university (in 1909–10 fewer than 9 percent of seventeen-year-olds were high school graduates) the men and women of the New York social science scholar-activist network were members of a comparatively small, elite, educated, American intellectual class.[5]

These were men and women of remarkable range and diversity of background. Kelley, general secretary of the National Consumers' League and a socialist, followed her father's penchant for politics and for action—he had been a radical Republican during the Civil War. Seligman, the patrician Columbia economist, was born and bred in New York City in one of the richest families in America but his father, a self-made millionaire, was a Jewish immigrant from Bavaria. Du Bois, the dazzling social scientist, social critic, and founding editor of the NAACP's periodical *The Crisis*, was an orphan from small-town western Massachusetts born into a family of free African Americans; his father, a barber and laborer, abandoned the family before he was two, and his mother, a domestic worker, died when he was sixteen. Frances Kellor, who took up leadership posts in the cause of poor black women and became a leading light of the 1912 Progressive party, came from an impoverished childhood in small-town Michigan to attend Cornell Law School and the University of Chicago's graduate program in sociology. The anthropologist Franz Boas, who demolished the illogic of racism, was an immigrant to America from Germany. Charles Beard, the famed

Columbia political scientist and historian, had grown up in rural Indiana. The social economist George Edmund Haynes, a founder of the National Urban League and Columbia's first African American Ph.D., was the son of a laborer and a domestic worker from southern Arkansas. Mary Kingsbury Simkhovitch, head of Greenwich House settlement, came from a middle-class intellectual New England home. Frances Perkins, who worked for Florence Kelley's National Consumers' League and later became the first woman in American history to serve in a presidential cabinet, was born into a middle-class family in Boston.

They wrote letters of encouragement and support to one another and served as trustees, presidents, vice presidents, and committee members in each other's associations, bureaus, committees, and leagues. When George Edmund Haynes, as a graduate student at Columbia, set out to found the National Urban League in 1910—initially called the Committee on Urban Conditions among Negroes—he drew support from the social science network in New York. The sociologist Frances Kellor agreed to merge the National League for the Protection of Colored Women, which she had founded, into the new Urban League, and Haynes tapped Edwin R. A. Seligman, one of his Columbia professors, to become the organization's first president. Haynes was also a member of the American Association for Labor Legislation, a supporter of the New York School of Philanthropy, a writer for Edward T. Devine's and Paul U. Kellogg's *The Survey*, and, as Professor of Social Science at Fisk University, an important figure in the histories of American social science, African American educational history, and social work.

The symbolic hub of the social science reform network in Manhattan was the United Charities Building at 105 East 22nd Street at Fourth Avenue (now Park Avenue South), a seven-story Renaissance Revival structure that Kathryn Kish Sklar calls "the single most important center of reform activity during the Progressive Era."[6] The wide round arch of its main entrance led to a large ground-floor assembly hall, locus of many public forums. Upper floors housed many of the city's reform organizations: the offices of the New York Charities Organization Society, the National Consumers' League, the National Child Labor Committee, the Association for Improving Conditions among the Poor, the editorial offices of the applied social science and reform magazine *Charities* (later *The Survey*), and offices for some of the Russell Sage Foundation's staff, among others. The New York School of Philanthropy conducted its first classes in the Charities Building. Early meetings of the American Association for Labor Legislation were held there; so was the two-day conference in 1909 which led to the formation of the NAACP. A dialogue among leaders of organizations with offices in the Charities Building—

particularly conversations between Florence Kelley and Edward T. Devine—led to President Theodore Roosevelt's call for the 1909 White House conference on children that led, in turn, in 1912, to establishment of the U.S. Children's Bureau.

Perkins, later a leading figure in the creation of the Social Security Act of 1935 and the Fair Labor Standards Act of 1938, said of the Charities Building: "You could hardly fail to become acquainted. Somebody introduced you to somebody in the elevator, said who you were, and so you became acquainted with the AICP people—the Association for Improving Conditions Among the Poor—the COS people—Charity Organization people—and the tenement house reform group. You knew everybody else that was operating. It was a small and sort of integrated professional world as there weren't so many of them. Mutual help and fairness prevailed and I remember it to this day."[7]

After a Charity Organization Society subscription drive in 1890, the first five stories of the Charities Building (two more were added later) were erected. John Stewart Kennedy, a banker and businessman, paid the entire cost of the site and the building. One of New York's great but forgotten philanthropists, Kennedy was an anti-Tammany good-government reform Democrat, a Scottish Presbyterian who devoted himself to good works. He served as vice president of the New York Charity Organization Society, as a member of the boards of the Presbyterian Hospital for the New York poor and the Metropolitan Museum of Art, was a benefactor of the New York Public Library (a bust of Kennedy is ensconced in a niche in the library's grand entrance), and Columbia trustee from 1903 to his death in 1909. He gave $500,000 to build Columbia's Hamilton Hall, and left a bequest of $2.5 million, Columbia's largest gift until that time.[8]

Social scientists met at a number of cultural crossroads in Manhattan, not only at the United Charities Building, but also on Columbia University's campus, in the offices of the Bureau of Municipal Research near City Hall, at the socialist Rand School for Social Science (a brownstone at 112 East 19th Street), and at the city's principal settlement houses, including Greenwich House (two blocks west of Washington Square Park), and at the University, College, and Henry Street settlements on Manhattan's Lower East Side, where women—forbidden full-time academic posts in the universities—created a kind of real-life campus of their own.

A cultural crossroads, organized in 1903 for men only, was the New York X Club at which social scientists and others met to eat and talk: "The New York X," Charles Beard called it, a dinner discussion club for "a group of men interested in social questions." Its name had been appropriated from a famous scientific dining club in Victorian London whose members included the Social Darwinist Herbert Spencer, the botanist Joseph Dalton Hooker (close friend of Charles Darwin), the physicist John Tyndall, and the botanist Thomas Henry Huxley. Some members of the London X Club were political conservatives, but those in "the New York X" were on the liberal left. In inviting one young scholar to a club meeting, W. J. Ghent, the club's founder, a socialist and author of a number of books of social analysis, wrote: "Everything is informal—dress, speech and manners. It is a round-table sort of thing." Meetings were held every few weeks, sometimes at Maria's, an Italian restaurant at 133 West 41st Street, sometimes farther downtown at the Aldine Club at 111 Fifth Avenue. Notified of meetings by casual post cards, members dined equally informally, "sparingly and expeditiously," said Morris Hillquit, the nation's leading socialist lawyer and an X Club member. They listened to speakers on "politics, science, religion, literature, and art," most often a club member, but occasionally an outsider (one in 1906 was the author H. G. Wells). "Each member, in the order seated around a long table, would make his contribution to the discussion." "Nobody was excused," Hillquit wrote, "Nobody wanted to be excused." The club "had no program and no object except to unite a group of chosen spirits for periodical talk-fests."[9]

Of the no more than forty members, social scientists, lawyers, journalists, publishers, and writers, no list appears to have survived, but among its social science members were three from Columbia University: Charles Beard, Edward Devine, and sociologist Franklin Giddings; the economist John B. Andrews, executive secretary of the American Association for Labor Legislation; and William H. Allen and Henry Bruère, directors of the New York Bureau of Municipal Research. Among the club's "literary members" were journalists Ray Stannard Baker, Lincoln Steffens, Upton Sinclair, and Charles Edward Russell, muckrakers all; Norman Hapgood, editor of *Collier's Weekly*; Hamilton Holt, managing editor of the *Independent: A Weekly Magazine*; the radical novelist Jack London; and the journalist William English Walling. In 1909 and 1910 Baker, Walling, Russell, and Steffens were among those who signed the Call that led to the founding of the NAACP. In his autobiography, Hillquit called some X Club members "just Socialists," and included among them W. J. Ghent, the club's founder; Robert W. Bruère, brother of Henry Bruère; Edmond Kelly, a sometime lecturer at Columbia and a civic reformer; Algernon Lee, founder—along with Beard, Ghent, and Hillquit—of the Rand School of Social Science; William Noyes, a chemist; and the wealthy reformer J. G. Phelps-Stokes. The New York X Club's one-hundredth meeting was held in 1911; in 1917, with members split bitterly over America's entry into the First World War, "a sort of personal hostility . . . caused people to shun one another," and the club broke apart, though it was revived, for a time, in the mid-1920s.[10]

Women and blacks were leaders in the progressive social science net-work in New York, but they had to make their way past obstacles. Cultural views on women's proper, submissive, place and on acceptable subordinate roles for African Americans, kept them from positions of leadership throughout much of the rest of America, but in New York City as social scientists they had opportunities available, though even here there were sharp limits on opportunity. Female social scientists were virtually shut out of full-time faculty appointments and other male precincts on campuses in New York as elsewhere, altogether from the X Club, and in some instances, even relegated to the sidelines in organizations they themselves had created or helped create. Excluded also from leadership posts in the nation's corporate boardrooms, pulpits, and offices of government, women social scientists found a path to power in social-science-grounded, issue-oriented groups of their own making. In the "voluntary group action," as Mary Kingsbury Simkhovitch called it, of organizations like the National Consumers' League, the settlement houses, the NAACP, as well as at the New York School of Philanthropy and elsewhere, women circumvented traditional male leadership. Women in academe held positions of power in the "seven sisters" colleges in New York (Barnard and Vassar), Pennsylvania (Bryn Mawr), and Massachusetts (Radcliffe, Smith, Wellesley, and Mount Holyoke) and, sometimes through domestic economics or hygiene programs, at research universities like the University of Chicago and Berkeley. Many had studied in the same graduate programs in the U.S. and in Europe as men, but instead of receiving full-time appointments they were exploited in part-time or adjunct posts in colleges and universities with low pay and little or no job security. (Between 1870 and 1900 women attending U.S. colleges and universities increased from a fifth to a third of all college students. By 1909–10, of the fewer than 3 percent of eighteen- to twenty-four-year olds enrolled in institutions of higher education, 141,000 were women and 215,000 were men—but with 28,762 degrees conferred upon men, 8,437 upon women.)[11]

Florence Kelley, who retained control of the National Consumers' League, made the League a stronghold for women. Women led at the College Settlement, at Greenwich House and at the Henry Street settlement. Mary White Ovington was a pivotal figure in the formation of the NAACP. Yet to give the impression that women worked apart from men, even in these organizations, would be misleading. Kelley's Consumers' League, a redoubt for women leaders, Pauline and Josephine Goldmark and Frances Perkins among them, enlisted men as well—in 1915 the

League's list of vice presidents included not only Mary E. Woolley, president of Mount Holyoke, but social scientists Lindsay and Seligman of Columbia, Jeremiah W. Jenks of New York University, Henry Carter Adams of the University of Michigan, Frank W. Taussig of Harvard, Richard T. Ely of the University of Wisconsin, and Arthur T. Hadley of Yale.

Mary Kingsbury Simkhovitch founded and ran Greenwich House settlement, and served on the executive board of her friend Florence Kelley's Consumers' League, but her settlement, too, was a place of leadership by men as well as women. Seligman was president of her settlement for several years. The philosopher John Dewey chaired its committee on education. Greenwich House's Committee on Social Studies included among its Progressive Era members Seligman, the anthropologist Franz Boas, the social economist Edward T. Devine, the political economist Henry Rogers Seager, the sociologist Franklin Giddings, and the economic historian Vladimir Simkhovitch (Mary Kingsbury Simkhovitch's husband)—all members of Columbia University's faculty.

The New York Research Council, too, was a point of intersection for both men and women of the social science network. Only three of the Council's thirteen members were not social scientists: John Mitchell (a labor leader), Felix Adler (founder of the Society for Ethical Culture), and Gaylord S. White (headworker of the Union Settlement). The other ten were among the brightest stars in the city's constellation of social science reform: Kelley, Kellor, Simkhovitch, Devine, John M. Glenn (executive director of the Russell Sage Foundation), Paul U. Kellogg (editor of *The Survey*), James B. Reynolds (previously headworker at the University Settlement), Seager, Seligman (the Council's chairman), and Lillian D. Wald (headworker at the Henry Street settlement). The Council sponsored publication of the 1911 *Civic Bibliography for Greater New York*, a "practical handbook" of civic reform compiled by graduates of the New York School of Philanthropy and Columbia's School of Political Science, published by The Russell Sage Foundation (itself founded in 1907 for social reform through social science research), and edited for the Council by Reynolds.[12]

A few African Americans—Du Bois and Haynes principal among them (Eugene Kinckle Jones, who worked with Haynes and held a master's degree in sociology from Cornell, was another)—overcame racial exclusion by their graduate study in universities and found in the social sciences in New York City a freedom from traditionalist strictures and a way to disseminate their new visions of race and society. In social science's focus on the authority of *science*, those who fought racism may have assumed that they had found an avenue for advancement, but traditional views on race, grounded in claims of the inferiority of blacks and in claims that the bible authorized slavery, tainted social science as well.

To put old prejudices to rout through science and social science would prove to be a massive and difficult undertaking. These male African American social scientists, like women, had to win space from those who sought to keep it from them—including many white male social scientists. African Americans found support in the New York network, as when, in an October 1905 issue of Edward T. Devine's *Charities*, articles of social science research and advocacy on race appeared by Boas, Du Bois, Kellor, Ovington, and others. At the same time, the professional chances for African Americans were sharply limited even in this community of opportunity. Du Bois and Haynes, both with doctorates, could find no academic appointments in Progressive Era New York City, only in the nation's historically black universities. Still, the social sciences proved to be a groundwork, if one bitterly contested, for great achievement and advance for women and blacks.

This story of social science is largely the story of the borough of Manhattan, for, even after the 1898 four-borough expansion of the city to include the Bronx, Queens, Brooklyn, and Staten Island, Manhattan remained the densest and busiest and most renowned and electric part of the city—by 1910, 2,331,000 people lived there. New York City, famous for remaking itself with every generation, was constantly in flux. There was, as H. G. Wells wrote in 1906, "a blindly furious energy of growth."[13]

At the turn of the twentieth century the United States was the richest nation in the world, and New York had evolved from its early seventeenth century beginnings as a Dutch harbor colony into an international center of finance, commerce, manufacture, and culture, competing on the world stage with London, Paris, and Berlin. But even as late as the 1870s the area around Central Park, now at the heart of Manhattan, was populated with wooden huts clustered "between blocks of imposing houses" (the Park was completed in 1876). The city's first mass transportation, steam-powered locomotives suspended above city streets (the "elevated" or "el") on lattices of iron and steel, pushed up Ninth, Sixth, Third, and then Second Avenue. The massive suspension Brooklyn Bridge was completed in 1883; the majestic Statue of Liberty, arrived from Paris, was installed in 1886; the Washington Arch at Washington Square Park went up in 1889 in celebration of the centenary of George Washington's New York presidential inauguration; Carnegie Hall opened in 1893. With new elevator technology, the city began to rise vertically as well: the 21-story steel-framed Flatiron Building of 1902 was eclipsed eleven years later by the 60-story Woolworth Building. Within several years of the 1882 opening of Edison's electrical generating station on Pearl Street, portions of the gas-lit city were bright with incandescent light. The first subway line opened in 1904 as automobiles vied for space on the streets with horse drawn buggies and carts.[14]

The City was ripe for the intervention of social science reformers. The Vanderbilts had transformed Fifth Avenue with French Renaissance architecture, and millionaires from the nation's railroad and steel industries—Henry Clay Frick, Henry Phipps, and Andrew Carnegie among them—had built palatial mansions along the Avenue, but, at the same time, multitudes elsewhere lived in squalor. The Lower East Side, by 1910 the most crowded neighborhood on earth, housed tens of thousands in ill-lighted, overcrowded tenements, many without running water, flush toilets, or electricity. New York, the world's largest port, was the point of entry for most of the nation's eighteen million immigrants in the quarter century before the First World War. New York City's 30,000 manufacturers employed over 600,000 employees, and ranked first in the nation's industrial output. By 1910, 87 percent of the 4,767,000 people in Greater New York were immigrants or the children of immigrants, and many of them were desperately poor.[15]

New York had no blanket-coverage local, state, or federal welfare programs, no systematized workmen's compensation, no workfare or welfare support for poor families with dependent children, no social security for the elderly or handicapped, no food stamps, only private charity and some municipal sponsored free coal for heat. (Federal veterans' pensions did supply aid for that fraction of the population who had served the Union army in the Civil War, but most of the city did not qualify.)[16] In the long tradition of private (most often religious) or county-sponsored relief (reminiscent of eighteenth-century English poor law practice), places of confinement, such as prisons, orphanages, asylums, and almshouses sheltered those in need and in distress.

But at the center of social scientists' reach toward leadership was an unresolved ambiguity in the meaning of social science itself, and of social science's relationship with democracy. Was social science to be herald of a reinvigorated democracy or an instrument of technocracy, or both? In this question lay a dual vision and an unresolved tension, the paradox of democratic elitism. What was the proper role of leadership for social science in a democracy? Were science and social science elitist enterprises of a privileged, educated community sharing a specialized and esoteric language? Were scientists qualified as experts to advise and lead where nonscientists could not? Did science know best? Ought scientists to be ceded a compelling authority in political policy decision-making and be permitted to wield a technocratic social control in the form of an autocracy? Or, alternatively, if science signifies an experimental method accessible to all, one that promotes undogmatic, open-ended, rational inquiry in which hypotheses and propositions can be evaluated by any observer who has access to the evidence, then science might prove to be a great democratizing force. Education need not belong only to the few.

This unresolved tension between science as elitist enterprise and science as democratizing force was a formative and unresolved paradox in the greatest social science laboratory. For science was understood both as a great leveling and equalizing force and, at the same time, as an elitist occupation of the learned. This ambivalence was reflected in the role of social scientists: were they to be intellectual paternalists wielding power or champions of democracy helping to wrest power from barons of wealth who were turning the country into an oligarchy? Indeed, Progressive Era social scientists' many references to the city as laboratory captures this unresolved tension and the ambiguity in social scientists' assumptions about progress, democracy, and science. In conceiving the city as social laboratory, social scientists offered their fellow citizens the view that the society in which they all lived, having been humanly made need not be viewed as fixed and immutable, but might be humanly remade; laboratories are places of experiment, and the densely populated city was a perfect place for research, tests, and trials. Viewing themselves as living in a great laboratory, citizens' imaginative and experimental energies might awaken to the possibilities of a democratic remaking of the social order and by their efforts fulfill the promise of American democracy. Yet the view of the city as laboratory for social experimentation might also mean that turn-of-the-twentieth-century activist intellectuals in the social sciences in New York might not only observe and analyze their city, but also diagnose, prescribe, and perhaps even seek to control the currents of its social, economic, and political future. Social scientists were inevitably a part of the society they sought to understand and improve; they were self-interested actors in the social laboratory of the city and might undo the very civic expectations they had raised and subvert the democratic aspirations of the public they believed they were serving. Their democratic aspirations conflicted with the contrary guiding principle of scientific expertise.

As Edmund S. Morgan has argued, the notion that the people are sovereign—the notion that "the people" direct policies of government through direct expressions of their voice and will—is the modern fiction that makes our Constitutional republic work.[17] Leadership remains central in American culture and politics, and American politics, locally and nationally, is a dialectical dance (and sometimes a fierce fight) between leadership elites, hemmed in, to be sure, by popular expressions of approval or discontent. The scholar-activists of New York frequently acted for the common people, but as their surrogate not chosen by them, and in accordance with their own beliefs about what was best for the common people. Bothered by the fear that their own expertise might be neglected by ill-educated voters, social scientists insisted that the people—or at least their elected representatives—must be educated. In this sense, the men and women of this community carried the scientific-secular, educated, and enlightened torch of the American intellectual elite, bearers of the flame of the eighteenth century Enlightenment. Some social scientists set out boldly to control the social policy agenda on one or another issue, holding fast to the view that they were not unlike medical doctors, alone qualified to prescribe cures which, though bitter, would result in a more healthy body politic.

The paradox of democratic elitism was expressed by James McKeen Cattell, the Columbia psychologist: "Political democracy does not mean government by the uninformed, but by those best able to serve the people. Representative and expert government is necessary." Edwin Seligman, in his moments of greatest worry about democracy, pointed out, as in his address to the freshman class at Columbia University's matriculation ceremony in 1916, that "the university spirit is jeopardized by democracy, no less than by autocracy. For democracy levels down as well as up, and is proverbially intolerant of the expert." Yet he was generally sanguine about democracy, holding in 1913 that "enrollment of the services of trained experts [was needed] to carry out social reforms," though precisely which social reforms to undertake were to be determined through electoral politics. Paul Kellogg, editor of *The Survey*, sought to resolve the paradox of democratic elitism by melding scientific expertise and democracy through the persuasive force of education, when he told a gathering of scholars at the 18 April 1912, meeting of the Academy of Political Science that the best hope was "to bring the knowledge and inventions of scientists and experts home to the common imagination, and to gain for their proposals the dynamic backing of a convinced democracy."[18] By expanding the social space in which they had opportunity to convince their fellow citizens, social science scholar-activists opened a venue for the exchange of ideas on both sides; social scientists' public efforts to bring their ideas home to the imaginations of their fellow citizens meant, practically, a commitment to deliberative democracy—a democratic form in which people do not reflexively and unreflectively vote their prejudices, but which, through discussion and debate that opens possibilities for discovery of new facts and new perspectives, allows for persuasion on both sides—even if imperfectly and within limitations that some find restrictive, others liberating.

Even John Dewey, at Columbia from 1904, the great philosopher of American democracy who shared the causes of the reform left throughout his life, reflected this unresolved conflict between democracy and an elite. In Dewey's view, "Because the public is so behind the scientific times, it must be brought up," that is, educated. But social problems, Dewey wrote in 1908, "are essentially *scientific* problems, questions for expert intelligence conjoined with wide sympathy," and modern conditions, "necessitate the selection of public servants of scientifically equipped powers." The modern age was characterized by an "almost religious faith in the need of progress and in the possibility of making it the ruling principle of human affairs." "The idea of progress . . . explicitly connot[es] change toward a more desirable state of affairs, something higher, better, more perfect." "Since progress is not automatic but requires trained intelligence and forceful character, progressive societies depend for their very existence upon educational resources. Moreover, the conditions that are favorable to progress are also favorable to the release of energy from the restrictions of customs and convention." In such a release of energy, Dewey said, "conditions that had previously been regarded as inevitable accompaniments of the human lot, political despotism, subjection of masses to intellectual authority, sickness and poverty were regarded as due to man's ignorance and lack of freedom, and as sure to pass away with the growth of science, and with economic and political freedom." Dewey traced the "clearness and force" of modern science to its roots in Francis Bacon's seventeenth century philosophy, and to the eighteenth century Enlightenment. Bacon, Dewey wrote, had "asserted both the need and the possibility of progress, to be brought about through a scientific knowledge of natural conditions and taking effect in inventions directed toward ameliorating the lot of man." Enlightenment thinkers had emphasized that in the application of science to everyday life, humans achieved "deliberate control of the means of reaching ends." With the rise of secular modern science, Dewey observed, the social stasis of the medieval world gave way to the dynamic, transformative progress of the modern. Science for Dewey was a problem-solving tool, useful to identify and solve problems that emerged from lived experience. In his view four stages of such problem-solving were to be accomplished in democratic forums in which the public would join with those of expert intelligence to puzzle out solutions to commonly agreed upon problems. Dewey's four stages were: defining the problem—including constraints on the solution, brainstorming solutions, choosing a solution, and implementing it. It was a savvy solution to the paradox of democratic elitism in social science, and one destined to have a wide influence.[19]

Yet the undertaking was often fraught with risk and failure. In their work with both the working class and the out-of-work destitute poor—in the settlement houses and elsewhere—social science-trained scholar-activists shepherded those who were willing, even eager, for education and for a chance to take control of their lives. But sometimes, as they set out to promote a reform agenda, they encountered opposition from among those they sought to help, who, exhausted by a twelve-hour-day (or longer) work schedule or for other reasons, had little zest or energy for efforts at social change and for being educated on how to live what their patrons saw as a better life.

The scholar-activists of the New York network of social scientists were heirs to the rise of modern science and the Enlightenment and makers of a continuing American Enlightenment. These public intellectuals declined to appeal to the church as an instrument of change as earlier generations had done and appealed, instead, to the authority of science. Grounding their views on evidence and argument, they relied on the continuing possibility of new evidence and new arguments for the social reconstruction of the modern world. Yet many had grown up in deeply religious households. James Bronson Reynolds, headworker at the University Settlement, for example, was the son of a minister from a small town in upstate New York. The father of sociologist Franklin Giddings was a Congregational minister. Henry Moskowitz's father, an emigre from Rumania to Manhattan's Lower East Side, though not formally ordained as a rabbi, headed a Jewish congregation. Religion was also a central part in the youths and, in varying degrees, in the adult lives of Mary Kingsbury Simkhovitch, Josephine Shaw Lowell, Mary White Ovington, George Edmund Haynes, and Samuel McCune Lindsay. Edwin R. A. Seligman was raised in the New York Ethical Culture Society, a society that expressed religious conscience in moral deeds but emphasized reason rather than an Almighty or scripture as the source of conscience.

For these men and women moral or religious fervor served as an ethical guide and as an impetus to civic action. They turned to the social sciences for authority and method, though with a fervor and commitment religious in character. That parents of some of these young social scientists were clergy is not surprising; in an age of rising science, ministers, priests and rabbis had to share the high cultural stage with physical and social scientists.

In 1785 in what the etymologists of the Oxford English Dictionary record as one of the earliest uses of the term "social science," John Adams, U.S. minister to Great Britain, wrote: "The social science will never be much improved, until the people unanimously know and consider themselves as the fountain of power." Adams was using social science as a near synonym for "politics." By the nineteenth century, social science was taking on a different meaning. The French intellectual Auguste Comte coined the term "sociology" in 1838—by it he said he sought "to replace all imperfect and provisional systems resting on the primitive basis of theology"—and the term "social science" sometimes appeared as a synonym for sociology. But toward the end of the nineteenth century, "social science" came most often to signal a broad project by which, in some degree, the secrets of human behavior and social interaction were to be unlocked in separate yet interrelated rational disciplines. Psychologists analyzed the vast complexities of brain and behavior; economists mapped production, distribution, and exchange of commodities and services; anthropologists studied and compared cultures; political scientists probed relations between individuals, classes, and states; historians reconstructed the human past; sociologists forged rational knowledge of individual parts of society and of the social whole grounded in empirical observation. But humans are richly complex animals and the lines demarking one social science discipline from another are not sharp: any social science discipline that ignores the others does so at its peril, and successful economists, of necessity, drew on psychology, political science, sociology, and history in constructing their theories and insights.[20]

Joining this community of scholars meant joining a research community dedicated to the careful collection of information about one or another aspect of the human condition. Belief in proportion to the evidence and the meticulous, arduous, trustworthy collection of that evidence were important keys to membership in the social science community of scholars. Equally important was the fitting of the collected evidence into something akin to a theory, if not a full-fledged, worked-out conceptual scheme that explained a group of collected information. Unlike the physical sciences of physics, chemistry, or biology, the "data" or phenomena of the social sciences usually did not fit into general or abstract principles undisputable in their meaning with predictive qualities, able to be replicated. (The word theory sometimes connotes an intellectual exercise not meant to have a practical purpose; in the social science scholar-activists' sense of the word, theory *was* linked to practice.)

The young men and women of the social science network in New York came of age, intellectually and politically, at a time of sharp change in America. Slavery had ended, and the industrial revolution had taken off. The concept of a fixed natural social order, a providential great chain of being, under assault since the eighteenth century Enlightenment, was, by the late nineteenth century, giving way before notions of experiment, change, evolution, and progress, fueled by Charles Darwin's theory of evolution and the new industrial market economy. Change was everywhere, and the ethos of the age was captured by Mary Kingsbury

Simkhovitch in 1902, in the *Political Science Quarterly*: "The order of the day is not an eternal order, but that what is can actually be otherwise."[21] It was to a mapping of the visions of just what that "otherwise" might be that Simkhovitch and other social science-trained scholar-activists gave their lives in work.

The social order of the day was now being interpreted, by some at least, as no longer stable and fixed, and longstanding social relations—of gender, race, labor, and the like—were or might be, in the light of modern science, open to a reinterpretation and remaking. Darwinian evolutionary theory, combined with the rapid evident changes in the industrializing market economy, signalled the possibilities. Besides, science and technology had fueled social and economic change through their insight and invention.

It was an age of scientific revolution, a time when the authority of, and reverence for, science grew with the legacy of its achievement. The physical sciences were yielding a vast bounty, and no one could deny that science and technology were revolutionizing human understanding and transforming everyday life. Contemporary developments included Charles Darwin's *Origin of Species* (1859) and his *Descent of Man* (1871), Wilhelm Roentgen's discovery of x-rays (1895), J. J. Thomson's discovery of the electron (1897), Max Planck's quantum theory of matter (1900), Albert Einstein's theory of relativity (1905), H. K. Onnes's 1911 discovery of superconductivity, and Ernest Rutherford's ground-breaking theory of the atom in that same year. Inventions were transforming everyday life, not only Tesla's alternating-current motor, Bell's telephone, Marconi's radio, but the Wright brothers' first airplane of 1903, Lee De Forest's triode vacuum tube of 1906, and Henry Ford's Model T of 1908. Advances in medicine were no less impressive. Marie and Pierre Curie's work with radioactivity and radium opened new vistas of biomedical diagnosis and cure. Between 1897 and 1910 human blood groups were classified, the whooping cough bacillus was isolated, viruses were identified, diagnostic tests for diphtheria, syphilis, and tuberculosis were developed, a typhoid vaccine was discovered, and aspirin went on sale.[22]

In such a world, where fixed notions about the natural world and the labors of everyday life were rapidly giving way to entirely new visions and procedures, it seemed to some natural that old notions of a fixed social order in which everything had its place, and in which a successful life was one that fulfilled a set place in a hierarchy of fixed powers, would give way to new possibilities. Those who believed that much in the social order was worth conserving held the view that the established rules of the competitive market economy and established social relations simply needed enforcing. Those at the opposite end of the spectrum held that the social sciences, in their measuring, counting, analyzing, and conceiving, provided a groundwork for a radical transformation in economy and society. In between were others, neither conservative nor radical, convinced that the social sciences might be used instrumentally and incrementally to reform the worst social and economic excesses through social initiatives and regulatory controls of government.

The terms "intelligentsia" and "intellectuals," coined in the nineteenth century in Russia and France, initially denoted those dedicated to a life of thought, but not thinking alone. They implied a stance of opposition to institutions built on force, power, doctrine—aristocracy, army, church.[23] New York City's social scientists, a part of what W. E. B. Du Bois called the "thinking classes," included conservatives, even reactionaries, but most were reform-minded and saw themselves as warriors against the entrenched and aggressive power of the wealth-elite, including the trustees and administrators of the academy itself.

Chapter 1
Competing Gospels: "Make Way for Science and for Light!"

At the heart of the social reform movement in New York City, "the greatest social science laboratory in the world" in the words of the New School for Social Research's founders, were private nonprofit institutions, from churches to universities, foundations, newspapers, magazines, publishing houses, settlement houses, and civil rights and feminist organizations. From the movement's origins in private civic-minded enterprise it moved on to the public realm of government and politics. But it took immense effort, many defeats, and many years to bridge the private and public worlds, to arouse the conscience of government and to move beyond social experiment and enterprise to legislation and large-scale city, state, and federal programs of implementation of reform in the city and in the nation.

A principal element of the reform movement started with the end of the nineteenth century and the rise of the social sciences, and began with the academy and an intellectual elite. The scholar-activists of the social laboratory in New York were drawn to the city as if it were a magnet, not only from New York itself but from New England and the upper Midwest, a number emigrated from Europe in the early years of the new century. New York City's universities, beginning with Columbia University, trained a pool of educated leaders and they, in turn, shaped the universities in unanticipated ways. They provided resources, measured and tested, compiled data on poverty and its effects on public health and on the consequences of the expanding and exploitative industrial revolution, and proposed, then initiated and implemented, the plans and programs that characterized the Progressive Era. They encountered powerful opposition not only from the bastions of wealth and power but from within their own ranks, from corporate trustees and administrators who sought to limit dissent, and from scholars committed to unchecked capitalism or the status quo or to a pseudo-science of eugenics that gave racism a scholarly face. But this community of dedicated and persistent men and women achieved social change that was not to be reversed.

But before this competition with the gospel of wealth and economic power, the gospel of scholarship and science had to win over institutions of higher education from the first gospel, from which the academy itself arose, the gospel of theology. The early colleges in the colonies and in the United States were founded not by secular institutions but by churches, and religious doctrine preceded science as their founding principle and the source of truth. Yet the establishment of colleges set in motion secular forces of scholarship committed to the free search for knowledge from whatever sources and to the emerging sciences that moved from study and explanation of the physical to the biological world and, in the mid and late 1800s and early 1900s, to the society itself. With this knowledge came the will to lead in efforts to reshape a rich and energetic but flawed American community.

"From the Study of Nature to the Knowledge of Themselves"

In 1754 the Anglican minister Samuel Johnson published an advertisement in the New York *Gazette* announcing the opening of a college on Manhattan Island: "To such Parents as have now (or expect to have) Children prepared to be educated." It was the plan for King's College (later renamed Columbia College, then Columbia University): "The chief thing that is aimed at in this college is to teach and engage the children to *know God in Jesus Christ,* and to love and serve Him in all *Sobriety, Godliness, and Righteousness* of Life, with a *perfect Heart, and a willing Mind,*" yet with "no Intention to impose on the Scholars, the peculiar Tenets of any particular Sect of Christians;" but rather "to inculcate upon their tender Minds, the great Principles of Christianity and Morality, in which true Christians of each Denomination are generally agreed." Daily attendance at chapel was required (there were morning and evening chapel services), though on "the Lord's Day" students could attend any place of worship "their Parents or Guardians shall think fit to order and permit." No doctrine was imposed, but compulsory chapel would not end until 1891.

Yet, from the beginning, the college accommodated not only theology and Christian virtue but the secular world of the eighteenth century age of Enlightenment's "Arts of *reasoning* exactly." And it accommodated, too, the Enlightenment's belief-in-accordance-with-the-evidence empiricism and emphasis on practical knowledge: "the Arts of *numbering* and *measuring,* of *Surveying* and *Navigation,* of *Geography* and *History,* of *Husbandry, Commerce,* and *Government,* and in the Knowledge of *all Nature. . . .*"[1]

The first classes at King's College met in the vestry room and schoolhouse of Trinity Church at Broadway and Wall Street, but by 1760 the college had left the precincts of the church and moved a few blocks uptown to College Hall, at Park Place and Church Street. It was the centerpiece of Columbia's campus for the next ninety-seven years. Important members of the nation's founding generation had studied at King's College, among them Alexander Hamilton, John Jay, Robert Livingston, and Gouverneur Morris. In 1784, the year after the Treaty of Paris ended the Revolution, the college symbolically freed itself, renaming King's College, Columbia College. The new nation's fifth oldest institution of higher education, it was preceded by Harvard, William and Mary, Yale, and the College of New Jersey, later known as Princeton; all were creatures of the church, Columbia and William and Mary of the Anglicans, Harvard and Yale of the Congregationalists, Princeton of the Presbyterians.

The college would move again in 1857, up to East 49th Street and Madison Avenue, near the city's northern limit, into the middle of the world of practical work—a livestock yard, a railroad line, a paper factory; in winter its classrooms and library were heated by fireplaces, two to a room. Seeking more open space, in 1897 the college moved again, to West 116th Street and Broadway, where, more than a century later, it still stands. At the core of its midcentury curriculum was the classical study of philosophy, mathematics, literature, and science, but social science and the professions were emerging. In 1857 Columbia College hired a German-born political scientist and jurist, Francis Lieber, to a chair of history and political science; in 1858 it established a school of law, in 1860 revived an earlier relationship with the city's College of Physicians and Surgeons, and in 1864 opened a school of engineering and applied science ("The School of Mines"). On 7 June 1880, the college's sixteen trustees assembled and voted to create a School of Political Science, Columbia's first nonprofessional graduate program. In the fall of 1880, the year the program opened its doors, a young Theodore Roosevelt entered Columbia's Law School, and registered "for all of the courses in political history, public law, and political science." By the end of the nineteenth century, Columbia College, and others as well, had been transformed into secular modern research universities. The academy was reaching out to the public world, collecting data, conducting research, spreading discovered truth to the world to be applied in that world.[2]

Columbia University's School of Political Science was part of a seachange in higher education, in which, Louis Menand has said, "science, not theology, was [to be] the educational core of the future." It was a time, as historian T. J. Jackson Lears has observed, when leading academics sought "to create and put to use a new 'science of man' that reflected their own experience and aspirations more accurately than the evangelical ethos had done." In creating that science of man Columbia would draw on European higher education, especially the German universities, Oxford and Cambridge, the Sorbonne, the College de France, and the Ecole Libre des Sciences et Politiques, where the spirit of science and reform was flourishing. All five of the first faculty members at Columbia College's School of Political Science studied in Europe—all in Germany, a few also in France. Study abroad had become the intellectually fashionable thing to do. Indeed, the social science reform network in New York was part of an international web of effort, as the historian Daniel T. Rodgers has demonstrated.[3]

Harvard-trained historian and black leader W. E. B. Du Bois would remember with delight his own studies in Germany in the early 1890s with Gustav Schmoller, Adolf Wagner, and Heinrich von Treitschke. Mary Kingsbury Simkhovitch, founder of Greenwich House Settlement, called her studies with German Historical School economists Gustav Schmoller and Adolf Wagner, "a yeasty period" that gave her "a roomier outlook on the social and economic scene of the planet." Many of the young Americans attracted to the German Historical School were keen to point out that the British Manchester School's laissez-faire, free trade strategy might work well for the powerful, dominant British economy, but that the developing German and U.S. economies would benefit from state regulation. While Marx and Engels called for revolution, the scholars of the German Historical School, wary of socialism, sought a "middle way." By 1871 the Historical School's younger members, *Katheder Sozialister*—"Socialists of the Chair"—were promoting the regulatory role of government, and social scientists as agenda-setting regulators. Gustav Schmoller set the tone: "convinced of the necessity of reforms, we preach neither the upsetting of science nor the overthrow of the existing social order, and we protest against all socialistic experiments." In 1873 Schmoller and others organized a coalition of academics, labor leaders, leading industrialists, and government officials under the umbrella of a new organization, the *Verein fur Sozialpolitik* (Association for Social Politics) to bring "the men of science and the men of practical affairs" together to discuss how best to use the state "as regulator and moderator of the contending industrial classes." Its perspective would guide the social science scholar-activists of Manhattan over the decades to come.[4]

Early U.S. social science graduate programs were established not only at Columbia, but also at Harvard, Johns Hopkins, New York University, Yale, and the universities of Chicago, Wisconsin, and Pennsylvania. Harvard elected a chemist and mathematician, Charles W. Eliot, as its president in 1869, and a pioneering elective system transformed America's first college into a distinguished research university. Daniel Coit Gilman, as the first president of Johns Hopkins in 1876, oversaw creation of the nation's first graduate university—the physical and social sciences at its core—along the German model. The University of Chicago, funded by John D. Rockefeller's oil, opened its doors in 1892, among its earliest programs the nation's first department of sociology.

In Manhattan, New York University (1831), called the University of the City of New York until the end of the century, and the public College of the City of New York (1847), joined Columbia as the city's principal institutions of higher education. After an initial fight in the 1830s between merchants and ministers at its Washington Square campus over what education to offer, Presbyterian and Dutch Reform minister-presidents led NYU into the early twentieth century. In 1858 New York University's Law School opened; in 1866, with money from the Shoe and Leather Bank of New York, an endowed chair was established in political science for the teaching of undergraduates; in 1886 a graduate program in political science, political economy, sociology, and constitutional law was established. By 1912–13 NYU was offering a variety of social science graduate courses, including "The Metropolitan City: Causes, Conditions, and Problems" and "Relation of Government to Business." In 1903 its politically progressive graduate, John MacCracken (son of NYU president Henry M. MacCracken and brother of Henry Noble Mac-Cracken, Vassar's president after 1915), with a doctorate from Halle-Wittenberg, became professor of politics at NYU. In 1904 Frederick Cleveland, later a principal figure in the New York Bureau of Municipal Research, who had studied at the University of Chicago and the University of Pennsylvania, was appointed to a post in NYU's Department of Economics and Finance. In 1912 Jeremiah W. Jenks, recent president of the American Economic Association, who studied at the University of Halle and taught political economy and politics at Cornell, was appointed as research professor in government and public administration.[5]

Columbia and NYU were competing for the sons of the intellectual and financial elite. The College of the City of New York, founded as a publicly funded Free Academy, located uptown at 138th Street and Convent Avenue after 1907 (it had earlier held classes downtown at 17 Lexington Avenue), drew students from the city's tradesmen, clerks, and professionals, and from the 1880s, increasingly, from "new immigrant" groups. The political scientist Stephen P. Duggan estimated that about 75 percent of City College students in the early twentieth century were Jewish, "recent arrivals from Eastern Europe or . . . the sons of recent arrivals. They were practically all poor and many of them had been badly persecuted in Russia, Poland, Rumania, and in Central Europe." Duggan, who had earned his own undergraduate degree at City College and his political science doctorate at Columbia, returned to teach at City College whose "first and most important function" was, he said, "to provide a higher education for the youth of the city who are going to become its political and social leaders."[6]

Parallel professional social scientific organizations were in process. The American Social Science Association (1865), was replaced by discipline-specific associations: the American Historical Association (1884); the American Economic Association (1885); the American Statistical Association (1830s, reorganized in the 1880s); the American Psychological Association (1892); the American Anthropological Association (1902); the American Political Science Association (1903); and the American Sociological Association (1905). The *American Economic Review* began publication in 1885, the *American Historical Review* and the *American Journal of Sociology* in 1895.

"Christian Sociology": "a New Spirit" for Social Science or "a Species of Venerable Quackery"?

The earlier American higher education, with its heavy dose of theology dispensed by college presidents and professors who were quite often members of the clergy, was giving way to an increasingly secular and scientific academy. James Leuba, professor of psychology at Bryn Mawr, found in a study that scientists and social scientists listed in *American Men of Science* in 1913–14 were far more irreligious or at least more unorthodox than the general population: that is, the majority did not believe in God or immortality.[7] Yet, church affiliation and religion as ethic were alive, not only in the academy but in social reform and social work as well. A 1906 survey of religious affiliation by the American Institute of Social Service of persons working in charities, social settlements, and social work reported that 74 percent responding to questions on religion said they were "communicants in some church"—Episcopalians, Presbyterians, Congregationalists, Methodists, Baptists, Catholics, Unitarians, and Universalists. (The survey did not mention Judaism.) The charity organizations reported that 92 percent of their workers were church members, settlements that 88 percent of their staff were.[8]

Some intellectuals of the era rejected modern science; some rejected religion; some saw science as requiring a commitment to a materialist or naturalistic ontology; others believed science could neither infuse life with meaningful purpose nor account for the world of the spirit. But with the advent of graduate programs in social science a structured secular alternative to the clergy's authority had arisen. In response, some clergy sought to subsume the authority of social science under the religious. The Reverend James F. Riggs of Bayonne, New Jersey, in an 1890 article, "Social Science and the Pulpit," wrote that "Social science is not Theology, yet it sustains a definite relation to it." "The Christian pulpit cannot ignore the facts of sociology, but those facts should be like the sugar put in a cup of tea. There ought not to be too much of it, and what there is should be perfectly in solution." James A. Quarles, in *Presbyterian Quarterly*, tried to merge Christianity and social science. "The science of Sociology," he said, "has not passed the embryonic stage," but religion and social science together could create a "Christian Sociology." Indeed, sixteen years earlier, in 1880—the same year Columbia's School of Political Science was founded—the Reverend J. H. W. Stuckenberg, in his book *Christian Sociology*, called sociology "a department of Christian theology." "By adopting sociology," he wrote, "theology enlarges its own domain and will, at the same time, infuse a new spirit into social science." In 1892, a chair of "Christian Sociology" was established at the Chicago Theological Seminary and filled by Graham Taylor, a minister famous for his "socioreligious" survey of conditions among the poor in Hartford, Connecticut. Taylor called upon "social science" to become, "the science of Christian society. Its field is the world, including all classes and conditions of men from all nationalities. Its work is to investigate the conditions of social and personal life, discover the causes of suffering and the sources of inharmonious relations." In Taylor's view the answer was "sociology with God left in it."[9]

A debate ensued in theological and social science circles about whether a "Christian Sociology" made sense or not. The Congregationalist Christian periodical *Bibliotheca Sacra* added the subtitle, "A Religious and Sociological Quarterly," to its masthead and published the replies of 125 "leading thinkers in the United States" (all male) to a survey it disseminated on the relationship between sociology and Christianity. The Reverend W. G. Ballantine of Oberlin College said that, "if Jesus alone can save his people from their sins—then the principles of Christianity are the fundamentals of Sociology." John Bascom, a graduate of Andover Theological Seminary, president of the new University of Wisconsin, and now professor of political science at Williams College, concurred: "Christian principles correctly applied to society and a correct Sociology are identical." But Jeremiah W. Jenks, then professor of political economy and politics at Cornell, had misgivings: "I believe Sociology to be a science dealing with definite facts and principles. I fear that the use of the expression, 'Christian Sociology,' may mislead many people regarding the nature of the science and will thus do harm, while I see no good that can come from its use. The expression 'Christian Biology' would, in my judgement, be as fit for current use as is 'Christian Sociology.'" Yet Jenks saw the principles of Jesus' teachings as relevant:

"As a student of social science and politics, it has been a source of satisfaction to me to see how many cases the principles laid down by him [Jesus] have made their way, often without the will of political or social leaders, into the scheme of our modern life. The Christian religion has proved itself practical in politics, and statesmen are realizing as never before that God cannot be left out as a factor in public affairs." A decade later, Walter Rauschenbusch, distinguished theologian of the Social Gospel movement, wrote that Jesus: "had the scientific insight that comes to most men only by training."[10]

Yet, to David S. Jordan, a professor of natural history and zoology before becoming president of Stanford University in 1891, "the word 'Christian' prefixed to the name of any science is a species of venerable quackery. Sociology is a science because its facts and inferences are true, not because they are the teaching of any authority." Franklin H. Giddings, Columbia professor of sociology, took a similar position: "Sociology is the natural history and natural philosophy of society . . . a descriptive, historical and explanatory account of natural communities, of animals and of men, savage, barbarian and civilized, as they have actually been, as they actually are. It affords data to Social Ethics. There can be a Christian Society. There can be a Christian Social Ethics, but a 'Christian Sociology' is as absurd as a Christian Chemistry or a Christian Astronomy." The next year, in his *The Principles of Sociology*, Giddings added: "Whether we like it or not, we must now throw over our illusions and must learn to substitute for them the truths of a rational sociology."[11]

A dozen years after the *Bibliotheca Sacra* survey, Seth Low, Columbia's president from 1890 to 1901, wrote in "What Facts Have to Do with Faith?": "It is hardly more than a generation, if so long, since teaching in every department of intellectual activity depended for its weight upon authority. Now, however, that sort of teaching is absolutely confined to the domain of Theology."[12]

The Dilemma of "Expert Intelligence" in a Democratic Society

Had a new "authority"—science—taken over from theology? Through the same methods employed by the natural sciences social scientists were now seeking to develop undogmatic, empirical, measured, fact-based knowledge about the psychological and social world. But just how "scientific" was that work? Social scientists sometimes claimed identity, or at least similarity, between their science and the work of physicists, chemists, biologists, and physicians. But what did similarity mean? And who was to assign authority to transform the public world to these new social scientists who stepped forward, with little modesty, to assume a role of leadership?

John Bates Clark, who had been an undergraduate student of political economy at Amherst when John W. Burgess, founder of Columbia's School of Political Science, taught there, wrote an essay in 1878 on "The Scholar's Duty to the State." In it he disparaged traditional case-by-case approaches to helping the poor as analogous to the efforts of pre-scientific agrarians. Like chemists, economists could offer a more broad-based impact: "The farmer who irrigates a number of acres may raise a crop. The chemist who discovers a means by which the alkali that now ruins the land may be converted into a fertilizer, will do more than a million farmers. So the economist who can devise a means of removing the cause of extreme poverty, with the consequent ignorance and brutality, will do more than many charitable associations for the permanent benefit of the poor." "This" Clark concluded, "is the highest service which the State now asks of its scholars." If "the popular disposition" was to "follow loud mouthed demagogues," such demagogues, Clark believed, ought be supplanted by social scientists. Lester Ward, the noted proponent of Reform Darwinism, later a professor of sociology at Brown University, agreed. "Proper intellectual guidance" was necessary for a democracy to flourish. "Before progressive legislation can become a success, every legislature, as it were," Ward wrote, "must become a polytechnic school, a laboratory of philosophical research into the laws of society and human nature. . . . Every true legislator must be a sociologist and have his knowledge of that most intricate of all sciences founded upon organic and inorganic science."[13]

To be sure, there were doubters. Leslie Stephen, president of the Social and Political Education League, wrote in 1892: "There is no science of sociology, properly scientific—merely a heap of vague empirical observations, too flimsy to be useful in strict logical inference." And though, like Stephen, later detractors would disparage efforts of social science, calling it "scientism," social scientists of the Gilded Age and Progressive Era claimed science as their own instrument and frequently adopted the terminology of the physical sciences. They collected "data," established social and economic "laboratories," sought etiologies, practiced quantitative statistical analyses, and sometimes predicted events and trends. Biological analogies and medical metaphors abounded. Sociologist William Howe Tolman, active in the municipal reform politics of New York City, compared social scientists to medical doctors and epidemiologists: "Our modern cities are so many great laboratories for the social scientist," he said. "The social, like the physical evils, exists in all our large cities, and there is no reason why it [the social evil] should not be studied scientifically, like small-pox, typhus, or other deadly and insidious diseases. . . . The social sciences are beginning to be made the subject of scientific study and are yielding most fruitful results." If physicians tended individual patients, the social science expert would care for the collective subject, the body politic. Paul U. Kellogg, editor of *The Survey*, the nation's leading journal of practical application of the social sciences, noted that: "The survey takes from the physician his art of applying to the problems at hand standards and experience worked out elsewhere." Nor was it only the progressive scholars who made such claims. Columbia's John W. Burgess, classical nineteenth century laissez-faire-liberal political scientist, saw his own approach as "an attempt to apply the method, which has been found so productive in the domain of Natural Science, to Political Science and Jurisprudence."[14]

Du Bois, then on the faculty of Atlanta University, wrote in *Some Notes on the Negroes in New York City* in 1903: "Since now scientists have begun to study men and conditions of group life so carefully, persons who would better the world in any way must study and learn from the material collected here, just as in other lines we use the wisdom of the geologist or psychologist." Columbia University's Charles A. Beard said: "Political science is to be the greatest of all sciences. Physics and politics are to be united, but the former is to be the bondsman." (Precisely how Beard intended to enslave physics to political science he did not say.) To Walter Lippmann, the influential journalist and social critic, who had studied social science at Harvard, "the scientific spirit" was "the discipline of democracy, the escape from drift;" "the discipline of science is the only one which gives any assurance that from the same set of facts men will come approximately to the same conclusions." Beard and Columbia historian James Harvey Robinson noted that, through "careful observation and experimentation" and by "laborious watching, musing, and calculating . . . men of science, not kings, or warriors or even statesmen are to be the heroes of the future." Editors of the May 1910 issue of *Cosmopolitan* magazine said: "the great mass of laymen which constitutes the public at large has accepted almost without question the dictum of science as to the necessities of its progressive growth. When the word has been passed that science demanded such and such a concession opposition has raised its head in vain. 'Make way for science and for light!' has cleared obstruction from every path. If there have been doubters they have been branded as foes to progress."[15]

In 1880, the first year of Columbia College's School of Political Science, eleven students took courses; by 1890 the number was ninety-eight. In 1882, an Academy of Political Science opened under auspices of the School of Political Science; its object, so its constitution said, was "the cultivation of the political sciences and their application to the solution of social and political problems." In 1886 Columbia's School of Political Science faculty began publication of the *Political Science Quarterly*, the "treatment" in a "scientific" forum "of political, economic, and legal questions." In the first issue Munroe Smith asked, what "are the methods of the social sciences?" His answer: "Statistics, comparative legislation, history—these are means and modes of accumulating facts for comparison."[16]

By 1910 Columbia had become the largest university in the nation and, in keeping with that growth, by 1911 the faculty in its School of Political Science was among the largest and best social science faculties in the nation, with nineteen professors, three associate professors, six assistant professors, and a lecturer—all of them men. From the first, they aspired not only to develop social science research and theory, but also, on an eminently practical level, to help end the corrupt political spoils system of Manhattan, and in particular, of Tammany Hall. The undergraduate newspaper, the *Columbia Spectator*, published a cartoon, "True Civil Service Reform," in October 1880—the month the new School of Political Science opened its doors—that captured the new school's intent. Faculty and administrators were in medieval armor and vestments, ranged behind the crenelated battlements of the college library's tower, led by the School's founder, John W. Burgess. With pike-wielding faculty allies, Burgess, bearded and jaw set, supports a standard emblazoned, "Civil Service Reform," the cannon at his command labelled "Political Science."[17]

Contrary to the laissez-faire view of the role of government held by John W. Burgess, founder of Columbia's School of Political Science and later dean of Columbia's combined graduate faculties, other Columbia faculty held an activist view of the role of government and social scientists in public governance. The 1894 "Report on a Department of Social Science at Columbia College" promised it would seek to ease the grinding poverty of industrial capitalism, and renew democracy in an age when wealth was in the hands of a few. They would begin with work on the city in which they lived. In 1894 the Department of Social Science was introduced within the School of Political Science, its "Principal" areas: sociology, political economy, social ethics and social reform, public and private charity, criminology, and the social effects of taxation. Some of its "Special" courses included: housing the poor, labor organization, theories of communism and socialism, ethics and social reform, and the study of comparative cultures; and among "Related" courses: political philosophy, psychology, history of philosophy, and sanitary science.[18]

Columbia's location in New York City, the largest American metropolis, provided an ideal arena for such research and analysis. As the faculty

report on creation of the new department had said: "The city is the natural laboratory of Social Science." In cities were, "in their most acute
forms," "the problems of poverty, of mendicancy, of intemperance, of
unsanitary surroundings, of debasing social influences." The faculty
report continued: "It would be of immense advantage to the student of
political economy and sociology . . . to study these conditions and these
efforts under the auspices of science and the best of practice. Such study
emphasizes all that is taught by theory, and like 'field work' in natural
science it trains the faculties of observation and makes the subject 'real.'
For the University it is like adding a great museum and laboratory, where
many of the questions it deals with theoretically are being worked out
practically." The founding of Columbia's School of Political Science and
Department of Social Science coincided with the rapid expanse of
industrial capitalism, as well as the beginnings of the southern and eastern European "new immigration," and the upward surge in New York
City's population, and made the School and its new department well sit-
uated for social science research. The new department of social science
was to supply undogmatic, nonpartisan, and precise facts and become
"a sort of scientific Clearing House," disseminating its findings in scholarly journals, in the classroom, and also in "popular lectures." It would
benefit "the simple citizen" and "the future statesman."[19]

"Expert Intelligence": Leaders or Public Servants?

The concept of an academic elite, of social scientists as experts to shape
and guide the citizenry, introduced a dilemma for New York's scholar-
activists. Could they assume leadership in a democratic society? Columbia University's department of social science, according to the "Report
on a Department of Social Science," "would diffuse accurate and sound
knowledge of the problems demanding solution, and would train up a
body of scientific and practical men for future leaders in those enterprises." Its professors would be the "competent scientific authority,"
and a student in the new department would "be made an expert in judging of the value of sociological evidence."[20] Modesty was not the new
department's strong suit. Social scientists would structure public percep-
tions and shape society. But would the opinions of the uninitiated citizen prove meddlesome in the making of appropriate public policy?
Would social scientists, using their research to control and shape social
policy, seize power from the ordinary citizen and reserve it for themselves? If science was to be at the core of the critique of the current social
order and also at the center of the quest to remake that order, what was
the proper role of the citizen?
    Social scientists' claims of expertise generated a conflict for intellectu-

als that still persists—between a commitment to democracy and a claim of the authority to lead.[21] Democracy's commitment to majority rule, in the U.S. context bounded by constitutionally guaranteed minority rights, is its admission that issues of policy are to be contested in the public arena. If the social scientists' view was to trump all other views then democracy might give way to a technocracy that resembles the older theocracies in which a small, self-elected, group of "truth knowers" run government, or an aristocracy, leadership by the "aristoi," the best men, that is, perhaps, the richest, brightest, or most powerful.

Mary Kingsbury Simkhovitch, one of the earliest women to enroll in the School of Political Science—she studied with Edwin R. A. Seligman, John Bates Clark, and Giddings, among others, in 1897 and 1898— wrote in the *Political Science Quarterly* that the scholar who "lives in a world of ideas" must take care not to exude "superiority" when talking to ordinary citizens, it was "alienating in its effect." But social scientists, generally, believed that their methods were objective enough to set them above special interests. They relied on measurable data and the discipline of the laboratory. The Columbia report that established the department of social science proposed a "statistical laboratory," fed both by "data" collected in the "field work" of faculty, fellows, and students, and raw, unanalyzed, data to be supplied by charity organizations, social settlements, and, as it would turn out, by the police department. The statistical lab was to be furnished with the latest "important apparatus": "drawing tables, instruments, calculating and tabulating machines and books, cards, charts, and a collection of statistical publications— everything necessary to put statistical data into scientific shape." Students were to be put to work compiling and analyzing numbers, on, for example, "the distribution of wealth," "the relation of classes," "the general statistics of population," and "the true significance of statistics of crime, vice and misfortune."[22] Complex social and economic questions were deemed reducible to laboratory analysis. The lab was up and running by 1895, and its first two reports were completed the next year.

Working closely with New York's Charity Organization Society (itself to undergo a transformation of sorts as social scientists grew to dominate its governance), the statistician Richmond Mayo-Smith and sociologist Franklin Giddings, the first hire of Columbia's new department of social science, created a Committee on Statistics in the Society. Into the university's statistical laboratory were fed numbers from five hundred casework files. The sociologist, the statistician, and their graduate students concluded that environmental circumstance, "social conditions or illness," caused 41.8 percent of the cases of poverty, moral failure and "shiftlessness" another 12 percent, the remaining 46 percent they attributed to a tangle of causes. A second, somewhat expanded, study covering 2,400 casework files "regarding homeless men," concluded much the same—a tangle of social forces and personal behavior patterns caused poverty.[23]

The social scientists were upbeat about their chances of turning poverty around: "The first fruits of our recent alliance with Columbia University," said a Charity Organization Society report, "and of its use of our Registration Bureau as a laboratory for the training of students in social science. . . . gives ground for hope that many problems will be solved and many practical remedies be evolved by the close and scientific study of the causes and conditions of dependence in this city."[24]

Who Was "Progressive" and What Was "Regression"? An Academic Quarrel

Social scientists were not a united body committed to a common purpose, for all their talk about objective science. They had competing agendas. On 19 November 1898, the New York *Tribune* demanded "Scientific City Government," its editors calling for "experts in the administration of city business" to replace "guesswork" by political party hacks. Two years later an editorial noted: "The brains engaged in university work are being utilized for the public service to an extent never known before. . . . University professors are actually exerting a power on legislation." Columbia had become "a 'progressive' university . . . whence the state and nation draw guidance and men for public service," said the editors of the *Tribune* in 1911. They anticipated that "Columbia's influence is bound to be felt more and more in the future."[25] But what, practically, did the claim that Columbia was "a 'progressive' university" mean? Classical liberals (conservatives in today's terminology), modern liberals, and socialists battled over the label "progressive," the dispute centering on the proper use of government. Conservative social scientists thought government regulation ought to be confined to laws that would allow corporations to flourish; modern liberals wanted to use the regulatory power of government as an instrument of human welfare while ensuring civil liberties. Socialists considered government the means of transforming the existing social order away from a market economy.

John W. Burgess, "tall, urbane, handsome" and "very charming," at thirty-two Columbia professor of political science and constitutional law, exemplified the classical liberal (conservative) vision of social science in politics that wanted government to refrain from interfering with those who ran society. He had arrived in the city in the 1870s with the goal of creating a school of political leadership training, the future School of Political Science, his philosophy of leadership rooted in his service in the Union Army. "Speeding through the dark forests" on horseback at seventeen, he had escaped from pro-slavery neighbors in his hometown in middle Tennessee to become a soldier in the Union cause, yet, like many soldiers fighting to preserve the Union, he was a racist—he saw American blacks as "ignorant barbarians"—and became convinced that the war's carnage might have been averted had the nation's politicians been better trained. (He embraced a Teutonic theory of racial superiority that was echoed by his Columbia colleague, historian William H. Dunning, who wrote racist histories of Reconstruction.) It was, Burgess said, this image of a failed statecraft that had motivated him to study the social sciences, and to found Columbia's School of Political Science. An undergraduate at Amherst, trained as a lawyer, a student of history, public law, and political science at the universities at Gottingen, Leipzig, and Berlin, and, by age twenty-nine, professor of history and political science at Amherst, he had come to Columbia well prepared for his grand purpose. He hired three of his former Amherst students as the core of the new School of Political Science faculty: Richmond Mayo-Smith in political economy, sociology, and statistics; Munroe Smith in Roman law; and Clifford Bateman in administrative law. At Bateman's death, he hired Frank J. Goodnow, one of his star pupils at the new School of Political Science.[26]

To Burgess "outreach" in public service meant not liberal social change but alliance with the economic leaders of society. In an 1898 essay, "Private Corporations from the Point of View of Political Science," he chastised those who considered emerging corporate power a bogey. "The prejudice of the masses" led them to misconceive corporations as "some alien monster that has nothing in common with the people and lives upon the sacrifices it imposes upon them—some Juggernaut that mercilessly crushes the people to earth under the wheels of his terrible chariot—some Moloch, in whose fiery embrace men, women and children are ruthlessly consumed." Burgess said "a private business corporation is, from the point of view of political science, a group of human beings, usually belonging to the best class of citizens, associated for the prosecution of some great enterprise and endowed with certain privileges and obligations." And, though populists, progressives, and radicals would insist that corporations generally failed to meet those "certain obligations," to Burgess an over-reaching government was worse. "What we mean by liberty in political science," he said, "is absence of government in a given sphere of individual or social action." "Keeping this meaning in our minds, it is easy to see how corporations are a great stay against paternalism in government."[27]

Burgess was conservative, too, in his views on the place of women in society. Brown, the University of Chicago, the University of Pennsylvania, and Yale had admitted women into social science graduate programs, but Burgess opposed their admission into Columbia's School of Political Science. When three women went to him in the mid-1890s and asked to be permitted to enroll, reportedly saying: " 'Professor Burgess, women can enroll in the graduate school of political science in Chicago,' " Burgess is said to have replied: " 'So much the better . . . let them all go there.' " In 1896, over his objection, women were admitted into courses in the graduate program at Columbia, but he continued to bar women from his own classes. By 1904, 14 percent of the graduate students in the School of Political Science were women, Burgess notwithstanding.[28]

In a 1912 essay, "What Is Real Political Progress?," Burgess derided both the activist regulatory state of modern liberalism and socialism. He bridled at the commitment of Theodore Roosevelt's Progressive Party to an active government that would regulate economic relations in the work place and offer transfer payments to the poor by taxing the rich. "The so called progressive platform," he wrote, "looks to a further centralization of governmental power." But, "the first question for us is whether this is progress, standstill or retrogression in the development of political theory and practical politics." His answer was "retrogression." "We dare not call anything progress . . . which contemplates . . . the expansion of governmental power," Burgess said. He argued "so-called progressives" must "show conclusively that the improvement and development of the system of popular education, the revival of the influence of religion, the restoration of a better family life, producing a more enlightened individual conscience and a more general conscientiousness, would not be the truer way, the American way, the real progressive way of overcoming the claimed failure of our system of civil liberty and of fulfilling the hope of history, instead of recurring to the governmental absolutism of earlier times."[29] In such a view, Burgess aligned himself with American Spencerians such as William Graham Sumner at Yale and E. L. Youmans, founder of *Popular Science Monthly*. As Youmans put it, social science was "pure investigation . . . the strict and passionless study of society from a scientific point of view." "Social science is but a branch of natural science," and properly understood, this "pure" and "passionless study" compelled laissez faire capitalism.[30]

Nicholas Murray Butler, Columbia University's president after 1901, who had been Burgess's student at Columbia, concurred with his teacher and friend in an essay entitled "What Is Progress in Politics?" In his view "limitations on the power of government" were essential. America "should push forward along the road already traveled. . . . and do so in a spirit that will not lead the individual to lean more heavily upon the community, but rather help him to stand up more surely and

confidently upon his own feet." Burgess's and Butler's classical liberalism was a celebration of the minimalist state and the relative freedom of
economic markets as spelled out in Adam Smith's 1776 *Wealth of Nations*:
individual "self-love" allowed to flourish in a competitive market economy will, Smith had argued, lead to dynamic and expansive economic
growth. The capitalist economy's inequitable distribution of wealth,
from the conservative capitalist perspective, was acceptable since the system's success provided, they argued, adequate provision for all. While
many have vastly less wealth than others, the poor, though at a relative
disadvantage to the rich, have more wealth than they might otherwise
expect. For all its flaws, the capitalist system provided greater freedoms
and more goods and services to more people than any workable alternative, so Burgess, Butler, and their conservative allies believed. Butler and
Burgess agreed with political conservatives that government ought to be
used in only limited ways, for example to dissolve monopolies and
ensure competition. Both defended the tradition of constitutional
republicanism. To them, efforts at direct democracy like the ballot initiative, referendum, and recall were anathema, reminiscent of the practices of direct democracy in the ancient Athenian agora, and a distortion
of the Founding Fathers' representative republic. To Butler the recall of
executive and legislative officials was "a stupid and foolish device of restless and meddling minds."[31]

Nicholas Murray Butler was rewarded for his sober conservative views
with the presidency of Columbia in 1902; promoted from professor to
president (after a year as interim president), he served until 1945. In
1904, a booster of the Republican party, he was considered as its candidate for governor of New York; when Republican president William
Howard Taft's vice presidential running-mate, James Schoolcraft Sherman, died on the eve of the 1912 election, Republican party leaders
chose Butler to replace him. The Taft-Butler presidential ticket served
as a conservative alternative to both the Democrats' politically progressive (in certain respects) social scientist nominee for president, Woodrow Wilson, and the Progressive party's candidate Theodore Roosevelt,
favorite of many in the academy and civic reform elite.

If Burgess, in hiring his former students to staff Columbia's School
of Political Science, had hoped to shape the school itself in his own
ideological image, he did not succeed. The School's main intellectual
current flowed away from classical liberalism toward visions of the modern liberal state, and what began as a trickle, with Goodnow and Seligman (both of whom favored expanded regulatory government), soon
became a torrent.

In contrast to Burgess and his conservative allies were the social scientists who viewed government intervention in social reform with favor.

The modern liberal, politically progressive, view was promoted (if sometimes inconsistently) by a core group of social scientists at Columbia, including Charles A. Beard in politics; John Bates Clark, Henry Rogers Seager, and Edwin R. A. Seligman in political economy; Edward T. Devine in social economy; Franklin H. Giddings in sociology; Frank J. Goodnow in administrative law and municipal science; Samuel McCune Lindsay in social legislation; James Harvey Robinson in history; and Vladimir G. Simkhovitch in economic history. Outside of the Faculty of Political Science were the psychologist James McKeen Cattell; the anthropologist Franz Boas; and the philosopher John Dewey, previously of Johns Hopkins, the University of Michigan, and the University of Chicago, at Columbia after 1904.

Seligman, for example, approved "the present tendency to centralization of power in the government," and Seager agreed that "efforts to reform industrial society in any fundamental way must prove abortive without the aid of society's most powerful organ, the state or government." In 1898 James B. Reynolds, a fellow in sociology in Columbia's School of Political Science and head resident at the University Settlement, wrote that "the best interests of society demand . . . the assumption by the general government of such powers as corporations have assumed in the interests and supposedly in the service of the public."[32]

William F. Willoughby, the Princeton political economist, summed up the point: "Modern liberalism, in the United States . . . looks to state action as the means, and the only practicable means now in sight, of giving to the individual, all individuals, not merely a small economically strong class, real freedom." Laws to regulate the industrial economic order—"public opinion, crystallized into law," as Seligman put it—could improve the lives of workers and the poor. Democracy itself suffered when unskilled but honest workers received wages so low that they and their families lived in "a condition of squalid misery." Liberty would be enhanced, not diminished, by the proper use of state power to expand social welfare functions. Seligman exemplified the ethos of modern liberalism, not only as a proponent of the regulatory state but also in his insistence on freedom from regulation in individual liberty and academic freedom, and on the rights of women and of African Americans. He practiced as he preached, serving as president of the American Economic Association in 1902, and of the New York Bureau of Municipal Research; as a founding member of the NAACP; as the first president, in 1911, of the National League on Urban Conditions Among Negroes (later the National Urban League); and as chair of a principal founding committee of the American Association of University Professors, which was organized to champion academic freedom. "A kind of universal scholar," said Alvin Johnson, one of his graduate students (thirty years later, Johnson and Seligman would coedit the fifteen-volume *Encyclopedia of the Social Sciences*).[33]

Seligman, born in Manhattan into a wealthy German-Jewish family, had been tutored to age eleven by Horatio Alger, son of a Unitarian minister. Alger's rags-to-riches stories, in which a poor but honest, industrious, and frugal lad finds himself, by dint of pluck and not a little luck, happy, married, and wealthy by story's end, no doubt seemed congenial to the Seligmans' family history. His father had emigrated to the U.S. from Bavaria, and had started life as an itinerant peddler, then dry goods merchant; by the mid-1860s with the aid of his several brothers he had become one of the nation's most successful bankers. President Ulysses S. Grant offered him the post of secretary of the treasury, but he declined.[34] Seligman matriculated at Columbia at fourteen, earned his degree at eighteen, undertook the intellectually fashionable pilgrimage to study in Berlin, Heidelberg, Geneva, and Paris, received a Columbia Ph.D. in economics in 1885, became a lecturer in political economy that same year, and became a full professor six years later. In his sixty-four years at Columbia, Seligman was always impeccably dressed for class, often in a white shirt, suit, tie, and pince-nez, his precise, patrician air balanced by earnestness and kindness. He wrote many tracts on taxation, the influential *The Economic Interpretation of History* (1902), and became editor-in-chief of the *Encyclopedia of the Social Sciences*.

In contrast to those who would reserve to the state "merely the night-watchman function" of classical liberalism, Seligman saw a "more positive duty of constructive achievement." Legislation could "safeguard the interests of all." "In politics we have liberty because there exists political equality [one man, one vote]. But in economic life, the equality in the parties to a contract is not always present. The liberty of the strong may become the license of the oppressor; the liberty of the weak may practically come to mean the subjection of the oppressed." When the freedom of the capitalist became "the license of the oppressor," the state could sensibly be used by "the weak" to counter that oppression. Government as an expression of the popular will—Seligman's "public opinion, crystallized into law"—might use legislation in small increments, not to subvert the dynamic growth of capitalist markets but, for example, to support the living wage. "Recognition by government of the doctrine of the living wage," he declared, "will not revolutionize the world. It will accomplish only a very little, but that little will be in the direction of progress." Seligman often debated socialists in public forums, though he offered a sympathetic summary of Marx's work as "brilliant and striking." If government promoted "certain common rules" for work, it would alleviate "the sufferings of the poor," and secure "the real blessings of modern civilization" for "every honest laborer," make possible "equality of economic opportunity," and thus help create "the conditions for the restoration of an ultimate and enlarged liberty." When the nation's poor lived "benumbing," "sordid," and "degrading" lives democracy itself suffered.[35]

Seligman was advocating a modern liberalism, capitalism within limited government regulation and with progressive taxation of incomes, inheritance, and corporate profit, "to apportion the burden more equally among the taxpayers." He became the country's leading expert on taxation and a leader in the movement for a federal income tax (achieved under President Wilson with ratification of the Sixteenth Amendment in 1913). An article, "The College Professor in the Public Service" in *South Atlantic Quarterly*, praised his activism, and in the late 1890s New York State Governor Theodore Roosevelt consulted with him on pending state tax bills.[36]

Social scientists in New York's great social laboratory were not all progressive, by any means. Within Columbia University defenders of capitalism contested with promoters of regulatory government. But both supported an active government, if not in those words. Burgess's appeal to the sanctity of liberty in minimalist government was actually an appeal to a government that upheld the interests of capitalists—government itself having sanctioned creation of the private business corporation. Though Burgess might have denied it, he was a scholar-activist of a sort, seeking an activist state that favored capital. Political progressives like Seligman looked to a state activism too, but one that, to a degree, favored labor. Modern liberals held that classical liberals had failed to comprehend the power of corporations. The exercise of too much power by the state could vitiate individual liberty, as in Europe it led to the corporatism of fascism and the statism of socialism. Yet the unregulated freedom of the rich in a capitalist economy could lead to an autocracy and plutocracy, a dictatorship of the wealthy. A proper balancing of freedom and power proved elusive in the academy and the world of social reform as in the courts and the nation as a whole. The often maddening effort at a dynamic balancing of regulatory government and civil liberties would prove to be a central characteristic of modern liberalism, and a central feature of modern politics.

The Limits of Dissent: Trustees and Faculty

Many colleges and universities were run by politically conservative trustees and presidents; the private academy depended on the generosity of economic benefactors and wealthy alumni to grow their endowments and fund capital improvements.[37] In the nexus between conservative administrators and politically progressive faculty campuses sometimes were hotbeds of political disputation. Professors who promoted gradual reform and modest regulation of capitalism tended to be tolerated, but some who moved into a more fundamental critique of capitalism were disciplined or cast out. Scholars of socialist or other radical views were often simply not hired, and those who ventured past an acceptable level of political reformism could find themselves out of work. Columbia's generally progressive faculty did sponsor the work of certain radical graduate students. Harry W. Laidler, for example, working for a doctorate in social economics in 1913, was an active member of the Socialist Party, and executive director of that party's Intercollegiate Socialist Society. Another socialist, Isaac M. Rubinow, studied under Seligman for his doctorate in economics.

An early example of the disciplining of dissent in the social sciences was the case of Daniel De Leon. Burgess said he "knew more international law and diplomatic history than any man of his age"—a graduate of Columbia's Law School, a graduate student in its School of Political Science, and in 1884 the Faculty of Political Science's first Prize Lecturer. De Leon had expressed allegiance to the Republican party at the time of his initial appointment, but in the New York City mayoral race of 1886 De Leon's politics turned radical and he campaigned for the single-taxer Henry George on the United Labor Party ticket (a race George nearly won). Columbia's outraged president, A. P. Barnard, proposed to the trustees that De Leon be dismissed; he was allowed to finish out the year but his lectureship was not renewed. De Leon denounced Barnard and the trustees and launched the Socialist Labor Party; his opponents defended their action on the ground that De Leon had deserved to be dismissed because told curious and contradictory tales about his genealogical origins and his educational background.[38]

In 1894 economist Richard T. Ely was forced to submit to an inquiry at the University of Wisconsin after offending a university regent with comments about workers' right to strike. The next year another economist, Edward Bemis, was compelled to resign from the University of Chicago for his support of the Pullman strike. At the University of Pennsylvania, Scott Nearing was "dismissed because of certain views on economic questions which were obnoxious to some of the trustees." At the University of Colorado professor of economics James Brewster's contract was not renewed after he gave testimony in 1914 before the U.S. Industrial Commission which the state's governor as well as members of the university's trustees considered too radical. Seligman observed that though "they were by no means the only ones," it was "teachers of the political and social sciences [who] were today primarily the ones on the firing line."[39]

At the end of 1913, troubled by instances of university administrators' denial of academic freedom to social scientists, the American Economic Association, the American Sociological Society, and the American Political Science Association passed identical resolutions calling for a committee to look into "the present situation in American educational institutions as to liberty of thought, freedom of speech, and security of tenure for teachers of Economics (Sociology or Political Science)." Six months later, with other academic allies outside the social sciences, the three committees became one, and Seligman, chair of the American Economic Association's committee, was elected to head the new joint committee on Academic Freedom and Academic Tenure. Soon "a large number of individual cases were brought to the attention of the committee." In another six months the committee published a "Preliminary Report of the Committee on Academic Freedom and Academic Tenure."[40]

In the wake of that report, the American Association of University Professors was organized, with John Dewey of Columbia as president, and Arthur O. Lovejoy of Johns Hopkins, like Dewey a philosopher, its secretary. In drawing up the AAUP's declaration of principles, the fifteen academics on Seligman's committee, the majority of them social scientists, emphasized the scientific nature of intellectual inquiry: "A university is a great and indispensable organ of the higher life of a civilized community . . . in which the faculties hold an independent place . . . and in relation to purely scientific and educational questions, the primary responsibility." They warned of "special dangers to freedom of teaching in the domain of the social sciences," and, in more than a dozen references, asserted the "scientific conscience," "scientific research," "scientific temper," "scientific inquiry," or "scientific spirit" of scholars as grounds for academic freedom.[41] In effect, they were appealing to the scientific—with its aura of objective nonpartisan data gathering and analysis—in demanding from college trustees and presidents that those faculty who disagreed with them be allowed to carry on unimpeded.

But the AAUP did not end ideological conflict in the halls of academe. When Burgess retired as professor and dean of Columbia's combined graduate faculties in 1912, President Nicholas Murray Butler—according to Charles Beard—made plain that, "no person with progressive or liberal views would be acceptable" to succeed him. A corporate lawyer, law partner of one of the university's trustees, was appointed. For another position, Butler "pointed out that a man of 'Bull Moose' [Progressive Party] proclivities would not be acceptable." When Leon Fraser, a young instructor in politics at Columbia, criticized the military camp at Plattsburg, New York, early in 1916 he was "hauled before the trustees," and, the following year, Beard wrote, the political science department was "warned not to re-nominate Dr. Fraser for re-appointment because he was not acceptable to Mr. Bangs, one of the trustees."[42] The department did renominate Fraser, but he was not reappointed. The years of the First World War heated the atmosphere of intolerance of dissent on campuses as in the public at large.

"It was," Charles Beard said in a statement to the *New Republic,* "the evident purpose of a small group of the trustees (unhindered, if not aided, by Mr. Butler) to take advantage of the state of war to drive out or humiliate or terrorize every man who held progressive, liberal, or unconventional views on political matters in no way connected with the war." Henry Wadsworth Dana, who taught comparative literature, was dismissed, as historian Robert A. McCaughey notes, "for sundry antiwar activities." After twenty-six years as professor of psychology, James Mc-Keen Cattell was fired in 1917 by Columbia's trustees and they refused payment of his pension. Columbia's first professor of experimental psychology, Cattell had not confined his energies to the psychological laboratory; his "A Program of Radical Democracy" (1910) argued for progressive taxation, old-age and disability pensions, universal health care, child welfare payments, the eight-hour day, a minimum wage, an end to child labor, votes for women, and, more ominously no doubt to the trustees, a $5,000 annual cap on individual income. He made this radical proposition: "The homes and tools of production to be owned by those who use them. The excess wealth to be owned by the locality, the state and the nation." In 1906 Cattell had begun publishing a series of articles that became the basis for his 1913 *University Control,* a book in which he upbraided university administrators and trustees and included 290 unsigned letters from academics from across the country calling for faculty administrative control of the nation's institutions of higher education. Sometimes gruff and irascible, Cattell had made his opposition to Columbia's administration a personal matter, circulating letters chastising President Butler among the faculty, and in other ways exacerbating his relations with the school's administration and many faculty. When, following America's April 1917 entry into the First World War, one of Cattell's sons, a part-time Columbia undergraduate, took part in an antiwar demonstration and was arrested, Cattell praised him. When Columbia administrators learned that Cattell had written to members of Congress in August that Americans opposed to the war ought not be sent into the fight, the trustees used the occasion to dismiss him.[43]

Beard fell under similar scrutiny. After his "wander days at Heidelberg" and graduate study at Oxford and in Columbia's School of Political Science, Beard had risen to the rank of professor of politics. His *American Government and Politics* (1910) was a pioneering textbook in its field. "When Beard strode into the classroom it was," one of his students wrote, "like a salty breeze blowing out the stuffiness from the room."

Tall, with red hair and striking blue eyes, daring and controversial, "in grave moments [his appearance] could give him the aspect of a worried eagle," the historian Richard Hofstadter later said. His trouble with the trustees arose with a 1916 speech before the National Conference of Community Centers, advocating the use of schools as centers for the discussion of public questions. After an inaccurate published account of his remarks accused him of approving flag burning, Beard wrote the city's newspapers, including the errant one, correcting the record. What had actually occurred, he said, was that, a few weeks earlier, a speaker who supported the use of schools for public forums was said to have said, "To Hell with the Flag." Beard did not agree with the sentiment but did believe "that the intemperance of one man should not drive us into closing the schools to others." The newspaper's inaccurate story had generated a public outcry and Beard was summoned before a committee of the university's trustees. "I complied," Beard wrote, "because I wanted to clear up any wrong impressions." "As soon as the committee of the trustees opened the inquiry I speedily disposed of the 'flag incident,' by showing that I had said nothing that could be construed as endorsing in any way the objectionable language in question. No one doubted my word. Indeed I had available abundant testimony from reliable men and women who had heard the address. The record was thus soon set straight." As he prepared to leave the room, two trustees, who were corporate lawyers, Frederic R. Coudert and Francis S. Bangs, stopped him. "I was utterly astonished to have Mr. Bangs and Mr. Coudert launch into an inquisition into my views and teachings." They "grilled" him for half an hour. "Mr. Coudert, who had once privately commended my book on the Constitution as 'admirably well done,' and opening up 'a most fertile field,' denounced my teaching in vigorous language, in which he was strongly seconded by Mr. Bangs." Beard was admonished "to warn all other men in my department against teachings 'likely to inculcate disrespect for American institutions.'" (Trustee Francis S. Bangs also targeted the progressive economist Seligman for sanctioning but, as McCaughey writes, he failed "to generate much enthusiasm for cashiering" him among other board members.) [44]

At several subsequent faculty caucuses "it was generally agreed that the proceedings of the trustees were highly reprehensible." Aroused faculty were calmed by President Butler and by a dean who told them, Beard said, that "the trustees had learned their lesson and that such an inquisition would never happen again." Yet the following year, 1917, the trustees "gave to the press a set of resolutions instructing a committee 'to inquire and ascertain' whether certain doctrines were being taught in the University." In response, the Faculty of Political Science resolved "that we will not individually or collectively lend any countenance to such an inquiry." Stymied by the opposition, the trustees agreed to work with a faculty committee to resolve cases in dispute, but Beard had had enough. In a letter of resignation he derided "a small and active group" of Columbia trustees who "dominated the university and terrorize the young instructors" as "reactionary and visionless in politics, [and] narrow and medieval in religion." A group of Columbia students called for "a protest against the resignation of Professor Beard and the 'autocratic' methods of the Trustees," and distributed handbills reading:

> As a Protest Against the Suppression of Academic Freedom
> By the Trustees of Columbia University,
> All Students are Requested to Cut Classes
> at 11 o'clock Wednesday Morning.

At the protest on the steps of Low Library, "about 500 students, many merely curious, responded." The president of the senior class tried to speak but other students, described by a *New York Times* reporter as "student patriots," "sounded three cheers for Columbia and the Faculty and gave the radicals what is known among students as the 'bum's rush'" and the rally was "dispersed more or less roughly by a small but vigorous group."[45]

The following year, Beard and his friend and colleague James Harvey Robinson—the two had created a school of historical interpretation called "the New History," drawing on American pragmatist philosophy—laid plans for an alternative institution for the study of the social sciences. By 1919 it had opened as the New School for Social Research. Another of its founders, Alvin Johnson, noted, "Every liberal in the city was excited by the novel venture of an institution headed by two such dynamic figures as Robinson and Beard."[46] Beard and Robinson were joined in the founding by Johnson, Dewey, Wesley Clair Mitchell, and Thorstein Veblen (Edwin Seligman was an early patron)—each in his own way an academic renegade. The school, initially housed in a rented brownstone on West 23rd Street, was conceived as "an Independent School of Social Science for Men and Women," where "teachers and investigators" could work "emancipated from suspected obligations to donors, trustees and university management in general." As the founders saw it, "The political and social problems forced upon the country by the economic development of the past twenty-five years call for a new type of leadership in every field of American life." With the "city, state and national Governments . . . undertaking new functions which require for their efficient administration experts," the New School would prepare such experts "through the Social and Political sciences," and thus become "the center of the best thought in America." The New School's founders, freed "from the narrow trammels of lay boards of trustees," would be run by the faculty itself. The founders declared: "this is the hour for experiment; and New York is the place, because it is the greatest social science laboratory in the world."[47]

To the political left of The New School, and antedating it by more than a decade, was the Rand School of Social Science. Despite the trashing of its offices and classrooms during the War and the Red Scare that followed it, the Rand School continued to teach radical visions of social science. (It closed in 1956.) Housed in a brownstone at 112 East 19th Street, the Rand School set out to train its students as lecturers, teachers, and organizers. It taught "political and social science from the standpoint of socialism." Graduates would "rally workers to establish a just social system." It had been funded by an endowment bequeathed by the Christian socialist Carrie Rand and by revenues from tuition and the sale of books and pamphlets. The school's founders—they called themselves the Board of Directors of the American Socialist Society—included Morris Hillquit, Algernon Lee, William James Ghent, and Charles Beard (one early organizational meeting of 5 April 1906 was held in Beard's Manhattan apartment). All four were members of the left liberal "New York X" men's dinner and discussion club that had been started by Ghent in 1903. Ghent taught "Introduction to Socialism," Hillquit "The History of Socialism," and Beard (while he also held a full-time teaching position at Columbia), "American Economic and Political History." The school's most popular lecturer in those early years was the Columbia sociologist, Franklin Giddings, also a "New York X'er", whose effusive and engaging personality captivated students in his course on "The Principles of Sociology."[48]

Women, unwelcome on the full-time social science faculties of most universities, were welcome at the Rand School: Florence Kelley, director of the National Consumers' League; Charlotte Perkins Gilman, socialist feminist; and Mary Ritter Beard, historian and wife of Charles Beard, were active at the Rand School. Kelley captured many socialists' criticisms of the social sciences in the nation's universities: "In medicine, in the natural sciences, the word of the day is, 'Investigation regardless of consequences; the truth at all costs!' But in the social sciences there comes always in some insidious form the misleading influence of personal or class interest." The very institutions—colleges and universities—in which the social sciences ought to be expected to proceed without interference, were themselves at risk. "Our colleges being institutions owned by the ruling class (even when founded with public money) for the training of the rising generation thereof, and manned by its carefully selected employes, the economic and sociological teaching done in them is such as the employers require." "Our college course of economic study," Kelley said, "usually affords us either no light on the subject or actual darkness, the teaching that should be in the direction of unprejudiced investigation being only too frequently dogmatic apology for the social system as it is to-day."[49]

Social scientists might broadly agree that they were an elite, the claim grounded in their shared embrace of science, but modern American social science was shaped on American campuses that were sometimes a haven, sometimes a den of conflict. Beyond broad methodological agreement the social sciences were caught in a tangle of disagreement, dissent, and repression based on conflicts of interest. Some social scientists, like the conservative John W. Burgess, reflected the established and dominant cultural ethos of the era, opposed social reform, and were insensitive on women's rights and racist in their views. Others, like the economist Edwin R. A. Seligman, supported social reform, women's rights, and racial equality. The conflict of views would structure the terms of debate over political ends in the social sciences.

Yet, despite the unresolved debates on economic theory and on politics, a group of men and women trained in the nation's new graduate schools of social science at the turn of the century created and led a vast number of voluntary, issue-oriented, liberal associations, committees, and organizations that went beyond critique to efforts to reform the repressive and unequal social order. In "the greatest social science laboratory in the world," an expanding network of scholar-activists sought to reconcile social science and democracy.

Chapter 2

From Noblesse Oblige to Social Reform in the "New Philanthropy" of "Scientific Charity"

Toward a "Science" of "Dealing with the Poor": "Mrs. Lowell's Society"

Josephine Shaw Lowell was a pioneer in the advancement of organized charity in the United States, a transitional figure between patrician noblesse oblige and the new social science in the tradition of liberal religious women of the mid-nineteenth century such as Dorothea Dix, who transformed asylums for the mentally ill; Clara Barton, a founder of the Red Cross; and Florence Nightingale, English crusader for hospital reform and founder of modern nursing. Shut out of university faculty appointments, the world of scholarship, science, and the professions, denied the vote, such women found a way into the public realm, where their education, aristocratic lineage, family money, and familiarity with the world of influence could have immediate impact in social reform.

Born to privilege in 1843 into two of Boston's wealthiest mercantile blue-blood Brahmin families, the Shaws and the Sturgises, Josephine Shaw Lowell spent four years in Europe, learning French, Italian, and German, before settling in New York City. Her parents were fiercely antislavery, active Unitarians, part of the Boston-New York liberal intelligentsia, acquaintances of Emerson and enthusiasts of the radical reformer Henry George.[1]

Lowell's career of public service began at nineteen, when she volunteered to serve as a nurse in Virginia during the Civil War with the United States Sanitary Commission, predecessor to the Red Cross. Her brother, Robert Gould Shaw, colonel of the Massachusetts 54th, the famous commander of the nation's first black regiment, was killed in battle in 1863. Her husband of only a year, Charles Russell Lowell (valedictorian of his Harvard class), led the Union attack at the battle of Cedar Creek in 1864 and died of his wounds the next day. Lowell wore widow's-black for the rest of her life, but she did not withdraw into private life. For five years, in her mid-twenties, she was secretary of the New York branch of the American Freedmen's Relief Commission, providing teachers and money to newly freed slaves in the South, and in 1876 she was appointed to the New York State Board of Charities, the first woman to serve on such a state commission. She founded the Charity Organization Society (COS) of the City of New York in 1882 and served as the first president of the Consumers' League of the City of New York.[2]

Lowell's venture into charity work was shaped by the noblesse oblige tradition of the European and American patrician elite in which, as historian Timothy B. Smith has summed it: "the rich and respectable vied with each other in good works, and no noblewoman was without 'her' poor." "I do not agree," she wrote, "that any province of life is outside the domain of the laws of the gospels: I hold that every relation of life should be governed by them." But Lowell was also a modern woman, and by her early forties she declared: "the task of dealing with the poor has become a science." "It can only be from 'economic science enlightened by the spirit of the gospel,'" that progress could be achieved.[3]

As a young woman, Lowell held the traditional view of the privileged: poverty was a consequence of moral failing; but over time she concluded that employers, consumers, and citizens were complicit in the creation and maintenance of poverty and responsible for the suffering that affected others. "Fearless, intelligent and devoted," Lowell aroused "strong indignation" with her "plain speaking," as two who followed her example would say later.[4] No one could intimidate or dissuade her from her course.

Lowell, like most young women of her time, had no practical opportunity for a college education, but she was said to have read John Stuart Mill's *Principles of Political Economy* three times on her honeymoon, and, as a nurse in the Civil War she met a number of members of the American Social Science Association. When her Charity Organization Society opened its Summer School in Philanthropy in 1898 to train young Americans in the practical application of social science in social work, she was an occasional lecturer.[5] She had learned on the job.

The Charity Organization Society—"Mrs. Lowell's society," its members called it—reflected a sense of dual responsibility, of each of the poor for their own conduct, and of the affluent for social reforms. According to the Society's constitution of 1882 it would "promote the general welfare of the poor by social and sanitary reforms," and "investigate thoroughly, and without charge, the cases of all applicants for relief which are referred to the Society for inquiry." It investigated applicants through the casework method of "friendly visits"; its "visitors" expected to "personally attend cases needing counsel and advice" and, "by the inculcation of habits of providence and self-dependence," seek to improve the character of the poor.[6]

"Mrs. Lowell's Society" undertook to coordinate and organize private charities, and in its first year it won the cooperation of 138—religious and secular—in New York City. It opened a "bureau of fraudulent cases" to keep "impostors" and double-dipping cheats from defrauding the city's charities, publishing dozens of "Illustrative Cases," among them: "An able-bodied Italian twists his legs so as to appear helpless. Has saved much money, and last year revisited Italy for pleasure. Another prosperous one hides 2 good eyes under goggles, and carries a sign, 'Help poor blind man.'" The poor should retain their dignity and not beg on the streets: "it is evident that the alms given to them only do them unmitigated harm; maintaining them either in a life of deceit and systematic fraud, or of the deepest physical degradation. In either case the injury to them and to society is deadly."[7]

A number of religious charities were dispensing evangelism along with food, but the Charity Organization Society constitution forbade "friendly visitors" to preach: "No person representing the Society in any capacity whatsoever shall use his or her position for the purpose of proselytism." In 1901, Edward T. Devine, Charity Organization Society executive secretary, reinforced the point: "This is not to say that the charity worker can be indifferent to the value of spiritual influence in the reconstructive work which he has undertaken. He simply consents to a division of work under which the giving of religious instruction and counsel devolves upon others."[8]

The casework system, with home visits, interviews, and counseling of the poor, was the Society's signature method. In its second year, it published an 88-page *Handbook for Friendly Visitors* (within a few years the term "friendly visitor" would be replaced by "caseworker"). "Charity Must," the *Handbook*'s title page declared, "Do Five Things":

1. Act only upon knowledge got by thorough investigation.
2. Relieve worthy need promptly, fittingly, and tenderly.
3. Prevent unwise alms to the unworthy.
4. Raise into independence every needy person, where this is possible.
5. Make sure that no children grow up to be paupers.

The *Handbook* admonished the poor to spend their money on clean dress, nourishing food, and well-ventilated living quarters, not on alcohol. (It offered a number of dietary tips; one read: "fish is better flesh-forming food than poultry, lamb, or veal but furnishes less heat.") Within a few years casefile cards for 3,400 families were indexed in a central filebox (a decade later there were, reportedly, 170,000). The Society set guidelines for its caseworkers' interviews with the poor, supplying $4^{1}/_{4}'' \times 10''$ stock cards with questions preprinted and space for inserting interviewees' replies. It asked, for example, who in the family was earning money, and how much. Was "Any other able to work?"; "Why are any out of work?"; "Has anything been saved in prosperous times?"; "Any thing in pawn?"; "Habits? as to intemperance, etc."; "Assistance most needed?" The Society helped families that had no ablebodied adult with "suitable and adequate relief for deserving cases," distributing small sums of relief, often $5 or $10 a week, sometimes for several weeks, on occasion for much longer periods, but Lowell admonished caseworkers not to give indiscriminate "relief" (money not earned by a person's own labor) lest it lead recipients to become addicted to unearned income and engender long-term dependency. *The Handbook* concluded: "Bear in mind that co-operation and consultation are fundamental principles of Organized Charity, and should govern all our intercourse. . . . Do not rely on your own or any single judgment. Remember our investigations will be investigated, and our conclusions often subjected to adverse criticism. Have no pride of your own opinion, and let all be done in a spirit of the broadest charity."[9]

The "Deserving" and the "Undeserving" Poor

Charity Organization Society "friendly" visitors were not always so friendly, and sometimes they were controlling and even, if in a genteel way, cruel. Clients who did not hew the line were rejected. "Mrs. Lowell's Society" drew on the old tradition from medieval times, of the English Poor Law, which made a distinction between the deserving and undeserving poor—the Ordinance of Labourers of 1349 held that ablebodied beggars "may be compelled to labour for their necessary living." "Paupers," in Lowell's vocabulary, and in the vocabulary of the Society, were those who refused to work, and none were to receive continuing alms lest they become accustomed to perennial indolence and be robbed of self-worth and the possibility of independent selfhood. The Scottish Reverend John Peden Bell had expressed a similar view in his 1853 book *Christian Sociology*: "one who willingly abandons labour, or who depends upon others while he could meet his own needs . . . throws himself under the power of evil." "Idleness is itself a fen for the growth of all that is noxious." Lowell herself said (her words would echo in the debates of later decades), "recipients of alms become dependent, lose their energy, are rendered incapable of self-support, and what they receive in return for their lost character is quite inadequate to supply their needs; thus they are kept on the verge almost of death by the very persons who think they are relieving them." Also: "It is the greatest wrong that can be done to him to undermine the character of a poor

man—for it is his all"; "almsgiving and dolegiving are hurtful—
therefore they are not charitable"; "the proof that dolegiving and almsgiving do break down independence, do destroy energy, do undermine
character, may be found in the growing ranks of pauperism in every city,
in the fact that the larger the funds given in relief in any community,
the more pressing is the demand for them, and in the experience and
testimony of all practical workers among the poor." Lowell did fault
"the pressure of the unjust social laws and legislative enactments which
produce hardship and cause more people to become idlers than would
otherwise be the case," but, "the usual cause of poverty," she wrote, "is
to be found in some deficiency—moral, mental, or physical—in the person who suffers."[10]

Families in which the adult or adults were unable to work because of
physical injury, illness or mental incapacity, or in times of sharp economic downturn that threw them out of work, were deemed by Mrs.
Lowell's Society "the deserving poor" and were helped. Although the
approach of the Society was suffused with self-righteousness, Mrs. Lowell
was intent not on condemning the idle but in putting them to work and
freeing them from reliance on charity. The paid staff and volunteers not
only assessed the worthiness of each individual who applied, but also lectured them and tried to find them jobs. They even hired many themselves. Women deemed employable were sent to wash and iron at a
Society laundry that opened in 1889 at 589 Park Avenue and moved to
the Society's Industrial Building at 516 West 28th Street in 1900. By the
early 1900s the laundry was training eighty or ninety women a month; it
was one of Lowell's pioneering successes. The sociologist Frances Kellor
wrote in 1904 that the system began first "over steaming wash-tubs,
advances them to starching and ironing, and graduates them with a recommendation after thorough instruction in the ironing of filmy lace
curtains and finest linen." The Society opened a wood yard in 1884 on
East 24th Street, where young male beggars were sent to test their will-
ingness to work. The Society sold tickets to the charitable for them to
offer to street beggars in lieu of cash—each ticket entitled its bearer to
a day's work in the wood yard. Beggars who showed themselves willing to
work were placed as jobs became available as domestic servants, factory
workers, janitors and furnace men, messengers and delivery boys, por-
ters, watchmen, drivers, dishwashers, bootblacks, and the like, the Society functioning more as an employment agency than as a traditional
charity.[11]

The Charity Organization Society did not content itself with its private
activities but took public action against what it perceived as New York
City's own indiscriminate charity. When the city persisted in distributing
free coal to the poor (a practice it began in 1875), the Society lobbied

legislators to stop it, and though thwarted by Tammany-connected coal merchants profiting from city treasury payments, it eventually got the practice stopped. It even urged the municipal government to follow the European practice of lengthening prison sentences for vagrants and street beggars. And when, in 1904, "a flurry of excitement over children who go breakfastless to school" created a movement to provide "free meals" at public expense, the Society opposed it in hearings before the city's special committee of the Board of Education. Two years later, another proposal was offered to "give eye-glasses to all for whom they were prescribed" among the city's school children, and the Society took a stand against it as " 'certainly unnecessary' " "in view of the admitted ability of parents in the very great majority of all cases to take care of their own children." The COS was stern but not heartless; it would "supply the needs of any child" whose family was truly unable to feed them or buy eyeglasses.[12]

Political bosses and their machines often stepped in when the Charity Organization Society declined to. Frances Perkins, the future U.S. Secretary of Labor, recalled just such an instance. When, as a young woman, Perkins lived in a settlement house in the Hell's Kitchen neighborhood on Manhattan's West Side, she went to the Society to ask that the family of a young man awaiting trial in prison, the sole means of support for his mother and two sisters, receive financial assistance. "Friendly" visitors met with the mother and sisters but found them unworthy, as Perkins understood it, because the mother drank excessively. Perkins marched indignantly from COS headquarters to the offices of Thomas J. MacManus, the Tammany Hall ward boss for Hell's Kitchen. She asked the men "milling about, talking, smoking and spitting" if she could see MacManus, and was directed inside. Did the boy live in his district? Mac-Manus asked; and did *she*? At the time as a resident of Hartley House, she was indeed in MacManus's district, and shrewdly gave her street address without mentioning that it was a settlement house. Three days later— she never learned just how—the young man was back at his job.[13] It was a harbinger of the sort of person Perkins was and of the public political role she would one day assume.

Lowell was a transitional person in the world of social reform from one age to another. Born only seventeen years after Thomas Jefferson's death, she had an early vision of work as builder of moral character that echoed Jefferson's own democratic vision of the small independent producer—the farmer and independent craftsman—fiercely proud of his independence. Yet, by her middle years, her perspective changed in response to the decline in skilled journeymen and the burgeoning increase in poorly paid industrial laborers in sweatshops, mines, mills, and factories at jobs that were hazardous, physically exhausting, and

brain-numbingly repetitive, with little leisure time for character building. With the same passion she had earlier brought to her lectures on
moral responsibility, Lowell now chastised a social order that destroyed
life choices. In 1885 in a blistering address, "On the Relation of Employers and Employed," before the Women's Conference of the Philadelphia Society for Organized Charity, she scolded industrial capitalists and
their corporations for ruining the morals and destroying the health and
household economies of working people:

In how many ways do not employers contribute directly to their degradation!
By overwork, driving them to the use of stimulants; by unhealthy surroundings,
sapping their strength; and by these and other means depriving them of all
chance of being free and independent men. . . . women who should be caring
for their children,—working in factories in bad air, working overtime, destroying
their own health, turning off their children to be drugged and abused by careless, brutal nurses. What hope can there be for the health and strength of children so born and nurtured? What hope for their characters, when they are left
to run in the streets until they too are swept into the unrelenting grasp of these
same dread factories? Employers are responsible for the deterioration of the
race because they allow such things.

Of the labor of children in factories Lowell said: "Here we see that
employers are guilty of a great crime, not only against their working people, but against the State, and this crime should be forbidden by law in
every State in the Union, and the laws when passed, should be
enforced." "Corporations especially" she declared, "are acknowledged
to be devoid of all conscience in their relations toward those who make
the wealth which they divide; the directors and officers convince themselves that their first duty is toward their stockholders, and that they are
bound to make every dollar possible, regardless of the means by which
it is done, the stockholders know nothing whatever of the methods
adopted, and the workers go down in the struggle." Nor was Lowell satis-
fied with chastising the hard-hearted or indifferent wealthy; she
expected government action: "Legislation is required in the interest of
the national health, to ensure that every man shall have at least one day
in seven for his sabbath, his day of rest, essential both for his body and
his soul."[14]
      Lowell was intent on changing the work place itself by use of private
power to influence public power. She was instrumental in founding the
Working Women's Society of the City of New York in 1886, its purpose to
investigate conditions faced by women workers. Observing that "public
opinion has a great influence in fixing the rates of wages," she became
a founder and first president of the New York Consumers' League, headquartered in Manhattan, its purpose to educate consumers to use their
power by purchasing only goods produced and sold in shops where

wages, conditions of labor, and hours of work were fair. Any consumer who bought at the lowest possible price regardless of the conditions under which a product was made would signal employers to drive wages and working conditions down, and overworked and underpaid workers would suffer a collapse of health and moral character. The Consumers' League was not, as some later might suppose, an organization out to lower prices; it sought, in effect, to raise them—in order to improve conditions and increase pay for workers. Lowell also supported the right of workers to form unions and profit-sharing workers' cooperatives.[15] Deterrent and disciplinary reforms to chasten employers could come from individual consumers wielding buying power in the cause, a strategy expanded beginning in 1899 into a national movement led by Florence Kelley, as executive secretary of the National Consumers' League (see Chapter 5).

By the spring of 1895, at fifty-one, Lowell was calling for enhanced "public relief," for government to establish fair hours, wages, and working conditions in the industrializing economy. In an address on "Poverty and Its Relief: The Methods Possible in the City of New York," delivered to the National Conference of Charities and Correction, she proposed that "the chronically 'homeless and unemployed'" become the responsibility of "a system of public relief, the exception being only made in favor of such private relief agencies as will bind themselves to take sole care, and permanent care, of such individuals as they undertake to deal with at all,—to provide home and work and education and religious teaching for them." Such "public relief" would provide decent lodging; a training school for teaching a trade (such training to last from six months to two years); but also "an asylum for moral idiots" "where men and women who have proved themselves incorrigible shall be shut away from harming themselves and others." While the object of the Charity Organization Society was "to make" men and women "workers and not idlers, and to educate them" to desire "a higher standard of living if they happen to have a low one," with "really sympathetic" attention—including, perhaps, a version of therapeutic counseling by caseworkers—it was crucial that employers provide reasonable working conditions, that government pass "legislative enactments," and that consumers buy only from shops where workers were treated fairly.[16]

In the last decade of Lowell's life (she died in 1905), Mary Kingsbury Simkhovitch, who worked with her, wrote, Lowell "came out for [the populist William Jennings] Bryan" in his bid for the presidency, and "championed" the advocate for labor "Joseph Barondess's candidacy for Congress in his socialist days, much to the amazement of some of her less seasoned uptown friends."[17] Her perspective was no longer the old elites' noblesse oblige or the maternal/paternal control of her own earlier years, but an equally unsentimental political strategy of transforming a society based on inequality.

"The New Philanthropy" with "the Rank of a Science"

In 1885 Josephine Shaw Lowell had been foresighted in acknowledging the importance of "our science" and of "economic science" in the work of her Charity Organization Society. A decade later, in 1896, with the appointment of Edward Thomas Devine as executive secretary of "Mrs. Lowell's Society" (a post he held for the next twenty-one years), social science took center stage. A credentialed—perhaps one might say "professional"—social scientist had been chosen by Lowell to head her Society. Charitable groups generally were the domain of the churches. Lowell was way ahead of her time.

Edward Devine, like so many of New York's scholar-activists a Midwesterner who came east, had received formal training in the new social science graduate programs, though he was born in a log cabin and raised on his family's farm in Iowa. His father was an Irish immigrant, his mother New England born. After attending Iowa's Cornell College, Devine taught Greek and Latin and was working as a high school principal until an almost by chance dinner conversation with Simon Nelson Patten, also an Iowa public school principal but soon to become a top sociologist and economist at the University of Pennsylvania, "determined my whole future." He went to Philadelphia to study with Patten, earned his doctorate in economics at the University of Pennsylvania and, at Patten's recommendation, studied for a year at the University of Halle in Germany. They remained life-long friends. Patten took a personal and engaged interest in a number of his students; for example, he lent $300 (about $5,000 in 2000 dollars) to William H. Allen, later a founder of the New York Bureau of Municipal Research, so he could pursue graduate study in Europe. Patten also urged Frances Perkins, who also studied with him at Pennsylvania, to continue her study of sociology and economics at Columbia University, and, with a letter of recommendation from him, she did. Patten's view of social cooperation rather than market competitiveness as the key to the success of the American economy influenced a number of his students. To Patten, the nation's riches were a socially produced surplus, and government ought to distribute that surplus fairly.[18]

In 1896, with Patten and Franklin Giddings at Columbia lobbying on his behalf, Devine won appointment as executive secretary to the Charity Organization Society of the City of New York. In 1905 he was appointed professor of social economy at Columbia University. Nicknamed "the doctor" by his Columbia students, Devine sought to raise philanthropy itself to a science, extending Josephine Shaw Lowell's own philosophy of the duty of the affluent with his own theory, research, and practical prescriptive problem-solving. Such applied social science was increasingly winning the label "social work," though a social work with a dual impulse, to integrate the lives of the poor into the rhythms and expectations of the established social and economic order, and to improve the order itself. Within a year, Devine had founded a journal, *Charities: A Weekly Review of Local and General Philanthropy* (in 1905 it became *Charities and the Commons*, when it absorbed *The Commons*, a small midwestern journal of social reform, and, in 1909 *The Survey: Journal of Applied Social Science and Social Work*). *The Survey* served for decades as the journal of record for charity and social work on the application of social science research to everyday life. Devine was also a leading figure in opening, under Society auspices, the nation's first school—initially a summer school—of social work, which in 1904 formally adopted the name New York School of Philanthropy, with Devine as its director. That same year Devine became a principal founder of the National Child Labor Committee (see Chapter 5) and recruited a sociologist at the University of Pennsylvania, Samuel McCune Lindsay, as its first executive secretary; he also helped found the National Association for the Study and Prevention of Tuberculosis. The following year he became Schiff Professor of Social Economy at Columbia University, a chair endowed by Jacob Henry Schiff of the powerful banking firm of Kuhn, Loeb and Co., a leader of New York's German-Jewish community and funder of Lillian Wald's Nurses' Settlement, later Henry Street Settlement. Devine's work was not limited to New York: he headed the American Red Cross relief work in San Francisco in the wake of the devastating 1906 earthquake and Red Cross disaster relief after major floods crippled Dayton, Ohio in 1913. During the First World War, he headed the American Bureau of Refugees and Relief in France, and by the mid-1920s he had become dean of the graduate school of American University in Washington, D.C.[19]

Devine had been hired by Lowell and the other members of the Charity Organization Society's central council in part because he shared much of her perspective on poverty and the poor. (In a long illness she described as "jaundice," Lowell wrote, on 9 September 1905, in what turned out to be her last letter to Devine, "I should like to stay on the [COS's Central] Council for 'sentiment.'" She died the next month at sixty-two.) Devine was a quarter century younger than Lowell, formally trained in the social sciences, as she was not, and also fired with passion about the possibilities of social science. In 1899 he wrote: "There is no charity in which anybody of standing and a moderate degree of brains believes except scientific charity. Unscientific charity is clearly as absurd and indefensible as unscientific medicine." He urged "the universal acceptance of scientific charity" as "rapidly as possible." Devine shared Lowell's sense of double causation of poverty and social decay: "the idea of charity," he said, was "bounded," on the one side, by "the existing economic and social order" and the "social conditions" within that order, and, on the other side, by "the faults and weaknesses of the individual."[20]

Devine rejected the Social Darwinian notion that society ought to allow the unfit to die rather than create a social network to aid them. "Charity reasonably bestowed," he wrote, "does not perpetuate the unfit but transforms the unfit into that which may profitably survive."

In the eighteenth century, and well on into our own, there was a prevailing school of thought that found all the explanation for misery and social inequality in the oppressive burden of government and its accompanying social institutions. Take off the burden, was their urgent cry. Man by nature is progressive, intelligent and good. He has been held down. Remove all these artificial restrictions. Let human society be left free to work out its own salvation, and all the woes we deplore will silently disappear. *Laissez faire, laissez passer.* Let everything alone, and there will be no trouble.

He rejected the classical liberalism of social scientists like John W. Burgess with its insistence on a minimalist state and on a noninterventionist, wholly free-market political economy. Laissez faire, Devine declared, "is fallacious and in practice of no value," rather, "the best thought of those who desire social reform and improvement is now crystallizing in the idea that liberty—social freedom—is not a state of nature, but a positively created condition in which the most active vigilance on the part of the community is needed."[21]

Devine wrote later in his autobiography, *When Social Work Was Young:* "The new confidence was in what might be accomplished by conscious social action." Academically trained social scientists hoped not merely to manage poverty but to end it. Government was to be called on to set a safety net.

Misery was in evidence, but its causes were believed to be discoverable and removable. The hardships and injustices under which the poor suffered were to be measured, analyzed, and dealt with. The prosperous were to be persuaded or compelled to share their prosperity. Child labor, sweatshops, preventable diseases, insanitary slums were to be abolished. Organized labor was encouraged to demand decent working conditions and living wages. The state was to be called in to fix the levels below which the exploitation of workers and consumers would not be tolerated, above which the principle of free competition might safely and advantageously be left free to operate.[22]

Social science was setting the terms for the conduct of society, in the private and public realms.

The new emphasis was on science as the preferred method of philanthropy and on philanthropy as preventative. Thus Albert O. Wright, a Wisconsin educator and student of the social sciences, told members of the National Conference of Charities and Correction that "The New Philanthropy" "claims as its own the recent rapid rise of the study of sociology in our institutions of learning. Philanthropy is thus raised to the rank of a science, the practical and theoretical are yoked together." Devine wrote, in his autobiography, of the "new view" of charity that it "makes of charity a type of anticipatory justice, which deals not only with individuals who suffer but with social conditions that tend to perpetuate crime, pauperism, and degeneracy." In 1906 he wrote to the Charity Organization Society's president Robert W. de Forest that "more attention in the future than has been given in the past" ought to be given to "preventative social work."[23]

The First School of Applied Social Science: The New York School of Philanthropy

In 1896, in Devine's first year as Charity Organization Society general secretary he initiated a cooperative venture with Columbia's Department of Social Science that would lead to the New York School of Philanthropy, the nation's first school of social work in 1898, teaming up Franklin Giddings and Richmond Mayo-Smith of Columbia to analyze hundreds of the Society's casework records. The Charity Organization Society arranged for a permanent seat on its central council for a member of Columbia's Faculty of Political Science, a seat Giddings occupied for many years. The very next year after the cooperative casework venture began, the School of Philanthropy offered its first classes in the intersection between traditional charity work and academic social science. Similar schools were soon to follow: in 1903, a school of social service, affiliated with the University of Chicago; in 1904, the Boston School for Social Workers, affiliated with Harvard and Simmons Colleges; in 1908, the St. Louis School of Philanthropy and the Philadelphia Training School for Social Work.[24]

The New York School's first classes were held during a six-week Summer School in Philanthropy known as the "training class in applied philanthropy" in the library of the Charity Organization Society's offices in the United Charities Building on East 22nd Street, the hub of the social reform movement of New York's scholar-activists. With an endowment of $250,000 from John Stewart Kennedy, the Society's vice president, a year-long curriculum was undertaken; in 1904 the name New York School of Philanthropy was adopted. In its first summer, twenty-six full-time students and "many visitors" attended, including "members of charity organization societies, residents of settlements, or leaders in social reform in their respective cities," representing eleven states from Massachusetts to California. Among those who taught there in its early years were James B. Reynolds, Mary Kingsbury (soon to become Mary Kingsbury Simkhovitch), and Columbia University social scientists Mayo-Smith and Giddings. The School's Progressive Era advisory council included, along with Devine and Lindsay—Lindsay assumed the School's directorship from 1907 to 1912—Columbia social scientists Henry Rogers Seager, Edwin R. A. Seligman, and Giddings. By an early agreement between Columbia and the School of Philanthropy, students who registered at either school could attend lectures at the other, and Columbia accepted course work at the School of Philanthropy as a minor for advanced degrees. Devine considered the university affiliation "ideal." Besides, John Stewart Kennedy's endowment had insisted on it.[25]

From its inception the School reflected the twin emphases of its institutional sponsors—social work and social theory. It set out to train students as social workers through the one-on-one casework method of investigation and counseling developed by the Charity Organization Society. It also taught social theory, research skills, and public speaking on broad-based questions of economy and society, convinced that persuading the public was part of its task. Graduates were to be equipped to offer insight into problems caused by the industrial capitalist social order, and to engage in political advocacy as "headworkers and assistants in social settlements," community organizers, legislative lobbyists, and government officials.[26] In 1919, though the emphasis on advocacy and reform remained alive, the School's name changed, to the New York School of Social Work. In 1940, the School assumed formal affiliation with Columbia University.

In the School of Philanthropy notions of noblesse oblige, elitism, leadership, and concern for participatory democracy clashed and contended with each other. That first summer of 1898, lecture topics ranged from "The Arrival and Disposition of Immigrants," "The Treatment of Delinquent Children," "The Abuse of Medical Charities in New York City," and "The Colored People in New York," to "The Savings of the Poor" and "The Financial Management of Charitable Institutions." The second summer, a "Friendly Visitors Course," on the casework method, was added. In the third summer, lectures were offered on, among other topics, "The Inculcation of Thrift," and "Co-operation between Public and Private Agencies in Caring for Children." The emphasis was on instilling solid middle class values, and on the dual role of government and private groups in improving the lot of the poor. Josephine Shaw Lowell spoke on "Civil Service Reform with Reference to Charitable Institutions"; Mayo-Smith of Columbia on "The Statistical Method in Social Work"; James B. Reynolds, headworker at the University Settlement", on "The Purpose and Scope of Settlements: How Far Are Their Objects Attained?" More than a decade later, Samuel McCune Lindsay taught on exploitation of wage workers, and "legislative experiments to protect the rights and promote the welfare of employes."[27]

The School of Philanthropy proved to be a key crossroads and meeting place for the vibrant network of New York scholar-activist social scientists. Seager lectured there on "A Program of Social Reform"; Russell Sage Foundation's Mary Van Kleeck on "Modern Industrial Conditions"; I.M. Rubinow on "Social Insurance." Frederick Cleveland and William H. Allen, co-directors of the Bureau of Municipal Research, and Charles A. Beard, Columbia's professor of politics, lectured on government corruption and municipal efficiency and planning, and Mary Kingsbury Simkhovitch on "the place of the settlement in a constructive social program." Devine, true to the emphasis of the time on science taught "The Scientific Basis of Social Work."[28]

One of the stars at the School of Philanthropy was Franklin Giddings, a founder of American sociology, "a big red-headed man" with a red beard, "scintillating eyes," and a complex intellect. Giddings, the son of a Connecticut Congregational minister, had fallen away from the orthodoxy of his youth because it depressed him, and turned to reading Darwin, Spencer, and Thomas Huxley. After dropping out of Union College in Schenectady and working as a newspaper reporter in Springfield, Massachusetts, in 1888 he replaced assistant professor of politics Woodrow Wilson at Bryn Mawr College as a lecturer on sociology. In 1891 he became part-time lecturer in sociology at Columbia. Three years later, though without a Ph.D., Giddings became Columbia's first professor of sociology and served in that capacity for the next thirty-four years.[29]

Giddings rejected Spencerian Social Darwinism, at least on the issue of laissez faire, writing in 1893, "Shall we give ourselves over to the belief that *laissez faire* is the last word of social science and the first law of ethics? Assuredly and most emphatically, no!" "A public and private philanthropy" should "be governed by the results of scientific inquiry," and society, in turn, "must . . . assume the regulation, by industrial and labor legislation, of those industries in which free competition displaces the better man by the inferior." Giddings was a socialist sympathizer. In 1906, the *New York World* reported his comment that "America has not one man in Congress to represent Socialism, but I want to see one there." "His views," said the 1910 edition of the *Encyclopedia of Social Reform*, "have often caused him to be classed as an independent Socialist and radical." With his Columbia colleague Charles Beard, he was a member of the men's dining club, the New York X, and, like Beard, he taught at the socialist Rand School for Social Science, his classes the most popular there. He served on the board of the University Settlement House, Greenwich House's committee on social studies, the School of Philanthropy's advisory council, and as vice president of the League for Political Education.[30]

Richmond Mayo-Smith, Giddings' Columbia colleague and co-investigator on the 1896–97 Columbia-COS cooperative analysis of poverty in New York City was also a principal figure at the School of Philanthropy, until his death in 1901 at forty-seven. Another Midwesterner, the son of a railroad developer in Ohio, he studied at Amherst, Berlin, and Heidelberg. In 1877 John W. Burgess brought him to Columbia to assist in founding the School of Political Science; seventeen years later he led the effort to set up a department of social science within that School. He helped revive the moribund American Statistical Association (and served as its vice president for the rest of his life) and was a founder of the American Economic Association and a founding editor of *Political Science Quarterly*. Part of the extensive network of Manhattan activists, he lived at the University Settlement for a time and served as a member of the central council of the Charity Organization Society and as one of its district chairmen. To Mayo-Smith what could be measured and quantified was most reliable and "the burning question in political economy" was "the distribution of wealth, especially in respect to the so-called laboring class. Does the laborer get his fair share of the wealth which his labor has aided in producing?" "If now we inquire how we shall determine what is the condition of the laboring class, the answer is: By statistics." Mayo-Smith compiled figures on school attendance "among children of the laboring classes," in a house-to-house canvass of four of the city's most squalid blocks.[31]

Another key figure in the social science activist circle was Samuel McCune Lindsay, a sociologist, who took over from Devine as director of the School of Philanthropy in 1907 but handed the reins back in 1912 to become a central figure in the new Progressive party (see Chapter 8). Passionate about regulatory reform of the economy, he had been raised on Chestnut Street in an elite neighborhood of Philadelphia, his father a real estate broker who rose to become president of the Real Estate Trust Company. He was graduated at twenty from the Wharton School of Economy and Finance at the University of Pennsylvania, and after graduate study there and, briefly, at Berlin, Vienna, Rome, and Paris, earned a Ph.D. from the University at Halle, where his mentors at Pennsylvania, Edmund J. James and Simon N. Patten, had studied before him. Lindsay became professor and chair of Pennsylvania's sociology program, and, as head of the Civic Club of Philadelphia's Committee of the Social Sciences, worked to improve the club's philanthropic work with the poor. President Theodore Roosevelt appointed him commissioner of education for Puerto Rico, and by 1904 he was executive secretary of the National Child Labor Committee, splitting his time between his classes in sociology in Philadelphia and his work in New York City with the Committee. Columbia hired him three years later as its first Professor of Social Legislation, and he held the post for the next thirty-two years.[32]

Lindsay was everywhere active in the activist network: in addition to the National Child Labor Committee, he was active on the American Association for Labor Legislation, vice president of the National Consumers' League, member of Columbia's Legislative Research Bureau, secretary of the New York Bureau of Municipal Research, and instrumental in establishing the U.S. Children's Bureau and the U.S. Commission on Industrial Relations. "Sam" to his friends, he conveyed an almost haughty air but he was a kind man who offered prudent advice— "When in search of world wisdom, I find myself turning to you as a matter of habit!" Florence Kelley wrote to him. His wife, Anna Robertson Brown, was the first woman to earn a doctorate (in English) from the University of Pennsylvania.[33]

"The Sensational Story of Industrial Pittsburgh": Social Science and Social Change

The Progressive Era's most ambitious single-city social science research study, the "Pittsburgh Survey," was proposed in 1907 by Edward Devine and Paul Kellogg, editors of the journal *Charities and the Commons*, and carried out with a grant of $27,000 (about $450,000 in year 2000 dollars) from the new Russell Sage Foundation, which dedicated itself to "the improvement of social and living conditions in the United States." Leading economists, political scientists, and sociologists, and a cadre of young and up-and-coming social science-trained men and women— about seventy in all—undertook what became the nation's first comprehensive social science portrait of an American city. By the mid-1910s, six large volumes of social science analysis were published; they served as a model for future sociological investigation.[34]

Devine himself said it was the New York Charity Organization Society and the journal *Charities and the Commons* that "decided on the Pittsburgh Survey and planned and undertook it." He was in a position to know. Kellogg, at twenty-eight, became the survey's director. The grandson of a Michigan lumber magnate who lost his fortune in the early 1890s' depression, Kellogg had attended classes at the Summer School in Philanthropy when Devine offered him a post at the journal. He had earlier been a reporter and city editor for the *Kalamazoo Daily Telegraph*, then attended Columbia University for a year. He never earned a college degree, but Devine promoted him to managing editor of *Charities*, and in 1912 he became editor-in-chief of its successor, *The Survey*, a position he would hold for the next half century.[35] To scholar-activists the journal was their key publication. Mary Kingsbury Simkhovitch, founder of Greenwich House settlement, ran its "Social Settlements department" for a time; Florence Kelley, general secretary of the National Consumers' League, reported on "Child Labor and Protection of Children"; John Andrews, executive secretary of the American Association for Labor Legislation, contributed articles; and the Harvard-educated sociologist and historian W. E. B. Du Bois wrote on "The Negro in the Cities of the North" in a 1905 volume dedicated to that theme.

A special issue of *Charities* on social and economic conditions in Washington, D.C., had inspired the Pittsburgh Survey. Pittsburgh itself was chosen for the survey as a "microcosm in industrial America," where the "forces that shape America's destiny and mold the American character" were "most fully at work," as Devine put it. Devine summed up that undertaking as "an attempt to study family life in an industrial and urban community—to offer a structural exhibit of the community as a whole." The survey found a city of hope and a city of despair, a polyglot industrial city, almost two-thirds of its population immigrants or children of immigrants. The survey found, Devine observed: "An altogether incredible amount of overwork by everybody, reaching its extreme in the twelve-hour shift for seven days in the week in the steel mills and the railway switchyards. Low wages for the great majority of the laborers. . . . Still lower wages for women. . . . never before has a great community applied what it had so meagerly to the rational purposes of human life." Frances Perkins later said, "The Pittsburgh Survey brought a terrific amount of material to our mill upon which to base knowledge of how many people were injured, and seriously injured, with no compensation, what the result was upon their family economic status, and so forth." Isaac Rubinow credited "the sensational story of industrial Pittsburgh," with opening "the door to the [workmen's] compensation movement."[36] The Pittsburgh Survey found no easy "scientific" solution, no clear course of political action, to the problems of poverty and oppression, but its extensive observations and considerable collection of data—its social science research—served as the groundwork for future activism and advocacy.

The movement from traditional noblesse oblige charity to the "scientific charity" of the new century signalled a decisive modern turn in the making of social policy. Traditional charity, grounded in a religious ethos that advised "the poor will always be with you" might be transformed by social science. One of the most vexed of human social problems, poverty, might, some Progressive Era social scientists urged, be radically reduced, even ended, by a science of the social that, through the careful collection of evidence crafted into a theory, would yield the needed insight. To be sure, not all social scientists shared in this vision. Some saw science as a means of gathering evidence but not as a transforming power, simply as offering techniques that would expand knowledge. But others employed that evidence, through an extensive network of private organizations of their making, to persuade others to redirect public policy by prescriptions proposed by the social science scholar-activists themselves. Yet, despite the emphasis on "scientific charity" and the need for structural social reform, the view of the poor as helpless, unable, unfit, and dependent survived, encouraging patriarchal control and shepherding of such persons, as Devine said, into the "normal community" through "rational social control."[37]

Chapter 3

Social Settlements as Neighborhood Democracy or Benevolent Paternalism?

The very notion of *helping others*, so dominant among social reformers, embodied an unresolved ambiguity. Did helping or aiding others mean aiding individuals to achieve ends that those individuals desired? Or did it mean reformers determining what was in the best interest of those they sought to help? Prescribing help for people who didn't ask for it, or who wanted something else, could, in combination with the notion of science as technical expertise with authority to guide policy decision-making, lead to undemocratic means and effective social control. In this it resembled the rationale of some elements of the Christian missionary movement and of the empires of the nineteenth century—bringing salvation and civilization to those judged to be in need, and considered subordinate or even racially inferior.

Could the new social science activists resolve that dilemma of means and ends? A group of young Americans trained in the social sciences, men and women, driven by a passionate sense of moral duty and fortified by training, went to the slums of lower Manhattan to create a sort of peoples' laboratory-campus of their own, the nation's first settlement houses. They bought or rented houses or tenements and moved in after graduation from Smith, Vassar, Amherst, Columbia, City College, and NYU, making homes there, primarily among immigrants, fueling discussions in settlement-sponsored clubs, mobilizing the community for political action. It was a humane, compassionate activism, far from the charity alms of past patrons of the poor, and a secular endeavor—though, to be sure, as the settlement idea subsequently spread, religiously-affiliated settlements were also founded.[1] With much talk of frontier settlements taming the wilds of the West, those who ventured into the nation's urban frontiers, in Chicago, Philadelphia, and Boston as well as New York, established settlements of another kind but with similar purpose, to create a civilized living space, a real community. But certain unresolved questions and tensions remained, the principal one of which was: in bringing social science to the slums, what was to be the relationship between the educated scholar-activist elite and the mostly ill-educated working poor?

"In Daily Personal Contact with Working People"

The settlement house movement had begun in 1884, at Toynbee Hall in London's impoverished East End, where students from Oxford and Cambridge universities educated and supplied social services to the city's working-class poor. The first U.S. outposts appeared soon after on Manhattan's Lower East Side; in 1886, in the Neighborhood Guild (later, the University Settlement), founded by Stanton Coit of Columbus, Ohio, a young graduate of Amherst and the University of Berlin; in 1889, in the College Settlement, founded by a group of young Smith College graduates. Within two decades there were more than four hundred such settlement houses in cities across the country, including Jane Addams' famous Hull House in Chicago, which opened the same year as the College Settlement.[2]

Stanton Coit, then twenty-nine, a member of Felix Adler's New York Society for Ethical Culture, spent two months in London at Toynbee Hall, and, on his return to the U.S. opened his settlement house in an apartment in a Manhattan tenement between the Bowery and the East River. Coit organized meetings of working men as an experimental grassroots movement for social change, and within several months the impromptu meetings evolved into America's first social settlement, the Neighborhood Guild. The Neighborhood Guild had moved three times by the end of the century, all within a four-block radius—in 1886, it was at 146 Forsyth Street; in 1893, at 26 Delancey Street ("no carpets on the coarse and undulating floors, no curtains at the windows, the window shades were broken and stained, [and] the gasjets lacked globes"), and, in 1898, at 184 Eldridge Street, in a five-story building of "pressed brick, simple and tasteful in design" on the corner of an immigrant hub, Rivington Street. Its work continues there to this day as University Settlement. It was deliberately set in New York City's poorest and most congested neighborhood, the Tenth Ward. Known variously as the Crooked Ward, the Typhus Ward, and the Suicide Ward, its immigrant population in the late 1880s and early 1890s consisted mainly of Germans, Poles, Russian Jews, and Rumanians. Helen Moore, a nonresident volunteer at the University Settlement, wrote of "fermenting garbage in the gutter and the smell of stale beer" and "a long panorama of heart-rending sights":

Every window opens into a room crowded with scantily-clothed, dull-faced men and women sewing upon heavy woollen coats and trousers. They pant for air, the perspiration that drops from their foreheads is like life-blood, but they toil on steadily, wearily, except when now and again one, crazed by heat, hangs himself to a door-jamb. . . . From a political, sanitary, and educational point of view it is the worst ward in the city, and social statistics offer no parallel in any city. It is twice as crowded as the densest part of London, our census of 1890 showing 522 human beings to the acre, and to the ward 57,514.

It was, the historian Kenneth T. Jackson has said, "the most crowded neighborhood in the world."[3]

The first six residents of Coit's settlement were male college graduates; several nonresident women volunteers ran its women's and girls' clubs. The 1910 edition of the *Encyclopedia of Social Reform* (it had first appeared in 1897, a sign of the times) described settlement houses as "homes in the poorer quarters of a city where educated men and women may live in daily personal contact with working people." By one estimate about nine out of ten settlement volunteers were college-educated. Some came out of curiosity, others to teach, and, no doubt, some because settlements offered cheap, dormitory-style housing in a congenial and familiar college-like atmosphere. But, in the first and most prominent settlement houses, most of the "educated men and women" came in search of "an active, positive, interested understanding" of the lives of the poor, and to help alleviate suffering. "It was," said one resident of the University Settlement, "an education just to live there."[4]

Eldridge Street, the final home of Coit's settlement, included, besides sleeping quarters for residents, clubrooms, classrooms, a sewing room, kitchen, gymnasium, library, and spacious assembly hall for neighborhood use. At any one time about a dozen college men lived there, some staying a few months, others several years. Columbia University professor of sociology and statistics Richmond Mayo-Smith "was so much attracted by the work of the University Settlement that he lived there at various periods in his career as a resident" until his death in 1901. Most residents and most nonresidents were unpaid volunteers; by 1903 Columbia University economist Edwin R. A. Seligman estimated that hundreds of Columbia students had volunteered at the settlement. So had "many" City College students, the political scientist Stephen P. Duggan reported. In 1905 there were between sixty and seventy nonresident volunteers, by 1911, 137 nonresident workers, eighty-three women, fifty-four men.[5]

While they were studying at Oxford, the group of young Smith College alumnae who would form College Settlement visited the Women's University Settlement in East London, just as Coit had Toynbee Hall, and came home, as one of them, Jean Fine Spahr, would write, "full of the thought, that what English women could do in London, American women could do here." In 1887 a small group formed the College Settlement Association, a year after Coit opened his Neighborhood Guild, and by the winter a physician, Dr. Jane E. Robbins, and Jean G. Fine moved into a tenement across from Coit's Neighborhood Guild. From this site they ran Girl's Clubs, and by September 1889—the same month Jane Addams opened Hull House—they opened the doors of College Settlement at 95 Rivington Street, several hundred yards north of the Neighborhood Guild, in a once elegant brick house "dingy and unattractive" outside but with two grand parlors inside framed by Corinthian columns and silver-mantled heavy mahogany doors and filled "with piano, pictures, and the books and magazines we had coaxed away from our families." Fine became the settlement's first headworker and Robbins its physician in residence.[6]

College Settlement, the second settlement house in the U.S., was staffed by women until 1907, when men were added to an auxiliary staff. This was a difference from the male-led Neighborhood Guild. Jean Fine, an 1883 Smith graduate from Ogdensburg, New York, had taught mathematics and science at Clinton College in Kentucky after college, and then had taken a post at the Neighborhood Guild in 1888, in charge of its women's and girls' clubs. The following year she became director of College Settlement, until, in 1892, she married Charles B. Spahr, the editor of *The Outlook* magazine, and resigned, to be succeeded as director by Jane E. Robbins, from Wethersfield, Connecticut, like Fine, a Smith College graduate. Robbins served five years, during the years of economic depression that hit the Lower East Side with special force. "It has seemed to us sometimes," Robbins wrote, "that the whole world was unemployed." Mary Melinda Kingsbury (Mary Kingsbury Simkhovitch after her marriage), a graduate student in economics and sociology in Columbia's School of Political Science, would follow Robbins as director.[7]

Like University Settlement, which early became associated with Columbia University, College Settlement, in its earliest years, was affiliated with a consortium of four women's colleges, Smith, Vassar, Wellesley, and Bryn Mawr. Eight months after its opening professors and students from these colleges formed The College Settlements Association, to promote settlement work nationwide. It opened other houses in Boston, Philadelphia, and Baltimore, and, after formal incorporation in 1894, added eight more colleges and universities—women's and coeducational—to its consortium: Barnard, Cornell, Elmira, Packer Institute, Radcliffe, Swarthmore, Wells, and the Women's College of Baltimore. New York City's experiment by women had seeded a corridor of settlements up and down the East Coast.[8]

Of the half-dozen to dozen female residents who lived on the College Settlement's second floor—"in our rooms it seemed as if we were back in college again," Jane Robbins said—some stayed for a month or two, others for several years. By 1905 there were 60 nonresident volunteers. An assortment of educational, social, investigative, and political clubs, not only for girls and women but for boys and men as well, were set up—by one count there were thirty by 1900. One club of young men devoted itself to the study of civil government and explored "various of the bills that have come before the New York Legislature."[9]

In a plan to form a special club for married women, as one of the settlement's volunteers said, "a social experiment," College Settlement women set out to visit the homes of neighborhood working class women and to invite them to a meeting. When some of the women came expecting to receive alms, they went away when none were offered, but several stayed to form the Women's Home Improvement Club. The club was to be run democratically with a president elected from among its members and events and activities planned by the women themselves. But it soon became clear that any grand vision of the club structure as the basis for sweeping social reform initiatives would have to be nurtured over time, for the club's first talk was not on grand issues of social welfare reform but on the question: "How long after the hair is out of curling-papers is it becoming?" The club's first activities were club dances scheduled for members' families. Nonetheless, the club's success, from the perspective of one of the College Settlement women, was profound; women otherwise isolated in their homes and disempowered, like women generally in society, learned through their experience in the club's participatory decision-making process that their voice mattered. Lillian W. Betts, one of the settlement's residents, observed that a neighborhood woman who at first had said club decisions "'don't make no difference to me,'" after a time, "grasped the idea that she was one of the many, but had equal rights with all."[10]

The settlement sponsored social science fellowships for educated women in social and economic research; inquiries conducted under its auspices led to important works of social science research and to political action as well. Isabel Eaton, a fellow at the settlement in 1893 and 1894, wrote a fastidiously researched account of garment workers in New York and Chicago, published in *Quarterly Publications of the American Statistical Association* and subsequently issued as a small book. Her research had taken her into managers' offices, sweatshops and factories, and union halls. Accompanied by a union representative as translator, she interviewed workers and inquired into their wages—those averaging $11 a week were among the best paid—and into their cost of living. In a day when the Gospel of Wealth and Social Darwinism were sustaining a popular conviction that poverty was caused by laziness or poor money management, Eaton's research offered persuasive evidence that such views were generally false. The tens of thousands of workers in the garment industry were living in crowded, dirty tenements not because they were lazy or poor managers, Eaton concluded, but because their meager wages offered no other choice.[11]

"Responsible Self-government," "Associating . . . as Equals" in a "New and Perfect City"

In founding the Neighborhood Guild, New York's and the nation's first social settlement, Stanton Coit brought a vision of communitarian, deliberative democracy, self-renewal, and social reform to what he described as "heart-rending" living and working conditions. The Guild was not to be imposed as a paternalistic enterprise, its central aim was, Coit said, "to organize the people of the neighborhood—men, women, children—irrespective of religion or political belief, into a set of clubs to carry out, or induce others to carry out, all the local reforms, moral, industrial, educational, which the social ideal demands. The principles thus put into practice are those of self-help and co-operation." "Responsible self-government" was to be the watchword.[12] The residents and volunteers did not see themselves as autocratic, but as responding to the people of the neighborhood: "There is no command from any authority above the united will and character of the club," Coit said. Neighborhood Guild club members included residents and volunteers from outside the neighborhood and the working men and women who lived there. Decisions were meant to be arrived at democratically. "It is," Coit wrote, "this independence and responsibility, this voluntary co-operation, which gives breath and breeze, freedom and expansion, to the atmosphere of the Guild." Coit first had to learn the lesson of deliberative democracy himself. At one club meeting, he disagreed with a course of action club members were contemplating that, as he put it, "surely they ought not." When Coit tried to redirect club members away from that path he was interrupted by a young worker: " 'We have often been told that this club is self-governing, and the printed prospectus of the club declares so. But of course that is only upon paper!' " Coit wrote, "I saw that he was right; and I yielded."[13]

But while settlements were the era's greatest success in investing the energies and enthusiasms of students of social science in the cause of communitarianism, their deliberative democracy had limits—headworkers and governing boards at the Neighborhood Guild and at College Settlement remained in the hands of educated elites. Nor were clubs open-ended forums for any desired neighborhood activity, but, as the title of the book Coit published in 1891 described them, *Neighborhood Guilds: An Instrument of Social Reform.* Nor was all membership free; it usually cost 5 or 10 cents monthly dues, a sum that could account for an hour or more's labor for the lowest paid—enough to keep away the truly destitute. Nor were the goals wholly set by the tenements' inhabitants. Joseph B. Gilder, journalist and founding secretary of the University Settlement Society in 1891, and himself for a time a University Settlement resident, said that "college graduates" and "university men" had come there "in the hope of successfully combatting" the evils they found, and to raise the people they found there "to a higher level of civilization." "Here men live for study and improvement of themselves and their fellow-men, and while enjoying much that has made their college days perhaps the best of their lives, do earnest, practical work under the incentive of association with others of like interests. Each man has his own rooms, and there is a common room for intercourse and society."[14]

Gilder's idea of the settlement, like Coit's, demonstrated ambivalence between the settlement as laboratory for its founders' vision of the future as a place where the common people were to be "bettered" and "raised up"—and the settlement as a place where "educated men and women, living and working among the poor," were "associating with them as equals." Gilder, like Coit, saw the settlement "as a field for social and economic study—as a social experimental station, so to speak,—a centre of work for college men in the tenement districts bears the same relation to Political Economy and Social Science that the hospital bears to Medicine, or field work to the study of Engineering."[15]

Coit's ideal society went only so far. The settlements were not intended to be isolated as a utopian community but part of the living city. His ideal did not call for the overthrow of the capitalist system; it was reformist not revolutionary. "Unlike the many utopian dreams of the earlier communism," he wrote, "the scheme I have been proposing does not seek to isolate a group of families from contact with their surrounding society, or to disregard the present conditions and motives of life. On the contrary, it plants itself in the midst of the modern city, believing that in it there is already room to lay at least the foundations of the New and Perfect City." The "New and Perfect City" implied a "new order of society."

It is . . . illogical to infer, as I have known more than one person to do, that, because the Neighborhood Guild scheme does not aim at overthrowing the wage-system and the private ownership of land and capital, it is therefore in league with the present order of society, and that its reforms are a mere patchwork of the dominant system. Instead of being regarded as a component part of the social mechanism of to-day, it should rather be classed with those various anticipations, in miniature, of a new order of society. . . . What else would men do with their leisure hours and increased means of enjoyment than forthwith proceed to the social reconstruction of their mental and moral life . . . ?

Coit's words repeat a dual impulse, an endemic tension, between the social settlement house as, on the one side, a democratic arena in which all citizens could come to the table to express their desires and speak their minds, and, on the other side, an arena of persuasion in which those who came to the table were to be persuaded by those educated in the ways of leadership to undertake the "social reconstruction of their mental and moral life."[16]

The settlement sought to promote what Coit called "social reconstruction" through educational and social opportunities, voluntarily offered and accepted. Hundreds of men, women, and children attended the Neighborhood Guild's events, classes for adults in music and drama, public lectures, a kindergarten and a library, history and literature clubs, dances and musical concerts, and a variety of sports. There was a "debating and general improvement club" for young men, and also an "improvement club" for women over eighteen. When one club member lay "dangerously ill" with typhoid fever, fellow club members "procured for him one of the best physicians in the city," and young women at the settlement dispatched "port wine, beef tea, delicacies and flowers." When a father of five was killed in a lift accident at a factory, club members investigated, discovered that witnesses who had claimed that the man was drunk on the job had been bribed, and issued findings that led the court to reverse its initial decision and to find "culpable negligence on the part of the employers."[17]

Two clubs in particular, the Social Science Club and the Tenth Ward Social Reform Club, went beyond tending to individual cases of illness or injustice to engage in social science research, investigation, and political action. The Social Science Club was organized "in the belief that meeting for intelligent and friendly discussion of social economic conditions should be mutually helpful and enlightening." "Uptown men" from colleges and trades unions spoke to the "downtown men" on a wide variety of topics, among them, "The History and Nature of Trusts," "Wages as Affected by the Eight-hour System," "Strikes," and "Anarchism." "It was hoped," wrote University Settlement volunteer Helen Moore in 1893, "that thus theorist and student, brought face to face . . . should learn what were actually the Problems of the Labor Question." But rancor and divisiveness of a class nature soon surfaced and the club collapsed: "Too often the up-town author of a thoughtfully prepared paper had not prepared himself nor allowed time for subsequent attack and question, and such seeming unfairness and lack of sympathy quickly alienated the down-town man who had prepared for and expected fair play and hearing of his side." As Moore said: "The failure of an experiment which promised great gains in knowledge of facts, of conditions, and of sentiments, and which should have made for the destruction of formalism on the one side and distrust upon the other, was likewise an injury to the humanitarian and social work in Forsyth Street."[18]

The Tenth Ward Social Reform Club, on the other hand, thrived by focusing on reform programs not talk. Its club members advanced "an immense programme of reform" through "legal steps" and "public agitation" in efforts "to procure small parks, public baths, laundries, kitchens, [and] co-operative stores," and in efforts to improve health and safety in the neighborhood through "sanitation, and sweat-shop investigation."[19]

James Bronson Reynolds, headworker at the University Settlement after 1894, noted with pride that, "in our long-continued work with the clubs of the house we have seen our young people grow up to manhood and womanhood, and it has been with peculiar satisfaction that we have witnessed many of them undertake work for their own district and for their own community."[20] One neighborhood boy, Henry Moskowitz, whose father had emigrated from Rumania to become head of a Jewish congregation on the Lower East Side and who grew up in and around University Settlement as a member of its Social and Educational Improvement Club, went on to earn a doctorate and to become head resident of Madison House Settlement. Moskowitz testified on living conditions in his neighborhood's tenements before the Tenement House Commission of 1900 and in so doing made a contribution to basic improvements in the city's housing code that year (the new code mandated flush toilets and running water in the city's tenements). Moskowitz enrolled at City College, then studied at Columbia University and at the University of Erlangen in Germany, in philosophy and the social sciences, earning a doctorate at Erlangen. "A settlement, to be a power for good in the neighborhood," Moskowitz said, "must be a center radiating social and political reform." He served as a civil service administrator for the City of New York, and in 1909 became one of the three initial founding members of the National Association for the Advancement of Colored People (NAACP). In 1912 he ran as a candidate for Congress (unsuccessfully) from the Lower East Side on the Progressive Party ticket. His wife, Belle Israels Moskowitz became an advisor to New York's Governor Al Smith. (From 1908 to 1910 she had worked in the Charity Building offices of *The Survey* during the hectic days of its sponsorship of the sociological research for the celebrated Pittsburgh Survey.) Like Stanton Coit, Moskowitz was a leading figure in Felix Adler's Society for Ethical Culture.[21]

The University Settlement Society's 1891 constitution had opened membership not to residents of the neighborhood but to elected undergraduates (annual dues, one dollar) and college graduates (annual dues, five dollars). Its executive council was dominated by social scientists from Columbia, among them Columbia professors Giddings and Seligman, Frank J. Goodnow (political science), and William M. Sloane (history), as well as by local philanthropists, Stephen H. Olin (a lawyer), R. R. Bowker (a publisher), and V. Everit Macy (a wealthy New York philanthropist). Presiding over the settlement's council was then Columbia president Seth Low. In May 1891, the Guild formally incorporated under the new name, University Settlement Society, its goal "to establish settlements, each working in a particular locality or neighborhood and occupying a 'Neighborhood House'—the present Neighborhood Guild being adopted as the first of these settlements." The journalist Joseph B. Gilder, the Society's founding secretary, called University Settlement Society a self-conscious imitation of "the organization . . . successfully adopted by the Women's College Settlement Society," a year earlier.[22]

The "Social Experiment" of Henry Street, and Greenwich House's "Passionate Attempt to Realize Democracy"

In the summer of 1893, four years after the College Settlement opened, a young woman came to live there for a short time, was inspired by what she saw, and set out to set up a settlement of her own. Lillian Wald was twenty-six when she arrived, a nurse dedicated to helping the poor, who had grown up in an affluent German-Jewish community in Rochester, New York, where her father was an optical goods merchant. Wald, moved by the poverty she observed in New York City's tenements on a home nursing visit had, together with a friend, Mary Brewster, rented the top floor of a tenement building for their work. Brewster had to withdraw because of poor health, but Wald stayed on, financed by Jacob Schiff, a wealthy financier, and opened the Henry Street Nurses' Settlement, at 265 Henry Street, several blocks south of College Settlement. Her goal was "to move into the neighborhood; to carry on volunteer nursing, and contribute our citizenship to what seemed an alien group in a so-called democratic community."[23]

Convalescent and "Fresh Air homes" became part of the settlement's work. By 1898 nine "visiting nurses" were working there, by 1906 twenty-seven, some "colored nurses," employed, in those days of prevailing racism, primarily to work with the African American community.[24]

The atmosphere was not simply clinical. Wald frequently held dinner parties at Henry Street, and not for the elite alone. As Frances Perkins later recounted: "Lillian Wald was a very, very agreeable hostess, as well as a very agreeable woman. When she had you to dinner at the Henry Street Settlement, you not only saw Lillian Wald, but you saw the neighborhood, you saw the neighbors ["the Pole, the Jews, the Ukrainians, and so forth"], you saw how a settlement operates." At one such dinner, Florence Kelley, who lived for many years at Henry Street, Frances Perkins, and Paul U. Kellogg, editor of *The Survey*, sought, as Perkins

United Charities Building, 105 East Twenty-Second Street at Fourth Avenue.
Built in 1892 as headquarters for philanthropy by the Charity Organization
Society with the cost covered by businessman John Stewart Kennedy, the
building served as a center of New York City's social science activist network.
It housed numerous offices, from the National Consumers' League and
National Child Labor Committee to the New York School of Philanthropy,
and was the site of American Association for Labor Legislation meetings and
the 1909 founding conference of NAACP. Frances Perkins said of it:
"Somebody introduced you to somebody in the elevator, said who you were,
and so you became acquainted. . . . It was a small and sort of integrated
professional world." Courtesy Library of Congress.

Josephine Shaw Lowell, 1880. Born into two of Boston's wealthiest families, the Shaws and Sturgises, she was the sister of Robert Gould Shaw, colonel of the Massachusetts 54th, the nation's first black regiment, and the wife of textile heir Charles Russell Lowell, who died at the battle of Cedar Creek. Lowell founded the Charity Organization Society in 1882 and was the first president of the Consumers' League of the City of New York. Courtesy Schlesinger Library, Radcliffe Institute, Harvard University.

Edward Thomas Devine, 1905. Born in a log cabin in Iowa, he became professor of social economy at Columbia University, applying "scientific charity" to social problems. He was Josephine Shaw Lowell's successor as executive secretary of the Charity Organization Society, editor of *The Survey*, and director of the New York School of Philanthropy. Courtesy Columbiana Collection, Columbia University.

Florence Kelley as an undergraduate at Cornell University around 1880. The daughter of radical Republican William Kelley, she was general secretary of the Consumers' League by 1889 and was a member of the executive board of the American Association for Labor Legislation. She helped shape the 1912 Progressive Party platform. Courtesy New York Public Library.

Sisters Pauline and Josephine Goldmark, daughters of Austrian immigrants and sisters-in-law of Louis Brandeis. Pauline (top) was secretary of the Consumers' League's New York City branch, director of the New York Child Labor Committee, and a leader in the New York School of Philanthropy (*The Survey*, 27 November 1915). Josephine (bottom) was secretary of research for the Consumers' League and a member of the New York Child Labor Committee. Courtesy Bryn Mawr College.

Frances Perkins as a student at Mount Holyoke College, 1901 or 1902.
Following social science graduate study at the University of Pennsylvania
and Columbia University, she taught sociology at Adelphi College and was
active in the Inter-Municipal Committee on Household Research and the
National Consumers' League. She became the first woman cabinet member
as FDR's Secretary of Labor. Courtesy Mount Holyoke College.

Mary Kingsbury Simkhovitch, 1907. After graduate work in the United States and Germany, in 1902 she was a founder of the Greenwich House settlement at 26 Jones Street on Manhattan's Lower West Side, a "passionate attempt to realize democracy" by working with the poor. She taught in Barnard College's department of sociology. Courtesy Columbiana Collection, Columbia University.

Frances Alice Kellor. From small town Michigan newspaper reporter to pioneering University of Chicago-trained sociologist, Kellor founded the Inter-Municipal Committee on Household Research and the National League on Urban Conditions Among Negroes, precursor of National Urban League; she was a leader in the 1912 Progressive Party. Courtesy Library of Congress.

Samuel McCune Lindsay, 1907. A Columbia sociologist and political advocate, Lindsay was the first executive secretary of the National Child Labor Committee, director of the New York School of Philanthropy, secretary of both the New York Bureau of Municipal Research and American Association for Labor Legislation, and a delegate to the 1912 Progressive Party convention. Courtesy Columbiana Collection, Columbia University.

recalled, to educate a wealthy dinner guest, Florence Jaffray ("Daisy") Harriman, to the conditions of the neighborhood. (Harriman, married to a cousin of the railroad mogul E. H. Harriman, was later appointed by President Wilson to the Federal Industrial Relations Commission.) Frances Perkins described the scene:

Miss Wald, with great skill of course, turned the conversation to life in the city of New York, the working people, where they lived, how they lived, the general living conditions of the area around Henry Street, why you had to have settlements. She would draw out of each one of us in a tactful way something about what we had been seeing. "Now, Frances, what did you see? I know you've been making that investigation into cellar bakeries with Raymond Fosdick [later active in the Wilson administration, and by the mid-1930s president of the Rockefeller Foundation]. I haven't heard you say what you found." Then it was my turn to deliver what I had recently seen of the living and working conditions of the people of the great city. One person after another would comment. Tenement house inspectors were there, as were people who knew about factories and factory life and arrangements. That was the kind of thing that went on.[25]

In the 1890s Wald worked with Josephine Shaw Lowell of the New York Charity Organization Society to provide work relief for the unemployed (see Chapter 2) and in 1897 the Henry Street Nurses' Settlement joined the University and the College settlements to investigate dispossessed tenants. In the first decade of the new century, in cooperation with the Neighborhood Workers Association and the Union Settlement on East 105th Street, the Settlement investigated New York City midwives and foster care, conducted an investigation of unemployment, cooperated with the city's street cleaning department to improve sanitation and collection of street refuse, and played a leading role in campaigns to eradicate tuberculosis, improve housing, and establish more parks and playgrounds. By 1911 scores of clubs for "both sexes and all ages" were meeting at Henry Street. Wald became a major figure in public nursing—she was the first president of the National Organization for Public Health Nursing—and, as head resident at Henry Street and through her association with Florence Kelley, who headed the National Consumers' League, she became an important figure in the developing social sciences. Wald received a gold medal from the National Institute of Social Sciences in 1912 and, about that same time, became one of its vice presidents.[26]

In the fall of 1902, at 26 Jones Street, two blocks west of Washington Square Park (a mile west and a dozen blocks north of Henry Street), Mary Kingsbury Simkhovitch founded the Greenwich House settlement. At the time Jones Street was the most densely populated street on the Lower West Side. Later a center of bohemian culture and the arts, Greenwich Village was at the turn of the twentieth century best known as

New York City's Ninth Ward, a neighborhood of factories, warehouses, workshops, stores, and tenements.[27]

Simkhovitch, from Chestnut Hill outside Boston, had studied the social sciences in graduate programs at Radcliffe, the University of Berlin, and, in 1896 and 1897, was one of the first women to study at Columbia's graduate School of Political Science, concentrating on sociology and statistics. In establishing the Greenwich House settlement she emphasized the complex interrelationship between the individual and society, convinced that the democratic future of the U.S. rested on the character of its citizens. The social order shaped the individual subject, but individuals constituted and maintained the social order. As she put it in her first "Report on Greenwich House," "The settlement is founded on a belief that the springs of beauty of character and of the best social development are to be found in the lives of our working people, and that, firm in that belief, it is our duty and privilege to work with them, so to change the outer conditions of their lives that those inner springs will have a chance to develop."[28]

The Charity Organization Society, founded in New York by Josephine Shaw Lowell in 1882, had been paying special attention to the unemployed destitute poor, but in Simkhovitch's settlement, as in the settlement house movement generally, the principal focus was on employed workers and their families. Robert Hunter, a sociologist of poverty and in 1902 head resident of University Settlement, said that settlements "marked out for themselves . . . educational work and fellowship with . . . that class of working people, of small but regular earnings, who most strenuously fight for economic independence, and stand in more or less constant fear of sickness, death or unemployment." Simkhovitch later explained: "We knew that the settlement could never be another aspect of charity, but it must be the nucleus of local democratic action, and that only as helping friends, workers, and neighbors formed one group, guided by daily contact with the human events taking place around one, could American democracy really come true in any neighborhood." Her work was, she wrote in 1915, "a passionate attempt to realize democracy."[29]

Simkhovitch would become one of the most influential women in the movement and one of the most important members of New York's social science scholar-activist network. She headed Greenwich House's "board of operators," and was its long-time head resident, first at Jones Street and, beginning in 1917, at 27 Barrow Street (where it remains to this day). Greenwich House was, in effect, her settlement. The neighborhood into which she and her husband, Vladimir Simkhovitch, then a lecturer in economic history at Columbia, moved was a working-class enclave, a polyglot community primarily of Irish and Italian immigrants and African American migrants from the South, plus a number of German and French immigrants and "Jewish shopkeepers." Mary and Vladimir married in 1899 and, with their infant son in tow, moved into the house on Jones Street on Thanksgiving Day 1902. Mary had been head resident at the Unitarian-run Friendly Aid House in the city, and before that, headworker at College Settlement.[30]

Simkhovitch wanted more than "a noisy clubhouse filled with various hybrid educational and social activities," and she set out to make something better. She believed that the arts were central to developing "beauty of character," and from the first Greenwich House was a place for the expression of artistic creativity as well as intellectual and moral improvement. She organized a small theater, a kindergarten and playground, neighborhood festivals, a library, and clubs and classes (including industrial education courses), all in a spirit of her philosophy of "social pragmatism." Three years after it opened, Greenwich House had seventeen residents: nine women, six men, and, Simkhovitch having given birth to a daughter in 1904, her own two children. The settlement was "a center for experimentation," its "chief activity," Simkhovitch wrote, "to act as the center for organization, to bring to expression the living hopes and interests of the neighborhood, to organize these vital instincts into groups which like snowballs increase as they roll along." "There were no religious qualifications of any sort, it was recognized that our work was wholly social in its character."[31]

In her director's report of November 1903, Simkhovitch made the following rather typical entry for the preceding month: "A neighbor's child was burned to death alone in a tenement house. A man was stabbed on election night by a drunken comrade. On Cornelia Street (the next block) the [Irish and Italian] Jones Street boys are fighting the colored boys nightly with one or two really serious results." Known as "Mrs. Sims" to neighbors, Mary Simkhovitch established an atmosphere of love, a sentiment that was sometimes reciprocated. Carmel Pecoraro, the settlement's janitor and occasional doorkeeper, for example, wrote to thank Simkhovitch for attending his wedding:

You cannot imagine what joy and what happiness I have to think the great honor I received Easter Sunday at my wedding. . . . Dear Miss Simkhovitch I thank you very much for all what you have done for me. . . . It was all so beautiful for the italian people to see you's American people meet my wife with happiness and joy.[32]

Her nondoctrinaire approach was part of her background. She had grown up in a liberal and well-to-do family near Boston; her father, Isaac Kingsbury, inherited property easing his modestly paid post in city government. Her mother, "primarily an intellectual person" and for a time, a school teacher, spoke several languages and read the classics. Both her parents were anti-slavery, and before the war her mother's family had sheltered runaway slaves; her father, a colonel, had been wounded at Cold Harbor in one of the fiercest battles of the Civil War. At the neighborhood apple orchard battles, Mary, as a child, had served as referee and doctor to the "wounded" from both sides who were brought, "under a flag of truce" to her "hospital" to be "anointed with Pond's Extract and wrapped in cotton bandages." And, in a scene that might as easily have taken place two hundred years earlier in the same New England countryside, when she presented herself at fourteen to her Congregational church deacons she was asked "if I were willing to be damned if it was God's will." She was willing, she said.[33]

By her senior year at Boston University, Simkhovitch was drawn to the social sciences. Borden Parker Bowne, an inspiring teacher, had denounced the ruthless Spencerian social philosophy of Social Darwinism; he "broke up our ill-considered and naive convictions of the hour, and gave us that valuable jolt." She volunteered at St. Augustine's Catholic Church in Boston to supervise a "colored girls" club, and was appalled by the wrenching poverty of their wooden shacks. She taught high school Latin for two years, but the stupid students bored her and she felt guilty at the favoritism she showed the bright ones—bored by having to "correct all the many examination papers that were required," she "often threw them away." Simkhovitch's "thirst for understanding" led her to enroll for a year at Radcliffe, where, she "began to grasp the interrelationship of health and welfare with labor and housing and education." Then, with a scholarship from the Women's Educational and Industrial Union of Boston she went to Germany, chaperoned by her mother, among the first American women to study the social sciences there, though "no credits for degrees were given to women at that time in Berlin." There she met her future husband, then a Russian graduate student of economic history, and made many friends, among them, Emily Greene Balch, a recent graduate of Bryn Mawr College, later a distinguished sociologist, political scientist, and economist, and winner of the 1946 Nobel Prize for Peace for her work with the Women's International League for Peace and Freedom. The two friends attended lectures together, read Kant in the park, attended operas in the evenings, and "regaled" themselves with sandwiches and beer. ("There is," Simkhovitch said, "something very balancing and harmonious about the combination of *Tristan* and beer.") In 1896–97 she enrolled in Columbia University's School of Political Science. "Here at Columbia a sort of mental precipitation took place."

Sociology and economics and history would surely turn out to have a reality and a validity for one if one could gain a wider personal experience. I was glad, therefore, when the opportunity now came for me to live at the College Settlement. I had given up the idea of a church settlement which I had vaguely thought of in Boston days, for I felt that there could hardly be such a thing. A church predicates dogma and a settlement was rather a tryout, an experience in which dogma might perhaps develop, but life would come first and dogma afterward. At any rate, and however that might be, I was drawn to the idea of plunging into life where it was densest and most provocative. There was no longer the divided allegiance in my mind between the University and the City.[34]

Mary Kingsbury Simkhovitch became head resident at the College Settlement for 1898–99, started a Sunday evening economics club there, and from 1899 to 1902 was head resident at the Friendly Aid House in the city. Working on Saturday mornings at the local district office of the Charity Organization Society she came to know Josephine Shaw Lowell, still dressed in black in memory of her husband's death in the Civil War, a "garb" that "like a nun's, gave her a continuity," Simkhovitch said, "an invariability in personal appearance that drove home to us her equal steadfastness in the pursuit of her social objectives." She listened with rapt attention to Lowell and during her "case conferences" learned of "the dingier aspects of East Side life." "Generally, at the Settlement," she wrote later, "we met either the hopeful, the progressive, or at any rate the normal, life of working families—or perhaps the dramatic episodes of tragedy and comedy that became a part of neighborhood knowledge. But in the case conference there was one hard luck story after another. We could not help seeing how fortunate we were to live in a house where all elements of local life were seen. We knew not only poverty and crime, but also the intelligence and ability and charm of our neighbors."[35]

Simkhovitch promptly moved from helping individuals into political activity. She canvassed for Columbia University's president Seth Low in his successful reform Fusion ticket bid of 1901 to become mayor of New York and that same year, working with John Elliott of the Hudson Guild (a social settlement on West 27th Street), she co-founded the Association of Neighborhood Workers of the city's principal settlement and other social-welfare leaders. She helped organize the Women's Trade Union League, a nationwide coalition of upper- and middle-class women reformers and women workers devoted to organizing and to educating the public about working conditions in factories, sweatshops, and stores. (Florence Kelley of the National Consumers' League, Mary Ritter Beard, wife of Charles Beard, and Jane Addams of Hull House were also early League members.) She was the mayor's appointee on the city's Committee on Women, chair of the city's Social Welfare Subcommittee, a member of the city's Recreation Commission for city children and of the American Association for Labor Legislation, and, from 1898 to 1917, on the National Consumers' League executive board.[36] During the presidential election of 1912 she supported Theodore Roosevelt and the Progressive party.

Housing—affordable, uncrowded, and clean—was one of Simkhovitch's most passionate causes; in 1907, with Florence Kelley, executive director of the National Consumers' League, she founded the New York Committee on the Congestion of Population. Focusing on the environment, not moral lapses, Kelley asked: "Instead of assenting to the belief that people who are poor must be crowded, why did we not see years ago that people who are crowded must remain poor?" Founding officers of the Committee on the Congestion of Population included three Columbia faculty, Seager, Seligman, and Felix Adler, professor of political and social ethics and founder of the Society for Ethical Culture, and others from the city's social science network, among them Lillian Wald, Mary Dreier, and Henry Moskowitz. Its salaried secretary Benjamin C. Marsh was a resident of Simkhovitch's Greenwich House, earlier a graduate student in economics at the universities of Chicago and Pennsylvania. The committee sponsored a public exhibit on urban overcrowding that toured New York State and went on to Washington, D.C., and Boston. In its aftermath, New York City's Mayor William Gaynor and New York's Governor Charles Evans Hughes appointed city and state commissions on overcrowding in urban areas, and a National Association of City Planning was formed.[37]

Simkhovitch delivered her first lectures at the New York School of Philanthropy (later to become Columbia University's School of Social Work) in 1898, but in 1907 Columbia's president Nicholas Murray Butler questioned her qualifications for appointment as Adjunct Professor of Sociology at Barnard College and asked sociology professor Franklin Giddings: "Has Mrs. Simkhovitch the intellectual capacity and special training to undertake such work creditably in Barnard College? Has Mrs. Simkhovitch any defects of temperament or eccentricities of opinion which would make her a difficult or un-welcome colleague, or one whose utterances would be likely unnecessarily to disturb and distress those interested in the higher education of women?" Giddings, who knew Simkhovitch from his work on Greenwich House's Committee on Social Studies, recommended her, though for an appointment not in sociology but in social economy, explaining: "in this university by established usage we employ the word Sociology to designate a theoretical and historical study of society. . . . For those studies of a practical nature upon which it is proposed that Mrs. Simkhovitch shall lecture we use the term Social Economy, and it is so used in designating the chair held by

Professor Devine." Thereupon she was appointed adjunct lecturer in social economy in the department of sociology at Barnard and taught courses on "Life of the Industrial Family," "The Standard of Living," and "Social Progress in Cities." Several years later, boosted by a letter of recommendation from Seligman, she began similar courses at Columbia's Teachers College.[38]

Mary Simkhovitch spelled out her philosophy of civic engagement as a continuum of education, social effort, and community improvement. A settlement, she said, had three functions to perform: "First, the democratic—the constant presentation of the life of working people to the community at large so as to form an effective protest against evils. . . . bringing together people of different origins, education, and social opportunity." A settlement's second function was to offer education: from kindergarten schools to manual training, domestic science, and music classes, and to serve as a meeting place for "self-governing social clubs." The third function was "local improvement. The settlement is a kind of village improvement society. . . . Each settlement household forms of itself a little local improvement board."[39]

Settlements had, Simkhovitch said, three stages: "social impression," "amassing of a body of knowledge gossipy, intimate, and interested" through daily contact between settlement residents and their neighbors; "interpretation," a reliance on social science research; and "scientific reports" (the settlement "has to tell what it finds of virtue and beauty, of hampered life, of tragic economic conditions"). It was her duty to be "on the job day after day to watch and report upon the actual workings-out of social forces."[40]

Simkhovitch's reflections on her purpose and goals reflected at their core a conflicted impulse, one she shared with other social science-trained scholar-activists—how to ensure a decision-making process that expressed the egalitarian democracy and self-realization of the people of a neighborhood without, at the same time, imposing the leaders' own goals. If the men and women of the neighborhood were, in some measure, broken by circumstances, then how were they to join effectively in the settlement's decision-making process? At the Greenwich House settlement, Simkhovitch wrote: "We went in and out of their homes and they came to us."[41] But was the democracy to stop at the door of the settlement's inner offices, where Simkhovitch and others trained in the social sciences and members of an intellectual elite would lead the way? The dilemma was a recurrent one for Simkhovitch and her activist colleagues, as for the social science intellectual culture broadly. Commitment to democratic inclusiveness would mean working people joining forces on an equal level with those of privileged background. It was a question never wholly resolved throughout the decades of the social reform movement in New York, as elsewhere at the end of the old century and the beginning of the new.

The settlement houses were not town meetings. When the views settlement leaders offered persuaded some in the community, community residents might be mobilized for political action. Some working-class women and men went with Simkhovitch "in the old Bleecker Street cars with their straw-covered floors to City Hall to stir up officials," and testified before the early tenement house commissions. Increased power for their powerless neighborhood was often the result, and so was the authority and power of the social science scholar-activists. But, as at University Settlement and College Settlement, so also at Greenwich House, the settlement's board (at Greenwich House called the Social Settlement Society) was run not by members from the community but by the educated elite. Thus Simkhovitch, in consultation with the board, made the final decisions. "We have [only] so much money to spend and we must spend it in the direction we think most important," she wrote.[42] Had those from the surrounding neighborhood hoped to use the funds and facilities of the settlement to promote a political party boss that Simkhovitch disagreed with or considered corrupt, or had they come asking that the building be sold and the money be divided equally among neighborhood families, they would have been rebuffed.

The passionate commitment of Simkhovitch and other leading settlement figures—benevolent or paternalistic-maternalistic—was to convince the poor that the settlement leaders' arguments were for the best, and to persuade, not compel, the poor to respond accordingly. As Simkhovitch put it, "much of it [the settlement's fund of energy and money] should be spent toward getting the community aroused to its needs." Not just any needs, though. As Simkhovitch said, when the settlement's board "undertakes to enlarge its own work," there must "always" be a determination in considering a particular course of action by two criteria: "1) Is it necessary?" And, "2) do people want it?" The precise calculus of board-determined necessity versus popular desire was left unspecified, but in the everyday life of the settlement what was "necessary" was generally what settlement leaders' said was so.[43]

To aid in her efforts, Simkhovitch drew together a group of social science scholars, cultural critics, and a philosopher: "Our friends at Columbia helped us in formulating our inquiries and indeed it would be fair to say that our little house on Jones Street was a center of intellectual and social energy. [John] Dewey and [E. R. A.] Seligman and [Henry Rogers] Seager helped us. Randolph Bourne [the young, Columbia-educated, radical social critic] was in our midst." Greenwich House's committee on education had John Dewey as chairman, and the committee on social studies included "our friends, Henry R. Seager, Seligman, and [Franklin] Giddings from Columbia as members." Seligman served as president of the settlement for several years. Dewey, originally from Vermont, had moved from the University of Chicago to Columbia University's faculty in 1904. He was, no doubt, drawn to Greenwich House, as he had been to Chicago's Hull House, out of his life-long empathy with the poor and his commitment to democracy and to the use of science in pragmatic problem-solving. Seager, a Columbia political economist, lived for a winter at the settlement, and when Simkhovitch asked him to address the National Federation of Settlements on "Social Insurance as a Necessary Step in the Democratization of Industry" she wrote, "My dear Harry. . . . Will you do this for the good of the cause?"[44]

The Greenwich House Committee on Social Studies (also called the Committee on Social Investigation) was chaired by Seligman, and members included a core group of Columbia faculty: the anthropologist Franz Boas, the professor of social economy Edward T. Devine, the psychologist-turned-anthropologist Livingston Farrand, the sociologist Giddings, the political economist Seager, and the economic historian (and husband of the director) Vladimir Simkhovitch. The first publication issued under the committee's auspices was Louise Bolard More's 1903 social science research study, *Wage Earners' Budgets*, a mass of statistics demonstrating that low-paid working class men and women lived in poverty not because they were spendthrifts or lazy or of debased moral character, but because they earned so little that, even with the best efforts at frugality, they could seldom make ends meet. More's study was a direct and purposeful attack on those in the conservative camp in the academy who held that the working poor were poor through some personal fault or from an inability to save.[45]

That same year, Emily Wayland Dinwiddie, a volunteer worker at Greenwich House, graduate of the New York School of Philanthropy and graduate student in sociology and economics at the University of Pennsylvania, compiled *The Tenant's Manual.* The manual "enlightened" the people of the neighborhood about "the law and how to get it enforced," Simkhovitch said, and was "one more step in social education." Settlement houses sponsored a number of publications and research projects. *Half a Man*, a 1911 study of African American life in New York by Mary White Ovington, a principal founder of the NAACP, was published under the auspices of Greenwich House's Committee on Social Studies, as was Mabel Nassau's 1915 *Old Age Poverty in Greenwich Village.* (Simkhovitch's *The City Worker's World in America* appeared in 1917 in Macmillan's American Social Progress Series.) The short-lived New York Research Council was a culmination of such research sponsorship and a meeting place for some of the brightest stars in the constellation of New York's social science scholar-activists: Columbia professors Devine, Seager, and Seligman joined Simkhovitch, Florence Kelley, Frances A. Kellor, Paul U. Kellogg, James B. Reynolds, Lillian D. Wald, and John M. Glenn (director of the Russell Sage Foundation) on the Council. Felix Adler (founder of the Ethical Culture Society), and John Mitchell (the labor leader) were also Council members. The Council sponsored James B. Reynolds's 1911 *Civic Bibliography for Greater New York*, "a practical handbook for workers." "Public and private agencies kept us busy and intellectually alert," Simkhovitch wrote, "by asking us for reports on various social phenomena, such as overtime for women in factories, which were incorporated in their own material used for practical measures of reform."[46]

Settlements as "Laboratories in Social Science": "A Scientific Attitude of Mind"

Settlements were "Laboratories in Social Science," Robert Woods, head of Boston's South End settlement house and a lecturer on social economics, told the first national gathering of settlement workers in 1892. Training in the "sociological pantheon" was crucial. "The regular work of the settlement from day to day," he said, "is done after the analytical and synthetic method of science." The men and women who worked in settlements, Woods held, had the responsibility to "take a scientific as well as a philanthropic interest in learning accurately and comprehensively just what the state of life is in their neighborhood." It was a persistent theme. An 1897 essay, "Scientific Value of Social Settlements," in the first volume of *Municipal Affairs*, called the purpose of settlements to find "the most scientific method of accelerating social progress," and an article in *Harper's Bazaar* titled "New Social Science Put into Practice" described settlements as "social reform centres" whose "workers . . . regard the slums as their material from which to take daily object-lessons in social science." Woods and Albert Kennedy's 1911 Russell Sage Foundation-sponsored *Handbook of Settlements* noted that the Neighborhood Guild-University Settlement "carried on for many years sociological studies into different phases of East Side life." James B. Reynolds, University Settlement head resident after 1894, said it "undertakes through its residents careful and scientific investigation of the social, moral and civic conditions of the lower east side." "We must put ourselves in a scientific attitude of mind," Reynolds wrote. In a 1901 article in *McClure's*, Theodore Roosevelt, U.S. Vice President-elect, wrote: "Only those who know the appalling conditions of life in the swarming tenements that surround the University Settlement can appreciate what it has done." He praised Reynolds and his fellow workers for their "work of sociological investigation," and for their "work hand in hand, shoulder to shoulder, with those whom they seek to benefit."[47]

Sometimes those "object-lessons" led volunteers to rethink the social order that had led to the desperate conditions they saw around them. Jacob Salwyn Schapiro, a recent graduate of Columbia University's School of Political Science, put it this way: "Intimate knowledge of actual conditions, even more than the study of sociology, forced these men and women, some of them conservatives by temperament, into the radical current." To avoid spreading themselves too thin, workers at the University Settlement each year concentrated on a single issue: in 1894 it was unemployment; in 1895, working women; in 1896, health problems and availability of medical treatment on the Lower East Side; in 1897, eviction of the poor from tenement apartments; in 1898, the work of benefit societies; in 1899, the adequacy of city playground and recreational facilities; in 1900, tenement housing. They published the results of these studies from time to time in periodicals and in a University Settlement Studies pamphlet series.[48] The spread of public knowledge was part of their central purpose.

But radicalism was not the usual response. "The many-sidedness of social reform," Reynolds held, calls for "progressive" government. "While not urging too hasty movement for the extension of governmental powers, the settlement believes that public interests among sanitary, educational and even some moral lines [e.g., prostitution], are better safeguarded by comprehensive public inspection than by the effort of private individuals." Its strategy, and that of many of the scholar-activists, was cooperation with allies not confrontation. But they did try to effect social change. Residents "brought about conferences between employers and working men to discuss labor and economic questions," rented out settlement rooms for use by union locals and the city's Central Federated Union (the umbrella organization of unions in New York City), and "co-operated with the unions in searching out and closing sweat shops." In testimony before state commissions and legislative committees, settlement residents pushed for improved factory inspection laws and supported state laws to regulate "the hours and conditions of labor of men, women and children." As Theodore Roosevelt put it in *McClure's*, the University Settlement "consistently labored to secure the settlement of strikes, by consultation or arbitration, before the bitterness has become so great as to prevent any chance of settlement."[49]

Probably as a result of these nonadversarial efforts, University Settlement leaders found themselves elevated to influential posts within the government itself. From 1910 to 1914 Charles B. Stover, a long-time University Settlement resident and head resident of the settlement from 1889 to 1891, served as New York City Parks Commissioner. Reynolds, the settlement's head resident from 1894 to 1902, was active in local, state, and national government, a member of the New York State Tenement House Commission of 1900, and of a number of good government organizations, including the Committee of Seventy and the Citizen's Union.[50]

Reynold's own stance was not paternalistic. In his 1899 report as headworker of the settlement he said the settlement must work "with" not "for" the community: "We must care enough for others to learn to understand them. And in our work for others we must meet our fellow men on the basis of equality, to consider with them mutual plans for the common good, and so labor with them for the intellectual, social, and moral improvement of our great municipality." "In our care to emphasize the value of the scientific spirit, and in our aim to work *with* rather than to work *for* our community, we endeavor not to lose sight of our ethical aims. These aims are expressed in terms of economists by the word *co-operation*; in terms of social life, by that of *friendship*; in terms of ethics, by that of *altruism*. They give our work its character. Without these aims, our scientific analysis and our economic theory would be in vain." One of Reynolds's friends noted that he "worked always—this is his own phrase—trying to work for co-operation and not control."[51]

Reynolds was a minister's son from a small town in upstate New York and a graduate of Yale who had taken up graduate study of the social sciences, first as a student in Paris and Berlin, and subsequently as a fellow in sociology in Columbia University's School of Political Science when he was head resident at University Settlement. He was appointed secretary to former Columbia University president Seth Low during Low's term as mayor from 1901 to 1903—Low had been president of the settlement's council—and worked for President Theodore Roosevelt (later describing himself as a member of Roosevelt's "Kitchen Cabinet"). With Charles P. Neill, commissioner of the U.S. Bureau of Labor, he investigated Chicago stockyards, prompting Congress to pass the 1906 Meat Inspection Act. After Roosevelt's presidency, Reynolds became an Assistant District Attorney for the County of New York.[52]

Stanton Coit himself, who had started University Settlement, by the early 1890s had turned the stewardship of University Settlement over to its executive council and left for London. He was a principal figure there as he had been in New York, in the Ethical Culture Movement and prepared a hymnal, *Social Worship*, for his London congregation, with hymns to "Democracy," "The Moral Ideal," and "The Law of Duty."[53]

Women Scholar-Activists: Frances Kellor's "New Sociology" and Suffrage

A number of alumnae of the College Settlement, founded by Smith College alumnae, became important civic leaders. Frances Kellor was among them. On her way to becoming one of the Progressive Era's most important scholar-activists, Kellor received two fellowships, one from the College Settlements Association and another from the Woman's Municipal League, which enabled her to take up residence at the College Settlement in 1902 and study at the New York School of Philanthropy. She continued research she had begun as a graduate student at the University of Chicago, where she had completed a study in criminology with a "new sociology" approach, published as *Experimental Sociology, Descriptive and Analytical: Delinquents.* Her analysis stood in contrast to the view popular in Europe, the U.S., and Latin America that physiology—head shape and other gross morphological features—signaled a genetic propensity to crime. Kellor's study of crime in the American South led her to a contrary conclusion, that the causal connection was environment not genetic inheritance or physical type. What caused crime, Kellor found, was lack of education, "distressed" experiences in childhood, and unemployment.[54] Women scholars, Kellor among them, seem to have been captivated by the racist-oriented eugenics movement less often than their male counterparts; they generally seem to have been more broadly liberal in their perspective and commitments.

Kellor herself had grown up poor, first in Columbus, Ohio, where her father abandoned the family before Frances was two, then in Coldwater, a small town in Michigan, where her mother worked as a laundress and Kellor helped, " 'collecting and delivering laundry in a little wagon.' " The town's two librarians, Mary A. and Frances E. Eddy, took Kellor under their wing at sixteen, after she had accidently shot herself in the hand "while shooting targets in the woods with some local boys." The trio attended Coldwater's Presbyterian church, where, historian Ellen Fitzpatrick has observed, the minister's "inspirational sermons stressing Christian responsibility for social problems," and "the informal 'sociological' discussions" led Kellor to "enthusiastically" embrace "the social gospel." Setting type and a part-time reporter for the town's local newspaper, the *Coldwater Republican,* at seventeen she wrote about "national and political conditions and evils." Supported financially by the Eddy sisters, she was admitted to Cornell University by examination, then earned a law degree in 1897, at twenty-three, from Cornell. She went on to the University of Chicago for graduate study in sociology and economics.[55]

Kellor turned her "new sociology" of environmental etiology to issues of employment and conditions of labor during her years at the College Settlement, publishing, in 1904, *Out of Work: A Study of Employment Agencies, Their Treatment of the Unemployed, and Their Influence upon Home and Business,* on the horrors of New York's privately managed employment agencies. Sociologist Charles R. Henderson, one of Kellor's professors at the University of Chicago, said that "no previous study has accumulated such a wealth of information on this vital problem." In New York, Philadelphia, and Chicago, Kellor had posed either as someone looking for employment or as seeking to hire an employee. In some offices she found that "girls are actually herded and treated like cattle." One woman waiting tables in a restaurant had her pay envelope torn open by the restaurant's manager who took half of her first week's wages, by prearrangement, so he said, with the employment office that had placed her. In another instance, "a negro girl was promised a position as a nurse by an agent at Richmond, Virginia. She agreed to have $12.75 for her fare deducted from her wages. . . . On arrival she was told there were no vacancies for nurses, and she must do general housework." When she refused, her trunk with all her belongings were kept by the agency. A "Jewish girl, sixteen years old," told by an employment agent that "she was going to a restaurant to work for two dollars a week and tips," discovered that she was to be sent to a brothel instead. The girl was saved when an unidentified "assistant" paid ten dollars to the agency for her release.[56]

After *Out of Work*, Kellor launched a legislative campaign to aid the unemployed, drafting legislation with Woman's Municipal League director, Margaret Dreier, a wealthy young woman who, like Kellor, attended courses at the New York School of Philanthropy. She became "deeply involved," Frances Perkins said, in the Women's Trade Union League. In 1904, Kellor joined Mary Dreier, Margaret Dreier's younger sister, in drawing up a bill calling on New York State's governor to license private employment agencies. (Kellor and Mary Dreier lived together in Brooklyn Heights for the rest of Kellor's life.) Two years later, the New York State legislature voted overwhelmingly to regulate the job placement industry. Kellor and Dreier organized the Inter-Municipal Committee on Household Research, bringing together social activists from New York, Boston, and Philadelphia to study domestic housekeeping, the single most widely held job by women; the Committee found that those so employed were subjected to low wages, long hours, and the prospect of sexual assault by male employers.[57]

As general secretary of the Inter-Municipal Committee on Household Research, Kellor recruited Mary Simkhovitch of Greenwich House; Edward Devine, Columbia professor of social economy; and Florence Kelley. By 1906 the Committee had become the National League for the Protection of Colored Women, a precursor to the 1910 National Urban League (see Chapter 7). A decade later Kellor was appointed to New York State's Commission on Urban Conditions Among Negroes. With others, she successfully lobbied New York Governor Charles Evans Hughes to appoint a "Commission to Inquire into the Conditions, Welfare, and Industrial Opportunities of Aliens" (the New York Commission on Immigration). Appointed director of the new Bureau of Industries and Immigration in 1910, she became the first woman to head a New York State executive department. In all these roles, Kellor helped expand the regulatory role for government. She was active in politics as well and in 1912 resigned her directorship at the Bureau of Industries and Immigration to head the newly formed Progressive party's National Service (see Chapter 8); after the party's collapse and until her death in 1952 at 79 she applied her law degree and her experience in the American Arbitration Association.[58]

Democracy "Only upon Paper"?: The Continuing Dilemma of Benevolent Paternalism

The women and men social science scholar-activists of the settlement house movement in New York City's great social laboratory, as in other American cities, struggled with issues of democracy and elitism, but in general they sought not to impose but to persuade. Nor did most of them have the economic or political power to impose, many of them women with long experience of using persuasion to win ground and with few other sources of power.

Settlements were redoubts of social science research into grim living conditions in the nation's cities, but they were not only laboratories for study; they were serious attempts to change society and, as Mary Simkhovitch said, attempts to "realize democracy." In the settlement movement itself, deliberative democracy and social science sometimes mixed uneasily. The men and women who took up the study and application of the social sciences in living and working in the slums of the city shared the dual impulse of altering the social order by aiding others to empowerment and the impulse to promote their own will-to-power, benevolent, generous, often courageous, but real. Social scientists in the academy as well found themselves struggling with the dual impulse, the paradox of democratic elitism. In the settlement house movement the social sciences were, in many ways, at their practical best: gathering evidence where people lived, offering the evidence of their research in manuals, books, lectures, clubs, and conversations to those they believed needed that knowledge for their own welfare, and carrying the message into the arena of industry and government to try to improve the lives of the poor and the oppressed, in keeping with the vision of science as harbinger of renewed democracy.

"A Science of Municipal Government": "Scientific Training" or "Agents of Wall Street"?

In 1884, Theodore Roosevelt, then a young New York State assemblyman, called the liquor sellers who were also New York City's aldermen—city councilmen—"the lowest stratum of New-York life," and protested that these men "who from their vices should be the lowest in the social scale are allowed to rule over us." Indeed, half of New York's twenty-four aldermen were, in the words of the *New York Times* in 1882, current or former "gin-mill keepers"; the other dozen, according to historian Jon Teaford, were "a jeweler, a shoe dealer, a hotelkeeper, a builder, a dealer in mason's materials, a real estate dealer, a retired real estate agent, 2 professional public officeholders, and 3 lawyers." Two decades later things had not changed; government, the Columbia University philosopher John Dewey wrote, was "almost hopelessly under the heel of party-politicians whose least knowledge is of the scientific questions involved."[1]

"An Era of Constructive Municipal Undertakings"

Anti-corruption efforts in New York were spearheaded in the late nineteenth and early twentieth centuries by clergy, lawyers, and businessmen, and, at times, by social science scholar-activists. In 1892 the Reverend Charles H. Parkhurst, Madison Square Presbyterian Church pastor, and his City Vigilance League initiated a decades-long investigation that exposed police corruption, including the madams' payoffs to police. In June 1907 leading Presbyterians, Episcopalians, Congregationalists, Unitarians, Jews, Catholics, and Ethical Culturalists met at the Union Theological Seminary to discuss "social-ethical problems," and "co-ordinate more closely" their own "moral and social reform" work. In 1912 Social Gospel spokesman Walter C. Rauschenbusch drew ministers and laypersons from across the country to Carnegie Hall to hear addresses on "The Church and the Social Evil" and "The Christ-Answer to the Cry of the City." Some in attendance urged that: "we must work out an order of industry and commerce . . . which shall embody Christ's law of love and sacrifice in the institutions of society."[2]

Parallel to the efforts of the churches, the City Reform Club of New York, dominated by the city's wealth-elite, including the young Theodore Roosevelt and financed by the powerful J. Pierpont Morgan, led good government investigations against corruption. Lawyers and businessmen reformers battled Tammany through the Chamber of Commerce, the City Club, the Citizens' Union, boards of trade, and other, often ad hoc, committees of middle- and upper-class New Yorkers. The City Club of New York was organized in 1892 as successor to the City Reform Club, with the plutocrats John Jacob Astor, J. P. Morgan, and Cornelius Vanderbilt among its most prominent members. By 1895 it claimed ten thousand members in twenty-four Good Government Clubs in New York City.[3]

Along with religious leaders and the bourgeoisie, social scientists, too, were assuming a role in public civic leadership. The National Municipal League was founded in 1894, the first such organization in which "university professors of political and social science figured prominently." Among its members were Frank J. Goodnow of Columbia University, Edward W. Bemis of the University of Chicago, A. Lawrence Lowell of Harvard University, Jeremiah W. Jenks of Cornell University, and Edmund J. James and L. S. Rowe of the University of Pennsylvania.[4]

During the Gilded Age and Progressive Era, Republican party bosses worked, sometimes in uneasy cooperation, with party "respectables"— Elihu Root and Charles Evans Hughes among them—to promote reform candidates in the city. But Republicans were generally heavily outnumbered in New York City politics by the Democrats' far more powerful political machine, Tammany Hall, that built its power on the votes of the city's immigrants and the growing working class. (Charles Beard, the distinguished historian and political scientist, noted that, in 1900, only 737,477 of the city's 3,437,202 population was native, the rest immigrants or their children.) Mary Kingsbury Simkhovitch, writing in the *Political Science Quarterly*, called the political boss's coercive power, "an interesting example of political tyranny."[5]

But corruption was not the sum of Tammany Hall's efforts. Its officers cultivated voters by distributing thousands of clerical, police, fire, and other city jobs, its political machine helped working-class and poor New Yorkers negotiate the legal system, and, in a time before the welfare state, it provided money, jobs, and gifts to families impoverished by the loss of a job, home or business in a fire or other unanticipated tragedy. Tammany bosses William M. Tweed, John Kelly, Richard Croker, and Charles Murphy, one after the other, instinctively following the Machiavellian adage that it is best to be both loved and feared, led an urban machine that was a savvy admixture of autocracy and democracy, corruption and social welfare.

In New York City, the coordinated effort of reform groups led to the election of Tammany-challenging reformers. In 1894, reform candidate and Republican William L. Strong, merchant and bank president, won election to the Board of Aldermen; in 1901 Columbia University president Seth Low, with the support of the businessmen reformers of the Citizens Union, among others, left the Columbia campus to win office as mayor on a Fusion party ticket; in 1913, John Purroy Mitchel, a graduate of Columbia University and New York University Law School, won the mayoralty on a reform Fusion ticket.[6]

Though social scientists were proving to be central to the work of the National Municipal League, "the science of municipal government" remained in "an early stage of development," in the opinion of Frank J. Goodnow, the Columbia political scientist destined to become known as "Father of Public Administration." A Brooklyn-born prodigy— Amherst A.B., Columbia LL.B., star pupil of John W. Burgess in Columbia's School of Political Science, and on Columbia's Faculty of Political Science by age twenty-four—Goodnow became Columbia's first Eaton Professor of Administrative Law and Municipal Science. In building the models for government on which his reputation rested, Goodnow made a simple distinction: he separated "the determination of public policy," from "the execution of that policy." Voters were to determine the direction public policy would take; experts were to execute the administration of government. It was something of a corporate business efficiency model of government, and it made him famous. The city-manager system of government (in which the city's mayor holds elective office, but cedes city administration to a skilled manager), and commission government (in which local government is run by a small group of commissioners), both systems adopted by hundreds of towns and smaller cities (and still popular to this day), owe a large debt to Goodnow's work. The National Municipal League, which Goodnow helped found in 1894, was dedicated primarily to developing models of expert government for cities, counties, and states. In 1903, the twenty-five scholars who formed the American Political Science Association chose Goodnow as the Association's first president; today the APSA's Goodnow Award for Distinguished Service remains one of its highest honors. In 1913 and 1914 Goodnow advised the revolutionary government of Yuan Shih-kai in China; in 1914 he became Johns Hopkins University's third president.[7]

Goodnow's younger colleague at Columbia, Charles A. Beard, another giant among scholars, thought Goodnow's model did not go far enough. Ferreting out corruption and waste, ending budgetary and organizational inefficiency, were insufficient. "Mere business efficiency in administration" and "good city government movements," were "to be considered as temporary, not permanent, advances in American politics," Beard said. Beard offered instead a class-based sociological analysis of urban conditions as the root cause of corruption. He wrote in his 1912 book *American City Government* of political scientists' need to consider "the social and economic functions of city government" (not just its formal structures) and take into account that the "working class, which forms the bulk of the population of the great industrial centers, is in the main a landless, homeless, and propertyless proletariate [sic]." "From the point of view of economic freedom," Beard wrote, urban workers were "but little removed from the condition of the black bondsmen or the indentured servants of colonial days." The disease, crime, and vice that threatened to overwhelm the nation's cities were rooted in the soil of those conditions. This, not structural efficiency, was the real root problem: "The separation of the workman from the ownership and control of his tools and instruments of production and the creation of two rather sharply marked classes in society—the capitalist class, deriving its incomes from the ownership, management, and manipulation of industries, franchises, and public utilities, and the working class, dependent upon the sale of labor power for a livelihood [was] most distressing to those Americans who like to look upon their country as a land where all are equal."[8]

For Beard, social scientists' role was to uncover the "blind" forces inherent in the capitalist industrial order as well as the perhaps not so blind conspiracies of power among some capitalists and to expose those forces and conspiracies in their writings and in classrooms. "Education cannot and must not become a mere servant to the production of commodities. In a democracy training for citizenship—the awakening of a deep and abiding interest in government and its manifold relations to social and private welfare—must accompany preparation for the process of securing a livelihood." And Beard practiced what he preached. In his introductory course "Politics 105, Party Government in the United States" at Columbia College, he lectured on, among other topics, "Assumption of Leadership by the Slavocracy," "Machines and Bosses," and "Imperialism." His students read Theodore Roosevelt's *New Nationalism*, Robert M. La Follette's *Autobiography*, Walter Lippmann's *Preface to Politics*, Herbert Croly's *Progressive Democracy*, and Lincoln Steffens's *The Shame of the Cities*. Beard, one of his students said, was a man "burning with passionate concern for the unfortunate and deprived."[9]

Like Goodnow, Beard was a major political scientist of his day, and in 1926, like Goodnow before him, he was elected president of the American Political Science Association. He was also the most widely read

American historian of the first half of the twentieth century—his forty-nine volumes in the field of history sold more than eleven million copies—and in 1933 he was elected president of the American Historical Association. A later academic star, C. Vann Woodward of Yale, summed it succinctly. "Beard," Vann Woodward said, "laughed aside academic rules, overroad the barriers between disciplines, invaded preserves of other specialists and mixed politics with economics and wit with both." Beard's background suited his academic stance. In Indiana his father was, at various times, a farmer, a building contractor, a school teacher, and a bank president; at sixteen Charles and his older brother Clarence were expelled, Charles from his Quaker preparatory school and Clarence from college, both apparently for publishing criticism of the faculty and administration of Indiana University in a small local weekly newspaper their father had bought for them to run. As an undergraduate at DePauw College Beard immersed himself in political philosophy and economics, and in the summer of 1896 he "was introduced to a new world" at Jane Addams's Hull House in Chicago. Soon after, he attended Oxford and co-founded Ruskin Hall there, a worker's college, before returning to study at Cornell. (His wife Mary Ritter, whom he met at DePauw, herself became an important historian and a feminist, and the couple collaborated on many projects.) Beard published his first book, *The Industrial Revolution*, in 1901 when he was twenty-eight. Two years later, he earned a master's degree, and one year after that a Ph.D. in constitutional law, at Columbia's School of Political Science. By 1915 he was professor of politics at Columbia. He resigned a mere two years later in a dispute with the university administration over issues of academic freedom, see (Chapter 1).[10]

Goodnow was a political progressive and an activist in the 1912 Progressive party; Beard's own political sympathies lay with the socialist cause, though he apparently never formally joined the Socialist party. He was a co-founder of the party's Rand School for Social Science in 1905–06. He was a member of the American Socialist Society, the Rand School's supervisory board, and while teaching full-time at Columbia also taught courses at the socialist Rand School. (His 1906 ten-lecture course at the Rand School of Social Science, "The Evolution of the State," cost students the school's standard $2.50 per-course fee, though, as the School's prospectus announced, "specially low rates will be given to members of the Socialist Party.") Beard was a member of the New York X, the progressive men's dining club in Manhattan. When the editor of the student-based *Intercollegiate Socialist* inquired about his attitude toward socialism, Beard replied that students should take an "intelligent interest" in it.[11]

Beard had so many interests and dimensions that he was, in effect, a laboratory and training school of his own: a writer and editor for the *National Municipal Review*, the Columbia-run *Political Science Quarterly*, and the journal of the New York Bureau of Municipal Research; a member of New York's Commission on Retrenchment and Reorganization in the State Government; author of a bill in support of the direct primary.

His most famous work, analyzing the property holdings of the Founding Fathers, *An Economic Interpretation of the Constitution of the United States* (1913), became one of the most controversial books in American history. Members of the 1787 Constitutional Convention, he wrote, were not working "under the guidance of abstract principles of political science" but under the same economic self-interest that undergirded modern social and political relations. (In his title Beard was self-consciously echoing his Columbia colleague Edwin R. A. Seligman's 1902 *The Economic Interpretation of History*, a commentary on Karl Marx's economic interpretation of history.) Beard's *American City Government* and other writings outlined many municipal reforms to which "thoughtful men and women" in "progressive cities" were committed, including government regulation of public utility companies. "To all appearances," he said, "the age of tinkering with political machinery and spectacular 'wars on bosses' is passing into an era of constructive municipal undertakings on a large scale."[12]

The Bureau of Municipal Research Versus Tammany Hall: "Intelligent Control"

As Charles Beard said, there was "a revolution," afoot in the "way of going at the problems of municipal administration," and in that revolution, the New York Bureau of Municipal Research, and its directors known as the "ABC Powers"—William Allen, Henry Bruère, and Frederick Cleveland—were to play an important part.[13]

In 1905 William H. Allen, a "general agent" with the Association for Improving the Condition of the Poor and a Ph.D. in political science, organized the Bureau of City Betterment under the auspices of the Citizens' Union of New York, an organization of largely upper-middle-class and elite New Yorkers formed in 1897 with help from the economist Frederick Cleveland, Henry Bruère, who had studied sociology but never earned a graduate degree, and Robert Fulton Cutting, a wealthy banker from an established New York family. In 1907, the Bureau split off from the Citizens' Union and the *New York Times* noted that the goal of the newly renamed New York Bureau of Municipal Research was to "substitute knowledge for indignation as a motive force in reforming the city's affairs."[14] Frances Perkins, a close friend of Henry Bruère's, said of the Bureau:

All of them at that time were pretty much tied to the idea of economical government—government based on honest bookkeeping. They were overcoming corruption that was so broadcast that it didn't even have a name. The heart and
soul of the work of the Bureau was to have things done honestly and efficiently.
They felt that you couldn't have any social utilization of the machinery of City
government if you weren't honest and right. I think they were all what I would
call socially-minded men, including William H. Allen and Cleveland. They were
in favor of all sorts of social reforms, but they didn't want to see any more money
appropriated until they got [for example] the hospitals under control so that
hospital-appropriation money was spent for the purposes of caring for the sick.[15]

   The Bureau's "Budget Idea" was, Cleveland wrote, "a reaction against
the results of irresponsible government, the political boss, log-rolling
methods, pork barrel legislation." Again, science was a keyword; the
Bureau's goal, as Allen described it in the *Political Science Quarterly*, was:
"To promote efficient and economical municipal government; to promote the adoption of scientific methods of accounting and of reporting
the details of municipal business with a view to facilitating the work of
public officials . . . to collect, to classify, to analyze, to correlate, to interpret and to publish facts as to the administration of municipal government."[16] The Bureau set out, as the subheading of its periodical, *Efficient
Citizenship*, declared, "To Promote the Application of Scientific Principles to Government." (Just what counted as scientific principles in the
Bureau's work would prove to be contested terrain.)
   The Bureau brought together social scientists, journalists, and members of the city's elite. Seligman became its president beginning in 1907,
taking over from Cutting. On its first board of trustees were Seligman,
Allen, Cleveland, and Cutting; Frank Tucker, a journalist and social
worker, and director of the Association for Improving the Conditions of
the Poor; George McAneny, secretary of the local civil service reform
league and president of the City Club, and Richard W. Gilder, editor of
The Century magazine, first vice-president of the City Club; and a member of the Council of the National Civic Service Reform League. Several
years later, the sociologist Samuel McCune Lindsay, professor of social
legislation at Columbia, became Bureau secretary and director of its
"New York State work." Charles Beard directed the educational program at the Bureau's Training School starting in 1915 and, beginning
in 1918, served for three years as the Bureau's director.[17]
   But it was the "ABC Powers," Allen, Bruère, and Cleveland, who actually led the Bureau in its early years. All three directors were Midwestern-
ers, as so often in New York City's social science network. William Allen
was born in Minnesota, Henry Bruère in Missouri, Frederick Cleveland
in Illinois. Allen and Bruère had studied at the University of Chicago,
and Allen earned his Ph.D. in political science at the University of Penn-

sylvania in 1900 after an intervening year at Leipzig and Berlin. Bruère went from the University of Chicago to Harvard Law School, but left in a year to direct the boy's clubs at Boston's Denison House settlement. Bruère had directed Boston's Highland Union Workingmen's Club for two years, and in his early twenties had returned briefly to Chicago as director of the McCormick Works Men's Club and Technical School, before taking a position in New York with the Association for Improving the Conditions of the Poor where Allen was the "general agent." When Allen began the Bureau, Bruère joined in. (He enrolled in graduate classes in Columbia University's School of Political Science, and continued at the New York University Law School.) Cleveland studied at DePauw University in Indiana, and the University of Chicago. He had studied and practiced law briefly before enrolling, like Allen and Bruère, at the University of Chicago, earning a doctorate in economics from the University of Pennsylvania in the same class in which Allen earned his in political science. By 1904, Cleveland was in New York as a lecturer, later professor of finance, at New York University, and before joining the Bureau he served as an appointee of Mayor McClellan, on a commission investigating city finances.[18]

Robert Moses, the future power broker of New York, who studied at Columbia University and worked and taught for a time at the Bureau, considered its directors tedious men who played with file cards—"the voluminous filing and cross-filing of all information was a waste of time," Moses said. Photographs show the three directors around the time of the Bureau's incorporation as prim and tidy men in stiff-collared shirts and suits, but others remembered the three as neither prosaic nor dull. Bruère was, in Frances Perkins's words, someone "whose advice I always asked about everything," a man of "plenty of nerve and plenty of courage," "an excellent administrator" and "a very tactful, diplomatic man" with "the natural qualities of a mediator"; Cleveland "was very precise and in a way academic," but shared the "sense of mission" that infused the Bureau's scrutiny of public records with "'not a little romance.'" Allen was, Bruère said, "a man of extraordinary mental agility," filled with "passionate conviction." A student at the Bureau saw its work in the heroic mode: "How would I sum up what we were doing? . . . We were fighting to make democracy work, that's what we were doing!"[19]

William Allen, a member of the American Academy of Political and Social Science, the American Statistical Association, and the National Municipal League—and who on occassion in the 1910s taught a course that paralleled the work of the New York Bureau of Municipal Research at New York University—was, like Charles Beard, a radical, though, as he said, "not socialistic." "Whether . . . we are to socialize capital by owning it or by controlling it, no one can now foretell," he wrote. But what was certain, he said in his 1907 book *Efficient Democracy*, was that: "Without intelligent control by the public, no efficient, progressive, triumphant democracy is possible." With Beard, and with Bruère, he was a member of the liberal left New York X. (At one X Club meeting in Manhattan he took part in a political debate with the social economist Edward T. Devine, who, like Allen, had been a student of Simon Patten at Pennsylvania.) Like Beard a feminist, Allen wrote *Woman's Part in Government: Whether She Votes or Not*, pointing out that women were "setting new standards of training for participation in government." The New York Bureau of Municipal Research and the New York School of Philanthropy, he said, were "illustrations of young women now training themselves for leadership and professional service."[20]

Henry Bruère sought to promote a progressive politics, writing in his 1913 book, *The New City Government*, that "only through efficient government could progressive social welfare be achieved." The Bureau's goal, he said, was "harnessing to the work of social betterment" the forces of city government. Good government did not consist of "the glad hand and cheap bounty in the form of a Thanksgiving turkey, shoes or burial money," but in "decent tenements, clean streets, attractive parks, pure milk, and educational opportunities," achieved through "intelligent action by an independent electorate." In 1912, under Bureau auspices and on a fellowship supplied by Columbia University's School of Political Science, Bruère went to Germany to observe city administrations; enroute he conferred about British social welfare reform with David Lloyd George, Britain's Chancellor of the Exchequer (four years later, British Prime Minister). Bruère described his own politics in a letter to Theodore Roosevelt in 1912: "I have not, like my brother Robert, joined the socialist party, because I believe that we can work out our social and economic problems in America step by step without committing ourselves to a pre-conceived reordering of our national life. The present developments in the progressive movement give encouragement to my confidence in this belief." Bruère was no revolutionary, but believed that through scientific administration the forces of government could within the capitalist system be harnessed for social betterment.[21]

Frederick Cleveland, who taught at the New York School of Philanthropy in the 1910s, was less politically liberal than either Allen or Bruère, but shared in the era's confidence, as he wrote, "that the activities of man may be reduced to a science; and that the various social activities may be investigated from a common basis," though the newness of that science meant that there was "an absence of an accepted method of procedure" to place "modern, social-scientific inquiry" on par with the "natural sciences." "Theoretical writings" were available to a botanist "to facilitate biological thought," he said, but "in seeking for such a point of view for investigation in the social and political field one finds little guidance in the theoretical writings of the past." He was prepared to accept limitations on democracy in his quest for more efficient government, laying responsibility for much government inefficiency at the feet of ill-educated, uninformed citizens. He supported as "most advantageous" state restrictions on the right to vote of new immigrants in northern cities and of "the 'poor whites' and negroes of the South." On the government ownership of gas, water, transportation, and other utilities, he sounded a note of caution: "should not the American people premise this request on an insistent demand for increased intelligence concerning the management of [government's] business affairs? Until adequate provision has been made for such intelligence, increased government control through public ownership and operation may not safely be undertaken."[22]

"Bureau of Municipal Besmirch" Versus Tammany: Applying Scientific Methods to Government

The directors of the Bureau of Municipal Research may have disagreed politically, but they were agreed on the need for decisive leadership. In 1906, with an expanding treasury and a growing staff, they undertook a high-profile, high-stakes investigation into the workings of Manhattan's borough government, and with the cooperation of the city comptroller, Herman A. Metz, they poured over Manhattan departmental budgets. The Bureau published the results in a pamphlet, *How Manhattan Is Governed*, with an overview of city expenditures on roads, public baths, and sewer systems. In response, Manhattan Borough's president and Tammany-man John F. Ahearn, less cooperative than the city's comptroller, forbad Bureau investigators to examine city records under his control. Thereupon the Bureau's staff examined records publicly available, and soon uncovered inconsistencies that signalled graft. Tammany, in retaliation, referred mockingly to the "Bureau of Municipal Besmirch," and Ahearn, in turn, sued the Bureau on grounds of libel claiming damages of $100,000. In response, Bureau directors publicized their findings and broadened their inquiry; John Purroy Mitchel, a twenty-seven-year old "good government" lawyer, trained at Columbia University and New York University, undertook an inquiry into Ahearn's administration. Mitchel discovered evidence of extensive corruption; after public hearings, New York State Governor Charles Evans Hughes, in an unprecedented move, dismissed Ahearn from the Manhattan Borough presidency for "official incompetency." Ahearn lost his libel suit against the Bureau, the Bureau's legal right of access to municipal records was affirmed, and the imprimatur of the governor's office had been affixed to the Bureau's work. A few years later, Governor Hughes would say, "in the careful research of the historian and the studies of the economists are the natural and necessary aids of the practical administrator. . . . I rejoice that we are drawing more and more to legislative service men who have had special training."[23]

In the aftermath of the Ahearn case, the Bureau gained the cooperation of many city officials, and the Bureau's staff was able to study the fiscal records and the structures of administration in a number of the city's departments, conducting meticulous investigations. For example, it introduced into the organization and accounts of the police, health, and parks departments, such innovations as itemized budgeting practices—previously all departments at the city had asked only for lump sum annual allocations—and it helped curtail nepotism and graft through analyses of city workers' salaries. It made recommendations to the city about needs it thought the city was failing to meet, in one instance recommending that a department of child hygiene be established; it was.[24]

The Bureau of Municipal Research cast its investigative net wide. It inquired into the city's housing codes and, finding a lack of enforcement of tenement safety codes, called on the courts to arrest landlords who violated those codes. Its investigation into irregularities in the city's water system led to a boost in municipal revenues of $2 million a year. It recovered $723,000 from the city's notoriously corrupt street-railway corporations and was instrumental in "cleaning up of immorality at Coney Island." "We had the police go after houses of prostitution," Bruère said.[25]

The Bureau's goal of "intelligent popular control" of the city's government by its citizens would be possible only if citizens knew the "*facts* respecting the acts of government." The Bureau set out to uncover those facts through social science research, and to display and publicize what it uncovered through public exhibits and in printed bulletins and pamphlets. In a series of public exhibits between 1908 to 1911—the most popular drew nearly a million visitors—the Bureau displayed large charts and graphics in publicly accessible halls so New Yorkers could educate themselves about the organizational structure of the city's administration and the inefficiencies of municipal government. In one early exhibit, in the City Investing Building in downtown Manhattan, the Bureau displayed ordinary coat hooks: "the main chart of the exhibit was the 'Six Cent Hook' and everybody stopped and examined that hook that the City paid sixty cents for, and we bought it for six." Another exhibit displayed erasers: the city had paid 30 cents for erasers the Bureau found available for a dime at an ordinary stationery store not far from City Hall. In its first decade, the Bureau published and distributed

780 bulletins and pamphlets on a wide spectrum of issues, in copies that ran well into the millions.[26]

"No More Important Laboratory for the Science of Administration": Schools Collaborate

In 1911, the Bureau's "ABC Powers" founded the Training School for Public Service as an adjunct to the Bureau, to train both men and women for public service. The School educated men and women "of executive ability for the study and administration of public business," and trained them to "lead communities and to apply scientific methods to government." It was intended to be the nexus between the theoretical work of the social sciences as taught in universities and the practical world of politics. Engineers, lawyers, physicians, accountants, teachers, social workers, and graduate students in the social sciences attended its classes. Nineteen women studied there in its first few years of operation, but most of the 184 students in the Training School's first four years were men. Its graduates became city managers, city planners, other top- and mid-level municipal administrators, university professors, school teachers, and organizers of research bureaus. Robert Moses, the future power broker of New York, worked at the Training School while studying for his doctorate at Columbia's School of Political Science. (Moses's mother was a cousin of Edwin Seligman, Bureau trustee.) Raymond Moley, who, during the early years of the New Deal, served as Franklin Roosevelt's chief policy advisor and headed Roosevelt's so-called Brain Trust of social scientists, studied at the Bureau's Training School in the 1910s, when he was pursing his doctorate at Columbia under Beard.[27]

One Training School student, L. E. Meador, later a professor at Drury College in Missouri, described his first assignment.

That assignment was to go to the City Hall and attend the meeting of the City Council; I was told to walk in and take my seat at the press table. I was a complete stranger in New York and had some difficulty in finding the City Hall and where the council met. The only thing the council did that morning was to discuss some routine matters and pass one resolution appropriating $25,000 for the paving of a certain street. I returned to the office of the Bureau and handed in my report, thinking that the task was ended. The next morning my assignment was to locate that street and to see if it needed paving. The street was more difficult to find than the City Hall but I finally located it over on the east side. I found that it had never been paved. I made this report in writing, feeling that my task was ended. The next morning my assignment was to go to the city clerk's office and search the records to see if the street had ever been paved before. I discovered that the street every year for 25 years had been paved. The Bureau saw to it that the street was paved that year. . . . At the beginning of every week we had two kinds of assignments, one was in text books and magazines which we were to read during the week, and the other was some practical task such as I have indicated above.

As a result of such exhaustive investigations the Bureau reclaimed $900,000 for the city on street paving alone within several years.[28]

Beard wrote in *American City Government* that the Bureau and Training School furnished "a connecting link between schools and colleges and municipal and other public departments for practical field work." He concluded in a 1913 evaluation for the American Political Science Association and the American Economic Association that "the Training School fulfills every requirement of a university. It aims to develop just those qualities which universities seek to develop." He recommended that students writing dissertations in municipal science "spend a portion of their time at the Training School while engaged in their investigations."[29]

In 1911, the same year the Bureau of Municipal Research founded its Training School, Beard created a "Politics Laboratory" at Columbia. The 19 October 1911 *New York Tribune* wrote that Beard's "Political Laboratory" encouraged the study of politics and political science "from a practical viewpoint." In this "lab," students studied state and municipal administration, party organization and bill drafting, and met with legislators on campus and on trips to City Hall and Albany. It was part of the larger social science "laboratory" movement of the late nineteenth and early twentieth centuries that included "the Committee on Statistics in the Society," developed by Columbia professors Richmond Mayo-Smith and Franklin Giddings sixteen years earlier; the "Historical Laboratory" Herbert Baxter Adams opened at Johns Hopkins in the late nineteenth century; and the "Wisconsin Idea" of state-university cooperation developed by Charles McCarthy and others at the University of Wisconsin in the early twentieth century.[30]

With the movement of social science out of classrooms and into the practical politics of public service ramping up, the stage was set for a national conference on social science in city administration; in May 1914 a National Conference on Universities and Public Service, titled "The College and the City," convened at the City Club building in Manhattan under the auspices of New York's Bureau of Municipal Research and the American Political Science Association's Committee on Practical Training for Public Service. (The American Political Science Association's committee which sponsored the conference included principal figures in the field of practical training for public service: Charles McCarthy of Wisconsin, Albert Bushnell Hart of Harvard, Benjamin F. Shambaugh of the University of Iowa, William F. Willoughby of Princeton, and Raymond G. Gettell of Amherst.) Scholars from across the nation addressed the conference—Frederick Hicks, dean of the School of Commerce at the University of Cincinnati, for example, spoke about the work of his university's sociology department with "charitable and philanthropic institutions of the city" of Cincinnati—but the conference's primary focus was on its host city, New York.[31]

New York City Mayor John Purroy Mitchel (his exposure of Ahearn and Tammany had made him a rising star in municipal politics) opened the two-day conference, urging "closer cooperation between the universities and the government of the city." "We have New York University, we have The City College and we have Columbia, all institutions within the limits of the City of New York, and with all of which such a cooperative plan would be feasible." Indeed, New York University, the mayor said, had recently "loaned to the city government" an instructor in government "now studying the technical resources of the city government and appraising the technical equipment that we have." Professors from New York City's three principal institutions of higher education addressed conferees, among them Jeremiah W. Jenks, professor of government and public administration at New York University, and Stephen P. Duggan, professor of political science and head of the education department at City College. Duggan noted that City College was doing little work with city government and it was, he said, "practically a virgin field as far as the college is concerned."[32]

Charles Beard, Columbia professor of politics, spoke on "New York City as a Political Science Laboratory." "New York," he said, "presents the greatest laboratory in the Western hemisphere" for the study of political science. "There is not a condition or problem of modern social life which is not represented here." "There can be no more important laboratory for the science of administration than this city," he said. "This term 'laboratory' is coming up in political science. It is a new thing and many of us are siezing upon it with great zeal as if we had discovered something which nobody had ever thought of in the history of the world. And we are assuming also that we can apply in politics some of those methods which are applied in natural science." And, though Beard was contributing to this idea of the city as political laboratory, he cautioned against over-reaching in the comparison with the physical sciences: "I want to enter here a *caveat*. While I do not want to put in a word of discouragement, I want to call attention to the fact that we cannot in the academic world, or in the world of fact, we cannot use politics in the sense in which we can use chemistry."

Columbia sociologist Samuel McCune Lindsay, speaking on "New York as a Sociological Laboratory," called the city "a Teeming Sociological Laboratory" of immigrants and races. He praised his Columbia colleague Franz Boas's recent anthropological work with the immigrants of

New York that had refuted eugenicists' claims of fixed genetic types that purportedly proved the superiority of northern European racial stocks. He spoke on the growing social science scholar-activist movement, and highlighted the need to join theory to practice through "legislative remedies." Such work, he said, in his judgement was "the highest service the universities can render both to government and to social reform, that we may hope to evaluate our social ideals and subject them to the competent criticism and reflection of educated and trained minds. . . . It is our duty to build the foundations for a scientific training for public service by harnessing the theoretical and the practical together . . . for ever more effective practical use."[33] In the months following the conference, putting action to their words, both Lindsay and Beard took up work with the New York Bureau of Municipal Research, Lindsay becoming its secretary and director of its New York State work, Beard, supervisor of instruction at the Training School for Public Service, and, in 1917, the Bureau's director.

Just as the National Conference on Universities and Public Service was calling for greater scholarly service in the public interest, the New York State Department of Efficiency and Economy invited the Bureau of Municipal Research to work with it, and the Bureau offered, without cost to the state, a staff of twenty, headed by Cleveland and Beard, to examine policies and procedures in many of the state's municipalities.[34]

Another Realm: "Women's Historic Function . . . Along the Line of Cleanliness . . ."

The scientific administration of city politics was a largely male counterpart to the municipal efforts of women in their central roles in the Charity Organization Societies, the National Consumers' League, the settlement houses, and elsewhere. Women did work at the Bureau of Municipal Research and attended classes at its Training School for Public Service, but they were largely kept on the sidelines, as in the field of government administration, generally. After all women could not yet vote or hold elective office (they gained the vote in New York State only in 1917, and not until 1920 in the nation as a whole); the entire representative government of the state and city, as elsewhere in the country, was run by men. Columbia University political economist Henry Seager observed, in 1904, that the common currency of the day was that "women should be confined as far as possible to the domestic circle." And, for all their contributions, women were never promoted to leadership posts even at the Bureau or its Training School. Mary Buell Sayles did join the Bureau's staff in 1907; she was a graduate of Smith College with experience at the College Settlement and the New York City Tenement House Department, author of articles in the *Outlook* and in the *New York Daily Tribune,* and of an important 1902 study of housing conditions, published in the *Annals of the American Academy of Political and Social Science.* But Sayles never gained a leadership post at the Bureau and left after five years for the Russell Sage Foundation. A book by the Bureau director William Allen, *Woman's Part in Government: Whether She Votes or Not,* made clear that he considered the role of women crucial to the reform of government; yet he did not act to promote those he supervised to positions of leadership. When Elsa Denison, among the Training School's first women students and for two years a volunteer worker at the Bureau, published a book *Helping School Children* in 1912 on public and private support of the nation's public schools based on the work of 400 cities and towns, Allen praised it as "an important contribution" but did not raise her to a leadership spot.[35]

Women did make important contributions to the field of municipal reform despite the obstacles, as Mary Ritter Beard, Charles Beard's wife, reported, in her 1915 book *Woman's Work in Municipalities*: "Women's historic function having been along the line of cleanliness, her instinct when she looks forth from her own clean windows is toward public cleanliness."[36] The Beards were one of the most eminent social science couples in Progressive Era America. They had studied together in England and at Columbia, but Mary Beard raised the couple's children and did not pursue a graduate degree as her husband rose to prominence at Columbia. She did write important books, co-authoring some of them with her husband, but she worked largely from the sidelines of the academy.

Limits of Research: Social Scientists as "White Slaves of Philanthropy"?

In 1907, when the Bureau of City Betterment officially became the Bureau of Municipal Research, contributions from the city's elite began to pour in, and with a budget of more than $38,000—it was $12,000 the year before—the directors' staff of eight grew to eighteen, and the Bureau's influence spread rapidly. Within a decade of its founding there were similar bureaus in twenty-one cities: Philadelphia, Chicago, Rochester, Detroit, Milwaukee, Akron, Indianapolis, Kansas City, Minneapolis, and San Francisco among them.[37]

In 1910 the Bureau's work and Frank J. Goodnow's own work were recognized when President William Howard Taft appointed a federal Economy and Efficiency Commission to do for the federal government's management and accounting methods what the New York Bureau of Municipal Research had done in New York and other cities. Frederick

Cleveland, appointed to head the new federal commission, took a leave from the Department of Economics and Finance at New York University and from his post as a director at the Bureau to take the position. Goodnow, also appointed to the commission, took a leave of absence from Columbia, and the two New Yorkers were joined in Washington, D.C., by William F. Willoughby, professor of political science and law at Princeton. Part of their official charge was "to more efficiently inquire into the methods of transacting the public business of the government . . . with the view of inaugurating new or changing old methods." From 1910 to 1913, and a $100,000 congressional appropriation, the commission engaged in a systematic "investigation of the departments of the national government." Beginning in the Treasury Department, commissioners drew up organizational charts and budgeting and accounting recommendations and advised the President on the competence and efficiency of personnel, on waste in government expenditures, and on more efficient procedural methods: for example, how to handle incoming and outgoing mail and purchases and accounts. It counselled, for example, that the cost of federal employee travel could be cut by not riding in first-class train compartments. It suggested that the federal government's annual $600,000 electricity bill could be reduced by 30 to 60 percent. In a special message to Congress, President Taft praised the commissioners work.[38]

When Cleveland was called to federal service, Bureau director Henry Bruère was summoned to service in the city. When John Purroy Mitchel, the Columbia and NYU-trained lawyer who had worked closely with the Bureau and its directors in investigating the Ahearn affair, was elected New York City mayor, he appointed Bruère City Chamberlain, a position traditionally synonymous in New York City with that of city treasurer, though Bruère acted more, as the *Brooklyn Eagle* put it, as Mitchel's "Vice Mayor." Frances Perkins said: "He was in everything. He had a roving commission to be in anything that was of interest." Labeled "A Servant to Public Servants" by *The Independent* magazine, Bruère set out to broaden the social welfare functions of city government. He investigated the city's social services and its police department, its food and milk inspection practices, and, in imitation of the European practice of city-run public employment bureaus, played a leading role in establishing employment bureaus in the city.[39]

The wealth-elite of New York City took a serious interest in the work of the Bureau of Municipal Research and, between 1906 and 1914, their contributions to the Bureau and its Training School made up the overwhelming majority of the Bureau's $949,424 in contributions: John Rockefeller, $125,400 (approximately $2,200,000 in 2000 dollars); R. Fulton Cutting, $116,785; Andrew Carnegie, $55,000; Mrs. E. H. Harriman, $51,500 (she endowed the Bureau's Training School); Kuhn, Loeb & Co., $41,000; J. P. Morgan & Co., $29,200.[40] To some social scientists funding by the nation's wealth-elite was a heaven-sent bonanza, but to others such funding seemed more ominous and suggested the possibility of future cooptation of their mission.

Bolstered by a new generation of wealth fresh from the post-Civil War industrial boom, the modern age of American philanthropy had its start early in the new century in New York City. John D. Rockefeller, the oil baron, set up the Rockefeller Institute for Medical Research (later renamed Rockefeller University) in 1901 in Manhattan, the Rockefeller General Education Board in 1903 and the Rockefeller Foundation in 1913; Andrew Carnegie, the steel magnate, established the Carnegie Foundation for the Advancement of Teaching in 1905 and the Carnegie Corporation of New York, a foundation dedicated to "the advancement and diffusion of knowledge and understanding," in 1911; Margaret Olivia Sage funded in 1907 the Russell Sage Foundation, also headquartered in Manhattan, a foundation she named after her late husband, a wealthy financier, dedicated to "the improvement of social and living conditions in the United States."[41]

This first generation of industrial era philanthropic giving was especially important to the New York Bureau of Municipal Research, whose top philanthropic contributors were, after all, among the nation's wealthiest elite. Some—Rockefeller, Carnegie, and Morgan in particular—were then being stigmatized as robber barons by muckraking investigative journalists like Ida Tarbell (a scholar, too—she had studied at the Sorbonne in the early 1890s). In her two-year inquiry into Rockefeller's rise to wealth and power, Tarbell had employed the same careful empirical examination of records that the Bureau's own staff had vis-à-vis municipal government. She concluded that Rockefeller had employed bribery, coercion, and special privilege in gaining his oil industry monopoly, and her articles in *McClure's Magazine* and her 1904 book *The History of the Standard Oil Company* led to a government investigation of the Rockefeller monopoly, and to the 1911 government-mandated breakup of the Standard Oil Trust.[42] This was journalistic social science of the most powerful sort. Women might not have the vote, but their research and writing carried greater weight than many men who won public office.

Critics of the Bureau's work were convinced that the work was being shaped by dependence on a philanthropic community whose wealth derived from the profits of the new industrial capitalist economic order. They saw the wealth-elite as ruthless and self-aggrandizing capitalists who had cheated workers of the full value of their labor in their amassing great baronies of wealth. Conversely, those who celebrated the nation's wealth-elite as captains of industry attributed to them responsibility for much of the expansive and dynamic growth that was rapidly making America the richest nation in the world, and viewed their philanthropic endeavors as benevolent civic stewardship. Viewed from one angle, the nation's wealth-elite was selflessly dispensing great fortunes they might otherwise have invested in personal pleasures but had chosen to use as magnanimous patrons of the public good. Viewed from the other side, the modern foundations were ploys to clear the stigma of ruthlessness from the names of the foundations' founders and replace that stigma with an image of selflessness, while simultaneously contributing to the shaping of a social order conducive to the continued expanse of the economic and social system under which they had accumulated their wealth. It was from those who held this latter perspective, and in consequence of the Bureau's funding by the wealth-elite, that, as William Allen noted, the Bureau and Training School had "frequently been charged with being agents of 'Wall Street,' 'capital,' etc."[43]

The Bureau's directors and staff had carefully observed, measured, and analyzed elements of municipal government, yet, in their observations and measurements, it is true that they had paid particular attention to certain elements of the social order while ignoring others. Bureau directors largely focused on allocation and expenditures from the public treasuries, limiting their definition of corruption to the willful stealing of money by public servants or to careless or incompetent appropriation. The Bureau's investigative eye never examined, for example, the inequitable distribution of wealth and power in the municipality, or the corrosive effects of such inequality on the ideals of American democracy in the functioning of municipal administration. They did not question whether the highly stratified distribution of wealth and inequalities of power in the industrial capitalist social order might be part of a larger corruption that dwarfed the willful stealing from public treasuries, nor did they propose remedies related to such a proposition. The Bureau never urged, for example, taxing the rich in order to help supply funds for expanded governmental programs to aid the poor.

Ironically, Jerome D. Greene, a trustee and secretary of the Manhattan-based Rockefeller Foundation, which became one of the first and most important modern philanthropies, said of the Foundation's goals that it was more important to "go to the root of individual or social ill-being and misery" than to deal with progress "of an immediately remedial or alleviatory nature, such as asylums for the orphan, blind or cripples" because the former would be "more far-reaching in their effects." The Foundation's statement of purpose, as explained in its New York State charter of incorporation, was no less than the sweeping: "To promote the well-being of mankind throughout the world."[44]

Soon after the Foundation was established a question of its ability to carry out that stated mission arose in questions about potential conflicts of interest. Three Rockefeller Foundation trustees—Rockefeller, Sr., Rockefeller, Jr., and Greene—were also principal administrators of the Rockefeller family fortune, their goal to ensure the profitability of its investments in the competitive market economy. Could these men simultaneously carry out the Foundation's mission of promoting the well-being of mankind while working to grow the family's fortune in the for-profit capitalist marketplace? Would their position as market-economy decision-makers taint or compromise decisions they might make as Foundation trustees on which projects the Foundation would fund and which it would not? Such questions soon moved to center stage. John D., Jr., and Greene, were, as it turned out, not only on the board of trustees of the Foundation, but also directors of the Colorado Fuel and Iron Company, one of the family's many for-profit corporate investments. Their dual decision-making posts soon proved to be fraught with problems when, in September 1913, 11,000 coal miners, backed by the United Mine Workers, struck the Colorado company's mines with demands for recognition of their union, for an increase in miners' wages from the average $1.60 a day, and for improved mine safety. Soon after the strike began, striking miners and their families were evicted from company-owned housing on coal company property. The company, employing private security guards and with the backing of Colorado's governor who sent in the state's militia, won the strike, but not before sixty-six strike-related deaths occurred, thirteen of them in what came to be known as "the Ludlow Massacre." (Two women and eleven children were suffocated in a fire as they hid in a dug-out under one of the colony's tents that housed workers' families during an invasion of the camp by state militia and company guards.) It was, at the time, one Rockefeller biographer has written, "the worst nightmare in Rockefeller history." Helen Keller called Rockefeller "the monster of capitalism. He gives charity and in the same breath he permits the helpless workmen, their wives and children to be shot down." But, in a private memorandum, Rockefeller, Jr., said: "while this loss of life is profoundly to be regretted, it is unjust in the extreme to lay it at the door of the defenders of law and property, who were in no slightest way responsible for it."[45]

Against this background a parallel conflict raised questions of the propriety of increased Rockefeller Foundation oversight of the Bureau of Municipal Research's own work. The Rockefellers were the Bureau of Municipal Research's largest donor, but ought the Foundation to be able to control the Bureau's agenda and methods? What was and what ought to be the role of wealth generally at the Bureau, and what were its effects on the emerging social sciences? Did science require detachment and neutrality on matters of social policy? Would neutrality mean avoiding a challenge to the wealth-elite? "There are," Bureau director William Allen said, "things being lauded throughout the world to-day that every scientific man knows are not true. We don't dare to tell the truth; we all want some of the money, we are all becoming the white slaves of philanthropy."[46]

Although, from early in the Bureau's existence, the Rockefellers had funded its work, and although when John D. Rockefeller, Sr., created the Foundation in 1913 that funding continued, the relationship between the Foundation and Allen at the Bureau began to sour. An October 1913 exchange of letters between William Allen and Greene reflects the dispute. Greene, a Harvard graduate, former Secretary to the Corporation of Harvard University (he had nearly become Harvard's president when Charles W. Eliot stepped down), was one of the Foundation's nine trustees.[47] Allen had inquired by letter if Greene had seen the Bureau's recent report on public school administration in Waterbury, Connecticut, adding, without elaboration: "you have disagreed with the method which we wanted to employ in New York."[48] The following day, Greene responded:

The only difference between you and me which may be of some significance is with regard to the proper function of a bureau of municipal research. It seems to me that in the long run the influence of such a bureau is enormously enhanced if it confines its function to investigation, study and recommendation, including such advice and help as may be necessary in securing the initial installation of improved methods adopted on its recommendation. You evidently, and quite logically consider that the Bureau has an additional function, namely that of promotion, persuasion and agitation.

Greene thought these last three functions

interfere with that scientific detachment from partisan strife which would seem to be absolutely necessary if the Bureau's services are to be availed of to the best advantage by the particular administration that happens to be in power. You will reply to this by pointing out the extent of your services in both Tammany-controlled and Fusion-controlled departments, and to the extent to which this is true, the Bureau certainly deserves great credit. My own opinion, however, is that if the Bureau abstains entirely from the promotion, persuasion and agitation side of its work, its power for good would, in the long run, be increased, though there might be need of calling into being immediately as its coadjutor some civic organization that would make this field its own.

He was writing "on my own responsibility," he said, and added: "As to this obvious difference of opinion between us, you are clearly entitled to stick by your own policy which is presumably acceptable to your Board of Directors."[49]

Greene's emphasis on the importance of "scientific detachment from partisan strife," and Allen's desire, in Greene's words, to promote, persuade, and agitate, demonstrated a fundamental tension about the function and role of the social sciences in Progressive Era America (and is an issue that remains contentious in the social sciences to this day). Allen was indeed interested in promotion, persuasion, and agitation for particular political ends. He had expressed those ends in his 1907 book *Efficient Democracy*: "intelligent control by the public" through a "progressive, triumphant democracy."[50] Were not Greene and his allies, though they cloaked their appeals in the mantle of political disinterestedness, equally interested in promoting political ends?

From its earliest days the New York Bureau of Municipal Research's directors had emphasized their work as scientific. One of the Bureau's first publications, *Purposes and Methods of the Bureau of Municipal Research*, promised that "the field of municipal government not only needs scientific study but will lend itself readily to scientific measurements" and assured readers that "the Bureau's staff are well fitted by academic training and by previous field work to apply scientific measurement."[51] But just what counted as "scientific study"? And what place did ethical and political valuations have in such study? If the social sciences were to ground their research and public prescriptions in the ethical and political judgements and advocacy of individual social scientists, how should those social scientists make their ethical and political judgements? What role should those who supplied the funds for social science research be permitted to play in shaping its policy prescriptions?

From the Bureau's earliest days a tension had existed within the Bureau itself, between Cleveland and Allen, on these issues. An unsigned memorandum, written after Allen's "retirement" from the Bureau in September 1914, discussed this breach, the author of the letter identified only as "one who has been fairly well informed in a general way concerning the activities of the Bureau." (Given the similarity in style of Greene's 9 October 1913 letter and the memorandum, the author might well have been the Rockefeller Foundation's Jerome D. Greene himself.)

Generally speaking, there were two points of view in regard to the work of the Bureau. One which might be called the Cleveland point of view, regarded it as the function of the Bureau to engage in constructive investigation of the various departments of municipal administration, with a view to their improvement and with a high degree of scientific detachment, making it possible for the Bureau to cooperate with the city administration, regardless of what political party was in power. The Cleveland point of view was not indifferent to the necessity for proper publicity, but it emphasized the educational, as distinguished from the agitating or propagandist type of publicity. . . . From Dr. Allen's point of view, Dr. Cleveland was in favor of a policy that was in danger of becoming coldly scientific and academic, and less likely to 'put things over', while from Dr. Cleveland's point of view, Dr. Allen's policy was highly undignified, calculated to create personal animosities, and to involve the Bureau in political feelings and entanglements.[52]

As early as 1905 Cleveland had written: "Science is a codification of exactly determined common-sense, i.e., common observation of facts, common analysis and common classification pertaining to a single subject of human interest. The end of science is to establish conclusions that may be accepted for purposes of research or instruction." Cleveland made much the same point in his battle with Allen for control of the Bureau: "The Bureau originally undertook to make inquiries into the organization and management of government, to find out what the government is doing, how it is doing its work, and what results are being obtained, without color or bias." But Allen wanted, Cleveland said, to include advocacy on issues like the proper organization and management of public schools, "to criticize educational theory and the ideals of professional educators."[53]

What had begun in an exchange of private letters reached a public denouement in 1914. Cleveland had returned from Washington, D.C., to take up his post again as a director at the Bureau, and had sought, as he put it, to "find a basis whereon an agreement could be reached with respect to Bureau work" with Allen, his co-director of nine years. "Finding that this was impossible," Cleveland "submitted his resignation to the board of trustees, recommending that the whole management be turned over to Mr. Allen." But Cleveland's resignation was not accepted. Instead, the chairman of the board, Edwin R. A. Seligman, was brought into the discussion and an agreement was worked out on "the division of work" between the two. By July 18 of that year, the *New York Tribune* was reporting that the "Rift" at the Bureau had turned into a "Real Row." The "'friction between Dr. Allen and Dr. Cleveland'" was intense: "so wrought up did Dr. Allen become over what he believed was undue control of the bureau by the Rockefeller Foundation" that he made "a further protest" to the Bureau's board. "However," the *Tribune* reported, "Dr. Cleveland won his side of the fight to the extent of seeing his administrative policies . . . approved by the board."[54]

In the midst of the ongoing controversy, R. Fulton Cutting, a long-time Bureau trustee, met on 10 April 1914, with John D. Rockefeller, Jr. to talk things over. Cutting had urged Rockefeller "to take up the question of another five-year subscription [to support the Bureau of Municipal Research], the last year of the previous one being about to expire."[55] Rockefeller, Allen now said, was replacing his long-standing conditions-free funding of the Bureau with funding predicated on a series of conditions that would uproot the scientific nature of the Bureau, reducing the value of its research and advocacy and rendering suspect the degrees its Training School awarded.

It is clear from a pamphlet written by William Allen, *Reasons Why Mr. Allen Believes That Mr. Rockefeller's Conditional Offer of Support to the New York Bureau of Municipal Research Should Not Be Accepted,* that he had gained the impression from Cleveland and Cutting that Rockefeller, Jr. would offer future financial support to the Bureau only on condition that it stop its "public school work," "divorce the Training School from [the] Bureau," "stop out-of-town work," and "stop [its] postal card publicity." Allen believed Rockefeller had spread word to other foundations to withhold their own funding until his conditions were met.[56]

On May 13 Allen spoke at length before Bureau trustees. "Mr. Rockefeller" (John D. Rockefeller, Jr.) was "imposing restrictions" on the Bureau's work and, "in the hope of preventing a change in motive and method" at the Bureau, Allen urged trustees "not to surrender its freedom." (Two years earlier, in *Modern Philanthropy*, Allen had cautioned that "the Right to Impose Conditions" was "denied by orthodox philanthropy in theory, but seldom in practice.") Allen now, in this privately published booklet, sought to dissuade the Bureau's trustees from accepting conditional funding: "Mr. Rockefeller's restrictions indicate to me that he does not understand the Bureau's program, method or result. To base the Bureau's future upon the misunderstanding of however liberal a giver, is bound to injure that movement."

Mr. Rockefeller's right to spend his own money as he wishes I do not question. I do question anyone's right, even that of our own board or our own directors, to call an emasculated program by the name of the whole program, or to surrender the right to do what this town and the whole country needs on any other condition than that money be provided to render those benefits. . . .

The Bureau of Municipal Research cannot afford to owe its existence to Mr. Rockefeller enthusiastic [sic]; much less can it afford to owe its existence to Mr. Rockefeller imposing restrictions.

What, indeed, would become of social science if self-interested funding came to dominate and direct its research and prescriptive advocacy?

To regard the acceptance of restrictions as a lesser evil than even a temporary suspension of New York's present unrestricted Bureau is, I believe, to misread the purposes and standing of the municipal research movement. Once before when Mr.— and Mr.— asked us (on threat of attacking our financial support) not to publish a report on the— department, our trustees unanimously agreed with Chairman [Edwin R.A.] Seligman's statement that accepting such a proposition from the outside would be 'the beginning of the end of the Bureau's influence in New York.' . . . We have frequently been charged with being agents of 'Wall Street,' 'capital,' etc. We have always had a conclusive answer. Personally

I do not believe that we shall ever again have a conclusive answer after the world knows that the Bureau men are being paid out of funds given with the proposed restrictions.[57]

After Allen's impassioned appeal, Bureau trustees "voted 'that no subscriptions or contributions be received subject to any contributions or limitations as to the future activities of the Bureau.'" It sounded like a victory of principle. But, to Allen's great consternation, "gifts of $55,000 from Mr. Rockefeller followed shortly, part for the Bureau, part for so-called 'scientific research' to be by Bureau men, but not under the trustees' direction." "The original conditions, however technically rejected, have in large part been lived up to," Allen protested in dismay. "On June 18th I wrote the trustees that I would rather be 'alone in New York with our old program than have Mr. Rockefeller's millions but minus our program.' What I still believe I then affirmed—'With little money but with our old program the Bureau can accomplish more during the next ten years than Mr. Rockefeller can hope to accomplish with his tens of millions. . . .'"[58]

On 18 July came the *New York Tribune*'s report of a "Real Row." Allen, however, was fighting a lone battle at the Bureau, and in September he wrote: "I can do nothing now but resign from the New York Bureau of Municipal Research and to record clearly and publicly the grounds of my protest against accepting money in exchange for the momentum of independence and unbound vision."[59]

At the end of 1914 Allen took a job as director of the University of Wisconsin Survey. But before he left for Madison, he found a way to make his point a matter of public record. He was serving as a consultant with the U.S. Industrial Relations Commission and in that role he helped lead an inquiry into the "method of operation, powers, and results" of the nation's principal foundations, including the Rockefeller, Carnegie, and Russell Sage foundations. Both Greene and John D. Rockefeller, Jr. testified. After the hearings concluded, Basil M. Manly, the commission's director of research and investigation, wrote that the commission had identified "possible influence" on the part of the Rockefeller Foundation in "the adoption of a definite line of policy by the Bureau of Municipal Research of New York to meet the conditions imposed by Mr. Rockefeller in connection with proposed contributions."[60]

Such debate and disagreement about how—from what source—social scientists were to receive funding for their work, and how a funding source, in turn, could shape social scientists' research topics, conclusions, and advocacy efforts, took center stage in the early years of the twentieth century. For University of Pennsylvania political science Ph.D.

William Allen the wealth-elites' part in administering the Rockefeller Foundation had powerfully negative implications. Could there be disinterested social scientific inquiry in a world of self-interested actors, or were people bound by their commitments or economic self-interest to tend to promote a particular line of inquiry or action?

"The Only Kind of an Expert That Democracy Will and Ought to Tolerate"

In the aftermath of the pivotal dispute at the Bureau of Municipal Research, Henry Bruère continued in government service and then turned to a job in the private sector while Allen and Cleveland founded competing organizations to continue their work. Allen organized and directed the short-lived Institute for Public Service (he later served as secretary of the New York City Municipal Civil Service Commission); Cleveland, who went on to a professorship at Boston University, organized the Institute for Government Research "to conduct scientific investigations into the theory and practice of governmental administration" (today the Brookings Institution).[61] Jerome D. Greene of the Rockefeller Foundation was on the new Institute's board, and "Father of Public Administration" Frank J. Goodnow, by then president of Johns Hopkins University, was chairman of the Institute's trustees.[62]

With all three of the Bureau of Municipal Research's founding directors having now moved on, Charles Beard became Bureau director. He was eager to take on the unresolved issue of informed intelligence—including social scientists—and democracy. In "Democracy and the Expert," a subsection of a 1916 article for *Annals of the American Association of Political and Social Science,* Beard wrote: "There can be no doubt that democracy distrusts the expert. . . . and there is no doubt also that much of this mistrust is well grounded and thoroughly justified. This is due partly to the air of unwarranted superiority which the expert too frequently assumes and partly to the fact that history presents a long record of self-constituted experts who have been discredited." Beard drew on history: "In earlier times there was an expert class in theology that proposed to do the thinking for the human race in matters religious." And, "There have been military castes, self-confessed experts who have succeeded more than once in imposing not only their professional but their class interests upon the civil population." In a spirit John Dewey would surely have applauded, and one that Allen must have enjoyed, Beard wrote: "The only kind of an expert that democracy will and ought to tolerate is the expert who admits his fallibility, retains an open mind and is prepared to serve."[63]

In 1921 the New York Bureau of Municipal Research changed its name to the National Institute of Public Administration. Beard, that same year, having difficulty raising funds, resigned as its director, his fund raising difficulties, he believed, a result of opposition from Columbia University's president Nicholas Murray Butler, who in 1917 had been rankled by Beard's political radicalism and now sought to dissuade contributors from continuing to fund the Bureau's work. Beard by this time had resigned from Columbia University and become a founder of the New School for Social Research, on West 23rd Street, as "an Independent School of Social Science for Men and Women," its goal to be "emancipated from suspected obligations to donors."[64]

Chapter 5
"To Look After the Nation's Crop of Children"

One morning in 1903 while Lillian Wald, head resident of the Henry Street settlement, and Florence Kelley, the general secretary of the National Consumers' League, were having morning coffee at Wald's settlement, they read a newspaper story about a fact-finding trip into the South by the U.S. Secretary of Agriculture to investigate agricultural pests—in particular, the boll weevil—and the cotton crop. "If the Government can have a department to take such an interest in what is happening to the Nation's cotton crop," Wald reportedly asked Kelley, "why can't it have a bureau to look after the Nation's crop of children?"[1] This version may well be apocryphal, yet it sums up, as such stories often do, the principal facts of the case.

"Clearly a Duty of the Federal Government": A Children's Bureau Based on "Absolutely Scientific Work"

Lillian Wald and Florence Kelley promoted the idea of a U.S. children's bureau to Edward T. Devine, then editor of the journal *Charities* and executive director of the Charity Organization Society of New York, and Devine, in turn, wired President Theodore Roosevelt. The president telegraphed back: "Bully, come down and tell me about it." Whereupon a small group, Wald and Devine among them, went to Washington to meet with the president. In the next seven years, with Columbia University sociologist Samuel McCune Lindsay shepherding the concept in meetings with Roosevelt and his cabinet, eleven bills to establish a federal children's bureau were introduced into Congress. Each bill was defeated, but grassroots support grew. Endorsements came from the National Child Labor Committee and the National Consumers' League, the American Association for Labor Legislation, the General Federation of Women's Clubs, the National Congress of Mothers, the American Association for Study and Prevention of Infant Mortality, and from a number of labor unions. In one pamphlet, *A Federal Children's Bureau,*

What is Proposed—30,000 copies were printed—Florence Kelley advocated for the bureau: "We need full, consecutive, trustworthy, current information concerning the children of our nation." Devine pronounced such a bureau, "Clearly a Duty of the Federal Government." Lindsay said a federal bureau would provide for "Systematic and coordinated inquiry, investigation and report . . . as a basis for legislative and administrative action."[2]

In early 1909, six years after Wald and Kelley's inspiration at morning coffee, President Roosevelt convened a "White House Conference on Dependent Children," and Kelley, Wald, Devine, and Lindsay, joined by Jane Addams and Owen Lovejoy, executive secretary of the National Child Labor Committee (as well as by liberal labor leaders, educators, and civic-minded reformers) testified before Congress. Wald told Congress that "the best scientific treatment" was required and that "children as such have never been taken within the scope of the Federal Government." Lindsay urged the government to "pursue the fullest possible scientific research." Roosevelt sent a message to Congress urging favorable action. It took three years, but finally, in April 1912, Congress passed, and President William Howard Taft signed into law, an Act creating the U.S. Children's Bureau.[3]

In turn-of-the-twentieth-century America some two million children in the U.S. were working—most on farms, but over half a million in "nonagricultural occupations." State laws, where they existed, were often weak and unenforced. Many states did not require children to attend school. Owen Lovejoy wrote that, "Boys of 10 years were common in the blinding dust of coal breakers, picking slate with torn and bleeding fingers, or sweltering all night in the glare of the white-hot furnace of the glasshouse; the incarceration of little 10-year-old girls in the dust-laden cotton mills of the South or the silk mills of Pennsylvania for 12 hours a day was looked upon with approval or indifference; tobacco and cigarette factories, canneries, sweatshops, the street trades, and the night messenger service all took unchallenged too from schoolhouse, playground, or cradle." In 1900 in the cotton mills of North Carolina, men's daily wage averaged $1.72, women's 48 cents, the 30,273 children 32 cents. In 1910 in New York City, tens of thousands of children labored for pennies an hour in many of the 12,000 tenement sweatshops licensed by the state for "homework." "Our little kindergarten children at Greenwich House," Mary Simkhovitch, the settlement's head resident, protested, "go home from school to help make artificial flowers and as late as eleven o'clock at night we have found their baby fingers still fashioning the gay petals."[4]

"It might be thought that considerations of common humanity would lead employers of children to fix hours and other conditions of employment that would not be injurious to them," the Columbia political economist Henry Rogers Seager had written in 1904. "Unfortunately," "this is not the case." It was a "cruelty," he said, "not only of employers, but even of [the children's] own parents." The practice was driven, for parents, usually by necessity; the New York City social welfare and public health reformer Homer Folks noted in a 1907 pamphlet, *Poverty and Parental Dependence as an Obstacle to Child Labor Reform*, that parents, particularly single parents, depended on the small sums their children earned to help feed and clothe their families.[5]

Julia C. Lathrop of Illinois became the U.S. Children's Bureau's first director, the first woman in the nation's history to direct a federal bureau. A Vassar graduate of 1880 who had worked in her father's law office in Illinois, at Jane Addams's Hull House in Chicago, and on the Illinois Board of Charities, Lathrop had contributed research on charity institutions to *Hull-House Maps and Papers* and was a cofounder of the Chicago Institute of Social Science (later the Chicago School of Civics and Philanthropy and, in 1920, the University of Chicago School of Social Service Administration). She had championed the idea of a children's bureau "based always upon absolutely scientific work." As she put it in a Bureau pamphlet in her first year as director, "Forty years ago, when the standards of public service were not so well established, a scientific bureau of this type would have been unthinkable. Yet now, it was easily possible to discover in the governmental service, by the regular methods of inquiry, persons who had had the best university training, together with special experience in governmental methods of inquiry and statistical research, glad to cast their fortunes in."[6]

An informal coalition of social scientists, organized labor, women's clubs, religious organizations, and others also drew public attention to the issue of child labor, collecting information about employer practices, proposing solutions, and acting to implement those solutions. By 1916 their hard work resulted in the Keating-Owen Child Labor Act, a federal law designed to end child labor, but two years later a conservative U.S. Supreme Court declared Keating-Owen unconstitutional. It would take another two decades and the coming of the New Deal before tenacious women and men social science scholar-activists, in concert with numerous allies and political leaders, won the Fair Labor Standards Act of 1938, which banned child labor (setting age 14 to be the minimum age for nonmanufacturing jobs outside school hours, 16 for work in nonhazardous industries during school hours, 18 for hazardous occupations).

Scholar and "Impatient Crusader": Florence Kelley and the National Consumers' League

A key figure in the fight for child labor laws, and for laws protecting women workers as well, was Florence Kelley, the first general secretary of the National Consumers' League. Josephine Goldmark, Kelley's close colleague at the League, wrote: "No painstaking natural scientist in his laboratory worked more faithfully to verify an experiment than did Mrs. Kelley in digging out and assaying the much more elusive, the far less verifiable data of the sociologist." Kelley was, said Julia Lathrop, "always by taste and attainments genuinely a scholar." Kelley wrote essays for *The Survey, Annals of the American Academy of Political and Social Science, Proceedings of the Academy of Political Science, American Journal of Sociology, Journal of Political Economy,* and a book, *Some Ethical Gains Through Legislation* (1905), that insisted on improved working conditions for all adults and child laborers. In a series of lectures at Columbia Teachers College that also became a book, *Modern Industry: In Relation to the Family, Health, Education, Morality,* Kelley urged men and women to "resist the inherent tendency of industry" to drive wages ever lower through the "solidarity" of labor unions and political-party organization. She pressed consumers to use their "power over industry" to prod capitalists to pay fair wages and to make work environments safe. "Thinking people," especially teachers, needed to prepare "the oncoming generation" for "the new ideal of the democracy of the future: the ideal of service performed not as philanthropy, not as charity, not alone in the care of childhood and old age, but in a transformed industry."[7] A visionary in the field of social action, Kelley had gone far beyond the older concept of noblesse oblige. She, like Lathrop and other strong pioneering women, was ahead of her time, and in many ways, ahead of her male allies.

Josephine Goldmark titled her biography of Kelley *Impatient Crusader,* and Kelley was indeed indomitable and relentless in drive and energy. In her Hull House days in the 1890s, Jane Addams's nephew, James Linn, said, Kelley had been "the toughest customer in the reform riot." She "hurled the spears of her thought," Linn wrote, with "apparent carelessness of what breasts they pierced." "A very powerful person," said Frances Perkins. Perkins herself learned how to negotiate the halls of power from Kelley. Working for Kelley's Consumers' League and lobbying the New York State legislature for a 54-hour work week for women workers, Perkins, around 1910, had agreed to a legislative compromise that achieved that goal, excluding women workers in the state's high pressure seasonal cannery industry. Returning from Albany to Consumers' League headquarters in Manhattan, Perkins approached Kelley with news of the compromise, "in fear and trembling," she later said, "thinking I'd probably lose my job." In Albany, she had told Pauline Gold-mark, "this is *my* responsibility. I'll do it and hang for it if necessary." "Instead, Mrs. Kelley fell on my neck with embraces because for the first time in years we'd got some limitation on the hours of labor of women."[8]

Kelley had learned toughness, dedication, and boldness from her own family in Philadelphia. She was born in 1859, a year and a half before the attack on Fort Sumter, to a Quaker mother, Caroline Bartram Kelley. Her father, William D. Kelley, was elected to Congress in 1861, and served three decades in the House, with the nickname "Pig Iron" Kelley for his support of protective tariffs for Pennsylvania's iron and steel industries and a reputation as a Radical Republican for his advocacy of civil rights for American blacks. There were strong public women, too, in Kelley's family; her great-aunt Sarah Pugh was a leading abolitionist and friend of Lucretia Mott, the women's rights activist. Kelley's crusad-ing spirit had been tempered by grief and suffering from her childhood; her earliest memory, at five, was "a voice of utter sadness," as her grand-mother reported the news of Lincoln's assassination. Before she was eleven all five of her sisters had died of illness in infancy or early child-hood, deaths, she said, that "robbed the sunshine of its glory." Kelley retreated from suffering into a life of books (from Dickens to Burke to Emerson), and then into a struggle for social justice. Accompanying her father, at twelve, on his political rounds, she was shocked to see boys younger than herself working in the scorching heat of the iron and steel furnaces. As an undergraduate at Cornell University, Kelley began her lifelong campaign to protect children. She organized a Social Science Club, and wrote her senior thesis "On Some Changes in the Legal Status of the Child Since Blackstone." After graduation she became an advo-cate of Marx and Engels's socialism at the University of Zurich, corres-ponded with Frederick Engels, and translated his *Condition of the Working Class in England* into English, a translation that remained a favorite of scholars well into the twentieth century.[9]

Back in the U.S. in 1887 at twenty-eight, she lived in New York City for a few years, joined the Socialist Labor Party briefly, and moved to Hull House in Chicago. Under her married name, Florence Kelley Wischnew-etzky (she would drop her ex-husband's surname after a divorce), she wrote a paper for the New York Association of Collegiate Alumnae on "The Need of Theoretical Preparation for Philanthropic Work," urging "college-bred women" to study "fundamental works of modern scien-tific political economy"; at thirty she published her first book, *Our Toil-ing Children*, on the "hopelessly inadequate" child labor legislation, and earned a law degree from Northwestern University. Illinois Governor John Peter Altgeld, impressed by Kelley's survey of Chicago's poorest neighborhoods (undertaken with statistician Carroll D. Wright), com-missioned further study of the city's labor problems, and the report she filed led to a state law prohibiting child labor and limiting women to an eight-hour day. She was appointed chief factory inspector under the new law she had helped enact, but within two years the Illinois Supreme Court declared the law unconstitutional on the grounds that it inter-fered with an individual's legal right to freedom of contract. Kelley, once again far ahead of men in power, was out of a job. Instrumental in initiat-ing the research for *Hull-House Maps and Papers* (1895)—she wrote its entry on "The Sweating System," and co-authored the entry on "Wage Earning Children"—and one who helped found the Illinois Consumers' League, she was offered the general secretaryship of the newly forming National Consumers' League. In 1899, at forty, Kelley packed up and moved to New York City, one more prominent social science activist to find greater space in that magnet city.[10]

The National Consumers' League was a national consolidation of sev-eral state Consumers' Leagues, the first founded in 1890 by Josephine Shaw Lowell, the indefatigable reformer, for seven years president of the Consumers' League of the City of New York.[11] By 1898 leagues in Illinois, Minnesota, Wisconsin, New York, Massachusetts, New Jersey, and Penn-sylvania sponsored creation of the new National Consumers' League. As its first general secretary, Kelley—like Edward T. Devine who had taken over Lowell's Charity Organization Society in 1896—became, in effect, heir to Josephine Shaw Lowell's legacy. The two were, in some ways, quite different; Lowell was a Christian, Kelley an atheist; Lowell, espe-cially in her early years, emphasized the responsibilities of the poor for creating their poverty while Kelley placed primary responsibility for pov-erty on the market economy; Lowell was a gradualist reformer, Kelley a socialist. Yet there were striking similarities as well. Both came from affluent families of social position; both were excluded from top faculty posts in universities; both had suffered the pain of great loss—Lowell, whose young husband was killed in the Civil War soon after their wed-ding, Kelley, whose childhood was marred by the deaths of siblings. Both were single parents. Both underscored the importance of ordinary American consumers taking responsibility for shaping, through their own shopping habits, the behavior of employers; both castigated employers for exploiting workers. Both chose a private voluntary organi-zation as the means by which to pursue their goals, though, in fact, there was no other instrument for women interested in social change. Both went beyond the traditional women's sphere, each ahead of her own time, to set a new mark for women's engagement in public offices.

Kelley expanded and modified Lowell's vision but she did not aban-don it. A League pamphlet published around 1907, after Lowell's death, reflected the aim of the League as Lowell had envisioned it almost two decades earlier: "What is a Consumers' League?" "An association of persons who in making their purchases strives to further the welfare of those who make or distribute the things bought. The act of shopping seems to many trivial and entirely personal, while in reality it exerts a far reaching, oft-repeated influence for good or evil." Kelley would write later "the interest of the community demands that all workers should receive, not the lowest wages, but fair living wages," and responsibility for debilitating workplace conditions "rests with the consumers who persist in buying in the cheapest markets regardless of how cheapness is brought about." Since "the task of enlightening and organizing the careless money-spending public," Kelley said, might take "a century," it was important to get started. As Frances Perkins, then secretary of the New York branch of the Consumers' League, put it: "The Consumers' League is an organization of persons who wish to improve the industrial conditions by utilizing the shopping power, the buying power of the con- sumers, who are banded together, that is, by pledging themselves in their shopping to do their buying in such a way as to improve conditions, rather than make them worse."[12] The laborers' world of production and the consumers' world of consumption were, in the Consumers' League work, inseparable.

Under Kelley's leadership the Consumers' League worked against industrial sweatshops and against sweated labor in tenements; it sought an end to child labor and to excessive hours and night work for women. In 1904 the League published a "Standard Child Labor Law" intended as a model for uniform laws across the country. Its "Consumers' League label" could be affixed to articles "made under conditions approved by the League." It published a "White List" (the reverse of a blacklist) of recommended retail stores, where working conditions were, by League standards, fair. Kelley championed state and federal minimum wage laws, and laws to regulate hours of labor. She counseled Christmas shop- pers to avoid buying toys made by children or overworked adults: "the association of cruel overwork with the Christmas holidays, is wholly the fault of the shopping public. There need never again be a cruel Christ- mas." And in an essay on "Woman Suffrage: Its Relation to Working Women and Children," in the National Woman Suffrage Association's *Political Equality Series,* she observed that the vote for women would enhance the possibility of laws to protect women and children workers. It was not "safe or sane to exclude" women "from a full share of power and responsibility" in the society.[13]

Kelley's principal assistants at the League were women—the Goldm- ark sisters, Pauline and Josephine, and Frances Perkins among them— but she enlisted men as well. Reform was a coalition-built enterprise and it was bad politics and a waste of resources to turn any allies away. Around 1915 the League's vice presidents, including Mary E. Woolley, president of Mount Holyoke, also included respected male social scientists, Lindsay and Seligman of Columbia, Jeremiah Jenks of New York University, Henry Carter Adams of the University of Michigan, Frank W. Taussig of Harvard, Richard T. Ely of the University of Wisconsin, and Arthur T. Hadley of Yale, again a mix of the Northeastern and Midwestern academic activists. Columbia economists John Bates Clark and Henry R. Seager served on the Consumers' League's advisory board; so did Robert Hunter, James B. Reynolds, and Mary Simkhovitch—all leading figures in and proponents of social science in settlement work.[14]

Kelley developed an elaborate and efficient group of League committees dominated by social science-trained women scholar-activists. Pauline Goldmark and Frances Perkins were officers of the League's state branch and on its Committee on Investigation, as was Mary Van Kleeck, director for many years of the Russell Sage Foundation's department of industrial studies, a 1904 Smith College graduate, who taught social research at the New York School of Philanthropy. On the Consumers' League Committee on a Living Wage were Van Kleeck, who chaired the Committee in the 1910s; Irene Osgood Andrews, of the American Association for Labor Legislation; Mary E. Dreier, the Woman's Municipal League director, who had trained at the New York School of Philanthropy; and two men, Walter Lippmann, the journalist and author of *Preface to Politics*, and John Mitchell, former United Mine Workers president. Kelley enlisted support from ministers and politicians as well. The League's first president was John Graham Brooks, the author of *The Social Unrest*, a Harvard Divinity School graduate who had left the Unitarian pulpit for economics. Newton D. Baker, Brooks' successor as League president, was city solicitor and a reform mayor of Cleveland. (Later Woodrow Wilson's secretary of war, he incorporated the practices of the Consumers' League into the work of the War Department with a factory inspection service to look into working conditions in munitions factories under government contract during the war.)[15]

Among the earliest and most important National Consumers' League committees, its Committee on Legislation was chaired by Pauline Goldmark, with members Kelley, Van Kleeck, Perkins, Simkhovitch, and Alice Hooker Day Jackson (like Goldmark, a Bryn Mawr graduate, treasurer of the New York Consumers' League from 1903 to 1906, from 1908 to 1911 a social science graduate student at Columbia, and by 1915 the National League's first vice-president). In 1915 alone, this committee of women sponsored letter-writing campaigns to legislators and governors, organized a mass protest rally, issued sixty-seven thousand leaflets, sponsored an exhibit portraying "by means of charts, pictures, etc., the work of the League," dispatched officers and staff on speaking engagements ("averaging two weekly"), and "placed on the desk of every legislator" in New York State's capital at Albany a "stirring poem in regard to the exploitation of women and children in canneries."[16]

Kelley stumped the country to rally support for the League, in her first year as general secretary delivering fifty-five addresses in ten states; by 1906 she had built up sixty-three Consumers' League locals, and by 1913 League membership stood at 30,000. She drew the General Federation of Women's Clubs, with its more than 150,000 members, into sympathetic alliance; at its 1904 biennial convention, the Federation urged its members to adopt the League's "Standard Child Labor Law," which called for a general minimum age of fourteen in most industries, and for an end to night work and child labor in hazardous industries. The Federation counselled: "That no children under sixteen years of age shall be permitted to work at night; that is, between the hours of 7 P.M. and 7 A.M. That no children shall be permitted to be regularly employed who cannot read and write simple sentences." When New York City's board of commissioners failed to enact legislation to improve conditions in city schools, Kelley wrote to her "loving old friend" Mary Simkhovitch, "please throw yourself into the breach, as though Greenwich House were on fire!" and "see not only your own [City] Commissioner, but everybody whom you can influence." In 1908 after Kelley attended the first International Conference of Consumers' Leagues, inspired by what she heard, she initiated a minimum wage campaign for women in the U.S. (An active member of the American Association for Labor Legislation, she represented the AALL at an international convention in Lucerne that same year. See Chapter 6.) It was, a League pamphlet later said, "through the efforts of the Consumers' League that the idea of a minimum wage for women was first introduced into this country."[17]

In Kelley's social science, reform was neither noblesse oblige nor Christian charity, as it had been in an earlier century. Instead "social justice is the best safeguard against social disorder," was the League's motto, its modus operandi: investigate, educate, legislate, and—once prudent labor laws were on the books—enforce the law. Kelley's approach to social ills as part of a larger inter-dependent web of "the whole texture of our national life," demonstrated a clear evolution from Josephine Shaw Lowell's earlier insistence on disciplining the poor and setting moral standards for them.[18]

"Sociological Jurisprudence": Kelley, the Goldmark Sisters, and the "Brandeis Brief"

In 1899, her first year as general secretary of the National Consumers' League, Florence Kelley hired as her assistant secretary Pauline Goldmark, who by 1905 became both secretary of the New York City branch, and director of the New York Child Labor Committee. During the 1900s and 1910s, Goldmark served on the League's executive committee, its legislative committee, and its committee on investigations, was active with the College Settlement Association, headed the Bureau of Social Research for the Russell Sage Foundation and the New York School of Philanthropy, directed social science research studies sponsored by the Russell Sage Foundation and *The Survey*, and lectured at the New York School of Philanthropy, in 1910 becoming an associate director at the school and supervisor of its research bureau. In 1912, Pauline, her sister Josephine (who had joined her at the League), and Kelley wrote for the League a pamphlet on *The Truth About Wage-Earning Women and the State*. It declared that "shortening working hours [for women] is not a matter of gallantry or chivalry, a gracious gift to please the ladies. It is essential to the life of the nation. For overworked women can not rear sons and daughters capable of carrying forward a democratic republic." The Goldmark sisters—Pauline was two years older than Josephine—were the last of ten children of Austrian immigrants, their father a physician and member of the Austrian parliament who had fled Europe to settle in Brooklyn after the failed revolution of 1848. Pauline and Josephine graduated from Bryn Mawr College in the 1890s; both went on to Barnard College for further study, then into the New York social science reform network and to work with Kelley's National Consumers' League. For Kelley and the Goldmarks the time of women on a pedestal but without power, or as a token for male knights in tournament, had long gone by. Women were to play an equal role, not only for their own sake but for the sake of the public good and the future of "a democratic republic."[19]

Like Kelley and Pauline Goldmark, Josephine Goldmark was vital to the world of public policy-making—a member of the New York Child Labor Committee, for over a decade secretary of publications for the Consumers' League, and author of two books, *Child Labor Legislation* and *Fatigue and Efficiency, a Study in Industry*. Josephine Goldmark's most important contribution was an innovative approach to legal argument—through *sociology*. She and Kelley initiated the sociological research that Louis Brandeis, the celebrated Boston lawyer and later U.S. Supreme Court Justice, incorporated as special counsel for the State of Oregon in his successful brief in the 1908 case, *Muller v. Oregon*, an argument and a case that established "sociological jurisprudence." *Muller v. Oregon* served as an unacknowledged precedent for the social research supported legal brief later used in *Brown v. Board of Education* in 1954. The "Brandeis brief" offered the Justices a 113-page document, most of it a sociological report seeking to demonstrate the deleterious effects of long hours of workplace labor on women. (In 1898 the Court, in *Holden v. Hardy*, had upheld a law limiting the hours of labor for Utah miners on the grounds that their health was at stake, but in 1905, in *Lochner v. New York*, it had struck down a New York law limiting men's hours of work in a bakery.) The Brandeis connection was not accidental: Alice Goldmark, one of Josephine and Pauline's older siblings, was married to Brandeis, and Kelley and Josephine Goldmark met with, and convinced the Harvard-trained Brandeis to take the case. He agreed on the condition that the sociological research at the heart of the brief be conducted by Kelley and Goldmark; they did so, together with a group of young social scientists, including Helen Marot, daughter of wealthy Philadelphia Quakers, secretary of the National Women's Trade Union League, and author of the 1899 *Handbook of Labor Literature*.[20]

Noting in its opening that "the decision in this case will, in effect, determine the constitutionality of nearly all the statutes in force in the United States, limiting the hours of labor of adult women" the brief presented hundreds of paragraph-length excerpts, almost in equal measure by American and European authors, quoting physicians, physiologists, sociologists, political scientists, economists, historians, and hygienicists (from work published in, among others, *Journal of the American Medical Association, Annals of American Academy of Political and Social Science*, and *Journal of Political Economy*). Anecdotal evidence, passages from factory inspection reports from England, Germany, and France, were interwoven with state bureau of labor statistics reports from California, Nebraska, Wisconsin, Massachusetts, New Jersey, and New York. National and international associations and conference reports, and governmental inquiries and legislative acts were quoted, among them the 1890 Berlin *International Conference in Relation to Labor Legislation*, the 1900 *Report of the U.S. Industrial Commission*, and the 1891 *Proceedings of the French Senate*. The brief quoted the measured, pioneering view of Sophonisba Breckinridge, University of Chicago political science Ph.D. of 1901 and law school graduate of 1904: "The assumption of control over the conditions under which industrial women are employed is one of the most significant features of recent legislation. . . . The object of such control is the protection of the physical well-being of the community by setting a limit to the exploitation of the improvident, unworkmanlike, unorganized women who are yet the mothers, actual or prospective, of the coming generation."[21]

Judgments that a later age would find not only clearly erroneous but also bitterly prejudiced were included as well, such as Havelock Ellis's observation in his *Man and Woman* that "there is more water" in women's blood than in men's, and hence women were "in rapidity and precision of movement . . . inferior to men." Columbia University physiologist Frederick S. Lee was quoted from the *Journal of the American Medical Association* as saying that "prolonged and excessive activity of the muscular and the nervous system. . . . may easily give place to pathologic action," an observation equally true for men, no doubt, as for women. The brief's authors ignored data that demonstrated the ill effects on men of excessive hours of labor, and based the need for legislation to restrict women's hours of labor on women's physiological differences:

Long hours of labor are dangerous for women primarily because of their special physical organization. In structure and function women are differentiated from men. Besides these anatomical and physiological differences, physicians are agreed that women are fundamentally weaker than men in all that makes for endurance: in muscular strength, in nervous energy, in the powers of persistent attention and application. Overwork, therefore, which strains endurance to the utmost, is more disastrous to the health of women than of men, and entails upon them more lasting injury.

They were using popular and scientific claims of female inferiority to improve the quality of women's lives and to reduce one area of gender oppression. Brandeis closed his January 1908 brief to the Court: "it cannot be said that the Legislature of Oregon had no reasonable ground for believing that the public health, safety, or welfare did not require a legal limitation on women's work in manufacturing and mechanical establishments and laundries to ten hours in one day." Brandeis argued that the state's police powers could properly be understood to extend to cover the health of Oregon's women workers. Persuaded by Brandeis, the U.S. Supreme Court made legal history and upheld Oregon's right to restrict women's hours of work.[22]

From a perspective other than pragmatism, *Muller* could be viewed as discriminatory, paternalistic; as earlier, in 1873, in *Bradwell v. Illinois*, the Court upheld a state's refusal to allow women to practice law on grounds that women's "natural . . . delicacy" made women "unfit for many of the occupations of civil life." Whether the strategy to invoke traditional gender-role paradigms against oppression of women in *Muller* was an error has been much debated by legal scholars, feminists, and historians.[23] But in 1908, when women had no vote and little standing under the law, *Muller* gave Kelley and her allies the leverage they needed. By 1919 more than twenty states had passed laws regulating the hours of women's work.

Frances Perkins: "I'd Much Rather Get a Law Than Organize a Union"

Frances Perkins, one of the most distinguished women of New York City's social science network, trained at the National Consumers'

League for what became a lifetime of public service. Born Fannie Cor-
alie Perkins, she changed her name to Frances at the age of twenty-five.
She had been born in 1882 into a comfortable middle-class family in
Boston; her father, a wholesale stationer, taught her Greek as a child. At
Mount Holyoke she majored in chemistry and physics (1902), "the so-
called social sciences were hardly taught. . . . I knew nothing about economics, sociology, anthropology." But an introductory course in American history made its mark. Perkins's teacher, Annah May Soule, "had a
brilliant idea of having a class of perfectly innocent girls—that is, innocent of the industrial process—go and look at some factories. . . . look
at paper mills, textile mills, and so forth. I was astonished and fascinated
by what I saw. I think she also opened the door to the idea that there
were some people much poorer than other people; that not everybody
had comfort and security; and that the lack of comfort and security in
some people was not solely due to the fact that they drank, which had
been the prevailing view in my parental society." "With a social sense of
what ought to be done," Perkins went "to New York right from college—I remember my father protested—and went to the Charity Organization Society, demanding to see Mr. [Edward T.] Devine whose name
I knew. Everybody else lower down the line tried to interview me, but I
insisted on seeing Mr. Devine. I sometimes laugh when I think of how
fresh and naive I was really." She told him she wanted a job in the Society: "What did I think I'd like to do? I said I understood that they had
visitors who went out to see poor families who applied for help, decided
if they got relief, gave them food, unravelled their problems."

To this day I can see the strange, mature smile on Mr. Devine's face. He said,
"Well, that's very interesting. What would you do if you were sent out to a family
who had applied for some help, and you came into their tenement, you found
the father drunk on the bed, the children done up with sore throats and sick,
no food in the house. The mother was rustling around pretty disheveled and
disorderly looking. The dishes were piled high in the sink. The father was drunk
and obviously had just beaten the wife. What would you do?" Promptly I said,
"Well, I'd send for the police at once and have the man arrested, of course."
The smile on Mr. Devine's face broadened and he said, "That isn't exactly what
we would recommend." He then opened to me briefly the door to the idea that
rehabilitation consisted in getting parents to work, keep sober and discharge
their responsibilities. Anyhow, he explained to me in words of one and two sylla-
bles that, in the first place, they wouldn't hire anybody so young as I was, and,
in the second place, I hadn't had enough life experience to have any judgment
at all about what to do with the poor, the needy, the forsaken and those who
were in trouble.[24]

Devine recommended that Perkins teach for a few years and read Jacob
Riis's *How the Other Half Lives*. Perkins did both, and more. She taught
high school science in Lake Forest, Illinois, lived at Jane Addams' Hull

House, and "wrote to anybody I knew who had any connection at all with charities to say I wanted a job, but had no experience." Learning of "a league of women's organizations," she wrote to Frances Kellor—the University of Chicago-trained sociologist, author of *Experimental Sociology*, and organizer of The Inter-Municipal Committee on Household Research to aid women migrants from the South (later the National League for the Protection of Colored Women). Kellor hired the eager young woman, and, for about $50 a month, Frances Perkins conducted "an investigation of the exploitation" of women, her charge "to devise ways to prevent it [the exploitation] or overcome it, either by social representations or by legislation at the municipal or state level." As Perkins described her task: "We were to investigate the lodging houses where they stayed and devise some way of correcting anything bad. We were to investigate and determine their standard of living, their wage, the employment offices that got them jobs, what kind of jobs they got, what their economic level was, what their social connections were."[25]

One night while trying to put one seedy employment office—many were simply brothels—out of business, Perkins was followed home by two men, one she recognized as the illicit business's owner: "He took quantities of money and regularly sent these Negro girls to bawdy houses. That was his trade; that was his business." Alarmed, she did what her father had recommended for such an occasion, turned suddenly with her umbrella extended, screamed and called out the man's name. "Heads popped out of windows and I stopped him in his tracks. They turned and ran. It was very funny, but it gave me the feeling if you put up a bold front people will turn and run. What else would you do? You can't run and let them stab you."[26]

Mary Richmond, director of the Charity Organization department of the Russell Sage Foundation, and author of *Friendly Visiting Among the Poor* and *The Good Neighbor in the Modern City*, recommended that Perkins take some courses in economics and sociology, and Perkins did so, first in Philadelphia at the Wharton School of Economics with Simon Nelson Patten, and then, at Patten's urging and with the help of a fellowship, for two years at Columbia University. By 1910 she was working for her master's degree in sociology—she studied with Seager, Seligman, Giddings, Clark, and Lindsay—lived at the Greenwich House settlement, taught sociology as a part-time adjunct "in the late afternoon" at Adelphi College on Long Island (New York State's first coeducational college), and worked with Florence Kelley, until 1912, as secretary of the New York branch of the National Consumers' League.[27]

Perkins, Kelley, and the League were concerned about the women who worked as clerks in the Fifth Avenue shops where sweatshop goods were sold. At the city's most prestigious department stores—Altman's,

Macy's, and Bloomingdale's—they earned, on average, a mere three dollars a week. The League alerted upper-class women who shopped in these stores to the wages and working conditions of women and children (children worked as "cash children, bundle-girls, wrappers and junior clerks"), and, one after another, women of means began to cancel their accounts, making clear to the store owners that they would resume shopping there only when they provided better wages and working conditions. The League's demand was $5 a week minimum, with additional pay for overtime work, holidays off, and an improvement in working conditions, including seats for sales clerks and allowing the clerks to sit on them.[28]

"Legislation," Perkins said, "is the most important thing. I'd much rather get a law than organize a union." Perkins's study of the social sciences at the University of Pennsylvania and Columbia University and her work with the Consumers' League had taught her the importance of regulatory legislation in improving the lives of working Americans; two decades later, as Secretary of Labor under Franklin D. Roosevelt, she would champion both the Social Security Act of 1935 and the Fair Labor Standards Act of 1938. Referring once to Rose Schneiderman, the New York labor activist and founder of the United Cloth Hat and Cap Makers' Union (later president of the Women's Trade Union League), Perkins said: "We could drag Rosie Schneiderman up and say, 'See, she's the president of a union.' But it was a pretty weak union back of her. It wasn't much and wouldn't hold up. . . . They would never have had their hours reduced, if we hadn't gotten the legislation first."[29]

The social science scholar-activists, especially women, and especially in New York City's great social laboratory, were moving from the private power realm of their private associations, leagues, committees, and bureaus, to the realm of public power through government legislation and enforcement.

"Effective Child Labor Law Efficiently Enforced"

"Legislation first" was an important part of the National Consumers' League's efforts to curtail child labor and achieve improved conditions for women workers (and men, too). In 1902, Florence Kelley urged the American Academy of Political and Social Science's annual conference to join her: "To form in every state, among the purchasers of the products of manufacture, a body of alert, enlightened public opinion, keen to watch the officers to whom is entrusted the duty of enforcing child labor laws, rewarding with support and appreciation faithful officials and calling attention to derelictions from duty on the part of the mere politicians among them."[30]

That same year, Kelley, joined by Simkhovitch, Pauline Goldmark, Robert Hunter (headworker at University Settlement and author of *Poverty*), and Lillian Wald, working through the Association of Neighborhood Workers (an umbrella organization of more than thirty New York City settlement houses—all of the above were members), formed a local committee on child labor. With the help of the philanthropist-reformer William H. Baldwin, Jr., Ethical Culture leader Felix Adler, professor of Political and Social Ethics at Columbia, and Edward T. Devine, Charity Organization Society executive secretary, they launched the New York Child Labor Committee.[31] By the following year, Devine was writing to one New York state senator "on behalf of the Charity Organization Society and the relief agencies which co-operate with it": "We think that it is the general sentiment of this community that children who are of school age should be kept in school, rather than at work, even if this means supplementing the earning of the mother for that purpose." Columbia economists John Bates Clark and Edwin R. A. Seligman, along with sociologist Franklin Giddings, added their names to "The Child Labor Evil in the State of New York," a 1903 pamphlet calling, in lieu of federal action, for enactment of state laws prohibiting child labor. Within two years of the founding of the New York Child Labor Committee a national organization, the National Child Labor Committee, was launched, on 15 April 1904, at a grand rally of its supporters in Midtown Manhattan's Carnegie Hall. Kelley, Adler, and Baldwin were appointed to its committee "for preliminary work."[32]

With its headquarters in New York City—yet another example of the city's role as an important laboratory for Progressive Era reforms—the National Child Labor Committee reached beyond the city to a nationwide effort, including more than a score of other "prominent and wealthy persons, of newspapers, and of religious and civic groups," including Jane Addams; Sarah Platt Decker of Denver, president of the General Federation of Women's Clubs; Hoke Smith of Georgia (Grover Cleveland's Secretary of the Interior); Judge Ben Lindsey of the Juvenile Court of Denver; Talcott Williams of the *Philadelphia Press*; Alexander Cassatt, president of the Pennsylvania Railroad; Isaac N. Seligman, the New York banker and older brother of Edwin R. A. Seligman; Bishops Greer of New York and Wilmer of Atlanta; Cardinal Gibbons of Baltimore; and Edgar Gardner Murphy, an Episcopal minister turned social reformer from Alabama. Samuel Gompers, president of the American Federation of Labor, though at loggerheads with social scientists on other issues of government—hours and wage regulations for adult male workers, the core of his organization's membership—strongly supported child labor laws. Soon after the organization of the National Child Labor Committee Gompers said: "It should be entirely superfluous for me to say that I am in hearty accord and in full sympathy with the purpose for which the National Child Labor Committee and the various committees throughout the country are organized."[33]

Three weeks after the founding meeting at Carnegie Hall, Edward Devine wrote to Samuel McCune Lindsay, then professor of sociology at the University of Pennsylvania, to offer Lindsay the executive secretaryship of the new group, "at least two days a week in New York City and more occasionally, if necessary. . . ." Lindsay agreed to serve. The National Child Labor Committee was incorporated by an act of Congress in 1907 to "promot[e] the rights, awareness, dignity, well-being and education of children and youth as they relate to work and working." It set up its headquarters on the fifth floor of the omnipresent United Charities Building on East 22nd Street—a floor below the offices of Kelley's Consumers' League and Devine's Charity Organization Society. "Investigation, and then fresh investigation, and always fresh and further investigation" was the new group's objective, said Felix Adler, a founder of the New York committee that preceded it, its goal "to awaken and stimulate an attitude of scientific statesmanship" on child labor. Its program emphasized "scientific research and an accumulation of expert evidence" as a key to arousing the American people to "revelations concerning the abuse of childhood."[34]

But just how to stimulate the "attitude of scientific statesmanship" and promote the cited rights, and in what governmental venue—in federal or state jurisdictions—would prove to be a contentious point. In early executive council meetings, Edgar Gardner Murphy, the Alabama minister who had been instrumental in creating the organization, and others tangled with Lindsay over strategy. Murphy and his allies were adamant that child labor laws were the responsibility of state governments alone, Lindsay and his supporters convinced that federal legislation was essential. In the National Child Labor Committee's early days, Murphy and those who sought state-by-state legislation, had the upper hand.[35]

Membership grew to 6,400 by 1911–12, with a staff of the nation's most vigorous lobbyists on behalf of federal legislation to end child labor, who knew how to be effective. *The Child Labor Bulletin*, its monthly, employed "expert investigators to study and photograph child labor conditions throughout the country," and by 1912 it offered "exhibits of photographs, charts, diagrams and samples of children's work," and speakers from its membership list to help build allies. Graduate students joined in the campaign, one of them William F. Ogburn, a fellow in sociology and statistics at Columbia University, whose book *Progress and Uni-*

formity in Child-Labor Legislation: A Study in Statistical Measurement was intended to "be of practical value, especially to legislators, who, it is believed, can better frame their laws on child labor after a thorough knowledge of the status of child-labor laws of the various states." "It is expected," wrote Ogburn, "that sociology in the future will be concerned largely with inductive studies in the theory of social control." (Ogburn later became professor of sociology at the University of Chicago and president of the American Sociological Society.) The philosopher John Dewey goaded primary and secondary school teachers from the pages of the committee's *The Child Labor Bulletin* to "awaken from the lethargy through which they have permitted non-educational associations to take the lead in measures for the amelioration of the condition of children."[36]

Successes in the first years were incremental. By 1913 some reduction in the maximum hours a child might work each week was achieved in ten states; here and there, night work for children became illegal and minimum age requirements were raised by a year or two.[37] But private action could not provide effective monitoring and policing, and when one state acting alone shortened hours or increased age requirements, a business might simply pack up and move to another state where restrictions were less stringent. Federal action was needed. It came in two phases, the U.S. Children's Bureau in 1912, and the federal Keating-Owen Child Labor Act in 1916.

Mothers' Pensions: A "Right and Not as the Dole"

At the same time that momentum was building for a U.S. Children's Bureau and a federal law prohibiting child labor, a push came for states to provide payments to families without a father in the home. Except for Civil War veterans' pensions for Union soldiers and their families there was no federal support of families. (By the early 1900s, Congress relaxed requirements and almost a million ex-Union soldiers or their widows—about 1 percent of the population—began to receive such pensions; confederate soldiers, not covered by the federal pension plan, received modest payments from southern states.) Jean M. Gordon, a National Child Labor Committee member and a former factory inspector, protested in a symposium in the *Child Labor Bulletin*: "I contend it is just as much the duty of the State to pension dependent mothers as dependent veterans. Certainly the mother does as much for the country in rearing her children as the veterans did in killing her sons!" "Public aid would have to be administered with intelligence and care," Mary Simkhovitch wrote in an essay, "Women's Invasion of the Industrial Field." "But the difficulty of developing the technique of such a plan is not to be compared with the difficulty the state will meet through the inadequate care of families."[38]

Meeting in New York in May 1911, the Conference of Charities and Correction set up a committee to examine "the advisability of extending governmental aid to dependent families." Florence Kelley and Edward T. Devine presented papers; Devine with the traditional caution of the Charity Organization Society urged restraint, but "the prevailing opinion of those testifying to the committee was in favor of some form of governmental aid." Private charity organizations alone simply could not feed and clothe all needy children. A precedent had been set by the state—if the truant officers could force children out of the factories and into the schools under increasing numbers of state laws on compulsory education, the new committee said, government had an equal responsibility for economic aid to poor families.[39]

In June 1912, with Julia Lathrop as chief, the U.S. Children's Bureau began a nationwide campaign for "Public Aid to Mothers with Dependent Children." Illinois and Missouri had legislated mother's pensions by 1911; by 1914 twenty more had programs; by 1919, thirty-nine. These programs, Florence Kelley said, "lift the burden from the widowed mother by giving her, as her right and not as the dole of a private charity . . . an allowance out of public funds on condition that she stay in her home and keep her children at home and in school." But state programs were far from uniform, and often terribly inadequate.[40]

Workers from private charity organizations were enlisted to help administer the new programs, and the Charity Organization Society's standards for moral fitness were sometimes employed. Thus, in Ohio, recipients were graded by casework investigators on a scale of worthiness A, B, C, or D (A the most deserving, D worthy of no aid at all). Most women with pensions under the state plans—historian Judith Sealander estimates that only 3 percent were African Americans—received less than $240 a year, though the Charity Organization Society estimated that it took $700 a year for a family of four to live at a subsistence level. Sealander and Theda Skocpol have both observed that mothers' pensions led to marginalization rather than empowerment of women. Some states prohibited mothers who received the pensions from working outside the home for more than one day a week and, as a result, many had to take in homework as seamstresses or other long-hours, low-pay positions. In 1913, noting the limitations of state-run mothers' pension programs, Mary Richmond, head of the Russell Sage Foundation's Charity Organization department (she had an office, like so many others, in the United Charities Building), proposed spending the funds instead to eradicate conditions that led to deaths from tuberculosis—at the time, an estimated 10,000 annually in New York City alone.[41]

Federal Child Labor Law: "The Evil of Premature and Excessive Child Labor"

The fight to turn the Keating-Owen Child Labor Bill into law, to forbid interstate shipment of the products of child labor, was a fierce battle, with many in support, not only from the National Child Labor Committee, the National Consumers' League, and at the U.S. Children's Bureau, but also from the ranks of organized labor. John Golden of the United Textile Workers of America said, "it is the earnest hope of the thousands of members connected with our organization that this bill will become law this year." Some business leaders, too, supported regulatory reform, assuming government regulation of child labor would level the competitive playing field by removing any advantage a competitor might achieve by employing children. So, for example, the Laurel Cotton Mills in Laurel, Mississippi, employed children, but the company's president, Wallace B. Rogers, supported federal legislation to end child labor: "No particular hardship," Rogers explained, "would accrue to any individual operator, so long as all were laboring under the same condition." With President Woodrow Wilson's active lobbying of southern Democrats, the Keating-Owen Child Labor Act became law in September 1916, and almost immediately was challenged in the courts. In *Hammer v. Dagenhart*, in 1918, the U.S. Supreme Court, in a 5–4 decision, struck it down as unconstitutional. In his famous dissent, Justice Oliver Wendell Holmes, Jr. wrote, "if there is any matter upon which civilized countries have agreed—far more unanimously than they have with regard to intoxicants and some other matters over which this country is now emotionally aroused—it is the evil of premature and excessive child labor." More than two decades later the Court, reversing its earlier decision in Keating-Owen, would rule child labor laws constitutional.[42]

In the meanwhile, proponents of reform regrouped. In 1919 Congress passed the Child Labor Tax Act, imposing a 10 percent tax on net profits of companies that employed child laborers, but in 1922, in *Bailey v. Drexel Furniture Co.*, the Court declared that tax, too, unconstitutional.[43]

It took sixteen more years for an effective federal child labor law to be passed under the New Deal, the 1938 Fair Labor Standards Act. Unlike its predecessors, the 1938 law withstood subsequent scrutiny by the Court. Federal aid to impoverished families with dependent children, too, was provided, in Title IV of the Social Security Act of 1935, which also set up an employer-employee contribution plan to provide a guaranteed income for the elderly. Both laws owed a great debt to the tireless work of that nationwide, and especially New York, community of persistent social scientists, especially women, who never gave up the struggle despite powerful adversaries in business, industry, and the courts.

"Self-Constituted Leaders or 'Teachers' Whose Principal Aim Is Domination"? Social Science, Organized Labor, and Social Insurance Legislation

"Life Material . . . Upon Which These Professional Social Workers Experiment"

"Among those experimenters who devote their time and energies to finding out 'what is good' for the workers," wrote Samuel Gompers, president of the American Federation of Labor in a scathing editorial, "Labor Must Decide Its Own Course," in the June 1915 AFL journal *American Federationist,* "are certain individuals who are associated in the organization known as the American Association for Labor Legislation. The avowed purpose of the organization is to secure legislation to *protect and safeguard* those who labor." The "professional social students" who led the American Association for Labor Legislation (AALL) were not, in Gompers' view, the "disinterested third party" they claimed to be.[1]

Before his *American Federationist* editorial, Gompers had written to John B. Andrews, executive secretary of the American Association for Labor Legislation, to protest its "scientific experimentation." The proximate cause of Gompers's letter was a bill sponsored by the Association before the New York State legislature to set up a five-member labor commission in place of the state's single labor commissioner. It was a comparatively minor matter, but it was, Gompers thought, an ominous trend. The social scientists who headed the American Association for Labor Legislation—mostly economists, sociologists, and political economists—persistently took stances on labor issues that differed from those of Gompers and his AFL allies. Gompers had been a vice president of the AALL from around the time of its founding in 1905 but had resigned his vice presidency and, in the spring of 1915, resigned his membership too, "to take place immediately." The AALL was trying to take labor down "The Wrong Road," Gompers concluded.[2]

This *American Federationist* editorial reflected opinion to which he had clearly devoted much thought. His feelings of outrage were deep; he saw the social scientists as meddlers who sought to control workers' lives under a cloak of objective philanthropy:

With insistence and avowed singleness of purpose some professional social students are circulating propaganda and agitation in the interest of a method for adjusting industrial disagreements. This proposed method is based upon the theory that there is a disinterested third party, able, willing and diligent to ascertain industrial justice and to establish it. It is proposed to give this third party entire control over industrial relations. . . . It is interesting to note that those who advocate this service and power for the third party are among those who expect to qualify for the office of third party. It is furthermore interesting that the propaganda is serviceable in establishing a tradition of the disinterestedness of those who do not earn wages and yet have no manifest association with workers or employers. But even were these "third party" agitators successful in establishing a belief in their disinterestedness in labor conditions they could not prove an alibi to the charge of very great interest in creating and securing employment for their class in connection with their *philanthropic* desires to regulate the lives of other men and women.

Social scientists "thought they understood 'the needs of the workers better than they themselves,' " but workers, said Gompers, resented "those who wish to 'uplift' or exploit them" by an "attitude of mind that regards them as experimental materials for trying the theories of sociological scientists." "Life material," Gompers wrote, "is the study upon which these professional social workers experiment." He bitterly denounced such "experiments" as "a form of human vivisection" and warned that labor "will brook no domination at the hands of either irresponsible or self-constituted leaders or 'teachers' whose principal aim is domination." Social scientists' actual intent was access to decision-making power and authority.[3]

Gompers had joined the American Association of Labor Legislation in the first place because he believed those who "studied industrial relations from the theoretical viewpoint" could help labor, but had been "gradually forced [to] the conviction" that the Association was led "not by the spirit of helpfulness but by the desire to dictate policies, purposes and principles of legislation supposedly in the interest of labor." In 1913 the AALL had declined to endorse two AFL-backed nominees for the new U.S. Commission on Industrial Relations. John Andrews and other AALL leaders had spoken against the AFL nominees and had sought to persuade U.S. President-Elect Woodrow Wilson (himself a political scientist and recent AALL vice-president) to appoint social scientists and reformers to the posts instead. Thereupon Gompers wrote Andrews in searing words that the AALL nominees were "dilettantes," and worse: "In all of the years of my long experience in the labor movement, whenever any professor, or student, or so-called social worker, many of whom have Ph.D. and other titles, desired any real information regarding labor and labor conditions, they have invariably applied to the men whom your Association characterizes as having little weight, and as reactionaries, and lacking in knowledge of economics. You should all be thoroughly ashamed of yourselves, and you will have cause to be for this piece of stupidity and arrogance."[4]

Gompers renewed the attack in two 1916 editorials in the *American Federationist.* In one, "Labor vs. Its Barnacles," he called intellectuals who thought they knew labor's business better than organized labor did "barnacles." And in a 1917 editorial, "Not Even Compulsory Benevolence Will Do," he observed that intellectuals' "enthusiasm for human welfare," varied in proportion to the power they could attain in high government office by administering "benevolent" social welfare policies. Gompers pledged "inauguration of a revolution against compulsory insurance"—AALL backed federal social insurance programs like old age retirement pensions and national health care programs. Gompers did not trust government because he was convinced government always sided with capital and, therefore, could not be entrusted with workers' welfare. Its regulation of the workplace would put labor relations "under the domination not of the people but of an oligarchy—a bureaucracy," a bureaucracy that, time and again, had ruled against labor.[5]

The consortium of predominantly skilled craft-workers trades unions that would become the AFL was organized in 1881, in the same period as Columbia's School of Political Science (1880), the New York Charity Organization Society (1882), and the nation's first settlement house (University Settlement, 1886), and it was a product of the same social trends and forces—industrialization, urbanization, and immigration among them. To meet the problems those forces imposed on laboring men and women, Gompers and the majority of AFL unions supported "voluntarism." Workers, through their unions, ought to seek redress for grievances directly from employers by bargaining as a collective unit or, when negotiation failed, by striking. They could not trust the courts to intervene. Gompers argued that the courts almost invariably ruled in favor of business and against labor, repeatedly agreeing to injunctions against workers for striking, not on employers for mistreating or underpaying workers.[6]

Gompers's embrace of the strategy of voluntarism had come from his own life experience. A cigar roller by trade, he had grown up on London's impoverished East Side, influenced by the British tradition of self-help mutualism practiced by thousands of British "friendly societies" in a spirit that extolled manliness, self-sufficiency, and independence. He emigrated to the U.S. in his youth and joined the New York cigar workers' union. That union tried to enlist government to end "tenement-house production" of cigars, and New York state legislators twice passed laws making tenement-house production illegal, but the state's courts had vacated those laws. In response, Gompers and his fellow cigar rollers had "harassed the manufacturers by strikes and agitation." Direct action achieved for skilled workers "what we had failed to achieve through legislation," Gompers said.[7]

The social science scholar-activists had a different view of government as a potential ally against the power of capital and industry that no private group could match. Frances Perkins had experienced AFL hostility to government legislation firsthand. As secretary of the New York Consumers' League from 1910 to 1912 and also as an AALL member, Perkins had tried "to sell" workers' compensation to New York craft-worker trades unionists, but in vain. At a Manhattan meeting of the New York City branch of the AFL she and Paul Kennaday, another AALL member and a Greenwich House resident ("a young man of . . . great moral passion," Simkhovitch said), "were almost run out" when they sought to persuade skilled white male union members to support workers' compensation legislation. "They were as near ugly to us as I ever met, because we were trying to enlist them," Perkins said.

They didn't care about the thousands of men who didn't belong to trades unions and the thousands of men who were injured under circumstances where they could not bring a suit against their employer. . . . They would rise and say, "Bill So-and-So worked in the carpenters' union and fell off a building. We, in the union, brought suit and we recovered $25,000 for him. Now, you can't beat that. You're proposing to give him a measly little $6,000, or you're proposing to give him a little income two-thirds of his weekly wage for life while he's disabled. What's that for Bill?" "Yes, but," we would say, "we're proposing to give it to everybody else who couldn't bring a suit."

Perkins noted: "I do differentiate between trade union legislation and the legislation we were fostering, because legislation that was prepared by a very small handful of skilled workers to protect their jobs was really special legislation for them. It was not legislation that benefitted all working people."[8]

To say that the AFL remained staunchly against any efforts to find an ally in government through the Progressive Era would, however, overlook the contest and ambivalence within its ranks. Labor's position varied from state to state and sometimes from trade to trade within a given locale. In 1906 the AFL sent "Labor's Bill of Grievances" to President Roosevelt and Congress and its executive council recommended that unions work to elect candidates sympathetic to labor. In 1908 and again in 1912 the AFL endorsed the Democratic party's candidate for the presidency, but repeated frustrations in gaining government aid sent Gompers and his allies in the federation back to voluntarism. When, for example, in 1910 the AFL endorsed workers' compensation bills in Massachusetts and Rhodes Island, both bills were defeated, and the following year, similar bills ran into opposition in the New York State legislature. When, that same year, Maryland passed a law to compensate injured miners, settlement sums were so paltry that even victory seemed defeat—miners who lost "both hands at the wrist joints," or who were blinded in both eyes, received only $750 compensation plus $6 a week for 26 weeks. Still, there were divisions within labor itself on the issue. In 1912 the United Mine Workers, the largest AFL-affiliated union, came out for government ownership of industries, and in 1914 John Mitchell, the UMW's one-time president and long-time AFL vice president, led a "prolonged and somewhat heated" attack on the philosophy of voluntarism at the AFL's annual convention. In the floor fight of words (floor fights had, on occasion, been known to break into fist fights), Mitchell championed labor legislation, while Gompers and his allies opposed it. A majority sided with Gompers, but the Mitchell-led opposition was significant, 8,107 to 11,237 on a resolution that read:

The American Federation of Labor, as in the past, again declares that the question of the regulation of wages and the hours of labor should be undertaken through trade union activity and not be made subjects of law, through legislative enactment, excepting in so far as such regulations affect and govern the employment of women and minors, health and morals; and employment by federal and municipal governments.[9]

Social scientists had formed the American Association for Labor Legislation, in part, precisely because they considered that voluntarism, in the sense of opposing government participation in social reform, was not working. They were frank about their agenda, as the name of their association said—they were *for* labor legislation. They were alarmed by the epidemic of workplace injuries and the paroxysms of labor violence. There were no federal minimum wage laws, no federal workplace health and safety regulations, no federal child labor laws, no government programs for poor families with dependent children, no comprehensive workers' compensation laws, few restrictions on hours of labor, no government-sponsored universal old age retirement insurance, and no universal health care. Yet the American economy of the late nineteenth and early twentieth centuries had generated vast wealth for the owners of mines, mills, fields, and factories. The workers who made that wealth possible labored, sometimes for seventeen hours a day, sometimes for seven days in a week—and in the infamous fortnightly swing shifts of the western Pennsylvania steel industry, for twenty-four hours straight. Thousands of workers died of work-related injuries or disease every year:

"an army of 15,000 men," by one contemporary estimate, killed at work by unguarded machinery, by unsafe rolling stock, or by fibrous-dust or coal-dust that caused the mill workers' deadly brown lung disease or the coal miners' deadly black lung.[10]

Capitalist markets rewarded managers' ingenuity and innovation, but competition led to a nightmare scenario in which, as one factory or shop slashed prices and speeded up work, others in the same industry—to remain competitive—did the same, often with a consequent downward spiraling of wages. Violence was the frequent response. In an 1892 steel workers' strike in Homestead, Pennsylvania, strikebreakers and strikers engaged in a pitched gun battle. In 1902 there was labor violence in the Pennsylvania-centered anthracite coal strike, and in 1914, in the notorious strike of Colorado mine workers, sixty-six deaths were recorded, including those of eleven children when state militia and company guards set fire to the striking miners' tent colony in the notorious "Ludlow Massacre."

Columbia University economist Edwin R. A. Seligman noted in a 1902 address on "Economics and Social Progress," in the wake of the violent anthracite coal strike, that the new "economic science" itself was "a product of social unrest." And, amid the paroxysms of labor violence, Columbia economist Henry Rogers Seager called for government intervention to regulate the economy, at the same time writing reassuringly in support of the capitalist system: "The revolt [of some wage workers], as I interpret it, is not against the wage system itself but rather against the legal restrictions [e.g. court injunctions against striking workers] which in practice hamper wage-earners at every turn in their efforts to improve their condition without putting any corresponding restraint on their employers." It was against such "legal restrictions" on workers (and to place "corresponding restraint" on employers) that Seager and others had founded the Association. "New economists," as Seager and Seligman considered themselves, were challenging classical British economic theory and rethinking established laissez-faire economic theories in favor of government regulation along the lines promoted by Gustav Schmoller and other members of the German Historical School, with whom so many American "new economists" had studied. Germany had initiated workers' insurance programs in the 1880s, earlier than any other country. Two studies of German poverty in 1885 found the major cause of poverty not, as many in the U.S., even some of the early social reformers, had held, the moral turpitude of the poor but rather the blameless incapacity of a family's principal breadwinner through illness, old age, disability, or death.[11] Old age social security programs were established in Denmark in 1891, followed by New Zealand, France, and Britain; and in 1913 Sweden offered the world's first universal, noncon-

tributory, old-age pensions and France the first national system of payments to impoverished families with children.[12] The U.S. was far behind.
Reform-minded social scientists, in New York as in other major urban
areas and universities, intended to do something about it. They were for
capitalism, its productivity and technological innovation, but not for its
unregulated and unplanned capitalist marketplace that failed to serve
the broader interests of society.

Voluntarism: Self-Determination or "Reactionary" Self-interest?

Gompers saw the social scientists as elitists who had no concern for democratic process while, he said, the labor movement was "the most democratically conducted movement in the world; it is of, for and by the
workers."[13] Gompers's claim that social scientists acted not from a democratic mandate but as an intellectual elite was uncomfortably on target.
In the settlement house movement, in the National Consumers' League,
and elsewhere, as in the American Association for Labor Legislation
itself, social scientists did consider themselves, and hoped to be
accepted as, leaders in shaping public policy. They saw themselves as
wise and informed guides of the people. No one else, in their view, had
the knowledge and skills—or the will—to undertake such a role.

But Gompers's democracy had limits of its own. Initially, as AFL president, Gompers had sought an inclusive labor movement; he even had
kind words for radical socialists, telling an 1890 AFL convention: "I say
here broadly and openly that there is not a noble hope that a Socialist
may have that I do not hold as my ideal." But he changed his view, and
in a speech to the 1903 national AFL convention, said: "I want to tell
you, Socialists. . . . I am entirely at variance with your philosophy. . . .
Economically, you are unsound; socially you are wrong; industrially you
are an impossibility." Early on, too, he had expressed some degree of
openness to racial inclusiveness; in 1890, speaking of African American
workers to white AFL members, he said, "as working men we are not
justified in refusing them the right of the opportunity to organize." But,
a decade later he had, as one historian has put it, "abandoned even the
formality of equal status for Negro workers." And, beyond African
Americans and socialists, the AFL did little or nothing to aid the organizing efforts of semi-skilled or unskilled workers, including the millions of
women and child laborers.[14]

Gompers's AFL was dominated by white male craft workers and
imbued with a culture of racial, gender, and craft exclusivity. Nor were
social science scholar-activists loath to make the point. Seager, president
of the American Association for Labor Legislation, had come to Columbia University in 1902 after studying political economy at the University

of Michigan, Johns Hopkins, Halle, Berlin, Vienna, and the University of Pennsylvania. From his vantage point, white adult male cigarmakers, printers, carpenters, steam-pipe fitters, bricklayers, stonemasons, and other craft-workers might well benefit from the AFL's philosophy of voluntarism, but there were relatively few noncraft union affiliates in the Progressive Era AFL (the United Mine Workers and the International Ladies Garment Workers Union both had large memberships but were a minority of AFL members). By 1910 only 5.8 percent of the nation's civilian labor force were union members, and not all of these were in AFL-affiliated unions; excluding agricultural workers, 10.2 percent of workers were union members. More than 94 percent of all U.S. workers were not in unions—and with millions of southern and eastern European immigrants arriving annually, organizing the unskilled and semi-skilled into unions had become all but impossible. Unskilled or semi-skilled workers who went on strike for better pay or better working conditions were simply replaced by unemployed new arrivals eager for work. The AFL's vigorous defense of voluntarism and its rejection of laws that would cover all workers was, in Seager's opinion, "reactionary." Voluntarism "takes no account of the great majority of adult male wage-earners who are still unorganized," Seager told a joint meeting of the American Association for Labor Legislation and the American Political Science Association in Washington, D.C., in late 1915.[15] The AFL did not represent the interests of all workers, but largely labor's aristocracy—white, male, skilled craftsmen. It was not the democratic voice of all working people.

"Erratic College Professors": "on the Ragged Edge of Socialism"

America's traditional association of liberty with minimalist government, Seager, Seligman, and others in the American Association for Labor Legislation concluded, must be modified, perhaps even abandoned. Freedom in a modern industrial and urban society would best be achieved through certain government regulation and legislation to provide an economic safety net. As social scientists wrote legislation, lobbied, advised government officials, and promoted creation of governmental commissions to initiate a modern American social policy with a social insurance program, they were attacked not only by organized labor but from the political right and the political left. Conservatives considered government labor and social welfare legislation "paternalistic," as interference with private owners' business. Many "American socialists, radicals, and even American labor unions" said Isaac Rubinow, a member of the AALL's Social Insurance Committee who held a doctorate in economics from Columbia and a medical degree from NYU, considered

government labor and social welfare legislation "a Machiavellian con-
spiracy against 'social unrest.'" Many capitalists, too, ironically like
Gompers himself, considered the social scientists dangerous dabblers.
Thus John Kirby, president of the National Association of Manufacturers
(NAM), warned that in "our American universities. . . . there are a number of men who have attained considerable eminence in the department
of economics who hang on the ragged edge of socialism and lack experience, poise and practical contact with industrial affairs," adding that
"we have more to fear from erratic college professors than any other
source."[16]

Among the "erratic college professors" who formed the American
Association for Labor Legislation were twenty-one social scientists—
most of them economists—who came together at the 1905 annual meeting of the American Economics Association. Henry W. Farnam, a Yale
political economist who had studied at Berlin, Gottingen, and Strass-
burg, was a prime mover. Richard T. Ely, the American Economic Association's first secretary, political economist at the University of Wisconsin,
became the AALL's first president. He had been a fellow at Columbia
University when John W. Burgess was laying the groundwork for its
School of Political Science. Among the other founding members were
Columbia's Seager, Princeton economist William F. Willoughby, University of Wisconsin political economist John R. Commons, Cornell political
economist Jeremiah W. Jenks, University of Pennsylvania sociologist
Samuel McCune Lindsay (within two years Columbia professor of social
legislation); Adna Weber, chief statistician for the New York State
Department of Labor, and Charles P. Neill, appointed that same year as
U.S. Commissioner of Labor.

There were no women in the organizing group, but by 1907 Jane
Addams of Chicago's Hull House and Florence Kelley of the National
Consumers' League in New York City were members of the AALL execu-
tive council. Josephine Goldmark joined the Association's administrative
council two years later, and the Michigan-born scholar-activist Irene
Osgood Andrews (one of University of Wisconsin political economist
John Commons's graduate students), served as assistant, then associate
secretary of the Association. In 1908 Kelley, representing the American
Association, attended a conference of the International Association for
Labor Legislation in Lucerne, Switzerland (some twenty years earlier she
had been a graduate student there), reporting back to the annual AALL
meeting: "We have much to learn and much to teach through the Inter-
national Association." Indeed, the AALL had been conceived of as an
American branch of the "strictly scientific in character" International
Association, which had organized during the Paris Exposition of 1900.[17]

The first executive AALL council meetings convened at the busy

United Charities Building in Manhattan, and from the outset the Association pursued a broad spectrum of government regulation on, for example, the legal maximum working day in mines, industrial poisoning, employment of children, and similar concerns. In its first year Samuel McCune Lindsay, AALL correspondence secretary, invited three leading social science organizations to join—the American Academy of Political and Social Science, the American Political Science Association, and the American Statistical Association.[18]

For 1907 and 1908 the headquarters was in Madison, Wisconsin, in the campus office of John R. Commons, the Association's secretary. But in 1908 the AALL moved to New York City, and the following year Lindsay cast his membership net wider to include "Bureaus of Labor, Departments of Factory Inspection, Trade Unions, American Federation of Labor, Child Labor Committees, Consumers' Leagues, Christian Social unions, and Church Departments of Labor." By 1913 Association membership peaked at 3,348; it would stay stable at around 3,000 over the next two decades; it dissolved, with some of its principal goals met by the New Deal administration, following the death of its executive secretary John Andrews and other figures who had energized its work, in the mid-1940s.[19]

During its forty years, decision-making power remained in the hands of a small group of social scientists and public figures. Half-a-dozen years after its 1905 founding Henry Seager was president, and its nine vice presidents were a professionally and geographically diverse group: Jane Addams of Chicago; Ely of Wisconsin; Jeremiah W. Jenks, Cornell political economist (at NYU after 1912); Robert W. Deforest, philanthropist and leading housing reformer in New York City; Louis D. Brandeis, the progressive Boston lawyer; Woodrow Wilson, at the time governor-elect of New Jersey; Republican Illinois Representative Morton D. Hull, Paul M. Warburg, the wealthy New York banker, and Samuel Gompers. The Association's advisory council, though a similar mix of social scientists and civic leaders, was dominated by members who lived in New York City: Edwin R. A. Seligman and Edward T. Devine of Columbia; Albert Shaw, the political scientist editor of the *Review of Reviews*; John M. Glenn, director of the Russell Sage Foundation; Florence Kelley, executive director of the National Consumers' League; Helen Marot, executive secretary of the Woman's Trade Union League; Felix Adler, Columbia professor of political and social ethics and founder of the Ethical Culture Society; and Henry L. Stimson, Secretary of War in President Taft's cabinet. University of Pennsylvania political economist Simon N. Patten joined the council in 1912.

In the early 1910s in New York State, Crystal Eastman, sociologist, lawyer, and bohemian, a leading figure in the grand Pittsburgh Survey initiated a few years earlier, was secretary of the AALL's New York State branch (the AALL discontinued local branches in 1916). John Mitchell, the mining union official who was at loggerheads with Gompers on voluntarism and labor legislation, served as a New York State vice-president. The branch was a nest of social science-trained scholar-activists. Among its Progressive Era executive committee members as of 1911 were Samuel McCune Lindsay and Vladimir Simkhovitch of Columbia; Pauline Goldmark of the National Consumers' League, James B. Reynolds, pioneer in the settlement house movement, and Carola Woerishoffer, also a pioneer in social investigation, a Bryn Mawr graduate who lived at the Greenwich House settlement and had used her railroad fortune legacy to help Florence Kelley and the Consumers' League establish a "Label Shop" at 4 West 28th Street, where the League sold its approved "White Label" goods. She was the shop's first president. Woerishoffer's uncle, a pioneer in Germany's labor legislation and factory inspection movements, had been a model for her. When she was twenty-seven she went undercover, disguised as a poor immigrant servant woman, to expose corruption in private employment agencies and one summer, as a laundress, encouraged fellow workers to unionize and bailed them out from jail when they were arrested. Seager offered Woerishoffer a post as investigator with the New York branch of the AALL, but on a trip to inspect labor camps west of Albany her car went off the road and down an embankment, and she was killed.[20] (Another young woman volunteer in the New York network also died in the line of duty. Isabel Dillingham, of an established New England family, who had been inspired by the sociologist and economist Emily Balch at Wellesley to take up work in New York's Greenwich House, died, at twenty-three, from a disease, its exact nature apparently unrecorded, contracted in her work among the impoverished poor around New York's Greenwich House settlement.[21])

In 1908 the American Association for Labor Legislation headquarters moved from Wisconsin to the massive Metropolitan Tower on West 57th Street, later to smaller and less costly space on East 23rd Street a block from the convivial United Charities Building. Irene Osgood and John Andrews, both Wisconsin-trained social scientists, went with it, and two years later the two were married. Osgood became head of the AALL's Woman's Work Committee and assistant, then associate, AALL secretary. Andrews retained his position as its executive secretary until his death in 1943.

Like so many New York City social science activists, Andrews and Osgood had Midwestern roots. Raised on his family's Wisconsin farm, Andrews graduated from the University of Wisconsin, earned a master's degree in economics from Dartmouth, and an economics doctorate from Wisconsin, and in New York became a lecturer on social science legislation at Columbia University. Irene Osgood, "Essie" to friends and family, was the daughter of a decorated Civil War infantryman, a shoemaker and farmer in Michigan, later a grocer and general merchandise store owner. She went from the University of Minnesota and the New York Summer School in Philanthropy to earn an A.B. from Wisconsin in 1905, where she researched and wrote *Women Workers in Milwaukee Tanneries*, then worked as head resident of Northwestern University settlement, as factory inspector in Wisconsin, and, at twenty-seven, as "special agent for relief work," in San Francisco after the 1906 earthquake. An active woman suffragist, she became a member in New York of the Women's Trade Union League (WTUL), edited the WTUL's periodical, *Life and Labor*, and wrote on labor issues for *American Labor Legislation Review*, *The Survey*, and *Political Science Quarterly*. Her book *Minimum Wage Legislation* was published in 1914 under the auspices of the New York State Factory Investigating Commission.[22]

With the AALL move to Manhattan came support from New York's social science network. Seager and Crystal Eastman, as noted above, became central figures in its work; the sociologist Samuel McCune Lindsay headed or served on several of its investigatory committees; economist Edwin R. A. Seligman worked on industrial health and safety issues; social economist Edward T. Devine chaired its all-important Social Insurance Committee and helped found the New York State branch. Economist and physician Isaac M. Rubinow was a principal member of the Social Insurance Committee, Josephine Goldmark of the administrative council, her sister Pauline of the New York State branch's executive committee, and Mary Kingsbury Simkhovitch of more than one committee. Other major figures in the New York social science network who were Association members included Frances Perkins; Mary Van Kleeck, teacher of industrial research at the New York School of Philanthropy and an important figure at the Russell Sage Foundation; Mary Dreier, a wealthy activist educated at the New York School of Philanthropy; Helen Marot secretary of the National Women's Trade Union League and ally of Kelley and Goldmark on the Brandeis brief; James B. Reynolds, leading figure in the settlement house movement; Paul Kellogg, editor of *The Survey*; and Columbia-educated African American social economist George Edmund Haynes.[23]

The AALL was a model of social science effort to regulate the nation's economy through research and lobbying by private issue-oriented organizations of social scientists. Its central purpose was to study U.S. labor conditions in order to lay "a scientific foundation for future legislation in this country." As its president Henry Rogers Seager argued in his 1904 *Introduction to Economics*, "protective labour laws" were necessary because "unorganized workmen do not bargain on terms of strict equality with employers." At its first annual conference in 1907, Seager outlined a wide-ranging agenda for the new Association, including health and safety in the workplace, reduction of working hours, workers' compensation insurance, unemployment insurance, disability insurance, and old age insurance. The Association, Seager said, could become a "means for exterminating poverty." Through its Committee on Social Insurance it was, by 1913, promoting national health care and old age pensions as just such a means.[24]

In 1914, William F. Willoughby, summed up the organization's "Philosophy of Labor Legislation" in an address to members: "We have again and again asked the state to exert its sovereign power to bring about a certain condition of affairs but we have never converted the people wholeheartedly to the principle that the determination of the fundamental conditions under which industry should be carried on . . . and labor performed, is, or should be, a prime function of the state. . . . Back in their minds the American public are still dominated by the dogmas of laissez-faire and individualism."[25]

In its efforts to achieve popular support for regulating laissez-faire in some measure by government, the AALL employed a strategy common to social scientists' reform endeavors generally: it gathered evidence and statistics, framed the problem and alternative solutions, studied pertinent state, national, and international laws, drafted legislation, and educated legislators and the public on the facts as it had first educated itself, publishing pamphlets, bulletins, and broadsides, distributing, it said, 150,000 copies of its literature in 1910 alone.[26]

"A Laboratory" of "Scientific" Legislative Drafting

The American Association for Labor Legislation had numerous allies in related professions. In 1910 a group of Columbia University law professors, among them Joseph P. Chamberlain, Thomas I. Parkinson, and Harlan Fiske Stone, founded a Legislative Drafting Research Bureau within the law school at Columbia. Columbia economist Seligman and sociologist Lindsay of Columbia's School of Political Science became active "affiliate-members."[27] Chamberlain, a wealthy man, but one "modest, retiring, and without ambition to appear in the headlines," funded the Legislative Drafting Research Bureau with more than $100,000 of his own money.[28] At the AALL 1913 annual meeting, he delivered a paper on "The Practicability of Compulsory Sickness Insurance in America," and was regularly a "guest" at AALL executive committee meetings and a member of its subcommittee on Social Insurance. Parkinson, a graduate of the University of Pennsylvania's Law School and on the staff of the New York Bureau of Municipal Research before accepting appointment as professor of labor legislation and administrative law at Columbia, headed the law school's new Department of Legislative Drafting, and directed the Drafting Research Bureau, "a laboratory of legislation and administration," a place where, through "careful scientific research," Parkinson said, "the problems of drafting effective legislation and securing its prompt and economical enforcement" might be confronted and "permanent improvement in our legislation and its administration" be achieved. "We realize, however," Parkinson warned, "that such research work may tend to become too theoretical, and to avoid this we have been applying the results of our research in the furtherance of actual legislative and administrative reforms." Frances Perkins, who worked with both the National Consumers' League and the American Association for Labor Legislation during the 1910s, said of the "bill drafting division" at Columbia: "you went and got a proper bill drafted." Parkinson, Lindsay said, had "seen the vision of what better legislative drafting would mean in the service of social reforms." Parkinson had worked closely with Allen, Bruère, and Cleveland at the New York Bureau of Municipal Research in ferreting out corruption and improving efficiency in the city's municipal government, learning that "administration *and legislation*" were both crucial, "neither one is of itself sufficient to accomplish an effective permanent reform."[29]

Harlan Fiske Stone later became a pivotal figure in upholding the constitutionality of the New Deal's labor and social welfare legislation as Chief Justice of the U.S. Supreme Court. In 1918, Columbia law school's Legislative Drafting Association mounted a vigorous defense of the prohibition of child labor established by Congress in the 1916 Keating-Owen Act, but the U.S. Supreme Court, in *Hammer v. Dagenhart*, held the law unconstitutional. It must have been a special personal pleasure for Stone to write in 1941 for the Court voiding *Hammer* as "a departure from the principles which have prevailed in the interpretation of the Commerce Clause both before and since the decision."[30]

At meetings on Columbia's campus or at AALL headquarters, lawyers of the Legislative Drafting Research Bureau worked with principal figures of the Association to create "greater scientific accuracy in both investigation and legislation." As Parkinson put it in a 1911 article in the AALL's *American Labor Legislation Review:* "by scientific study of conditions, the details of the law are intelligently determined."[31]

The First Success: Ending Phosphorous Poisoning

Legislation on workmen's compensation and employers' liability law was the Drafting Bureau's first focus. The Bureau worked closely with the

AALL, the National Child Labor Committee, the National Consumers' League, and other reform organizations to draft legislation to curb industrial accidents and to prevent lead poisoning.[32]

The AALL's first real success came in the match-making industry, to stop American manufacturers' use of white phosphorus in the manufacture of matches. As early as the 1870s Finland and Denmark had outlawed its use; in 1897 two French chemists discovered that phosphorus sesquisulfide, a nondeadly compound, could substitute for it, and after 1906 the International Association for Labor Legislation persuaded seven European countries to ban white phosphorus in match production.[33] U.S. companies, however, continued its use, in part because the Diamond Match Company had acquired sole U.S. patent rights to sesquisulfide.

The AALL's executive secretary, John Andrews, made an intensive study of white phosphorus. What he found appalled him. Among workers in some of the fifteen match-producing factories he studied, Andrews discovered eighty-two cases of phosphorus poisoning, and he filed a report replete with statistics and comparative tables of analysis and the powerful personal stories of suffering workers. Workers had inhaled white phosphorus in poorly ventilated manufacturing rooms and had sometimes licked phosphorus-laden brushes to sharpen them as they painted the toxic chemical mix on matchheads. After months or years, workers had rotten teeth, decayed jaws, horrible facial deformities; some died in agonizing pain.[34] In a conference billed as the "First National Conference on Industrial Diseases," and with the "zealous advocacy" of the Federation of Women's Clubs and other organizations, the AALL persuaded the U.S. Congress to call public hearings. Andrews and Seager testified on white phosphorus's disfiguring and deadly nature, while Samuel McCune Lindsay lobbied legislators behind the scenes. Henry W. Farnam, AALL member, Yale economist and personal friend of President William Howard Taft, informed Taft about the matter, and the President recommended that Congress cancel the Diamond Match Company's patent and make sesquisulfide available to all. The Diamond Match Company, motivated no doubt by public exposure, decided to withdraw its patent right. In 1912 Congress enacted legislation, drafted by the Legislative Drafting Research Bureau and the AALL, to impose a prohibitive tax of two cents per hundred matches on manufacturers who persisted in using white phosphorus—violators of the act faced up to $5,000 in fines and three years imprisonment. The AALL's social science research and political activism, in collaboration with the Bureau's legislative drafting skill, had paid off.[35]

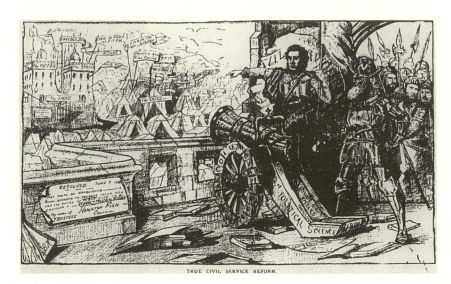

TRUE CIVIL SERVICE REFORM.

Columbia Spectator cartoon, "True Civil Service Reform," 8 October 1880. On the opening of the nation's first graduate School of Political Science. John W. Burgess, political scientist and school's founder, is shown directing "Political Science" in cannon fire on political corruption, supported by pike-wielding graduate faculty.

"ABC Powers," 1908. William Allen (above left), Henry Bruère (above right), and Frederick Cleveland (bottom), three directors of the Bureau of Municipal Research, all from the Middle West, applied social science to counter municipal corruption and waste. They quarreled over philanthropy's purpose in funding social science research. *Review of Reviews*, February 1908.

Charles A. Beard, 1910. An American historian and political scientist from rural Indiana, Beard was cofounder of the socialist Rand School for Social Science and the New School for Social Research and director of the Training School for Public Service. He resigned from Columbia during the First World War in a dispute with university administration over issues of academic freedom. Courtesy Columbiana Collection, Columbia University.

Franklin Giddings, 1893. After newspaper work in New England, Giddings became a founding figure of American sociology; he was a faculty member at Columbia University, the Rand School for Social Science, and the New York School of Philanthropy. He used Charity Organization Society casework files in a statistical study of poverty's causes. Courtesy Columbiana Collection, Columbia University.

Henry Rogers Seager, 1905. A lawyer's son from Lansing, Michigan, he was a political economist at Columbia University. As president of the American Association for Labor Legislation, he proposed regulations to protect workers and the aged. Courtesy Columbiana Collection, Columbia University.

John A. Andrews, c. 1910. Andrews, as executive secretary, and his wife Irene Osgood Andrews, as assistant secretary, of the American Association for Labor Legislation, promoted workers' rights. Courtesy Library of Congress.

W. E. B. Du Bois (1909) and George Edmund Haynes (page opposite; 1927?), pioneering scholar activists. Du Bois, leading social scientist, son of a Massachusetts barber and a domestic worker, became Harvard's first African American Ph.D. and a cofounder of the NAACP. Special Collections and Archives, W. E. B. Du Bois Library, University of Massachusetts, Amherst. Haynes, son of a domestic worker and a laborer in Arkansas, became Columbia's first African American Ph.D., a social economist, and founder and first executive director of the National League on Urban Conditions Among Negroes, later, National Urban League. Courtesy Schomburg Center for Research in Black Culture, New York Public Library.

Edwin R. A. Seligman. A Columbia economist, son of Jewish immigrants from Bavaria, he was vice president of the Consumers' League, president of Greenwich House, first president of the National League on Urban Conditions Among Negroes, and a founder of American Association of University Professors. Courtesy Columbiana Collection, Columbia University.

Franz Boas. A German immigrant and the era's most influential anthropologist, he was a founder of Columbia's anthropology department (the first in the United States) and a leader in discrediting eugenic theories of racial superiority. Courtesy, Columbiana Collection, Columbia University.

Mary White Ovington, 1902? Born in Brooklyn three days before Lincoln's assassination to parents who were vigorous advocates of black emancipation and women's rights, and introduced to the social sciences at Harvard Annex (Radcliffe College after 1894), she was a social science researcher on African Americans and a founder and executive secretary of NAACP. Courtesy Walter P. Reuther Library, Wayne State University.

"A Pride in the Enactment": Employer Liability and Workmen's Compensation

The social scientists of the American Association for Labor Legislation also singled out workmen's compensation for government regulation. They found it comparatively easy going because employers saw in workmen's compensation laws a way to minimize exposure to potentially disastrous legal suits filed by injured workers. It would be, employers concluded, more economical to pay out small monthly sums into a state-mandated but privately run workmen's compensation fund than to worry lest an injured worker win a large cash settlement in court and bankrupt the company.[36] In 1909 Henry Rogers Seager and Crystal Eastman of the AALL were appointed to the New York State Commission on Employer's Liability and the Unemployed, the "Wainwright Commission."[37] Crystal Eastman, the commission's salaried secretary and author of its report, was one of the strong group of women in New York's social science network who played an advanced role in civic activism even though excluded from posts at universities as also from the vote and from political office. A founding member and secretary of the New York Branch of the AALL, author of its pamphlet *Employers' Liability: A Criticism Based on Facts* and a book, *Work-Accidents and the Law,* part of the six-volume Pittsburgh Survey, Eastman was six feet tall, a dashing, graceful, athletic woman, a figure of elegance and a bohemian free-spirit.[38] Born in Marlboro, Massachusetts, Eastman's parents were both Congregational ministers. Eastman grew up, "confidently expecting to have a profession and earn my own living, and also confidently expecting to be married and have children." She did all of these, and "never wavered" in her "feminist faith." After graduation from Vassar in 1903, Eastman moved to Greenwich Village as a recreation worker at Mary Simkhovitch's Greenwich House settlement, at the same time earning a master's degree in sociology (in 1904) from Columbia's School of Political Science. In 1907, she graduated second in her class from the New York University Law School and became an active member of Alice Paul's Congressional Union for Woman Suffrage. She was also a leading pacifist, helping to organize the Woman's Peace party (later the Women's International League for Peace and Freedom), and serving as executive director of the American Union Against Militarism (on the Lower East Side, established during the First World War by the Henry Street Settlement's Peace Committee—Lillian Wald was president; Florence Kelley, and Paul U. Kellogg were members). She was among the earliest members of the 1917 National Civil Liberties Bureau (renamed the American Civil Liberties Union in 1920) and after the war organized the nation's "First Feminist Congress," one of the original proponents of the 1923

Equal Rights Amendment. Eastman died in 1928, at only forty-six, but in two decades she had achieved more than most men and women in far longer lifetimes.[39]

Under earlier employer liability law, a worker seeking compensation for an injury at work could only sue for damages under the common law and had to prove negligence. An employer could argue in defense that an injured worker (1) had contributed to the accident by carelessness— "contributory negligence"; (2) had agreed to accept the risks of the job as part of a free and uncoerced act and with the contracted acceptance had assumed all risks that came with the job—"assumption of risk"; or (3) had been injured as the result of a fellow worker's negligence—"the fellow-servant rule." So, though between 1885 and 1910 most states had enacted employer liability laws, most employers won in the courts. Indeed, the Wainwright commissioners found that of 115 married men killed at work in Erie County, New York in 1907–8, families received no compensation from employers in 38 of the deaths; less than $500 in 43 cases, and "no substantial recovery" in the remaining 34. Commissioners concluded "that the present legal system of employers' liability in force in this state . . . is fundamentally wrong and unwise and needs radical change." With passage of a broadly backed state constitutional amendment, new worker's compensation laws were soon on New York's books. John Andrews noted, in a December 1913 letter to AALL members, "If there was little opposition to the amendment when it was submitted to the people last November, it was in no small degree in consequence of the campaign of education which the Association had carried on during the preceding two years." Members were "equally influential in determining the form of the bill that has just become a law and in defending it before the committee of the Legislature." They "may well feel a pride in the enactment of this law."[40]

The Triangle Fire: Safer Working Conditions, a Minimum Wage, and the Opponents of Both

On 25 March 1911, Frances Perkins was having tea at a friend's apartment just around the corner from the Triangle Building, on the northeast corner of Washington Square Park in Manhattan, when she heard commotion outside and, drawn by curiosity, rushed out into the street, to witness one of the deadliest workplace fires in the nation's history. Fire was engulfing the ninth and tenth floors of the Triangle building, and scores of men and women, who minutes before had been sewing garments, were suffocating from smoke inhalation, burning to death, or dying on the street and sidewall below as they leaped to escape the flames. When the bodies were counted, there were 146, most of them young women.[41]

The city and the nation were horrified and, amid the cries of outrage, state officials mounted a public inquiry into the fire and beyond, into factory conditions across the state, with the New York State Factory Investigating Commission. Only one commissioner was a member of the New York social science network, Mary Dreier, but a number of members of the New York network of social science gave testimony or served on Factory Investigating Commission subcommittees. Mary Dreier, the commission's only woman, daughter of a prosperous iron company owner and former student of sociology and social work at the New York School of Philanthropy, was an AALL member, and had succeeded her older sister, Margaret, as president of the Women's Trade Union League, an organization of middle- and upper-class women reformers and women workers. Florence Kelley headed a commission subcommittee on the "Minimum Wage," Pauline Goldmark, one on "The Abolition of Home Work," and Henry Moskowitz, another on "Day of Rest in Seven."[42]

Social scientists from the New York City network flooded the Factory Investigating Commission with their testimony. Seager, president of the American Association for Labor Legislation, urged proper ventilation in work spaces and proper state licensing and inspection of factories. Lindsay, director of the New York School of Philanthropy and president of the Academy of Political Science, called for adequate factory inspection, registration, and licensing, adequate workmen's compensation laws, and a board of advisory experts ("if there was a little more chance of their receiving appointments" women who had trained at the School of Philanthropy "would make a very superior staff of inspectors"). Moskowitz, a member of the city's board of sanitary control, demanded automatic sprinklers and factory doors that opened outward so in future fires fewer lives would be lost. Frances Perkins, speaking as secretary of the New York Consumers' League, testified on the need for a central bureau of inspection. Edward E. Pratt, associate professor of economics at the School of Philanthropy, and John Andrews, AALL executive secretary, spoke on lead poisoning. Lillian Wald, headworker at Henry Street Settlement (she received a gold medal from the National Institute of Social Sciences the same year she gave her testimony before the commission), discussed conditions in tenement sweatshops and called for an end to child labor. Mary Simkhovitch testified on low wages, Mary Van Kleeck on the millinery trade; James Bronson Reynolds on the relationship of low wages to prostitution, Irene Osgood Andrews, on the need for a state medical bureau and a bureau of safety, and "the registering of all factories." Henry Bruère, co-director of the New York Bureau of Municipal

Research, said the city's government ought to be restructured to enforce current and future labor law. Josephine Goldmark, publications secretary of the National Consumers' League, recommended working hours' limitations and a minimum wage for women workers. Her sister Pauline, "in charge of the Bureau of Social Research connected with the Russell Sage Foundation and School of Philanthropy," was asked by commissioner Dreier, "what is your suggestion of a practical method of obtaining beneficial results [on working conditions for women]?" Goldmark replied, "we should publish clearly worded standards . . . capable of effective enforcement."[43]

Robert F. Wagner, a state senator, later U.S. senator, was the commission's chairman, and Alfred E. Smith, state assemblyman and later Democratic nominee for president, its vice-chairman. Both were Tammany-Hall Democrats, and neither, Frances Perkins said, "too hot about social legislation," nor, for that matter, very knowledgeable about labor issues. Wagner, Smith, Dreier, and the other commissioners decided to see things for themselves. With social scientists sometimes in tow, they traveled across the state and were shocked by what they found: poorly lighted, poorly ventilated, noxious-smelling work rooms; child employees hidden by factory owners in locked rooms or in elevator cars stopped between floors. The Factory Investigating Commission's final report went well beyond localized fire and workplace safety to propose that the state expand its regulatory function and take up many of the labor and social welfare reforms the AALL had been championing for years, including: state administration of labor exchanges, unemployment insurance, disability and old age insurance, and an extensive recodification of state labor law. Samuel McCune Lindsay termed the Commission's proposals "epoch making"; Lillian Wald called them "a step toward intelligent, scientific supervision of industrial conditions."[44]

The experience changed the lives of the commission's chairman and co-chairman, both lukewarm or indifferent to the issues of labor before their service, both now staunch proponents of an activist state and among the Democratic party's most dedicated pro-labor champions. Senator Robert Wagner would become a leading architect of the modern welfare state, and, in 1935, sponsor of the Social Security Act and the Industrial Labor Relations Act. Al Smith became one of the state's leaders in industrial reform, convincing party stalwarts to embrace fundamental reforms on child labor, hours of work, and occupational health and safety. Beginning in 1912, Smith and his fellow Democrats in the New York State Assembly introduced no fewer than thirty-six labor and social welfare laws—a new model for the American workplace and soon to become a groundwork for a newly reconstructed Democratic party. As governor in the 1920s, Smith would rely on the advice and counsel of the social science network, in particular of the progressive Belle Moskowitz.[45]

Social scientists from the New York network initiated a related undertaking of their own: a minimum wage. Seager had urged support for "minimum rates of wages in all trades" in his 1907 AALL "outline of a program of social reform." In the years that followed Kelley wrote on "Minimum Wage Laws" for the *Journal of Political Economy*, Seager a book on *The Theory of the Minimum Wage*, and Lindsay articles on the subject. Irene Osgood Andrews's *Minimum Wage Legislation* appeared in 1914, and her husband, John Andrews, teamed up with their old teacher, John R. Commons at Wisconsin, to publish *Principles of Labor Legislation.* Howard B. Woolston, City College professor of political science, directed a survey on minimum wage practices in New York State, drawing on research gathered by Mary Van Kleeck from settlement house workers, social workers, the New York Charity Organization Society, and the Consumers' League.[46]

The social scientists' campaign met opposition from both organized labor and organized capital—the American Federation of Labor and the National Association of Manufacturers. The AFL feared that a wage minimum might become a wage maximum; employers were convinced that the market, not government, should determine rates of pay. The social scientists persevered, and at their urging the state Factory Investigating Commission held hearings on the minimum wage. Seager, Devine, and Columbia economist John Bates Clark gave testimony, as did Kelley, Simkhovitch, Reynolds, and Josephine Goldmark. From across the country, Scott Nearing, the radical economist from the University of Pennsylvania; Edward A. Ross, sociologist from Wisconsin; Frank W. Taussig, the Harvard political economist; and Commons of Wisconsin all appeared before the New York commission.[47] But in the end the social scientists' minimum wage initiative failed. Not until 1938 did the Fair Labor Standards Act establish a national minimum wage—25 cents.

"What Next?": Government Aid for the Elderly, Unemployed, and Ill

Social scientists of the AALL promoted some of the Progressive Era's most daring social welfare legislation, primarily through its Social Insurance Committee and its call for government programs to care for the nation's unemployed, sick, and elderly. In 1913, in Chicago, the AALL sponsored the "First American Conference on Social Insurance."[48]

A 1908 article, "Old Age Pensions," in *Charities and the Commons*, by Henry Rogers Seager, had promoted broad-coverage government payments to the elderly poor. Why could not this government of, by, and for the people, support a pension program for the aged as Germany and Denmark already did, and as was being contemplated or enacted in Britain, New Zealand, Belgium, France, and Australia? There were Civil War pension payments to veterans of the war—such payments must, Isaac Rubinow noted, "be considered as a part of the American system of provision for old age"—but nothing beyond this.[49] Seager and others at the AALL found an ally in the otherwise less than friendly AFL, spurred on by John Mitchell and the United Mine Workers to endorse, between 1909 and 1914, noncontributory old-age pensions at the national level.[50] But there was not enough support to form an effective coalition for old age social security payments. Although by 1930 New York State had joined a few other states in enacting some old age coverage, not until the Social Security Act of 1935 did old age social insurance, funded by a tax on workers' wages, become a reality in the U.S.

On the issue of government-run unemployment compensation, the AALL's Social Insurance Committee joined its Committee on Unemployment, with John R. Commons at Wisconsin a particularly fervent advocate, in entering the ongoing European debate on the same issue and sponsoring, in 1914 and 1915, two national conferences to promote public bureaus of employment and state-sponsored vocational training schools. AALL executive secretary John Andrews observed: "We are beginning to recognize that unemployment is not so much due to individual causes and to the shiftlessness of 'won't-works,' as [it is] . . . inherent in our present method of industrial organization." Along with the sociologist and activist Frances Kellor, Andrews appeared before Congress to promote "governmental machinery" for a federal jobs-finding bureau, including labor exchanges, where unemployed workers could learn about job openings and apply. Offices were set up in New York City and elsewhere but not until 1932, in the midst of the Great Depression, did the first state, Wisconsin, enact a compulsory unemployment insurance act. That same year the AFL reversed its earlier opposition to government-run unemployment compensation programs, and in the years that followed unemployment compensation programs were established in every state.[51]

The AALL Social Insurance Committee's most ambitious effort was its tenacious and fervent, though ultimately unsuccessful, push for universal health care. Why, these advocates asked, in the world's richest nation were so many sick and injured people getting inadequate medical attention, and why could not a health care program with universal coverage be administered by a government in which the people were the sovereigns? The movement for universal government-run health insurance was initiated, Isaac Rubinow later wrote in *The Quest for Security*, in "a very deliberate way": "When a small group of such experienced social workers and social reformers (a title not yet discredited at the time) as Addams, Devine, Paul Kellogg, Joseph P. Chamberlain and John B. Andrews came together in 1915 in a conference, in which it was the writer's great privilege to participate, to consider the question: 'What next?' the inevitable conclusion was that health insurance *logically* came next." Rubinow was being modest; in fact, it was he more than any other member of the social science community who led the Progressive Era effort for national health care. He knew the European experience with government-backed security programs. A product of the classical department of the German Petri-Pauli-Schule in Moscow, Rubinow had emigrated at seventeen with his family, graduating from Columbia College in 1895 and, three years later, from New York University's Medical School, then from Columbia's School of Political Science with a Ph.D. in economics—he had studied with Seligman, Seager, and Lindsay. In the 1910s he was a member of the AALL's Social Insurance Committee and executive secretary of the American Medical Association's own short-lived Social Insurance Committee. He lectured on social insurance at the New York School of Philanthropy, served as an economist for the U.S. Bureau of Statistics, the Department of Agriculture, the Department of Commerce and Labor and, in the private sector, as chief statistician for the Ocean Accident and Guarantee Corporation.[52] In his 1913 book, *Social Insurance: With Special Reference to American Conditions*, written to educate and influence "all coming legislation" to raise the "standard of living of the neediest and productive classes," Rubinow noted that "many university professors of economics and social science are most active" in the social insurance movement.[53] He was a member of the Socialist Party of America—almost from the time of its founding, he once said. Like Florence Kelley and other socialists, he held a radical view of the capitalist system, but chose nonetheless to work within it.

The AALL's Social Insurance Committee introduced health insurance bills before the New York and Massachusetts legislatures, and its work led to the first congressional hearings on a national health insurance initiative. By 1915 it rallied behind a slogan it made famous for a time: "'Health Insurance—the next step in social progress.'" The bills it initiated proposed coverage for all wage workers—except only those highly paid or part-time workers at home—with medical, surgical, nursing care, and medical supplies, and two-thirds of a worker's lost wages to be paid as a cash benefit, the government to cover 20 percent of the cost, the balance to be shared equally by employers and workers.[54] "Night after night," John Andrews wrote in November 1916, "we are meeting with special committees appointed by employers, by employees and by the medical profession." For a brief few years it appeared that since no employer could gain a financial advantage because all employers would be equally taxed—the strategy had worked in the field of workmen's compensation—the proposal might gain the support of the National Civic Federation, the National Association of Manufacturers, and even the American Medical Association itself. But by the late 1910s, in the middle of the First World War, it was clear that no comprehensive system of health insurance would be adopted. The AMA Committee on Social Insurance, which Rubinow headed, had "aroused such violent protests" within the medical community itself that it was disbanded. Strong opposition had arisen also within the National Civic Federation and various Chambers of Commerce and manufacturers' associations. "The opposition," Rubinow observed in frustration, "was strong enough to kill even the agitation, the very thought of it for many years."[55]

In 1916 Andrews, Rubinow, and Chamberlain (from Columbia University's Legislative Drafting Research Bureau) appeared before Congress to urge federal health insurance, old age insurance, and "social insurance generally." But in the midst of a general debate on whether or not to join in the Great War in Europe, social reforms would have to wait.[56] After the war the nation was caught up in a feverish self-centered time of consumerism, constraints on civil liberties, racial oppression, and isolationism. Not until the Great Depression of the 1930s would the suffering of the poor and disenfranchised rise to the surface of national attention and would the federal government act. And not even then would there be universal medical insurance.

By the start of the millennium, in 2000, universal health care would become standard in virtually every industrialized state in the world except the United States. Progressive social scientists, without public will behind them, had insufficient power to transform the nation's practice. Dominant elements within both the AFL and the NAM had ranged themselves on the same side, opposing government initiatives and regulations. The NAM, for example, declared governmental regulation would bankrupt employers, lead to higher prices, or steer the country toward socialism; the AFL and organized labor in the aggregate persisted in their reliance on voluntarism.[57] It was social scientists, not labor leaders, who championed the use of government in aid of the welfare of American workers. They failed to implement a broad range of legislative reforms, workmen's compensation laws for industrial accidents their only legislative success during the Progressive Era, but at least they had placed labor law and social welfare issues before the public.

While, in the late nineteenth and early twentieth centuries, organized labor was led by socially conservative forces, insecure about their power, ambivalent about expanding power outside established precincts, and divided about the practical possibility of achieving laws to improve the hours, wages, and conditions of American workers that would pass muster with the courts, social science scholar-activists had no such ambivalence, ambiguity, or uncertainty. And, though opposed by their more conservative colleagues, they sought to enlist the power of the state to rectify economic and social injustices they knew private power would not, and could not, advance on its own. With colleagues and peers as co-strategists and with no dependent and restless oppressed constituency to serve or appease, the social scientists were freer than labor leaders to maneuver. For most academics and scholar activists their livelihood and freedom to take a public role were secure. But, though often skillful in political maneuvering, and confident in their wisdom about significant social change, many were naive about the currents and ways of political and social power. They did understand that their own private realms of philanthropy, their private issue-oriented organizations, and the academy would not be enough to achieve broad public change without alliance with the movers of the public realm. Science could identify problems and suggest solutions; it could educate and empower; but it could not win the biggest political and economic battles alone. Social science could set forth ideals and publish evidence and propose an agenda. Activists could move into the public world to testify, lobby, and accept appointments on commissions and many, in the New York community especially, did so. But there were limits to their power to implement their dreams and their agendas. Knowledge needed political and economic power to achieve transformative social change.

Chapter 7

Social Science and "the Negro Problem": From "Nordic Myth" to the NAACP and National Urban League

Social scientists, even those liberal or radical in their philosophy and their practice, were not wholly consistent on matters of value or on matters of scientific method. They were sometimes more creatures of their age, less pioneering than they imagined on fraught issues that touched nerves in their society. The prime examples of moral ambiguity were race and class, but race most contentious of all. On one hand, members of New York's scholar-activist network were leaders in the creation of the two most important organizations in the nation's history established to fight for the rights of blacks: the NAACP and the National Urban League (both were founded, and had their headquarters, in Manhattan). On the other hand, a number of social scientists promoted views essentially racist in perspective that muddled the evolving identity of social science as enlightened, scientific, modern, progressive, and reformist.

Eugenics and the "Science" of Racism

Most American and most New York social scientists who considered nonwhite races inferior, despite the cautionary principles of their disciplines, resorted to an ancient Teutonic theory that, combined with the new eugenics movement in academic circles that advocated selective breeding of the human species, was reflected in the Aryanism of a later Germany. Their views were undoubtedly shaped by their own intensive studies in England and Germany, where such perspectives were in vogue. Ever since the first-century Roman historian Tacitus ascribed to Teutonic peoples courage, simplicity, and a passion for freedom, the theory of exceptionalism has haunted the Western world. In 1881 historian Herbert Baxter Adams, in a paper before the Harvard Historical Society, held that American democracy and freedom had its origins in ancient and medieval Saxony, that "the Pilgrim fathers" were "merely one branch of the great Teutonic race," and that the direct democracy of the New England town hall meeting had been inherited from "the Village Community system of Ancient Germany."[1] From an environmental theory of higher and lower cultures evolved a theory of genetically superior and inferior races.

Two years after Adams's paper, Francis Galton, a British scientist and a cousin to Charles Darwin, coined the word "eugenics" to describe his theory that some genes are better than others and that good genes, through selective breeding, will lead to a higher type of human. Galton and his followers had been influenced, in turn, by the work of an American anthropologist, Samuel George Morton of Philadelphia, who, in 1849, classified human races in a *Catalogue of the Skulls of Man and the Inferior Animals*, measuring and mapping head size and shape to demonstrate the intellectual superiority of northern Europeans, by ascending order of size—bigger was better. Morton identified to his satisfaction a pyramid of five types, from Negro, at the bottom, up to American Indian, Malay, Mongolian, and Caucasian, in that order. Caucasians, Morton said, had the largest skulls and, among the Caucasians, Teutons the largest of all.[2] Skulls, in turn, were equivalent to brain size and hence to brain power. Morton's measurements and conclusions were later shown to be riddled with errors, but combined with Galton's eugenics they proved a powerful and ominous combination in Western social science for a half-century and more. The new biology and anthropology were said by some to confirm both the eugenic and Teutonic theories, and by the late nineteenth century some social scientists boldly declared that peoples of northern European descent were superior to those from southern Europe, Asia, Latin America, and Africa.

One of the leading Teutonic-theory proponents in the United States was John W. Burgess, founder and dean of Columbia University's School of Political Science. Burgess saw the Germanic peoples—also called Teutons, Anglo-Saxons, Nordics, or Aryans—as at the pinnacle of the human genetic and cultural pyramid, with everyone else below. "The national state" itself, "the most modern and complete solution of the whole problem of political organization," was "the creation of Teutonic political genius." Teutonic nations had the authority, even the duty, "to assume the leadership in the establishment and administration of states." Stephen Duggan, one of Burgess's students in the late 1890s, said Burgess "was infected by . . . the 'Nordic myth.' He [Burgess] advocated an alliance of some kind between Great Britain, the United States, and Germany, which was to be the guarantor of order, security, and civilization generally." Alvin Johnson, another of Burgess's students, reported that Burgess promoted the view that "only Nordics could be anything. Burgess would talk about how all the Latin nations were degenerate. . . . England, America and Germany were vital. It was their right and their duty to divide up the world."[3]

Burgess's embrace of the Teutonic theory facilitated his harsh assessment of American blacks as "ignorant barbarians" and the Reconstruction Acts as a "blunder-crime." Burgess's Columbia colleague, the historian William H. Dunning, wrote contemptuously of the "credulity and general childishness of the blacks" in the years of Reconstruction who "exercised an influence in political affairs out of all relation to their intelligence or property." But the Teutonic theory of race and the embrace of eugenics were not limited to political conservatives like Burgess and Dunning. Edward T. Devine, Columbia professor of social economy and executive secretary of the New York Charity Organization Society, even as he recommended W. E. B. Du Bois's scholarship to readers of the social science and social work magazine he edited, and, even after publishing an entire issue of *Charities* on race and racism, declared that "there is much of this eugenics program with which social workers may sympathize and in which they should clearly cooperate." So, too, Franklin Giddings, the Columbia sociologist, in his textbook, *The Principles of Sociology*, adopted a theory part environmental, part genetic, that, "deprived of the support of stronger races, he [the Negro] still relapses into savagery, but kept in contact with the whites, he readily takes the external impress of civilization, and there is reason to hope that he will yet acquire a measure of its spirit." "The Negro," Giddings said, was "plastic," hence racial inferiority could respond to environment but he doubted their capacity to become "a truly progressive type," since to be progressive required "strength of character to make independent advances."[4]

Even the noted political scientist and historian Charles A. Beard, in his youthful 1898 senior class oration, "The Story of a Race," at DePauw College in Indiana, pronounced the "anglo Saxon race" the "race of progress" and contrasted superior Anglo-Saxons with "the cringing miserly dago." Unlike some of his Columbia colleagues, Beard did abandon such views in his mature writings and by 1912 was writing of persecution of minorities and of the poor, of "slaves torn from African wilds for the profit of slavers and planters." Nor did he share the anti-immigrant prejudice prevalent in political and labor, and even academic, circles at the time. "No fair-minded American sanctions the . . . notion that the evils of our city government are due to the foreigners," Beard wrote.[5]

In the minds of a number of activist scholars social reform had gotten confused with establishment of racial purity, "race betterment." The Yale political economist Irving Fisher—"the prime mover in the American Eugenics Society"—declared in the *Journal of the National Institute of Social Sciences* in 1915: "The most vital problem before the world to-day is the problem of preventing race deterioration"; "the movements for eugenics and race betterment are the ones directed most definitely against race deterioration."[6] The statistician Frederick L. Hoffman argued in his book *Race Traits and Tendencies of the American Negro* (1896), one in a series of publications of the American Economic Association, that people of "Aryan descent will prove the superior" to "the negroes . . . solely on account of [the Aryans'] ancient inheritance of virtue and transmitted qualities which are determining factors in the struggle for race supremacy."

The lower races, even under the same conditions of life, must necessarily fail because of the vast numbers of incapables which a hard struggle for life has eliminated from the ranks of the white races, are still forming the large body of the lower races. . . .

Intercourse with the white race must absolutely cease and race purity must be insisted upon in marriage as well as outside of it. . . . The compensation of such an independent struggle will be a race of people [the Negroes] who will gain a place among civilized mankind and will increase and multiply instead of dying out with loathsome diseases.[7]

Proponents of eugenics were finding support in the Carnegie Institution's Station for Experimental Evolution at Cold Spring Harbor on Long Island, New York (headed by the zoologist and eugenicist Charles Davenport) and in Dr. John Harvey Kellogg's Race Betterment Foundation of Battle Creek, Michigan. Edward Devine's philosophy of "scientific philanthropy" moved to a dangerous course, to a eugenics that assumed some groups superior to others and the right of the superior to control the inferior, even their breeding. Some humans were simply "unfit," Devine wrote in 1909 in *Misery and Its Causes*: "Degenerate offspring of feeble-minded, alcoholic, or syphilitic parents come into the world with a just grievance against society." In 1912, in *The Family and Social Work*, Devine wrote of control of breeding, even by "permanent segregation, during the reproductive years," and of separating into "colonies" "incapables," "criminals," and the "hopeless." "Incapables and criminals are now supported by society in the most expensive and extravagant manner. To bring them into carefully planned and well-managed colonies where we could separate the improvable from the hopeless, and where we could accurately count the cost of their maintenance and forecast the probability of their reintegration, would require initial investment and for a time larger annual appropriations than we have been making. But the economy and wisdom of such investments would speedily become apparent." In *Misery and Its Causes*, Devine promoted a Lockean social contract theory but one modified by his own sense of social norms. By "common consent," Devine wrote, the structure of the "normal community" (he also called it the "ideal community") could be agreed upon. In *The Family and Social Work*, he described the "normal community" as one whose members worked, were physically healthy, and led a "normal family life." Those outside must be shepherded into it, through private and public agencies whose "direction . . . should be entrusted to experts of the first rank," culled, in turn, from the new profession of social science-trained social workers. Thus the development of a rationale for racism and eugenics was justified as benevolent social reform.[8]

Environment was key. In his *Social Forces* (1910), Devine emphasized that one must understand the "social forces" that give rise to poverty, as a physicist or engineer must understand natural forces to control them. He told the U.S. Commission on Industrial Relations that "charity of itself is no cure, and never can be, for industrial evils." Devine referred, enigmatically, to "a moderate exercise of rational social control." And yet for all of the ominous overtones later generations might reasonably read into his notion of isolating those outside the "normal community" into government-run camps, the thrust of his leadership of the Charity Organization Society was along the lines of moderate reform: under his leadership, sociological research sponsored by the Charity Organization Society contributed to the expansion of public housing and public health movements. The first publication of the COS Committee on Social Research was Lilian Brandt's *Five Hundred and Seventy-Four Deserters and Their Families*, a book that while compiling data on families that might well be considered outside Devine's "normal family life," painted sad, sometimes desparate, portraits of deserters and their families, and made no mention of isolating them.[9]

Franklin Giddings, too, was persuaded by the eugenics view of superior and inferior peoples. A strident imperialist, "his idea was, we had to have colonial possessions, as the English had, to save our democracy," Alvin Johnson said, "convinced that nobody amounted to anything in the world if he wasn't Nordic." Johnson's oral history interview in the Columbia University archives recalls that "Giddings . . . had real anti-semitism. Giddings's jokes to this effect [the mentioned jokes are not included in the interview] made Edwin Seligman and other Jewish social scientists profoundly uneasy." When Seligman proposed that Franz Boas, the distinguished anthropologist, join Columbia's Faculty of Political Science, "Giddings used his veto," Johnson reports, to keep Boas out, citing as his reason that "anthropology belonged with the physical sciences and not with the social sciences," but Giddings's stated reason, Johnson thought, "covered up the real reason, which was that Boas was a Jew."[10]

Giddings's most noted theory, "consciousness of kind"—promoted in his *The Principles of Sociology* and elsewhere—came in an age when scholars were coming to terms with Darwinian evolution, not itself Social Darwinism, in its description of biological evolution. Giddings sought to account for human social behavior through a naturalistic ontology, attributing "similar feelings" and "likemindedness" to common environment and social context as well as, so it seems (he was never wholly clear on the point), to genetic sources. He saw some "natural communities" as "savage, barbarian," others as "civilized."[11] "The ultimate aim of such study [of sociology] is to create a scientific basis for the conscious control of human society, to the end that evolution may be transformed into progress both for the race and for the individual." He argued that: "The key to the solution of the social problem will be found in a frank acceptance of the fact that one portion of every community is inherently progressive, resourceful, creative, [and] capable of self-direction," and "if, then, the masses of men are to be enlightened and made just, the outward conditions to which their lives will be conformed must themselves embody justice and must nobly provoke the mind. To create such conditions is democracy's great task." In a public forum in Vermont he made clear the importance he placed in the role of the intellectual elite in enlightening the masses: "Dr. Giddings held that it was perfectly certain if we are to have successful democracy the great masses of the people have got to take guidance and direction from a capable small minority. The shaping up of things must be effected by persons who have brains, intelligence, cleverness in the best sense of the word."[12]

On the other side of the heated debate were social scientists, especially several of European Jewish and African American descent, intent on obliterating the racist elements in eugenics. The anthropologist Franz Boas, after 1899 Columbia University's first professor of anthropology, a German Jewish immigrant with an 1881 doctorate from the University of Kiel, and W. E. B. Du Bois, Harvard educated and the leading African American social scientist of his day, were the most conspicuous of the opponents. Boas was the era's most influential anthropologist and leader of a school of cultural-environmental anthropology. (Deep scars on his face were said to be either a result of "cancer of the cheek" or of a duel of honor with a German student over an anti-Semitic remark.) Differences in pigmentation or hair texture, Boas asserted, had nothing to do with "inferior ability." Culture dominated genetics in shaping individual lives. In May 1910, at the Second National Negro Conference held in New York City, where scholar and civic activists would adopt the name The National Association for the Advancement of Colored People (NAACP), Boas addressed "The Real Race Problem." "The biological evidence," Boas held, "does not sustain the view, which is so often proposed, that the mental power of the one race is higher than that of the other."

Any one who is familiar with ethnological facts will recognize that the conditions under which the American slave population developed is apt to destroy what little culture may have existed. The complete break with the African past; the imposition of labor, in the results of which the slave had no direct interest; the difficulty of assimilating the elements of civilization by which they were surrounded, all tended equally to reduce to a minimum the amount of independent cultural achievement of the group.[13]

In 1911 Boas published *The Mind of Primitive Man*, his most influential rebuttal to the Teutonic theory, calling into question "how far we are justified in assuming . . . that the North European type . . . represents the highest development of mankind." "Anatomical and physiological considerations do not support," Boas said, "the common assumption that the white race represents physically the highest type of man." That same year Boas, though he himself did not attend, supplied a paper, "Instability of Human Types," for the first Universal Races Congress, convened in London. "Environment," Boas wrote, was central to the way in which humans develop. "The old idea of absolute stability of human types must . . . be given up," he wrote, "and with it the belief of the hereditary superiority of certain types over others." Attending the London Congress was W. E. B. Du Bois, the Manhattan-based editor of the NAACP's periodical *The Crisis*. He reported that Boas's work was celebrated by participants and added: "words quietly spoken" at the "epoch-making" Congress "went toward undermining long and comfortably cherished beliefs" on race. It was "a glance across the color line or . . . a sort of World Grievance Committee."[14]

The Universal Races Congress had been the idea of Columbia University professor of political and social ethics Felix Adler, whose Society for Ethical Culture promoted a humanistic ethics free of religious superstition and dogma. Adler set Gustave Spiller, one of the Ethical Culture Society's most able intellects in London to organizing the Congress. In late July 1911 a thousand people from fifty or more countries had come to the University of London to hear "leading anthropologists and sociologists," "professors of international law," government officials, religious leaders, and political activists discuss "in the light of science and the modern conscience, the general relations subsisting between the peoples of the West and those of the East, between so-called white and so-called colored peoples, with a view to encouraging between them a fuller understanding, the most friendly feelings, and a heartier cooperation."[15]

In the *Papers on Inter-Racial Problems Communicated to the First Universal Races Congress*, whose publication preceded the meeting, Spiller assembled more than fifty papers, eight from U.S. authors, more than thirty from Europeans, the rest from China, Japan, India, Egypt, South Africa,

Haiti, and the Middle East. Du Bois's own essay, "The Negro Race in the United States of America," offered an encyclopedic overview rich in history and statistics. "There are some signs," Du Bois wrote, "that the prejudice in the South is not immovable, and now and then voices of protest and signs of liberal thought appear there. Whether at last the Negro will gain full recognition as a man, or be utterly crushed by prejudice and superior numbers, is the present Negro problem of America." Du Bois reported in *The Crisis* that "a distinct feeling of uplift and hope" pervaded the sessions. On that same London trip, Du Bois was also a featured speaker at the Sociological Society in London and the city's Lyceum Club; at the latter gathering he "described conditions in America, the denial of civil rights, the insults and humiliation the colored man and women must face" and urged that "science to-day places no meets and bounds to the development of races given the favorable environment and there is no scientific proof that an individual of any race may not reach the highest. For this reason is it not the wisest and best course to refuse to tread the paths of exclusion and human despisery and to see that the gates of opportunity are absolutely closed in the faces of no race or people?"[16]

A month after the conference Du Bois wrote: "There was one thing that this congress could do of inestimable importance. . . . it could make clear the present state of scientific knowledge concerning the meaning of the term 'race.'" It was, he said, "unscientific to assert that mulattoes and Eurasians were degenerate in the absence of all scientific data." If "scientific sanction" were to be granted to racist eugenics, then racism and racists would employ that sanction to bolster its views and to promote political action. Had racist views "remained merely academic opinions," Du Bois wrote incisively, "it would not be necessary to recall them, but they have become the scientific sanction for widespread and decisive political action—like the disfranchisement of American negroes, the subjection of India and the partition of Africa."[17] Du Bois's warning was a powerful and prescient rejection and warning of the two-faced authority and appeal of science and the moral ambivalence of many of the scholar activists in Progressive Era America. If the grounds for debate on race in the early twentieth century were now to be centered not in biblical authority, folkloric claims, or traditional bigotry but in science and in the name of liberal and progressive social reform, Boas, Du Bois, and their scientific and social scientific allies would first have to win the debate of ideas.

In the opening decades of the century some in New York's social science network worked with members of the African American community to fight the pervasive racist epidemic. Alarmed social scientists, men and women, in the early 1900s emerged from the rich matrix in Manhattan to join Du Bois and Boas in setting the agenda and establishing the institutions of the modern civil rights movement. Samuel McCune Lindsay, Frances Kellor, Mary Kingsbury Simkhovitch, Henry Moskowitz, Mary White Ovington, Isaac M. Rubinow, Edwin R. A. Seligman, George Edmund Haynes were among those who joined Du Bois and Boas in this passionate struggle for justice.

They had to counteract not only top social scientists who were intellectual rationalists of racism, but a number of America's leading politicians, including progressives. President Theodore Roosevelt, whom many of the most liberal social scientists saw as their hero, did invite the moderate black leader, Booker T. Washington (whose gradualist reform was opposed by Du Bois in a famous and ongoing debate), to dine with him at the White House, but five years later, in 1906, he refused to reconsider his concurrence in the dishonorable discharge of 167 black soldiers in the Brownsville Affair, and at the 1912 Progressive party convention, then former president, he refused to allow the seating of black delegations from certain southern states. In 1916, Roosevelt wrote to Henry Cabot Lodge, a leader among Senate Republicans, that the "great majority of the negroes in the South are wholly unfit for the suffrage." Nor was this view found only in the Republican and Progressive parties. President Woodrow Wilson, political scientist and former president of Princeton University, wrote to the editor of the *Congregationalist*: "I would say that I do approve of the segregation that is being attempted in several of the departments." (The U.S. Post Office Department, the Bureau of the Census, the Bureau of Printing and Engraving, the Treasury Department, and other federal offices were segregated during his presidency.)[18]

The judiciary branch, too, paralleled the persistent racism of the executive and legislative branches. The 1896 U.S. Supreme Court ruling in *Plessy v. Ferguson* endorsing so-called "separate but equal" accommodations in railroad travel—and, by extension, in other venues as well—was not overturned until the unanimous *Brown v. Board of Education* decision on 17 May 1954. Jim Crow shaped Southern society and, to a considerable extent, de facto segregation in the North. The simplest interracial overtures often met public reproof. When President Roosevelt dined with Booker T. Washington in the White House in 1901, news of the dinner aroused a hailstorm of protest. New York City itself was a racial battleground. In August 1900, a race riot erupted in the aftermath of the killing of a white police officer by a black; with police connivance anti-black violence swept across Eighth Avenue between West 27th and 42nd Streets in midtown Manhattan.[19] In Atlanta in late September 1906, when white mobs attacked blacks and their places of business in the wake of a gubernatorial campaign that emphasized race supremacy, Du

Bois, then a professor of economics and history at black Atlanta University, stood, rifle in hand, on the porch of his house to protect his family from the mob. He wrote later, in a letter to Mary White Ovington, a founder of the NAACP, "The riot was a premeditated and planned affair."[20]

Those progressive social scientists who understood progress to include racial justice followed the principles and practice of their disciplines and resisted the myths and errors of social scientists imbued with the pervasive attitudes of a racist society. They investigated, described what they found, published, and encouraged strategies for remedy. In articles and books, in classrooms and public lectures, they began to challenge the seductive and popular premises of eugenics on U.S. campuses and attacked the legal notion in *Plessy* that separate could mean equal. They were following the established method of the social science elite in using their intellectual and cultural authority to shape opinion and to influence the public policy agenda, but they also adhered to a moral imperative, considering it part of the duty of those who sought knowledge based on evidence.

An interracial group of social scientists, ministers, journalists, and other civic leaders joined to resist the post-Reconstruction tidal wave of bigotry—intellectual and political. Among them were Joel Spingarn, Columbia professor of comparative literature until 1911, not long afterward a founder of Harcourt, Brace and Company (the NAACP's prestigious Spingarn Medal is named for him); Charles Edward Russell of New York City, American socialist and "chief of the muckrakers"; Oswald Garrison Villard, publisher of the *New York Post*, later owner and editor of *The Nation*; Ida B. Wells-Barnett of Chicago, prominent African American journalist who led an anti-lynching campaign from the 1890s; black ministers William Henry Brooks of New York's St. Mark's Methodist Episcopal Church and Bishop Alexander Walters of the African Methodist Episcopal Zion Church; William H. Bulkley, New York's only black public school principal; John Haynes Holmes, Unitarian minister of the Church of the Messiah (later renamed the Community Church of New York); and Rabbi Stephen R. Wise of the Free Synagogue of New York.

Harvard and Columbia's First African American Ph.D.s in "the Great Social Laboratory of New York City": Du Bois and Haynes

In New York by 1910 two African American social scientists, Harvard and Columbia universities' first African American Ph.D.s, assumed leadership of two new civil rights organizations, the NAACP and the Urban League. Whites, liberals in the scholar-activist and civic leadership of New York, had worked in alliance to organize and support both pioneering organizations. A century later they are still the two principal national black organizations.

Most noted of the two, and the top black intellectual of the twentieth century, was William Edward Burghardt Du Bois, who in 1903 published his famous *The Souls of Black Folk*. In New York, beginning in 1910, as founder and editor of the NAACP's magazine *The Crisis*, Du Bois became the nation's leading voice for racial justice.

The second, who has received far less acclaim than he deserves, was George Edmund Haynes, twelve years Du Bois's junior, and whose career paralleled and shadowed Du Bois's. As a Columbia graduate student he became a charter member of the NAACP and a founder and first executive secretary of the National League on Urban Conditions Among Negroes which became the National Urban League.[21]

Neither of the two, as was true of so many white scholar-activists of New York, was born and bred in New York. As the best place in the U.S. from which to lead a national social movement, New York drew them in as a magnet. Du Bois had been born in Great Barrington, Massachusetts, in 1868, to a family of free blacks of African, Dutch, and French Huguenot ancestry. His father, a barber and laborer, Alfred Du Bois, abandoned the family before Du Bois was two; his mother, Mary Burghardt, a domestic worker, died when he was sixteen. The principal at Great Barrington High School and the town's local Congregational Church raised money for a college scholarship, and Du Bois graduated from Fisk University in Nashville, a leading post-Civil War black university, returning to Massachusetts to enter Harvard as a junior. By age 27, in 1898, Du Bois had accumulated a Harvard B.A., M.A., and Ph.D.—his dissertation was on "The Suppression of the African Slave Trade."[22]

George Edmund Haynes was born in 1880 in Pine Bluff, Arkansas, son of a domestic worker, Mattie Sloan Haynes, and a laborer, Louis Haynes. His mother encouraged him to go to the Agricultural and Mechanical College in Normal, Alabama, and, at Fisk University afterward, he earned an A.B. Then, attending Yale on a tuition scholarship, he earned a masters degree in sociology in one year, enrolled at Yale's Divinity School for a year (he did not return the second year, in order to help finance, through work as secretary for the Colored Men's Department of the International Committee of the YMCA, his younger sister's education at Fisk's Preparatory School). Haynes visited the nation's black colleges and universities during his work for the YMCA and for two summers studied at the University of Chicago, where he took courses in the history of political economy, New Testament theology, experimental psychology, and "Race Development of Mind" (taught by white sociologist William Isaac Thomas, whose ground-breaking book *Sex and Society* was published in 1907). In 1908 Haynes moved to New York City for graduate work at the New York School of Philanthropy and in the social sciences at Columbia University; four years later he graduated with a Columbia Ph.D. in social economy, but even before finishing his dissertation he was appointed professor of social science at Fisk. After a wartime leave as director of Negro economics for the U.S. Department of Labor in Washington, D.C., he too was drawn back to New York City and served until 1947 as secretary of the Department of Race Relations for the Federal Council of Churches (the continuing Race Relations Sunday held each February was his initiative). Haynes served as a trustee of the State University of New York, and in his final decade taught courses on black history and international race relations at the City College of New York.[23]

The two black leaders had come from different backgrounds, each representing a different history of the black experience in America, one in the North, one in the South. Their education pattern varied—Du Bois's study of the German historical school of economics at the University of Berlin followed the same trajectory as many American social scientists at the time; Haynes did not study abroad. But in social activism, as in social science, their lives were linked. Both used social science as an instrument for reform of the conditions of the Negro, though as aspiring young social scientists both were barred by the color line of racial segregation from appointment to the faculties of any but the nation's historically black institutions of higher education despite their Ivy League educations. Had Du Bois been white he would likely have been appointed to the faculty at Harvard. Had Haynes been white he might have been appointed at Columbia.

One white member of the social science network, Samuel McCune Lindsay, proved especially critical to both Du Bois and Haynes. Lindsay, as assistant professor of sociology at the University of Pennsylvania in the 1890s, aided Du Bois, and as professor of social legislation at Columbia and director of the New York School of Philanthropy, he supported Haynes. Lindsay recruited Du Bois to undertake research as a part of a citywide study the University of Pennsylvania was conducting, and, accepting the assignment, Du Bois subsequently, in half-a-dozen letters, sought Lindsay's advice. "My plan," he wrote, "is first to get acquainted with the geography of the ward [Philadelphia's Seventh Ward] and the general haunts and characteristics of the people, and to supplement this by a study of the methods employed in such work by [Charles] Booth [author of *Life and Labour of the People in London*], [Jacob] Riis [author of *How the Other Half Lives*], the U.S. Census, etc." Du Bois's preface to his noted *The Philadelphia Negro: A Social Study*, published in 1899 in the University of Pennsylvania series in Political Economy and Public Law, thanked Lindsay "for aid, advice and sympathy, without which the work could hardly have been brought to a successful close." Years later Du Bois said: "If Lindsay had been a smaller man and had been induced to follow the usual American pattern of treating Negroes, he would have asked me to assist him as his clerk in this study." Lindsay, in turn, wrote the introduction to Du Bois's book, praising the "delicacy of an artist" in Du Bois's social science research.[24]

Lindsay supervised Haynes's research at Columbia. For his doctoral dissertation, Haynes, like Du Bois, conducted a sociological analysis of a city, in his case New York, through the New York School of Philanthropy's Bureau of Social Research, published as a book in 1912, *The Negro at Work in New York City: A Study in Economic Progress*. And as Du Bois had done in *The Philadelphia Negro* thirteen years earlier, Haynes's preface thanked Lindsay, for his "interest, advice and sympathy," to which the book's beginning and "its completion is largely due."[25]

The social sciences were paramount to both Du Bois and Haynes. For *The Philadelphia Negro*, Du Bois conducted a door-to-door canvass of 2,500 black households, noting income, property, housing, education, health, crime, and "pauperism and alcoholism." "That the Negro race has an appalling work of social reform before it need hardly be said," he wrote. "It is right and proper that Negro boys and girls should desire to rise as high in the world as their ability and just dessert entitle them." He looked toward the day when "all men, white and black, realize what the great founder of the city meant, when he named it the City of Brotherly Love."[26] In his 1903 autobiography, *Dusk of Dawn*, Du Bois wrote of that research, "The Negro problem was in my mind a matter of systematic investigation and intelligent understanding. The world was thinking wrong about race, because it did not know. The ultimate evil was stupidity. The cure for it was knowledge based on scientific investigation." Du Bois's biographer David Levering Lewis writes that Du Bois "had something of Herbert Spencer's confidence in both objective social science and in real-world application of its findings but without the British sociologist's mechanical determinism." "More than any other leading American sociologist during the decade after 1898, Du Bois undertook for a time the working out of an authentic objectivity in social science, 'to put science into sociology through a study of the conditions and problems of [his] own group.'" In his "Program for a Sociological Society," Du Bois adopted what historian Adolph L. Reed calls "an unambiguously positivistic model of social science and a pragmatic-like commitment to the wedding of knowledge and action."[27] In a paper, "A Program for Social Betterment," which Du Bois read before the First Sociological Society of Atlanta in 1898, he identified social science, especially sociology, as the principal means of achieving "social betterment."

Sociology is the science that studies the actions of human beings and seeks laws and regularities among these actions. Perhaps few if any exact laws of human action will ever be discovered, but many tendencies and uniform movements have already been pointed out, and that the study and inquiry in this field yields much of value and interest is not to be doubted. . . . Since now scientists have begun to study men and conditions of group life so carefully, persons who would better the world in any way must study and learn from the material collected here, just as in other lines we use the wisdom of geologist or psychologist. This consideration is characteristic of the modern methods of social reform—it is not enough to-day to want to do good or to reform criminals or to relieve poverty; we must know *how* these things can best be done. Now the first step toward this *knowing how*, is to learn what have been the results of careful study of crime and pauperism; then to study efforts and experiments made by others to lessen these evils and finally to experiment ourselves. . . .

The program of a society for social reform therefore must consist of three parts: *First*. Study—i.e. careful inquiry into the results of sociological research. *Second*: Knowledge of the work of others—i.e. an attempt to profit by the experience of other workers and reformers. *Third*: Actual Effort—i.e. careful tentative endeavor to better social conditions in limited localities and in definitely limited respects.[28]

Du Bois agreed with the larger social science reform community that it would take an active government to promote the good society.[29] In *Dusk of Dawn* he criticized the eugenists' view of race:

I could not lull my mind to hypnosis by regarding a phrase like "consciousness of kind" [Franklin Giddings' sociological theory of group difference] as a scientific law. By turning my gaze from fruitless word-twisting and facing the facts of my own social situation and racial world, I determined to put science into sociology through a study of the conditions and problems of my own group.

I was going to study the facts, any and all facts, concerning the American Negro and his plight, and by measurement and comparison and research, work up to any valid generalizations which I could, primarily with the utilization object of reform and uplift; but nevertheless, I wanted to do the work with scientific accuracy. Thus, in my own sociology, because of firm belief in a changing racial group, I easily grasped the idea of a changing developing society rather than a fixed social structure.[30]

Before the U.S. House of Representatives' Industrial Commission on Immigration and Education in 1901, when a congressman asked Du Bois, "How can the General Government draw lines of race or color?" Du Bois answered that the federal government ought to fund state schools "in proportion to illiteracy" not to race; "Say nothing about color in it [a law to provide federal funding in education]. In some cases it might go to help the whites." And in a 1903 article in *The Outlook*, "The Training of Negroes for Social Power," he called for funds for schools from government at all levels, state and federal, and for support for colleges "from private philanthropy and the United States Government. I make no apology for bringing the United States Government in thus conspicuously. The General Government must give aid to Southern education if illiteracy and ignorance are to cease threatening the very foundations of civilization within any reasonable time."[31]

Samuel McCune Lindsay, sponsor of Du Bois's earlier work in Philadelphia, wrote Du Bois in 1907, praising him as "an expert in sociological research," and urging that the Atlanta University conferences that Du Bois had, since 1897, been organizing "for the study of the negro problem [not be] given up or in any wise weakened." He "had been particularly impressed with the scientific spirit" of the investigations and with "the practical value of the results secured." After the Atlanta riots of 1906, Edwin R. A. Seligman wrote to Du Bois: "I was amazed & disgusted at the happenings in Atlanta. But perhaps I did not realize the horror of it all, until I read your beautiful poem in the Outlook. It must indeed be a tragedy for men like you. . . . Let us hold to the things that are eternally true, & let us seek within ourselves the compensation for the things that are withheld by an unthinking and uncivilized world." "If you ever come to New York," Seligman said, "kindly let me know in advance, so that I may have a chance to greet you." When Du Bois visited the city, Seligman did greet him. In this, and a multitude of similar ways, the network of social scientists in New York nurtured one another and reached out beyond the city.[32]

Du Bois was, in turn, active in the social science network, and he often praised the work of his fellow social scientists. Thus, he recommended to his readers in *The Horizon: A Journal of the Color Line*, a short-lived periodical he founded and edited, Edward T. Devine's *The Principles of Relief* as among the "good books for serious reading" and praised Boas, who he said "supplied intellectual reinforcement at a critical point."[33]

Politically, Du Bois, like a number of other social scientists drawn to New York City's social laboratory, was on the liberal left; in graduate school at the University of Berlin he attended Socialist Party meetings, but in 1904 he wrote to Isaac M. Rubinow: "I would scarcely describe myself as a socialist" though he had "much sympathy with the movement & I have many socialistic beliefs." By 1911, then in New York, he had joined the Socialist Party in the U.S. To Du Bois as to whites like Mary White Ovington and William English Walling—both founders of the NAACP—socialism offered a telling critique of the capitalist system. Still, Du Bois, in politics as in social science an astute pragmatist, supported Woodrow Wilson, not the Socialist candidate, Eugene Debs, or the Progressive, Theodore Roosevelt, in the 1912 election. Ovington, too, who had joined the Socialist Party in 1905, practiced, as the historian David Levering Lewis has put it, "a well-mannered and rather patient variety of it."[34]

In his classic *Souls of Black Folk* (1903), Du Bois called for the "talented tenth" among black folk, its "thinking classes," to step forward and lead.[35] No gradualist, in 1905, along with Harvard's first black Phi Beta Kappa, William Monroe Trotter of Boston, Du Bois founded the Niagara Movement, advocating bold strategies based on full equality, in direct opposition to Booker T. Washington's gradualist and vocationally based plan for Negro improvement.

George Edmund Haynes like Du Bois saw social science as a key ally for African Americans. "The problem of social uplift," he wrote, "is so great that, in addition to expert social workers, all Negro ministers, doctors, lawyers, teachers, and others should have the benefit of instruction in scientific methods and the new social point of view." Haynes became one of the first funded fellows of the Bureau of Social Research, the research organization orchestrated by the New York School of Philanthropy with the New York Charity Organization Society and the Russell Sage Foundation. To supplement his $50-a-month stipend Haynes worked part-time for the Committee for Improving the Industrial Condition of Negroes in New York (an organization pioneered by William Bulkley, the city's only black school principal), to place young black men in jobs. The result was his *The Negro at Work in New York City*, completed under Lindsay's mentoring, a detailed study of demography, entrepreneurship, and electoral strength in New York City's black population.[36]

Haynes wrote that he enrolled at Columbia University after his 1904 sociological studies at Yale: "for more grounding in the social sciences, I found my way into the great social laboratory of New York City." Working with Samuel McCune Lindsay and Edward T. Devine, both on the faculties of Columbia and of the New York School of Philanthropy, Haynes participated in a study of the migration of populations to U.S. urban centers, "as a basis for pioneering some kind of public employment-finding agency." His own assignment was "the migration of the negro population" from the rural South into urban centers in the North. His assignment became the seedbed of the National Urban League.[37]

Social scientists Devine, Seligman, and Frances Kellor—the University-of-Chicago-trained sociologist whose interests and activism spanned issues of race, poverty and crime—offered counsel during Haynes's graduate years in New York. In 1910, when Haynes was considering whether to take the job at Fisk, Devine advised: "Why not . . . focus your educational work with the students at Fisk University as a scientific foundation for their further education in social welfare and the organization of city agencies into which these trained workers might be introduced?"[38] Accepting Fisk's offer as Professor of Social Science, Haynes began to divide his time between Nashville and New York and married a fellow 1903 graduate of Fisk, Elizabeth A. Ross of Montgomery, Alabama. She earned a master's degree from Columbia University in 1923, and became a civil rights leader, community activist, school teacher, and author.[39]

Compelled by the prejudices of northern white universities to build his reputation in the South, like Du Bois at Atlanta University, Haynes founded and directed Fisk's Department of Social Science to train "Negro men and women" in "economics, sociology, labor problems and social work," with special training "in methods of social work and in research and investigation."[40] He established a sociological center for the study of the South, and set up a rigorous social work program, modeled on the New York School of Philanthropy's program, with an emphasis on field work and statistical training.[41] Writing in *The Survey* in February 1913, Haynes declared that the "social order" must be grounded in "economic and social justice." That "means that every individual should have an opportunity for physical, mental, and moral development to the limit of his capacity. It waives the question of superiority and inferiority of individuals or races and vouch-safes to all the chance for self-realization. It means equal opportunity."[42]

Prefiguring the later civil rights movement and the programs of affirmative action, Haynes wrote that, for "permanent progress," there must be an "equal chance for the Negro to get work, to hold work, to develop his capacity for work; equal protection of life and property; equal opportunity to educate his children to the limit of their varied capacity and to provide such a home for his family as his taste dictates and his purse allows; equal opportunity in sharing political responsibilities and of responding to the duties of citizenship, conditioned by character only, are fundamental conditions without which permanent adjustment cannot be made. . . . A police force and judiciary in which he can have no part, regardless of his attainments, produce lukewarm loyalty; and political life from which color alone excludes him ties a millstone about the neck of democracy."[43]

Disdaining the Spencerian Social Darwinian notion of a natural order of survival of the fittest, which his Yale professor William Graham Sumner had supported, Haynes wrote that: "Competition, which tends to eliminate the weak is not more fundamental than co-operation which calls upon the strong to help the weak to attain strength. In fact, such just and sympathetic consideration is the purchase price exacted of the strength of the strong."[44] For reasons unclear, this pioneering social science crusader has yet to receive the visibility and recognition his pioneering work deserves.

Mary White Ovington and the Call

Black leadership made common cause with white leaders unencumbered by social bias. One such white leader was Mary White Ovington, whose commitment to the African American community was part of a family legacy. Born in Brooklyn three days before Lincoln's assassination to Unitarian parents who were vigorous advocates of black emancipation and women's rights, she recalled that one of her grandmothers had been a friend of the abolitionist William Lloyd Garrison, "my childhood's greatest hero." She was influenced as a youth by the rational philosophy of John White Chadwick, minister of the Second Unitarian Church in Brooklyn and by the radical economist William Ashley, who introduced her to the social sciences at the Harvard Annex (later Radcliffe College)—several years later he also influenced Mary Kingsbury Simkhovitch. Ovington had worked as Ashley's research assistant, and from him she learned how "impartial history could become a tool of social reform."[45] After three years at the Harvard Annex, when her father's merchandising business failed, Ovington had to return to Brooklyn. There she began a life of social reform, first, as a founder and headworker, from 1895 to 1903, at the Pratt Institute's Greenpoint Settlement in Brooklyn, where she met working class immigrants and "saw the struggle for jobs, the boycott and the tragedy of the unemployed."[46] In 1903, her last year as headworker at Greenpoint Settlement, Ovington heard Booker T. Washington and a Negro physician address the Social Reform Club, and "The Negro and his problems came into my life," as she wrote in her memoirs years later. She decided "to be of some help to this neglected element." Her friend Mary Kingsbury Simkhovitch, headworker at Greenwich House, whom Ovington called "one of my wisest settlement friends," advised her how to begin. "You know nothing about the people you want to work with," Simkhovitch said, and arranged for a fellowship from Greenwich House's Committee on Social Investigation so Ovington could "study the Negro in New York."[47]

The principal members of Greenwich House's Committee on Social Investigation, which awarded Ovington's fellowship, were Seligman, Boas, Devine, Giddings, Henry Rogers Seager, Vladimir Simkhovitch, and Livingston Farrand, all at Columbia University, all social scientists. Seligman, committee chairman, was, Ovington said, "genuinely sympathetic and anxious that I should find out some means of material and social betterment for the Negroes here in New York."[48] Her research led to a 1911 book, *Half a Man: The Status of the Negro in New York*. Boas, in the Foreword, called it "a refutation of the claims that the Negro has equal opportunity with the whites, and that his failure to advance more rapidly than he has, is due to innate inability."[49]

Mary White Ovington corresponded with Du Bois, lectured at Atlanta University at Du Bois's invitation, and like him joined the Socialist Party. An early "Du Bois enthusiast" since reading his essays in the *Atlantic* and in the *Outlook*, Ovington had written to him in 1904 that she had chosen to study "the economic opportunities for young Negro men and women in New York," and hoped he would direct her "to data on the subject or might tell me to whom to go." She did not want to "trouble" him, but sought his advice on her plan to open "a Settlement in the Negro quarter in New York—an idea in which I know you have been interested." Du Bois had "talked to me through your writings for many years and have lately made me want to work as I never wanted to work before, but I need now to ask directly for advice."[50]

When Du Bois published his acclaimed "Credo" a few months later in 1904, Ovington wrote to him of her own sadness, despair, and hope, and Du Bois sent back a comforting note: "I am sorry you ached over it, for after all there are wonderful compensations in all this thing." In his Credo he had written: "I believe in Liberty for all men, the space to stretch their arms and their souls, the right to breathe and the right to vote, the freedom to choose their friends, enjoy the sunshine and ride on the railroads, uncursed by color; thinking, dreaming, working as they will in a kingdom of God and love."[51]

Beginning in 1905, Ovington published her work in numerous articles, such as "The Negro Home in New York," in *Charities*; "The Colored Woman in Domestic Service in New York City," in *Household Research Bulletin*; and "The Negro in the Trades Union in New York," in *Annals of the American Academy of Political and Social Science* (only 5 percent of black workingmen were union members, she observed).[52] By the next year, she was covering the Negro community for Oswald Garrison Villard's *New York Evening Post*. From Harpers Ferry, Virginia, "where John Brown made his stand for freedom," she reported on a meeting of the Niagara Movement, precursor to the NAACP, founded by Du Bois and William Trotter. She wrote years later that she had been "whole-heartedly in accord with the platform of these insurgents."[53] At Du Bois's invitation, Ovington, like Frances Kellor, lectured at the Conferences he directed at Atlanta University in the early 1900s.

Two brutal days of rioting in Abraham Lincoln's hometown of Springfield, Illinois, in the summer of 1908 led to the founding of the NAACP. Ovington read a moving account of the Springfield riot, "Race War in the North," written by a journalist she knew, William English Walling, the son of a wealthy, former slave-holding family from Kentucky, who had taken graduate courses in economics and sociology at the University of Chicago and lived at New York's University Settlement when Ovington was at the Greenpoint Settlement. Walling wrote that "race hatred," was the cause of the riot. "We must come to treat the Negro," Walling wrote, "on a plane of absolute political and social equality." "Within the hour" of reading Wallings' eloquent account, Ovington wrote from her home "in a New York Negro tenement on a Negro Street," and Walling proposed that they meet, as in early January 1909 they did, at Walling's apartment on West 39th Street in Manhattan. Henry Moskowitz joined them; himself raised in the settlement house culture of the Lower East Side, he was a graduate of the College of the City of New York and a student of economics at Columbia University and the University of Erlangen in Germany. The NAACP, as Ovington later wrote in a pamphlet, "was born in a little room of a New York apartment. It is to be regretted that there are no minutes of the first meeting, for they would make interesting if unparliamentary reading." Knowing "something of the Negro's difficulty in securing decent employment in the North and of the insolent treatment awarded him at Northern hotels and restaurants," Ovington wrote, "I voiced my protest." Walling had spent "some years" in Tzar Nicholas II's empire and it was his opinion, Ovington recalled, "that the Negro was treated with greater inhumanity in the United States than the Jew was treated in Russia." Moskowitz, she wrote, spoke from his own "broad knowledge of conditions among New York's helpless immigrants." "And so we talked and talked, voicing our indignation."[54]

The three—Ovington, Walling, and Moskowitz—decided that the next month, on 12 February, the centennial of Lincoln's birth, they would issue "a call for a national conference on the Negro question."[55] A group of about sixty social reformers agreed to join their initiative for a meeting, and signed a "Call" that read in part: "The celebration of the centennial of the birth of Abraham Lincoln . . . takes no note and makes no recognition of the colored men and women to whom the great emancipator labored to assure freedom. Besides a day of rejoicing, Lincoln's birthday in 1909 should be one of taking stock of the nation's progress since 1865." Were Lincoln to observe events in 1909 "he would learn . . . [of the] disfranchising of the negro," "that taxation without representation is the lot of millions of wealth-producing American citizens"; that "black men and women, for whose freedom a hundred thousand of soldiers gave their lives, [were] set apart in trains, in which they pay first-class fares for third-class service, in railway stations and in places of entertainment, while State after State declines to do its elementary duty in preparing the negro through education for the best exercise of citizenship." The Call concluded: "this government cannot exist half slave and half free any better to-day than it could in 1861. Hence we call upon all the believers in democracy to join in a national conference for the discussion of present evils, the voicing of protests, and the renewal of the struggle for civil and political liberty."[56]

"From the Standpoint of Modern Science, Are Negroes Men?": Founding of the NAACP

In 1905, Edward T. Devine's *Charities*, precursor to *The Survey*, as a central journal of record, published twenty-three articles in a special issue on race in northern cities. Boas wrote on "The Negro and the Demands of Modern Life," Du Bois on "The Black Vote of Philadelphia," Kellor on "Emigration from the South—The Women," Ovington on "The Negro Home in New York," Booker T. Washington on "Should Negro Business Men Go South," William Bulkley on "The School as Social Center," Lilian Brandt, a Wellesley graduate and member of the New York Charity Organization Society's Committee on Social Research, on "The Make-up of Negro City Groups."[57]

This was part of the network, already in place among social science activists,who responded to the Call in 1909. Among the fifty-seven signatories to the letter were whites and blacks, men and women, leading journalists, religious leaders, and social critics, including Jane Addams of Chicago's Hull House, Oswald Garrison Villard of the *New York Evening Post* (grandson of abolitionist William Lloyd Garrison), New York Unitarian minister John Haynes Holmes, Rabbi Stephen Wise, Florence Kelley of the National Consumers' League, Lillian Wald of the Henry Street Settlement, philanthropist and activist Mary E. Dreier, Jane E. Robbins, the physician head of College Settlement in Manhattan, and Helen Marot, secretary of the National Women's Trade Union League and ally of Kelley and Goldmark in the 1908 Brandeis brief. (Boas, Seligman, Haynes, and James B. Reynolds, not signators, became early participants in the NAACP.)[58]

Ovington apparently used her extensive personal connections, both within and outside the New York social science network, to enlist as co-signers Du Bois; William Bulkley, black principal of a New York public school; Ida Wells-Barnett, the African American journalist and co-founder of the National Association of Colored Women, the Reverend William Henry Brooks of St. Mark's Methodist Episcopal Church, Bishop Alexander Walters of the African Methodist Episcopal Zion Church, Mary Eliza Church Terrell, first president of the National Association of Colored Women, muckraking journalists Charles Edward Russell, Lincoln Steffens, and Ray Stannard Baker, and the wealthy reformer J. G. Phelps-Stokes. The latter four were fellow members, with William English Walling, of the liberal left men's dinner and discussion club, "The New York X."[59]

The landmark National Negro Conference began on the evening of 30 May 1909, with an informal reception at Lillian Wald's and Florence Kelley's Henry Street Settlement on the Lower East Side. The next morning participants settled in for two days of addresses and discussion in the United Charities Building on East 22nd Street, focal point of so much New York social reform. Of the thousand who had been invited, by Du Bois' count two to three hundred came. There was, he said, "a visible bursting into action of long gathering thought," though he thought many blacks "looked into each others faces with apprehension." Ovington reported that "the white people" in attendance "received a stimulating shock and . . . did not want to leave the meeting." This invitation-only conference was followed by an open public forum in the spacious ground-floor auditorium at Cooper Union at East 7th Street and Third Avenue, with an audience Du Bois estimated at 1,500, the same number said to have attended Lincoln's famous 27 February 1860 speech on sectionalism and slavery there.[60]

Science was center stage and eugenics was a central target. The conference began, Du Bois said, by "emphasizing the very points around which the real race argument centers today, viz., from the standpoint of modern science, are Negroes men?" At the first morning session, a neurologist, an anthropologist, economist, philosopher, and sociologist spoke. Burt G. Wilder, professor of neurology and vertebrate zoology at Cornell University, addressing "The Brain of the American Negro," declared that human brains of all races are vastly similar, and distinctly different from brains of other primates. Livingston Farrand, professor of anthropology at Columbia University, said that " 'the term 'race' '" is at the "present time in hopeless disrepute. We do not know what it means and are unable to agree upon an arbitrary definition of it." "It is absolutely unjustifiable," he said, "to assert that there is trustworthy evidence for the view that marked differences of mental capacity between the different races exist."[61]

"The more scientific we are, the less prejudice we have," the economist Edwin R. A. Seligman told the audience. "Social environment" was important in the shaping of social behavior. It was, his "fervent hope" and "confident expectation" that "the forces of science and the ethical forces which after all are deep down in the heart of everyone of us, white and black—that those forces will continue to grow in their influence and finally achieve their desired and deserved success. . . . Let us be prepared to face the future as it comes; but let us be prepared also to put up a good fight." The philosopher John Dewey told the audience that, "in the matter of this scientific discussion," the best "biological science" shows "there is no 'inferior race,' and the members of a race so-called should each have the same opportunities of social environment and personality as those of a more favored race."[62]

Celia Parker Woolley, headworker at Chicago's Frederick Douglass Centre, spoke on "Race Reconciliation"; Du Bois on "Politics and Industry" (on the transforming impact intelligent black male voters could have on southern politics); Walling on "The Negro and the South"; and Bulkley on "Race Prejudice as Viewed from an Economic Standpoint." Du Bois spoke again, on the "Evolution of the Race Problem"; Bishop Walters on the "Civil and Political Status of the Negro"; Wells-Barnett on "Lynching Our National Crime"; and Oswald Garrison Villard on "The Need of Organization."[63]

Newspapers covered the conference, including the *Washington Post*, *Brooklyn Eagle*, and *New York Sun*. One headline in the *Sun* read: "Demands Justice for Negro, Prominent Men Hold Conference and Disparage Race Prejudice and Inequality, Mass Meeting at Cooper Union. . . . Scientists Discuss Problem and Dismiss Natural Inequality of Black Man."[64] (The *Sun's* headline ignored prominent women participants and organizers.)

The conference established a "great central committee," to organize the work of the organization they were forming. The National Negro Committee then created various subcommittees, for example, on "legal advice," "social investigation," and "political propaganda." In a resolution for wide circulation conferees voted: "We denounce the ever growing oppression of our 10,000,000 colored fellow citizens as the greatest menace that threatens the country." They demanded that the President and Congress take three "first and immediate steps."

(1) That the constitution be strictly enforced and the civil rights guaranteed under the fourteenth amendment be secured impartially to all.
(2) That there be equal education opportunities for all and in all the states, and that public school expenditure be the same for the Negro and the white child.
(3) That in accordance with the fifteenth amendment the right of the Negro to the ballot on the same terms as other citizens be recognized in every part of the country.

The "net result" of the conference, Du Bois reported in *The Survey*, "was the vision of future co-operation, not simply as in the past between giver and beggar—the older ideal of charity—but a new alliance between experienced social workers and reformers in touch, on the one hand, with scientific philanthropy and, on the other, with the great struggling mass of laborers of all kinds whose condition and needs know no color line."[65]

The year after the historic conference, Seligman helped organize a second National Negro Conference, in Manhattan 12–14 May 1910.

Franz Boas's address, "The Real Race Problem," argued that the biological evidence did not sustain the view that the mental power of one race was higher than that of others, and implied that the real problem was eugenics and eugenicists. At about this same time (the archival copy of the text carries no date), the "Report of the Preliminary Committee on Permanent Organization" of the National Negro Committee was "Respectfully submitted" to the membership by Seligman, Du Bois, Walling, Villard, Charles Edward Russell, and *New York Tribune* reporter John E. Milholland. On the NAACP's seventy-two-member first "General Committee" were members from Illinois, Ohio, Pennsylvania, Massachusetts, Virginia, and Georgia, but a majority were from New York—Seligman, Kelley, Moskowitz, Ovington, Wald, and Dewey among them.[66]

Women played a central, if unpublicized, role, Ovington especially, at the first conference and in the founding of the NAACP, though by the custom of the day they were shunted away from the more influential political work. In December 1910, *The Crisis* announced that Mary Kingsbury Simkhovitch and Lillian D. Wald, "Mrs. John Dewey," "Mrs. E. R. A. Seligman," and other "patronesses" were sponsoring a morning "N.A.A.C.P. Lecture Recital" by black musical artists, soprano Emma Azalia Hackley, well known for her operatic "voice of surpassing sweetness," and Mary Church Terrell, a founder and first president of the National Association of Colored Women.[67] Mary Church Terrell, and Ida Wells-Barnett were the only two African-American women among the fifty-seven signatories to sign the 1909 Call; fifteen white women signed. Though largely unacknowledged publicly, women were nonetheless key to the new association's success.

"A Union" of "Opposition" to "the Forces of Evil": The NAACP

"What is the National Association for the Advancement of Colored People?" asked an editorial in the second issue (December 1910) of *The Crisis,* issued from the NAACP's national headquarters at 20 Vesey Street in lower Manhattan, unsigned but with all the hallmarks of Du Bois's style.

It is a union of those who believe that earnest, active opposition is the only effective way of meeting the forces of evil. They believe that the growth of race prejudice in the United States is evil. It is not always conscious evil. Much of it is born of ignorance and misapprehension, honest mistake and misguided zeal. . . . To treat all Negroes alike is treating evil as good and good as evil. To draw a crass and dogged undeviating color line in human affairs is dangerous—as dangerous to those who draw it as to those against whom it is drawn.

We are organized to fight this great modern danger. How may we fight it?

1. By the argument of the printed word in a periodical like this, and in pamphlets and tracts.

2. By the spoken word in talk and lecture.

3. By correspondence.

4. By encouraging all efforts at social uplift.

5. By careful investigation of the truth in matters of social condition and race contact—not the truth as we want it or you want it, but as it really is.

6. By individual relief of the wretched.[68]

Social science had shaped the NAACP's emerging goals and strategies at every step. Indeed, without the men and women scholar-activists of New York City's network, the NAACP would have taken an altogether different form. Not only did social science, allied with clergy, journalists, and other reformers, mostly white intellectual elites, organize its earliest conferences and serve on its committees and subcommittees, but social science representatives spoke out forcefully and often against racism in their own ranks and in the society at large, at its conferences and in print.

Du Bois had moved from Atlanta University to Manhattan to serve as the NAACP's Director of Publicity and Research and as the only black officer of the NAACP's board of directors. His intellectual and political vision shaped the new organization from the outset. Within a few months Du Bois began to publish the new NAACP magazine, *The Crisis*, and, beginning in 1919, he organized the first of several Pan-African Congresses, resigning in 1934 to return to Atlanta University. A decade later he was back in New York. In the aftermath of the Second World War, embittered about the pace of change in the U.S., Du Bois lived his last two years in Ghana, where he died in 1963 at 95.

"Equal Opportunity . . . Conditioned by Character Only": The National Urban League

Just as W. E. B. Du Bois had called for the training of a black intellectual class, the "talented tenth," so his social science colleague-in-arms George Edmund Haynes set about training that elite. Haynes's photographs show a distinguished man with chiseled features and eyes framed by rimless glasses; Haynes became a second great crusader for civil rights, but with a style different from Du Bois's. In 1910–11 he was a founder and first director of the National League on Urban Conditions Among Negroes (shortened in 1919 to the National Urban League). This was not a grassroots membership organization like the NAACP, but a policy advisory group, to business and industry especially. Like the NAACP, it placed the theory and practice of the social sciences at the center of its work. (Indeed, Whitney Young, who took over leadership of the National Urban League in 1960, had been trained as a social worker.) An editorial (probably by Du Bois) in *The Crisis* said that the training of social workers was, "in the opinion of the league and its director [Haynes], 'the very foundation stone for work among the negro people.'"[69]

The Committee on Urban Conditions Among Negroes (National Urban League) was created in 1910, the same year Du Bois left Atlanta for New York, and a year after the NAACP was organized, with a merger of two New York City-centered organizations, the National League for the Protection of Colored Women, pioneered by the sociologist Frances Kellor, and the Committee for Improving the Industrial Condition of Negroes in New York, pioneered by the black educator William Bulkley. Haynes, who had worked for Bulkley's Committee for Improving the Industrial Condition of Negroes when he arrived in New York several years before, played a principal role in orchestrating the merger.

The National League for the Protection of Colored Women had begun as the Inter-Municipal Committee on Household Research, founded by Kellor in 1905 and renamed within a year, an organization of committees to provide travelers' aid, lodging, education, employment, and finances for black migrants coming North. With its headquarters at 43 East 22nd Street in Manhattan, not far from the United Charities Building, and with Ruth Standish Baldwin—the widow of a railroad magnate, passionate promoter of civil rights, and the aunt of Roger Baldwin, founder and first director of the ACLU—joining Kellor at the League's head by 1909, the organization rapidly expanded from New York to additional chapters in Baltimore, Chicago, Philadelphia, Washington, D.C., and Memphis.[70]

The National League for the Protection of Colored Women reflected Kellor's own social science research. Kellor had overcome an impoverished childhood to earn a law degree from Cornell University, with further graduate studies in sociology at the University of Chicago. She had attended the New York Summer School of Philanthropy in 1901 and the following year became a fellow of the College Settlements Association. Her first book, *Experimental Sociology, Descriptive and Analytical: Delinquents*, published in 1902, challenged the view of Italian criminologist and physician Cesare Lombroso, whose physiological criminal taxonomy argued, as Kellor put it, that "the born criminal" conforms "to a criminal type," a companion theory to the eugenics of race. (Lombroso had argued from early in his career that irregular facial characteristics such as asymmetry, receding forehead, or large jaw signaled that a particular individual was a "throwback" to the apes and criminally inclined.) Society, not physical type, Kellor maintained, was implicated in crime. "The purpose of criminal sociology," she wrote, "is to investigate crime scientifically: to study its origin and causes, and to determine, if possible, what proportion of responsibility belongs to society and what to the criminal." Social programs had "prevented criminality," among them "vacation schools, social and industrial organizations, employment bureaus, societies in cities for the protection of women, mothers' aid associations, women's club movements, manual training schools, substitutes for saloon, [and] libraries." Early childhood intervention would do more to prevent future criminals than an expanded penal system. "Department store schools" should be conducted "each morning from 8 until 10 o'clock"—to educate the many boys and girls who worked as clerk-assistants and stock-boys in New York City's and other urban centers' multiplying new department stores.[71]

The League, however, concentrated its work on the plight of Southern black women migrants, most of whom, by Kellor's count, took up jobs as domestic servants when they arrived in Baltimore, Philadelphia, and New York. Alerted to the imminent arrival of a young woman at a pier on the Hudson River or at a railroad depot, National League members would arrange to meet her there; in repeated dramatic scenes, they raced to intercept the bewildered arrivals before recruiters from houses of ill repute could take them over. League volunteers guided young women to safe houses, and alerted them to the tactics used by labor agents to entice or deceive new arrivals into a life of prostitution. By 1909 its staff had sent 3,639 letters to Southern ministers and civic leaders hoping to enlist them in informing women of the peril, and in New York it set up a travelers' aid bureau to assist sick or disoriented travelers; secured day-care for children of working mothers; and arranged "fresh air" country vacations for children in urban slums. Kellor modelled her group's efforts to aid "the Negro women imported from the south," on New York City's Jewish community programs that met and helped Jewish immigrants arriving at Ellis Island. It reported disreputable employment agencies to the city's Licenses Commission, and its members testified before it, generating Commission reprimands to several of New York City's employment agencies.[72]

The second group in the merger that created the National Urban League was the Committee for Improving the Industrial Condition of Negroes in New York, initiated by the school principal William Bulkley in 1906. Mary White Ovington was assistant secretary of the Committee, and Haynes an active member. Bulkley's Committee focused on locating well-paid work in industry for black men—"a square deal in the matter of getting a livelihood." It established social centers and trade schools and sponsored a night school and an employment locator service, public forums, and publications.[73]

William Bulkley, the Committee's leader, born in 1861 as the Civil War began, was the son of free black parents in Greenville, South Carolina. He worked his way though Claflin College in Orangeburg, South Carolina (the oldest historically black college in South Carolina), and later attended Wesleyan College (now Wesleyan University) in Middletown, Connecticut, before earning a doctorate in Latin and Greek from Syracuse University after a year's study in Strasbourg and Paris. In 1901 he accepted a post as principal of public school P.S. 80, in what was at the time a largely African American district, "The Black Tenderloin," running along Eighth Avenue from West 23rd up to 42nd Street. A founding member and treasurer of the New York Association for the Protection of Colored Women, and member of the Charity Organization Society's subcommittee on tuberculosis, Bulkley had joined Ovington in her 1906 campaign to arrange for "fresh air" vacations for Negro children, and, with Du Bois and other black intellectuals, had been a founder of the Niagara Movement of 1905 and a member of New York's 1909 National Negro Conference.[74]

The Committee on Urban Conditions Among Negroes itself was launched a year after the NAACP, on 19 May 1910, at the initiative of George Edmund Haynes. Frances Kellor and Ruth Standish Baldwin, Haynes wrote later, "responded favorably to my scientific conclusions about Negro migration and what should be done to train Negro workers for urban life and service. Seeing eye-to-eye we soon joined hands to pioneer the urban movement." Haynes, then associate professor of social science at Fisk University in Nashville, agreed to split his time between Nashville and New York City—traveling from Nashville to New York for short visits during the academic year, and spending his summers in New York. He served for eight years as the organization's first executive director. Seligman, one of Haynes's professors at Columbia, accepted Haynes's invitation to become the new organization's first president; in 1915, Ruth Standish Baldwin succeeded him. Frances Kellor was a member of the first executive committee. On the new National Urban League's executive board along with Kellor, Seligman, and Haynes was Edward Ewing Pratt, Haynes' fellow graduate student at Columbia University, just then completing his dissertation on "Industrial Causes of Congestion of Population in New York City," while teaching economics and statistics at the New York School of Philanthropy.[75]

In the economic recession in 1914–15 that was a consequence of the war in Europe, the Urban League helped find work in New York for hundreds of black men and women, training women as domestic servants, one of the few available jobs, and placing 400 men, and women, too, with the New York Transit Authority and its contractors. It prepared lunches for needy families with food purchased from a local black grocer. With continuing wartime mass migration of tens of thousands of black families to other cities as well, it established affiliates in Philadelphia, St. Louis, Nashville, Baltimore, Memphis, and Louisville.[76]

On the question of economic justice, "a long stride toward securing economic justice can be made," Haynes asserted bluntly in 1913, by labor unions "extending a welcome to the Negro." He phoned a New York AFL affiliate to inquire what the American Federation of Labor was doing to organize black workers. The local could not answer but Haynes was soon invited to address the AFL executive board, and he asked for AFL help in organizing "Negro working men." Haynes wrote in his 1913 director's report that fall that Samuel Gompers, AFL president, had assured him that the AFL was "making every effort to reach those who have not yet adopted the ideas of organized labor," but it "considered the Negro's rights and needs just as much as they considered the rights and needs of other classes of working men but no more than the others."[77]

Why Two Organizations? Dividing the Mission

Both great American civil rights organizations, the NAACP and the National Urban League, were led by social scientists committed to strategies of research, education, legislation, and legal challenges as the most effective means of social reform. But why *two* national organizations? Those who created them asked themselves that question when, in late 1910, Haynes and Du Bois met to discuss ways of working together, and, on 9 February 1911, met again, at the offices of the NAACP in Lower Manhattan, to talk about programs and goals, this time with key members of their organizations. "The result of the conference," the League's report said, "was that there was to be co-operation between the two committees and no overlapping." The NAACP was to "occupy itself principally with the political, civil and social rights of the colored people, while the Committee on Urban Conditions [the National Urban League after 1919] shall occupy itself primarily with questions of philanthropy and social economy." It was agreed that "these two committees interchange monthly reports on their activities and plans."[78] Representing the Urban League at the conference were Haynes, Seligman, Edward Ewing Pratt, and a Mr. Wood (almost certainly L. Hollingsworth Wood, New York civil rights and civil liberties attorney, later president of the National Urban League for twenty-six years). Representing the NAACP were Du Bois, Ovington, and an unidentified Mrs. McLean.

The primary focus of each of these two groups over the decades to come would remain, essentially, as the 1911 meeting had set forth. The principal work of the League would be in "social economy"—aiding black workers in their training and finding them work; the Association would concentrate on African American "political, civil and social rights." The Urban League functioned, as it was sometimes later quipped, as the "State Department," a more elitist organization, and the NAACP, which eventually became a wide network of grassroots membership branches, as the "War Department" of the civil rights movement.[79]

The NAACP gave priority to research on discrimination in education, labor unions, and public programs; it resorted to the courts for redress, and to public protests and political action where negotiating proved ineffective. The National Urban League, under the influence of social scientists Haynes, Kellor, Seligman, Eugene Kinckle Jones, and others, rejected the traditional almsgiving charity of earlier organizations to aid the poor to commit itself, as its Constitution put it, to "promote, encourage, assist and engage in any and all kinds of work for improving the industrial, economic, social and spiritual conditions among Negroes."[80] Toward this end the National Urban League would conduct social science investigations of urban life, promote self-help programs, seek legislation to provide decent housing and decently paid employment, and promote development of Negro businesses. It would train social workers who would study with Haynes at Fisk and through other programs. League members would learn how to counsel black migrants from the rural South in work codes, dress, hygiene, and care of the home in the urban North. Over the years, it came to concern itself especially with a relationship with business and industry intended to improve job prospects for blacks.

Social science principles and methodology detached from moral commitment had not led to agreement among New York's scholar-activists on what public policies to pursue. American social science as a whole was certainly not united on the issue of race, and many could say it was still not even a century later. The leading social scientists in the Progressive Era who asserted Teutonic myths and theories of racial superiority, who defended the darker side of eugenics, or who simply assumed that differences in achievement were based on worth and intelligence, were challenged by other fervent and tenacious social scientists, white and black, who countered such claims as unscientific and who promoted racial equality. Over the next decades the latter became the dominant voices and led the way in racial justice in the public realm. In the end those who believed in equality won the debate in the academy, and in public policy as well. Individually, and through social science research and arguments and organized public education and action, this dedicated band of New York-centered intellectual and social activists had seen loyalty to knowledge and science as consistent with humane goals. Their crusade would culminate in the civil rights revolution of the 1950s to 1970s, the anti-poverty programs and affirmative action initiatives of the second half of the twentieth century, and continued effort on into the twenty-first century.

"Our Ideas Will Become Common Currency": Social Science Political Engagement in the Election of 1912 and Its Aftermath

The men and women scholar-activists of New York City's network in "the greatest social science laboratory in the world" had worked essentially from the private-sector sidelines. But in 1912 a series of events thrust them into the thick of electoral politics with adoption of a "Social Science Platform" in Cleveland, Ohio, at the annual meeting of the National Conference of Charities and Correction.

In Chicago, on 22 June, Theodore Roosevelt, recognizing that William Howard Taft had effectively blocked his bid for the Republican presidential nomination, signalled his supporters at the GOP's national convention that the time had come to make a break. At his word his supporters marched, cheering and singing, down the aisles and out of the convention hall. The Progressive party was born. Six weeks later, at the new Progressive party's national convention, the Cleveland "Social Science Platform" was ensconced as a centerpiece of the new party's economic platform. Social scientist activists of New York, who had been prominent in drawing up that platform, now became principal figures in the new third party.

Democrats, meeting at their own convention in Baltimore in July, and smelling political blood in the water, nominated Governor Woodrow Wilson of New Jersey as their presidential candidate. On economic and social welfare issues Wilson was a political progressive and his nomination effectively spoiled Roosevelt's chances of distinguishing himself as the sole progressive alternative to the politics of the established parties. Wilson was elected that November, and by 1916 Theodore Roosevelt's Progressive party was moribund. But during the summer and fall of 1912—in a four-way race among Wilson, Roosevelt, Taft, and Socialist Eugene Debs—Theodore Roosevelt and the newly formed Progressive party grappled with the vexed question of civil rights for African Americans, promoted women's suffrage, and placed before the nation the agenda articulated in the "Social Science Platform." It defined new frontiers of economic reform in modern America, and its ripples would extend far beyond the election itself.

"Political and Sociological Experts" in "the Stern Arena of Political Action"

"The product of 'political and sociological experts,' " as the sociologist Frances Kellor, of the new Progressive party's decision-making inner circle, described the party's platform to a group of women gathered in the home of A. E. Robinson, president of the women's suffrage organization of Coldwater, Michigan, Kellor's hometown. In what the local newspaper in August of 1912 called "an interesting account of the Chicago convention held by the Progressive party," Kellor told the group: "Perhaps everyone does not know that the party platform was not actually formulated by Mr. Roosevelt. He endorsed it, but political and sociological experts framed the various planks. . . . Various women served on different committees, men and women working in harmony." The Columbia sociologist Samuel McCune Lindsay, who had been at Cleveland that June, wrote with pride of, "our little committee that took so active a part in the formulation of the [Progressive party] platform." Paul Kellogg, editor of *The Survey*, declared that: "The men and women identified with child labor committees, consumers' leagues, charity organization societies, settlements and the like who drew up at Cleveland in June a series of labor planks which they could stand for collectively, little thought that in less than two months their platform would be adopted bodily as the practical economic gospel of a new political party. Yet that is the way the event has turned." Henry Moskowitz wrote to Lillian Wald, headworker at the Henry Street settlement, whom he had known since childhood, that, "our ideas will become common currency."[1]

Jane Addams of Chicago's pioneering Hull House, a founder of the new party, noted the sense of exhilaration in the ranks: "Perhaps we felt so keenly the uplifting sense of comradeship with old friends and co-workers not only because we had all realized how inadequate we were in small groups but because the very sentiments of compassion and desire for social justice were futile unless they could at last find expression as an integral part of corporate government." S. J. Duncan-Clark, editor of the *Chicago Evening Post*, extolled the "Value of Sociology Recognized" in the leadership in the new party: "The libraries and the laboratories in the colleges are being rediscovered as assets of value to the common good. Academic learning, the gibe of the professional politician, is being harnessed to the service of the state."[2]

Many scholar-activists in New York offered an outpouring of support for Roosevelt's new party. James Bronson Reynolds, former headworker of New York's University Settlement, wrote to Roosevelt: "I am of course heart and soul with you, and will do anything in my power" for "our new party." Henry Bruère, director of the New York Bureau of Municipal Research, told Roosevelt: "I have not, like my brother Robert, joined the socialist party, because I believe that we can work out our social and economic problems in America step by step without committing ourselves to a pre-conceived reordering of our national life. The present developments in the progressive movement gives encouragement to my confidence in this belief." Columbia economist E. R. A. Seligman sent Roosevelt a handwritten note: "I thought that you might like to know that I propose to cast in my fortunes with you and the new party. I admire Wilson, but I cannot share the Democratic views; & I do not believe that either Mr. Wilson or Pres. Taft is alive to the fundamental issues of modern political & economic life, as are you." Mary Kingsbury Simkhovitch, head resident at the Greenwich House settlement, pledged her support: "If there is any way in which I can help, count on me. This is the first time since the Civil War that there have been great political issues. My 1st fourteen years spent in Social Settlements have forced me to a knowledge of our social needs which life alone can give. At last to see these needs recognized and tackled by a political party is to fill me with thanksgiving." Nine months later she wrote Roosevelt again, inviting him to dine at Greenwich House, and adding: "my husband and myself are ardent Progressives."[3]

From its founding in 1874, the National Conference of Charities and Correction had served as a national forum for social scientists, social gospellers, labor leaders, women's club leaders, philanthropists, physicians, public health officials, lawyers, philosophers, and reform-minded politicians. Its agenda reflected their vision of progressive reform for the nation. The new party's agenda was a fulfillment of a quarter century's work of a national coalition of reformers. At the 1909 annual meeting of the National Conference, three years before its "Social Science Platform" would be drafted at Cleveland, Simkhovitch had spoken on raising "the standard of living," Florence Kelley on women's wages, Jane Addams on the work of the Conference's Immigrants Committee, Graham Taylor of the Chicago Theological Seminary on "The Neighborhood and the Municipality," and University of Chicago philosopher and social psychologist George Herbert Mead on "The Adjustment of Our Industry to Surplus and Unskilled Labor." The seeds of a new committee, the Standards of Living and Labor Committee, were sown, and members of this committee became the principal figures in the drafting of the influential "Social Science Platform."[4]

The journals and annual meetings of social science associations were abuzz with similar issues—the American Economic Association, the American Political Science Association, and Columbia University's Academy of Political Science among them. The January 1912 issue of the *Proceedings of the Academy of Political Science in the City of New York*, for example, carried articles by Samuel McCune Lindsay on "The Basis of Government Regulation," by Henry Rogers Seager on "The Relation of Government to Business," and by Edward T. Devine on "Workmen's Compensation Legislation." Its July issue included an essay by Columbia economist John Bates Clark on "A Federal Commission on Industrial Relations— Why it is Needed," and another by Henry Rogers Seager on "Labor Legislation a National Social Need."[5] (All three of the Academy of Political Science's executive board members in 1912—Columbia University professors Lindsay, Seligman, and Frank J. Goodnow—became ardent Progressive party supporters.)

The Twenty-Three Standards of the "Social Science Platform"

Contemporaries referred to the twenty-three standards of the "Social Science Platform" variously as "the standards of life and labor," the "Social Standards for Industry," the "Platform of Industrial Minimums," or simply "the Cleveland program." The incorporation of the Social Science Platform into the Progressive party platform had been well thought out by the delegates: "The Progressive Party . . . devoted hours of discussion and consideration to the recommendations of this great National Conference [of Charities and Correction] and made measures of social and industrial justice and health the foremost features of its platform." "A Comparison of the Platforms of the Progressive Party and of the Social Scientists—as to Social and Industrial Justice," a pamphlet with no author indicated, underscored the interrelationship: "Having read the foregoing platform of these great economists and social scientists read the Social and Industrial Justice Planks in the Progressive Platform. You will find that every idea in the Cleveland Platform is found in the Progressive Platform." Lindsay, Kellor, Moskowitz, and Mary Dreier were delegates to the National Progressive party convention. George W. Kirchwey, a professor of law at Columbia, former dean of the Law School, and a member of Columbia University's Legislative Drafting Association, which helped the American Association for Labor Legislation and the National Consumers' League draft labor legislation—brought copies of the twenty-three standards to the party's platform committee.[6]

Just who put pen to paper and who was in the room in Cleveland as members of the Standards of Living and Labor Committee set down the

twenty-three standards of the Social Science Platform has gone unrecorded, but subsequent accounts make clear that New York social scientists were at the center. On the committee were Devine, Kelley, John B.
Andrews, executive secretary of the American Association for Labor Legislation; Pauline Goldmark, associate director and supervisor of the
research bureau at the New York School of Philanthropy, and a leading
figure in the National Consumers' League; Benjamin C. Marsh, a resident of Greenwich House and director of the New York Committee on
Congestion; and Owen Lovejoy, executive secretary of the National
Child Labor Committee. Samuel McCune Lindsay, professor of social
legislation at Columbia, not himself a member of the Standards of Living and Labor Committee, also helped draw up the standards.[7]

Religious, philanthropic, and labor reformers, were also on the draft-
ing committee: V. Everit Macy, New York philanthropist; Julius Henry
Cohen, New York lawyer and urban development specialist; Lee K. Frankel, chemist and member of the American Association for Labor Legislation; Walter Rauschenbusch, noted "social gospel" theologian of the
Rochester, New York Seminary; John A. Ryan, the "labor priest" from
St. Paul, Minnesota; Charles S. Macfarland, executive secretary of the
Federal Council of Churches, headquartered in Manhattan; Dr. Alice
Hamilton, physician and pioneer in industrial disease; William B. Wil-
son, chairman of the Congressional Committee on Labor (ex-secretary-
treasurer of the United Mine Workers, and soon to become the nation's
first Secretary of Labor); Elizabeth Lewis Otey of Chicago, author of *The
Beginnings of Child Labor Legislation*; Margaret Dreier Robins, president of
the National Women's Trade Union League, co-founder of the Women's
Municipal League of New York City, the committee's vice-chair; and
Julian W. Mack, a Chicago judge and reformer, the Conference's president for 1912.[8]

The Social Science Platform preamble set forth its premiss:

The welfare of society and the prosperity of the state require for each individual
such food, clothing, housing conditions, and other necessaries and comforts of
life as will secure and maintain physical, mental and moral health. These are
essentially elements in a normal standard of living, below which society cannot
allow any of its members to live without injuring the public welfare. . . .

The community should bring such subnormal industrial conditions within the
scope of governmental action and control. . . .

Such minimum standards in relation to Wages, Hours, Housing, Safety and
Health, Term of Working Life, and Workman's Compensation are . . . counseled
by physicians and neurologists who have studied the effect of fatigue and over-
strain upon health; by economists who have analyzed the extravagance of
unskilled labor, excessive hours, and low pay; and by social workers who deal
with the human waste of industry through relief societies, or through orphanages, hospitals, insane asylums, and alms houses.[9]

Among "the Standards" were "A Living Wage" and "Eight-hour Day." (See Appendix for the text of the standards.) To give one example:

The Right to a Home. Social welfare demands for every family a safe and a sanitary home; healthful surroundings; ample and pure running water inside the house; modern and sanitary toilet conveniences for its exclusive use, located inside the building; adequate sunlight and ventilation; reasonable fire protection; privacy; rooms of sufficient size and number to decently house the members of the family; freedom from dampness; prompt, adequate collection of all waste materials. These fundamental requirements for normal living should be obtainable by every family, reasonably accessible from place of employment, at a rental not to exceed 20% of the family income.

Six weeks after these standards were drawn up in Cleveland, the "social and industrial justice" planks of the Progressive party's national platform were drafted in early August at the party's Chicago convention. Reflecting the Cleveland standards these planks included a call for legislation on the prevention of industrial accidents and occupational diseases, "overwork, involuntary unemployment"; "minimum safety and health standards . . . and the exercise of the public authority of State and Nation, including the Federal control over inter-State commerce and the taxing power, to maintain such standards." The new party called for prohibition of child labor, minimum wage standards for working women, prohibition of night work for women, an eight-hour day for women and youth; "one day's rest in seven for all wage-workers," "abolition of the convict labor system" "compensation for death by industrial accident and injury and trade diseases which will transfer the burden of lost earnings from the families of working people to the industry, and thus to the community," and "protection of home life against the hazards of sickness, irregular employment and old age through the adoption of a system of social insurance adapted to American use."[10]

"The concentration of modern business, in some degree," the Progressive party platform granted, "is both inevitable and necessary for National and international business efficiency," but it sought federal regulation to "preserve the good while eradicating and preventing its evils." What was needed was "a strong National regulation of inter-State corporations." The platform excoriated the "Old Parties" as "the tools of corrupt interests which use them impartially to serve their selfish purposes," and declared that "an unholy alliance between corrupt business and corrupt politics" was subverting the will of the American people.[11]

The new party's progressive inheritance tax policy—"We believe in a graduated inheritance tax as a National means of equalizing the obligations of holders of property to Government"—drew on the work of Seligman, the Columbia economist, and other new economists; Seligman's 1894 *Progressive Taxation*, well-known to Roosevelt, had promoted just such a view.[12] The party platform's emphasis on efficiency in government was a long-standing concern of political scientist Frank J. Goodnow, as well as Allen, Bruère, and Cleveland of the New York Bureau of Municipal Research. The platform's call for "governmental action to encourage the distribution of immigrants away from the congested cities . . . and to promote their assimilation, education and advancement" were key elements in Simkhovitch's, Kelley's, and Benjamin C. Marsh's New York Committee on Congestion.[13]

The Progressives billed their platform as "A Covenant with the People." In a radical break with Democrats and Republicans, the Progressive party demanded votes for women: "The Progressive Party, believing that no people can justly claim to be a true democracy which denies political rights on account of sex, pledges itself to the task of securing equal suffrage to men and women alike."[14] "To me," Henry Moskowitz, the young scholar-activist from New York's Lower East Side, said, "this third party movement is infinitely bigger than any man. It represents a sort of American crystallization of two of the great movements of our time—the social movement and the woman movement . . . [it is] the psychological moment in which these movements have been crystallized Nationally and brought into politics."[15]

Theodore Roosevelt himself boasted that the Progressive platform was "much the most important document promulgated in this country since the death of Abraham Lincoln. It represented the first effort on a large scale to translate abstract formulas of economic and social justice into concrete American nationalism."[16]

Roosevelt and "the Best People"

Theodore Roosevelt's ties to New York City's scholar-activists had been years in the making. In 1908, Samuel McCune Lindsay wrote to Roosevelt: "Dear Mr. President. . . . We feel the rising tide of socialistic agitation, and we see in your social and economic program the only hope of stemming this tide and preserving the integrity of our American institutions." Roosevelt responded: "the best people in university circles, the social workers and the like—[these are] the men of all others whom I am most anxious to see take a leading part in Republican politics."[17]

John A. Kingsbury, general director of the New York Association for Improving Condition of the Poor, noted that Roosevelt had "conferred freely" with a "distinguished group of social engineers," among them Lindsay, Devine, Moskowitz, and Paul Kellogg. In July 1912 Roosevelt invited these men to lunch at his home on Sagamore Hill on Long Island to discuss "what he proposed to say" on "social and industrial justice" at the National Progressive party convention in Chicago. Kellogg, editor of *The Survey*, later recalled that hot July day when he and a "small company of eight to ten" made their way to Roosevelt's "open veranda and in the shadows of his trophy room." Kellogg wrote to Jane Addams after the convention, "This report [including the twenty-three standards drawn up by the Living and Labor Committee] was all grist to T. R.'s mill in launching the Progressive Party during that summer. Through the initiative of Kingsbury we had a session with him out at Oyster Bay. I wrote some paragraphs which he more or less put into his keynote speech at the Chicago Convention; and he took over the Cleveland program of the standards of life and labor practically bodily, and it was, as you know, incorporated into the Progressive platform."[18]

Formally introduced to the social sciences in his undergraduate years at Harvard in the late 1870s with "An Introduction to Political Economy" and "Political Economy 3," Roosevelt had continued as a student in the Columbia University Law School in 1880 and 1881, where, as the School's dean later recalled, he took "all of the courses in political history, public law, and political science" that the new School of Political Science had to offer. While New York City commissioner of police and as Governor of New York State, Roosevelt kept in touch with the social scientists through conversations and correspondence, and before becoming President he praised the University Settlement's "work of sociological investigation."[19] As President, he had supported Devine, Wald, Kelley, Lindsay, and their allies in their call for creation of a U.S. Children's Bureau (see Chapter 5).

Roosevelt was quite willing to turn away from traditional laissez-faire notions toward an active use of federal government in behalf of social and economic reform. He conceived of government not as a bogey to liberty but as an agent of public service to meet citizens' needs. Becoming President on the assassination of William McKinley in 1901, he had backed expansion of federal regulatory authority through prudent application of the Sherman Anti-Trust Act: in 1902 he ordered his attorney-general to prosecute the Northern Securities Company, and in his two terms his administration filed another twenty-five anti-trust lawsuits. Roosevelt used his executive authority to resolve the 1902 anthracite coal strike, extended federal regulatory power over railroads, increased the power of the Interstate Commerce Commission, and backed the expansion of federal oversight of meat and drug processing facilities through the Meat Inspection Act and Pure Food and Drug Act.

Roosevelt was influenced by a compelling book, *The Promise of American Life*, by Herbert Croly, who had attended the City College of New York and Harvard and had been influenced by the works of Seligman, Simon Patten, and Richard Ely. Croly argued that the nation's ideals could best be achieved by "a government for the people by popular but responsible leaders," in particular political leaders "of intelligence" who would use the power of the state to regulate the central actors in the unfolding drama of the new industrial order—capital and labor, trusts and unions. Roosevelt wrote to Croly: "I do not know when I have read a book which I felt profited me as much as your book on American life. . . . I shall use your ideas freely in speeches I intend to make." In the October 1912 *Outlook*, in an article, "How I Became a Progressive," Roosevelt wrote that "social workers and others who were expert" had been the greatest influence on his thinking on issues of "social and industrial justice."[20]

The Progressive party, like many in the social science elite, did not call for socialistic overthrow of the capitalist system but rather for regulation of its workplaces and markets, as Roosevelt said, through "wise and moderate control." Jeffersonian democracy, based on an agrarian economy accompanied by a minimalist state, was, he said, in need of revision: "Our purposes are the purposes of Thomas Jefferson when he founded the Democratic Party; although the lapse of a century has shown that the extreme individualism and the minimized government control which in that day served to achieve his purposes are in our day no longer serviceable." "All we wish to do on behalf of the people is to meet the nationalization of the big business by nationalized government control," Roosevelt told a lively crowd of supporters in Denver in 1910. The state must become a senior partner in economic affairs: "All that I ask—I do not ask it, I demand it—on behalf of the people is that these corporations submit to such supervision and control as shall insure that . . . there shall go good to the public." He called for employer liability laws, child labor laws, abolition of sweatshops, laws to restrict the hours of labor, and praised the importance of trade unions and "a rate of wages sufficiently high to enable workmen to live in a manner comfortable to American ideals."[21]

Progressivism or Betrayal? Race and the Progressive Party

In the days before the party's convention in Chicago, encouraged by the reports of Jane Addams, Henry Moskowitz, and Joel Spingarn, W. E. B. Du Bois had drafted a plank for the platform:

The Progressive party recognizes that distinctions of race or class in political life have no place in a democracy. Especially does the party realize that a group of 10,000,000 people who have in a generation changed from a slave to a free labor system, reestablished family life, accumulated $1,000,000,000 [in] property, including 20,000,000 acres of land, and reduced their illiteracy from 80 to 30 percent, deserve and must have justice, opportunity and a voice in their own government. The party, therefore, demands for the American of Negro descent the repeal of unfair discriminatory laws and the right to vote on the same terms on which other citizens vote.

An additional sentence had been added to the proposed plank by the time it reached the convention: "The National Progressive Party, therefore, assures the American of African descent of its deep interest in his welfare, and in the gradual recognition by North and South of the principle that the colored man who has the same qualifications that are held to entitle the white man to political representation shall receive the same treatment."[22]

Joel Spingarn, a leading figure in the NAACP, presented Du Bois's plank to Roosevelt in a private meeting at the convention. Roosevelt, the *New York Times* reported, "heartily indorsed" the statement, but the *Times* wrote, "instructed the platform committee to ignore the Du Bois plank," and told Spingarn privately to be "'careful of that man Du Bois."[23]

In the days leading up to the 1912 convention, Alabama, Florida, Georgia, and Mississippi had each contemplated sending, or actually sent, two contested delegations, one that included blacks and one that did not. At the convention Roosevelt threw his support to the white delegates from states with dueling delegations, and the party's credentials committee, in a close 17 to 16 vote, sided with him.[24] Northern and Upper South state delegations that had no dueling groups—border states of Tennessee, Kentucky, Maryland, and West Virginia—sent black delegates to the National Progressive party convention and they were seated without incident, but the black delegations from the four Deep South states were excluded.

Roosevelt had urged a prudent strategy. Only by recognizing the political realities of white racism in the South, with whites' control of the polls, and by devising a plan to cope with such realities, could the Progressive party win the national election. The black delegates from the Deep South states, Roosevelt said, "represent absolutely nothing in the way of voting strength." True, blacks had been systematically disfranchised in the South since Reconstruction, but to change anything, Roosevelt's rationale went, he needed to win the presidency, and to win he needed the South's electoral votes. Yet, in late July, four days before the convention opened, Roosevelt had written a lengthy and widely-publicized letter to Julian La Rose Harris, son of Joel Chandler Harris, author of the famed Uncle Remus stories. It read in part:

In this country we cannot permanently succeed except upon the basis of treating each man on his worth as a man. We can fulfill our high mission among the nations of the earth, we can do lasting good to ourselves and to all mankind, only if we so act that the humblest among us, so long as he behaves in straight and decent fashion, has guaranteed to him under the law his right to life, to liberty, to protection from injustice, his right to enjoy the fruits of his own honest labor, and his right of the pursuit of happiness in his own way, so long as he does not trespass on the rights of others. Our only safe motto is 'All men up' and not 'Some men down.' For us to oppress any class of our fellow citizens is not only wrong to others but hurtful to ourselves; for in the long run such action is no more detrimental to the oppressed than to those who think that they temporarily benefit by the oppression. Surely no man can quarrel with these principles. Exactly as they should be applied among white men without regard to whether they are rich men or poor men, men who work with their hands or men who work with their brains; so they should be applied among all men without regard to the color of their skins.

It was, "essential that we should not [act] in such a way as to make believe that we are achieving these objects, and yet by our actions indefinitely postpone the time when it will become even measurably possible to achieve them." Roosevelt said, "I believe that the Progressive Movement should be made from the beginning one in the interest of every honest, industrious, law-abiding colored man, just as it is in the interest of every honest, industrious, law-abiding white man."[25]

"Our object must be the same everywhere," Roosevelt said, "but the methods by which we strive to attain it must be adapted to the needs of the several states, or it will never be attained at all." In Rhode Island, Maryland, New York, Indiana, Ohio, Illinois, New Jersey, and Pennsylvania, "to speak only of States of which I have personal knowledge"—it was politically possible, Roosevelt said, "at the present moment to bring the best colored men into the movement on the same terms as the white man."

We are now starting a new movement for the betterment of our people, a movement for social and industrial justice which shall be nationwide, a movement which is to strive to accomplish actual results and not to accept high-sounding phrases as a substitute for deeds. Therefore we are not to be pardoned if at the outset, with the knowledge gained by forty-five years' experience of failure [the Republican party's experience in the years since the Civil War], we repeat the course that has led to such failure [since the new party was engaged in] the effort to make the movement for social and industrial justice really nationwide.[26]

When Roosevelt arrived in Chicago for the convention, he found delegates up in arms "over the Negroes." The *New York Times* reported: "When told that scores of negroes were threatening to bolt the new party," Roosevelt replied with a "show of anger." S. D. Redmond, "Chairman of the negro delegation from Mississippi," declared he would "stump the State for Wilson, if the negroes were not given their rights by the Colonel." African American leaders from Chicago, Arkansas, and elsewhere joined the protest. Jane Addams, accompanied by "several others, who were also members of the National Association for the Advancement of Colored People," went to the Committee on Resolutions, then crafting the Progressive party platform, and, the *New York Times* reported, "lifted her voice on behalf of the negroes and warned the new party to 'stop, look, and listen,' before disfranchising in their convention the negroes of the South."[27] Still, after long discussions, Addams acceded to Roosevelt's strategy. Writing in the NAACP's magazine *The Crisis* later that fall, she would say, "I asked myself most searchingly whether my Abolitionist father would have remained in any political convention in which colored men had been treated slightingly." To hold to an ideal stubbornly and narrowly without weighing the practical consequences was not only impractical but short-sighted, hence she decided to stay. Invoking William James' philosophy of American pragmatism, Addams wrote: "moral ideals formed under the influence of new knowledge" might practically mean that it was necessary to embrace a short-term "bad" (the exclusion of African American delegates) for a middle- and long-range "good" (improved living conditions for black and white workers under the auspices of the new party):

The action of the Progressive party had at least taken the colored question away from sectionalism and put it in a national setting which might clear the way for a larger perspective. . . . Imbedded in this new movement is a strong ethical motive, and once the movement is crystallized, once as a body of people it gets a national foothold, once as a propaganda the rank and file are transfused with the full scope and meaning of social justice, it is bound to lift this question of the races, as all other questions, out of the grip of the past and into a new era of solution.[28]

A group of twenty-three black delegates to the Progressive party convention, in an "Official Statement" of support for Roosevelt and the party, asserted that: "The charge of lily-whitism against the Progressive Convention is false." "We heartily welcome the leadership of Theodore Roosevelt—a man of courage, convictions and unquestioned integrity."[29] But other black leaders did not buy it and walked out. "We've been with the Colonel because we expected fair play,'" said G. B. Ellis, a black delegate from Chicago. "'If we don't get it the Colonel don't get our votes.'" The party's Council of Chairmen of the Progressive Service took up "the negro problem" at an April 1913 meeting but: "No definite conclusion . . . was reached." Du Bois, hoping for the "possibility of an arrangement with the Democrats," supported Wilson instead.[30] But no "arrangement" came along after Wilson's victory. Indeed, Wilson was complicit in segregating the offices of the federal government (see Chapter 7).

"From the Women in Political Bondage: Vote the Progressive Ticket to Make Us Free"

Women, another disenfranchised group, fared better than did blacks with the Progressive party and its leaders. Women played a central role in leadership positions in the party, though a role still generally unrecognized. Jane Addams, for example, seconded Roosevelt's nomination at Chicago, "stirred by the splendid platform adopted by this Convention."

Measures of industrial amelioration, demands for social justice, long discussed by small groups in charity conferences and economic associations, have here been considered in a great convention, and are at last thrust into the stern arena of political action. A great party has pledged itself to the protection of children, to the care of the aged, to the relief of overworked girls, to the safeguarding of burdened men. Committed to these humane undertakings it is inevitable that such a party should appeal to women, should seek to draw upon the great reservoir of their moral energy so long undesired and unutilized in practical politics—one is the corollary of the other; a programme of human welfare, the participation of women in political life.[31]

In a note of thanks to Addams the day after the convention, Roosevelt wrote: "I prized your action, not only because of what you are and stand for, but because of what it symbolized for the new movement. In this great national convention, starting the new party, women have thereby been shown to have their place to fill precisely as men have, and on an absolute equality."[32]

Women in six far western states had the right, by their state constitutions, to vote in national elections—Wyoming, Colorado, Utah, Idaho, Washington, and California. In a close election the electoral votes of those states might swing the presidency to the Progressive candidate. A leaflet, "To the Women Voters of the United States from the Women in Political Bondage: Vote the Progressive Ticket to Make Us Free," signed by Frances A. Kellor, Jane Addams, Mary Dreier, and fifteen other women, appealed to women in those six states.

[The Progressive party represents] those humanitarian measures, for which women in their clubs and associations and trade unions have worked for so many years. . . . Now, for the first time in the history of our country, a great party has assembled these measures and is urging a program of social and industrial legislation for which women have so long been striving. The Progressive party is the only party that has pledged itself to work for suffrage, so that for the first time, the women of the six equal suffrage states have an opportunity to vote for candidates who are committed to extend suffrage to women throughout the Nation.[33]

In the *Progressive Bulletin* an article by Kellor, "What Women Can Do for the Progressive Cause—Why They Should Do It," urged women to organize "in every district, however small," for the new party offered an "unparalleled opportunity for all women interested in civic and social life to participate in an active, nation-wide campaign to win the things for which they have worked individually."[34]

Who was "Truly a Progressive"? Social Scientists on All Sides in the Election

Not all social scientists in the New York network supported Theodore Roosevelt. "I presume," Henry Rogers Seager, Columbia political economist and president of the American Association for Labor Legislation, wrote to John B. Andrews, AALL executive secretary, in mid-August 1912, "you have seen the platform of the Bull Moose party, but enclosed one on the chance you have not. As a platform it is a splendid grist for our mill & Lindsay and others are enthusiastic about it. However, I cannot shake off my doubts as to Roosevelt and I intend to help Wilson into the White House all I can though apparently he is going to need little assistance." Wilson not only supported the work of the American Association of Labor Legislation but had, until his term as governor of New Jersey began, been one of its vice presidents, and as governor Wilson had demonstrated that he was an aggressive proponent of government intervention in the public interest. He had supported a workman's compensation law, worked to regulate corporate trusts in the state, and backed state regulation of public utilities. Indeed, *The Outlook*, for which Roosevelt was a contributing editor, had endorsed Wilson's 1910 run for governor as "not only the representative but the champion of the progressive movement" in New Jersey. Wilson's gubernatorial candidacy, said *The Outlook*, showed that progressivism cut across party lines; after his victory in 1910, the magazine repeated that he was "truly a progressive," "a man of broad Progressive views."[35]

Wilson was a dark-horse candidate for president at the 1912 Democratic party convention, and had surfaced as the actual nominee only after an intense five-day, forty-six ballot battle. At a crucial juncture William Jennings Bryan threw his support to Wilson. The party's nomination of this Virginia-born political scientist with a Johns Hopkins Ph.D. was not the result of a cool calculus about who was likely to defeat Roosevelt in the fall election, but it might as well have been. For with Wilson's nomination Roosevelt was robbed of the possibility of running against a more conservative Democrat in the fall election. Following Wilson's nomination, some of Roosevelt's own staunchest early supporters began to have second thoughts. Oscar King Davis, the newspaper reporter turned Progressive party activist, wrote later that, with Wilson's nomination, "it was clear to us at Progressive headquarters that there was no practical possibility of victory for us at the election."[36] (If the Democrats had held their party convention before the Republicans they might—without knowledge of a Roosevelt third-party run—have nominated a more conservative candidate; if they had met first and nominated Wilson, Roosevelt might well not have bolted the GOP.)

Wilson, former professor of political science at Bryn Mawr College, Wesleyan University, and Princeton, was a prolific author, among his books, *Congressional Government: A Study in American Politics* (1885), *The State: Elements of Historical and Practical Politics* (1898), and a popular five-volume *A History of the American People* (1902). Aided in drawing up his campaign strategy by "the people's lawyer" Louis D. Brandeis, also a vice president of the American Association for Labor Legislation, Wilson adopted "The New Freedom" as his campaign slogan. He accused Roosevelt of seeking to destroy individual freedom through an overreaching federal government that, while regulating trusts and monopolies, would become an intrusive behemoth. Yet, the "New Freedom" itself, while it stressed states' rights over federal control, called for an active federal government to break up corporate trusts. Roosevelt condemned Wilson's "rural toryism," by which he meant his advocacy of the break-up of corporations. In Roosevelt's view Wilson held a too aggressive stance on large corporations, favoring dissolution not mere regulation, an uninspired return to the small producer ideology of the nineteenth century, which would lead back to the same competitive practices that had led to long hours, lower pay, and unsafe working conditions in a market saturated with many small producers.[37]

Wilson, for his part, portrayed Roosevelt as dangerously radical. "The history of liberty is the history of the limitation of governmental power," Wilson said in mid-September. Roosevelt was proposing to remove historical limitations on the regulatory power of government and create a master state that would crush individual liberties. Roosevelt replied that Wilson's logic would mean "that every law for the promotion of social and industrial justice which has been put upon the statute books ought to be repealed." He told a crowd of 16,000 in New York's Madison Square Garden in the closing days of the campaign: "We are for liberty. But we are for the liberty of the oppressed, and not for the liberty of the oppressor to oppress the weak and to bind the burdens on the shoulders of the heavy laden. It is idle to ask us not to exercise the powers of government when only by that power of government can we curb the greed that sits in the high places, when only by the exercise of the government can we exalt the lowly and give heart to the humble and downtrodden."[38]

Some social science activists in New York supported neither Wilson nor Roosevelt but the socialist Eugene Debs. As it had in the previous three elections, the Socialist party ran Debs on a platform that adapted a Marxian sociology and economics to American circumstances. After Debs was sent to jail in 1894 for violating a court injunction against striking with the American Railway Union, he read social theory—specifically, the works of Karl Marx—and was converted to socialism. His American Socialist party supported many of the worker-benefit and social insurance programs Roosevelt and the Progressives were to champion in the election, but not in a regulatory state within a free market economy; he called for the overthrow of capitalism itself as "utterly incapable of meeting the problems now confronting society," and "incompetent and corrupt."[39]

The philosopher John Dewey served briefly as co-director of the Progressive party's Committee on Education—the committee sought to bring "progressive education" to the public schools—but he said he voted for Debs.[40] Charles A. Beard, a director and lecturer at the socialist Rand School for Social Science and associate professor of politics at Columbia, while sympathetic to the Progressive agenda preferred the political left, and he may also have gone for Debs. Florence Kelley, a member of the Socialist party, who had helped draft the "Social Science Platform" in Cleveland, also held political views to Roosevelt's left, although as a woman she was not eligible to vote. (Her friend and fellow Henry Street Settlement House resident, Lillian Wald supported the Progressive party.)[41]

On the other side of the political spectrum, and outside the liberal left, John W. Burgess, the politically conservative dean of Columbia's School of Political Science, supported William Howard Taft, the Republican party nominee. Burgess celebrated Taft's conservative agenda and wrote disparagingly of "the so called progressive platform [that] looks to a further centralization of governmental power."[42] When Taft's vice-presidential running-mate, James Schoolcraft Sherman, died only six days before the November 5th election, Nicholas Murray Butler, Columbia University president, himself a supporter of a politically conservative social science, replaced Sherman on the Republican ballot. Butler's address, "What is Progress in Politics?," before the Commercial Club of Chicago the month after the election argued that Progress meant that America "should push forward along the road already traveled. . . . and do so in a spirit that will not lead the individual to lean more heavily upon the community, but rather help him to stand up more surely and confidently upon his own feet."[43]

"Defined by Scientific Laws and . . . Manned by Experts"

With the Progressive party's national headquarters in the Manhattan Hotel at 42nd Street and the corner of Madison Avenue, many scholar-activists of New York were active in party affairs. Frances Perkins, executive secretary of the Consumers' League's New York branch, said of Roosevelt that: "the sufferings of the poor, the neglected, the oppressed . . . and the right and duty of those who were advantaged to do something about that, he understood." "That was why," Perkins explained, "all the young people of my generation thought he was wonderful."[44] A number attended both the national convention in Chicago and the New York State convention, held a few weeks later, in Syracuse where New York City social science activists took the lead in writing the state political platform. Lindsay and Henry Moskowitz wrote drafts of the platform, Seligman, a member of the state party's Committee on Resolutions, penciled in suggested revisions.[45] (Plank 16 on "Social and Industrial Justice," followed "the recommendations of a committee of the National Conference of Charities and Correction"—i.e., the Living and Labor Committee which had drawn up the Cleveland Social Science Platform—calling for an end to child labor, " 'living wage' for working women," and for a constitutional amendment on workmen's compensation, and for "radical and persistent attack on congestion of population, bad housing, and all other preventable causes of poverty."[46]) The drafts were combined under Roosevelt's watchful eye: a few days before the state convention, William H. Hotchkiss, a prominent lawyer and the party's state chairman, wrote Moskowitz with an air of urgency: "I have tried to get you on the telephone several times since you were here today. Colonel Roosevelt is very anxious to see the preliminary draft of the [New York State] platform on Sunday and I expect to go there with it, hence, tried to get you on the 'phone and also tried to get in touch with Mr. Lindsay."[47] At the New York State convention, Seligman delivered the principal speech in support of the platform. "We are not opposed to wealth, to capital, to industry, to liberty," he declared. "On the contrary, we realize that they in conjunction have helped to make this country what it is." The Progressive party was heading "the ship of state in the right direction," away from "plutocratic Republicanism" and ineffective Democratic rule, he said. "The need of a new party in New York is especially urgent."[48]

Some scholar-activists, like the sociologist Frances Kellor, who headed the party's important Progressive Service, were members of the party's decision-making inner council. Columbia political scientist Frank J. Goodnow served on the party's national Legislative Committee. Henry Bruère and William Allen of the Bureau of Municipal Research sent copies of their recently published books—Bruère's *The New City Government*, and Allen's *Modern Philanthropy*—along with notes of support, to Roosevelt, no doubt hoping to influence policies.[49]

Henry Moskowitz, who had been active in the social science network for years, not content with influence in inner circles, ran as the Progressive party candidate for Congress from the twelfth congressional district in Manhattan. He was a man of "intellectual polish" who talked "with fire and conviction." In one of his campaign speeches he said, "'industry wears out the body and does not feed the soul. . . . Worst of all . . . is the fact that the law, which operates instantaneously to protect property, moves with leaden feet when measures are proposed to lighten labor's burdens. . . . the law is weighted against the working man.'" He lost his bid for Congress to Henry M. Goldfogle, the Democrat.[50]

Frances Kellor, sociologist and lawyer, did perhaps more than any other for the new party, as a delegate to the Chicago convention, a member of the party's national committee, and as leader of its Progressive Service, the core organization that, after the election, would hold party hopefuls together and plot a path for its future. "One of the finest souls I ever met," Roosevelt wrote in 1913.[51]

After Wilson won the election—Roosevelt had placed second, Taft third, in the popular vote—the Progressive party structure needed shoring up, and Kellor undertook the challenge. She herself had proposed the plan for the Progressive Service and was asked to direct its research, education, and legislative efforts.[52] Lindsay, Kirchwey, Moskowitz, and Kellogg joined her "Council of Chairmen," and an outpouring of support came from others in the social science network. Wald, Lindsay, Moskowitz, Goodnow, and Cornell professor of economics Walter F. Willcox served on the new party's national Legislative Committee; Jane Addams headed the Social and Industrial Justice Committee, and Devine, Kellogg, and Walter F. Willcox served with Addams. George W. Kirchwey, the Columbia law professor who had run unsuccessfully on the 1912 Progressive ticket for judge of the New York Court of Appeals, headed its Legislative Reference Bureau and its Child Welfare Committee.[53] Lindsay, who had chaired the party's New York State Committee on Resolutions, led a major group in the Service's Bureau of Education, with several distinguished social scientists on his staff. Active also on the party's 1913 Progressive National Convention Platform Committee and on the party's Child Welfare Committee, Lindsay promoted initiatives on minimum wage, unemployment, compensation for industrial accidents, sickness insurance, unemployment, and old age until he was sidelined by typhoid at the end of that year.[54]

The Progressive Service sought to "keep the promises of the platform," as "a scientific organization which studies political and social conditions; which prescribes remedies in the form of laws; which arouses public opinion through an understanding of the conditions revealed and the remedies proposed." Its methods, not surprisingly, were those of the social sciences—research, promulgation of findings, and lobbying for legislation. Kellor hoped that the party's agenda might be "'defined by scientific laws and . . . manned by experts.'" With all this in mind, the Progressive Service produced literature, organized a Lyceum Service of public speakers, supported a Committee on Education, drafted legislation, lobbied, and sent members to testify at government hearings. It worked to implement the party platform on workmen's compensation, hours, and wage legislation at both state and federal levels and in 1913 initiated a "Progressive Congressional Program" of sixteen legislative acts in an effort to implement various planks of the 1912 party platform.[55]

As Wilson's first term progressed, it became apparent that one of the likeliest places to find the votes he needed for a second term was among Roosevelt's former supporters. With Democratic party majorities in both houses of Congress, Wilson achieved much of the Progressive party's own legislative agenda, expanding the scope and regulatory authority of the federal government. He signed into law an act establishing a Federal Trade Commission with power to stop unfair business practices; the Clayton Anti-Trust Act, expanding the federal government's authority to act against monopolistic practices; the Keating-Owen Child Labor Act (1916), the first federal law barring goods made by children from interstate commerce; the Adamson Act, establishing an eight-hour day for employees on interstate railroads; a workmen's compensation act covering federal employees; and a Federal Aid Road Act providing funds for state highway construction. Wilson had appointed to the newly created post of Secretary of Labor William B. Wilson, a former miner and secretary-treasurer of the United Mine Workers, who had been a member of the Living and Labor Committee of the National Conference of Charities and Correction that had drawn up those twenty-three standards in Cleveland. He appointed the celebrated liberal lawyer Louis D. Brandeis to the U.S. Supreme Court, ally of social scientists in the *Muller v. Oregon* case. By September 1916, Wilson would claim: "We have in four years come very near to carrying out the platform of the Progressive party."[56]

The Kansas journalist William Allen White, friend of Theodore Roosevelt and Progressive party supporter, wrote: "So long as the Democratic party continues its present progressive leadership there is no chance for the Progressives, and so far as that goes, we don't care for the offices while the Democrats carry out the principles of the Progressive platform."[57] And when, in the summer of 1914, the First World War broke out in Europe and the economic downturn that had plagued the economy was reversed in war-related prosperity, White noted: "The Bull Moose party, which was founded upon a demand for distributive justice, using government as an agency of human welfare, lost its cause. . . . Our little army of colonels drilled lonesomely on the parade ground of a lost cause."[58]

In the Progressive Service Frances Kellor and other social scientists in the New York network had worked earnestly, hopeful that the Progressive party might take root at the local level, but the anticipated growth never materialized. By 1915, after repeated losses in state-level mid-term elections, the Progressive party was in shambles and dead by 1916. Still, its 1912 platform remains a crucial document in American political history, its influence felt not only in Woodrow Wilson's two presidential terms, but also in the regulatory state of the social welfare and labor programs of Franklin Roosevelt's New Deal, Harry S Truman's Fair Deal, and even, perhaps, John Kennedy's New Frontier, and Lyndon Johnson's Great Society.

The 1912 presidential election had been, in part, a referendum on which of four politicized uses of social science—John W. Burgess's conservative vision, Eugene Debs' socialist agenda, Woodrow Wilson's "middle way" political science approach, or Theodore Roosevelt's progressivism— could best lead an industrializing nation, now the world's richest. Social scientists on the liberal left, as the pamphlet comparing the social scientists and the Progressive party's 1912 platforms said, "spent a quarter of a century in promoting [their agenda] utterly without encouragement or help from either of the old parties."[59] Social scientists and social science had now moved from the political periphery to center stage in American party politics. The 1912 presidential election was not only a watershed in American political history, it was also an important juncture in the history of the social sciences and in the history of the rise of social scientists into a position of influence, even power. Yet those who honored science and learning knew that politics could taint that search. The goal was to influence the political world without losing independence or being coopted. Powerful forces of industry and politics could only be persuaded or compelled to social justice by public backing.

Epilogue

In a whirlwind of advocacy and research in Progressive-Era America, social science practitioners along with professors at New York's leading universities joined to make their city "the greatest social science laboratory in the world." And yet the new departure made possible by social science was, from the outset, characterized by intellectual and ethical ambiguities and dynamic, unresolved tensions. A remarkable group of people, these brilliant and daring men and women of New York City's social science scholar-activist network were frequently of no like minds.

They all made instrumental use of social science, some committed to the view that a coherent science of the social could be achieved and that through that science human society might be re-constructed. But the transformation they sought was often stymied, and, as they discovered, their social science research could tell them only so much. It could tell them how many were poor, or how much money was siphoned out of the city's treasury by a corrupt administration, or how many children labored in sweatshops, but it couldn't tell them—in any traditionally understood scientific sense as physics, chemistry, or biology defined it— what to do about it. Although they sometimes argued about the facts—as when Franz Boas and W. E. B. Du Bois disagreed with those who assumed the inferiority of certain ethnic and racial groups—they much more frequently disagreed about the framework within which to interpret the data and on the ends they wanted to achieve. The social world, contingent and uncertain, eluded a commonly agreed upon understanding of it, and divided temperaments, biases, and backgrounds led to divergent views on means and on ends.

On the contested terrain of Progressive-Era New York City, progressive social science scholar-activists disagreed among themselves, and also with social scientists of a more conservative persuasion. Quarrels on principle and tensions between dissenters were commonplace. Thus, politically conservative social scientists such as Columbia political scientist John W. Burgess held firmly to the view that minimalist government if combined with the energies of a competitive market economy would yield the greatest liberty and promote the good society. Burgess painted a vision of corporate capitalists as leaders of that good society and corporate power as aegis against overbearing government, as described in his 1898 essay, "Private Corporations from the Point of View of Political Science."[1] But in that same year, James B. Reynolds, head resident at University Settlement on Manhattan's Lower East Side and fellow in sociology at Columbia's School of Political Science, answered back that, to the contrary: "the best interests of society demand . . . the assumption by the general government of such powers as corporations have assumed in the interests and supposedly in the service of the public."[2] It was a bitter disagreement, and one that divided social scientists throughout the Progressive Era in New York, as it divided social scientists nationally and internationally, then and still. New York's progressive scholar-activist network generally promoted middle-way economic, social, and political solutions, urging abandonment of laissez-faire doctrines. Government was not a bogey, they said, and guided by social science could be a truly useful instrument for mitigating poverty and improving people's lives. Theirs was a vision that engrossed the participants in Manhattan's era of social reform.

But even among those scholar-activists who dismissed the conservative perspective as untenable there was disagreement about just how to craft the good society. The radicalism of Florence Kelley and others conflicted with the modern-liberal reformism of Edwin R. A. Seligman, Mary Kingsbury Simkhovitch, and others. Such differences were reflected in the city's institutions of social science as well, from the socialist Rand School of Social Science to Columbia University, where modern liberal and conservative social science perspectives flourished together. But even at Columbia those who ventured into radicalism could find themselves unemployed, pushed out by the university's conservative Trustees and President. Charles Beard resigned, but socialist Daniel DeLeon and others had been pushed out.

Yet the necessity of working within the realpolitik of the current order drew radicals and moderate reformers together in common cause. Their politics was most often based on practical consideration and the principal framework for their actions was reformist. Florence Kelley, director of the National Consumers' League, was a socialist, but her National Consumers' League advocated consumer responsibility in making purchases and lobbying for government regulation, not revolution. In the Manhattan offices of the New York Bureau of Municipal Research near City Hall, as in the corridors of Columbia's social science departments on Morningside Heights and elsewhere, scholars joined to condemn the corrosive corruption of Tammany Hall and to scrutinize the power of Wall Street, but they gave primary attention to making government less corrupt and more responsive to citizens' needs, despite some thinly veiled words of bitterness exchanged between radicals like Charles

Beard and William Allen and moderates like Frank J. Goodnow and Frederick Cleveland. The economists and sociologists of the American Association for Labor Legislation sought to expand the regulatory nature of government to help workers, not overthrow the capitalist system, even as some of the wealth-elite, whose power and privilege they challenged, claimed they were "on the ragged edge of socialism." Isaac Rubinow, a socialist, dedicated himself to achieving a government-run universal health care system, not to proletarian rebellion. The NAACP and National Urban League sought to resist the national tidal wave of bigotry by promoting equal justice before the law and by developing economic opportunity with goals of inclusion and resolution, not revolution—even though at least two of its principal founders, W. E. B. Du Bois and Mary White Ovington, were Socialist Party members. In the New York Charity Organization Society, the New York School of Philanthropy, and the city's settlement houses, where notions of noblesse oblige elitism clashed with concerns for deliberative democracy, revolution was off the agenda. The Progressive Party's "Social Science Platform" did not demand workers' ownership of the means of production, distribution, and exchange; it sought rather a new governmental activism of regulation.

With the advent of graduate programs in social science a structured secular alternative to the clergy's authority had developed, in the late nineteenth century modern research university, and with it, possibilities were opened up for revisiting traditional views on which the social world was constructed—the social place of men, women, and children, of wealth-elites and the poor, and of blacks and whites might all be reassessed. Intellectual heirs of the secular and scientific eighteenth century Enlightenment, New York City's social scientists were part of a larger national and international culture of belief-in-proportion-to-the-evidence science that clashed with religions' other-worldly beliefs. Some practitioners of science or social science dismissed a conflation of science and faith—as did the president of Stanford University, David S. Jordan in 1895, when he wrote that "the word 'Christian' prefixed to the name of any science is a species of venerable quackery."[3] But in New York's network, the relationship between religious belief and instrumental use of social science was somewhat more complex. Scholar-activists in New York were often nonreligious in practice—as were Frances Kellor, W. E. B. Du Bois, Franklin Giddings, Edwin R.A. Seligman, and Henry Moskowitz. But many were men and women of strong, if often unorthodox, religious faith—as were Frances Perkins, Josephine Shaw Lowell, Mary Kingsbury Simkhovitch, George Edmund Haynes, Jeremiah W. Jenks, and Samuel McCune Lindsay. Indeed, it is one conclusion of this book that in New York's social science network of research and reform, the Jamesean tough-minded joined with the tender-minded in common cause for achievement of a society characterized by humanistic values.

Philosophically physicalistic, materialistic, and observation-based, social science itself could generate claims on the nature of reality, but could offer no sure duty or *ought*. Moral imagining—imagining that racism should and could be smashed, or that children should have the chance to learn in school instead of wasting away in life-rotting industrial labor, or that, in some other ways, the current social order might be remade—was essential. Social scientists' emphasis on reform was made possible, in part, because their observation of social relations had demonstrated to them that those relations had once been *formed* by humans and so might be reformed (literally, formed again) by them. Observation of everyday human interaction made plain the socially constructed nature of the social. But the idea that social relations were socially constructed and so might be reconstructed was not derived in this way only. The U.S. Constitution had been written in light of the seventeenth and eighteenth century propositions of Hobbes, Locke, Hume and others, that legitimate political authority derives from humans, not from God; and it was an extension of that Enlightenment worldview—that social relations were of a similar nature—that social scientists promoted. In modern American democracy, it was plain, social relations were shaped by citizens' views and votes (and sometimes their guns). And, so shaped, could be reshaped. But it was not only an extension of Enlightenment philosophy and politics that gave rise to an understanding that what was made by humans might be remade by them, it was also the sheer fact that traditional social relations were—quite separate from social science scholar-activists or the Enlightenment Constitutionalism of the national polity—being wrenchingly remade in the caldron of the market revolution.

Social science scholar-activists and their fellow citizens were the inheritors of a moment in human history unlike any before it, inheritors of a rapidly changing economic order in industrial revolution—itself a complex of market forces and innovative ideas in science and applied science—that was churning abundant and rapid social, economic, and intellectual change. The rapid shift away from an overwhelmingly agrarian society—in 1800 more than seventy-five percent of men worked full-time in agriculture, less than two percent of the American population does so today—to an industrial and later postindustrial one signaled that much *was* new. The blister of overlapping and mutually reinforcing revolutions—industrial, urban, immigrant, scientific, technological, communication, and transportation primary among them—had made the world a different place and in a variety of ways remade human social relations.

In unsettling traditional social relations, the market revolution had made plain the malleable nature of social relations. Life's expectations, and its cadences and rhythms, were alterable—not by theorizing the possibilities but by actually changing them.

These convulsions of change were nowhere more in evidence than in Progressive-Era New York City. The slow moving, weather-dependent agrarian life of sowing, harvesting, milking, and mending was absent in industrial and commercial Gotham—workers performed tasks rather than making complete products, they were "hands" tending seasonless, never-tiring machines. By 1913 the U.S. was turning out a third of the world's industrial output, and New York City with its 30,000 manufacturers, ranked first in the nation's industrial output. In the Progressive Era's innovation and change, excitement grew about social science as a tool that could help make sense of the swirl and point to a direction that could understand and control the changes. If, as was common in the Progressive Era, citizens could make toast in electric toasters, or substitute automotive horsepower for horse power, could they not also revise the hours a man, woman, or child ought to labor in factories and consider outlawing tenement sweatshops? Might not even the social place of blacks and women be reassessed? Might not the market revolution be regulated by social controls of government, and government, in turn, be democratically directed by the people and civic and intellectual leaders?

If there was to be reform, the next question was how. Federalism—the American system of government in which individual states (there were forty-eight by February 1912) and the federal government shared sovereignty—could make reform a maddeningly complex affair. On a particular issue, in what branch of government—federal, state, or local—did actual decision-making power lie? The Constitution's supremacy clause clashed with its Tenth Amendment guarantee of states' rights time and again. Which branch of government had primary jurisdiction over, for example, child labor law: the president, Congress, federal courts, governors, state legislators, state judicial systems, or a government appointed commission? Reform sometimes appeared to be a continuous game of musical chairs—who could know, when the music stopped, whether the federal or state governments had final authority, or if, after a law was enacted, the U.S. Supreme Court would find it unconstitutional.

Sometimes historians have argued that the reformers of the era began with local efforts and that over time their efforts grew into national ones, and to some degree this is true. But intellectuals are smart people, and the New York network of scholar-activists, studied as they were on how decisions are made and where power lies in the polity, took a multi-tiered, action-at-all-levels approach that saw them make use of efforts at every level of government.

Social science scholar-activists sought a multiplicity of lines of advancement for the causes they held dear, approaching the nation's rich, if frequently maddening, decision-making matrix with an understanding of its musical-chairs quality. They enlisted the president as ally in creating the U.S. Children's Bureau in 1912 (the successful effort set in motion when Edward T. Devine—from his offices in the United Charities Building, and at the urging of Lillian Wald and Florence Kelley— sent President Theodore Roosevelt a telegram about the need). They enlisted the Supreme Court as ally in upholding the legislature's right to make laws regulating industrial capitalism (for women, at least) as in their 1908 "Brandeis brief" in *Muller v. Oregon* (prepared by Josephine Goldmark, Florence Kelley, Helen Marot, and others of the New York social science network). They enlisted Congress on issues from phossy-jaw phosphorus poisoning to women's rights in repeated appearances before congressional committees. Frances Perkins's face-to-face lobbying of New York State legislators paid off in a bill that reduced women's hours of work in industry. The New York Bureau of Municipal Research initiated efforts to discover and end corruption at Manhattan's City Hall. They used party politics to help achieve their goals, as when, in the 1912 Progressive Party key members of New York's social science network captured coveted seats at the party's inner circle. They made direct appeals to ordinary citizens, promoting their research, analysis, and solutions through books, articles, pamphlets and letters, and in public and private conferences, meetings, and lectures. It was on their shoulders—a legacy of the social science scholar-activist's Progressive-Era efforts—that the social policies and the regulatory government of Franklin Roosevelt's New Deal, Harry Truman's Fair Deal, John Kennedy's New Frontier, and Lyndon Johnson's Great Society stood.

In their voluntary associational organizations the social science scholar-activists of New York served not only as formative thinkers, but as political actors as well: community organizers, lobbyists, and legal strategists. And in their role as advocates they often tangled with the powerful who came to see them, at times, not as allies but as opponents. Just as, in their role as university trustees, the wealth-elite disciplined dissent by firing social science faculty members they judged too radical, so, in the emerging world of the modern foundation, wealthy trustees of the nation's new private philanthropies tangled with social scientists who sought foundation money without ideological strings attached—as was the case in the acrimonious relationship between the political scientist William Allen and trustees at the Rockefeller Foundation in 1914.

Sometimes opposition to social scientists arose from leaders of other alternative and competing institutions, as from Samuel Gompers, the American Federation of Labor's president, who considered the efforts of the "sociological scientists" of the American Association for Labor Legislation "attempts to exploit the wage-earners." And when social scientists stepped in to end municipal corruption and re-direct the role of government in New York, some public officials resisted, well aware that social change would lead to their ouster.

For women and for African Americans New York's social science network offered a way to break through traditional barriers of ignorance and inequality. The many white women and the smaller number of African American men who were members of New York's social science scholar-activist network broke new ground for modern feminism and civil rights. Still, they were also fiercely resisted by the continuing prejudices of the day. Yet it was in the milieu of social science scholarship that women and blacks achieved greater advancement than in any other aspect of that society. Fraught with potential hazards and traps of purported scientific claims of racial and gender inferiority, the social sciences—empirical, and observation-based, and disallowing firm certainty of dogmatic belief—allowed the possibility of new paradigms of knowledge and new constructions of the social world. Josephine Shaw Lowell's and W. E. B. Du Bois's challenges to the established social order opened up new chances for those who followed after them. The achievement of Florence Kelley built on the foundations of Josephine Shaw Lowell; George Edmund Haynes's advances benefited from Du Bois's labors.

The relationship between social science and democracy remained in unresolved but dynamic tension between the concept of social science as a great democratizing force and as an elitist enterprise. The paradox of democratic elitism remained unresolved. "Social control" was much written about in Progressive-Era America, in fundamental ambiguity. On the one side, social control was used to signal the fact that humans might, for the first time, broadly as a culture, gain conscious control over the social world. On the other side, social control implied that some one or another group in society was seeking dominance over ordinary citizens, either through subtle manipulation or even by force. Were the evidence and results of social scientists' empirical research accessible to all as a common ground for democratic decision-making and hence of an enhanced deliberative democracy? Were social scientists guides for democracy, their role, as Paul Kellogg had put it, "to bring the knowledge and inventions of scientists and experts home to the common imagination, and to gain for their proposals the dynamic backing of a convinced democracy"?[4] Was social science a leveling tool against traditional hierarchical authorities of bourgeoisie and clergy? Or did the dominant model for Progressive Era intellectuals herald a dissolution of democracy under a technocracy of technical, social scientific expertise? The puzzle was unresolved in Progressive Era New York City and remains unresolved to this day, a central tension in modern political, economic, and social life, and in the academy, a tension suggesting the need for persistent vigilance.

The young intellects drawn to New York in the Progressive Era built a cross-disciplinary associational network linking their efforts not only with other social science scholar-activists outside the city, but with the era's other reformers—the social gospellers, reform-minded journalists, women's club members, and so on.

The scholar-activists in New York fed on and fed a larger web of knowledge and action—simultaneously learning from and teaching like-minded men and women in Chicago, Philadelphia, Boston, and Baltimore, and also in Berlin, Halle, Paris, and London. This book examines the core of that rich activity, "the greatest social science laboratory in the world" of New York City, the ferment of affiliation in a time of extraordinary change, in a place of boundless energy. In that laboratory they had, as Mary Kingsbury Simkhovitch said, made "a passionate attempt to realize democracy."[5]

Curious, reasoning, and dedicated to the work of scholarship and of the good society, many in the small group of men and women who built the social science scholar-activist network in New York City and worked in its social laboratory were not New Yorkers to begin with but had come from small towns in the Midwest, New England, and the Mid-Atlantic states and as emigrants from Europe. It was a fundamentally American network, Jews, Christians, and atheists, women and men, black and white—despite the severe restrictions on equal opportunity of the day and within the network. They had been drawn to the country's leading metropolis because it was, as a group of them said, "the greatest social science laboratory in the world."[6] And when it came time to lead, in the public realm using the fruits of their research and study, they did not shy away from the responsibility. This generation of social science trained and dedicated intellectuals and intelligentsia took their energies and effort into the public realm and, in doing so, helped transform their city, and to a considerable degree, the nation.

Appendix

The twenty-three standards of the "Social Science Platform," adopted at the June 1912 annual meeting of the National Conference of Charities and Correction, held that year in Cleveland, Ohio. Source: "A Comparison of the Platforms of the Progressive Party and of the Social Scientists—as to Social and Industrial Justice," printed pamphlet (n.p., 1912?), 2–3, Theodore Roosevelt Collection, Houghton Library, Harvard University.

The Standards

A Living Wage. A living wage for all who devote their time and energy to industrial occupations. The monetary equivalent of a living wage varies according to local conditions, but must include enough to secure the elements of a normal standard of living; to provide for education and recreation; to care for immature members of the family; to maintain the family during periods of sickness; and to permit of reasonable saving for old age.

Minimum Wage Commissions. Many industrial occupations, especially where women, children, and immigrant men are employed, do not pay wages to maintain a normal standard of living. Minimum wage commissions should therefore be established in each state to inquire into wages paid in various industries, and to determine the standard which the public will sanction as the minimum.

Wage Publicity. Properly constituted authorities should be empowered to require all employers to file with them for public purposes such wage scales, and other data as to earnings as the public element in industry demands. The movement for honest weights and measures has its counterpart in industry. All tallies, scales, and check system should be open to public inspection and inspection of committees of the workers concerned. Changes in wage rates, systems of dockage, bonuses, and all other modifications of the wage contract should be posted, and wages should be paid in cash at least every two weeks.

Eight-Hour Day. The establishment of the eight-hour day for all men employed in continuous industries, and as a maximum for women and minors in all industries.

Six-Day Week. The work period limited to six days in each week; and a period of rest of forty consecutive hours each week.

Night Work. Night work for minors entirely prohibited; an uninterrupted period of at least eight hours night rest for all women; and night work for men minimized wherever possible.

Investigation. An investigation of the Federal Government of all industries, on the plan pursued in the present investigation of mining, with a view to establishing standards of sanitation and safety and a basis for compensation for injury. This should include a scientific study and report upon fire-escapes, safety-appliances, sanitary conditions, and the effects of ventilation, dust, poisons, heat, cold, compressed air, steam, glare, darkness, speed and noise.

Prohibition of Poisons. Prohibition of manufacture or sale of poisonous articles dangerous to life of worker, wherever harmless substitutes are possible, on the principle already established by Congress in relation to poisonous phosphorus matches.

Regulation According to Hazard. In trades and occupations offering a menace to life, limb, or health, the employment of women and minors regulated according to the degree of hazard. No minor under 18 employed in any dangerous occupation, or in any occupations which involve danger to fellow workmen or require use of explosives, poisonous gases, or other injurious ingredients. Un-skilled craftsmen who do not read and understand the English language forbidden to handle the dangerous machinery or processes known to be extra hazardous.

Standardized Inspection. Inspection of mines and work places standardized either by interstate agreement or by establishment of Government standard. All death, injuries and diseases due to industrial operations to be reported to public authorities as required in accident laws of Minnesota, and with respect to some trade diseases in New York.

The Right to a Home. Social welfare demands for every family a safe and a sanitary home; healthful surroundings; ample and pure running water inside the house; modern and sanitary toilet conveniences for its exclusive use, located inside the building; adequate sunlight and ventilation;

reasonable fire protection; privacy; rooms of sufficient size and number to decently house the members of the family; freedom from dampness; prompt, adequate collection of all waste materials. These fundamental requirements for normal living should be obtainable by every family, reasonably accessible from place of employment, at a rental not to exceed 20% of the family income.

Taxes. To protect wage earners from exorbitant rents and to secure for them that increased municipal service demanded by the massing together of people in thickly settled industrial communities, a greater share of taxes to be transferred from dwellings to land held for speculative purposes the value of which is enhanced by the very congestion of these industrial populations.

Home Work. Factory production to be carried on in factories, whenever work is given out to homes, abuses are sure to creep in which cannot be controlled by any known system of inspection or supervision.

Tenement Manufacture. Tenement house manufacture is know to be a serious menace to the health, education, and economic independence of thousands of people in large cities. It subjects children to injurious industrial burdens and cannot be successfully regulated by inspection or other official supervision;. Public welfare, therefore, demands for city tenements the entire prohibition of manufacture of articles of commerce in rooms occupied for dwelling purposes.

Labor Colonies. In temporary construction camps and labor colonies, definite standards to provide against over-crowding, and for ventilation, water, supply, sanitation, to be written into the contract specifications, as now provided in the New York law.

Employment of Children. Prohibition of all wage-earning occupations for children under 16 years of age.

Employment of Women. Prohibition of employment of women in manufacturing, commerce, or other trades where work compels standing constantly. Also prohibition for a period of at least eight weeks at time of childbirth.

Intermittent Employment. Any industrial occupation subject to rush periods and out-of-work seasons to be considered abnormal, and subject to governmental review and regulation. Official investigation of such intermittent employment and other forms of unemployment as a basis for better distribution of immigrants, for guiding seasonal laborers from trade to trade, and other methods for lessening these evils.

The Unemployable. The restrictions upon employers set forth in this platform will lead them to refuse to engage any to fall below a grade of industrial efficiency which renders their work profitable. An increased army of industrial outcasts will be thrown upon society to be cared for in public labor colonies or by various relief agencies. This condition will in turn necessitate a minimum standard of preparation, including at least sufficient educational opportunity to abolish illiteracy among all minors and to train every minor over 16 years of age to some form of industrial efficiency.

Compensation Demanded. Both social and individual welfare requires some effective system of compensation for the heavy loss now sustained by industrial workers as a result of unavoidable accidents, industrial diseases, sickness, invalidity, involuntary unemployment, and old age.

Accidents. Equitable standards of compensation must be determined by extensive experience, but there is already ample precedent for immediate adoption as a minimum the equivalent of four years' wages in compensation for accidents resulting fatally. Compensation for accidents resulting in permanent disability should not be less than 65% of the annual wage for a period of fifteen years.

Trade Diseases. For diseases clearly caused by nature and conditions of the industry, the same compensation as for accidents.

Old Age. Service pensions or old age insurance whenever instituted so protected that the person who withdraws or is discharged from the employment of a given company does not forfeit his equity in the same.

Notes

Archival abbreviations are used in the notes as follows:

AALL Papers—American Association for Labor Legislation Records. Kheel Center for Labor-Management Documentation and Archives, Cornell University Library

CUOHROC—Columbia University Oral History Research Office Collection

CSS Papers—Community Service Society Papers, RBML

GHC—Greenwich House Collection, Tamiment Library, New York University

Lindsay Papers—Samuel McCune Lindsay Papers, RBML

RFA—Rockefeller Foundation Archives, Sleepy Hollow, New York

RBML—Rare Book and Manuscript Library, Columbia University

Wald Papers—Lillian B. Wald Papers, RBML

Introduction, "The Greatest Social Science Laboratory in the World"

1. "We need men . . .": "Letter in reply to a questionnaire reported in L. L. Bernard, 'The Teaching of Sociology in the United States,'" *American Journal of Sociology* 15 (September 1909): 196 (emphasis in the original); quoted in Seymour Martin Lipset, "The Department of Sociology," in R. Gordon Hoxie et al., *A History of the Faculty of Political Science, Columbia University* (New York: Columbia University Press, 1955), 287. "If political economy . . ." "There is one . . .": Henry Rawie, *The Principles of a New Political Economy* (Indianapolis: Wm. W. Hampton, 1900), 11, 14. "The future of . . .": Edward T. Devine, "Economic Science in America," *University Extension Bulletin*, 10 May 1894, 88.

2. "The city . . .": "Report on a Department of Social Science at Columbia College," *Charities Review*, April 1894, 288. "the greatest . . .": *A Proposal for an Independent School of Social Science for Men and Women* (New York: Marchbanks Press, 1918?), 10, Archives of the New School University.

3. U.S. Department of Commerce, *Statistical Abstract of the United States, 1920* (Washington, D.C.: Government Printing Office, 1921), 50–53.

4. "Columbia Leads in Registration," *New York Times*, 6 October 1914.

5. Educational statistics: Thomas D. Snyder, ed., *120 Years of American Education: A Statistical Portrait*, National Center for Educational Statistics (Washington, D.C.: Government Printing Office, 1993), 55, 75, 76, 80, 82–83.

6. "the single most . . .": Kathryn Kish Sklar, "Two Political Cultures in the Progressive Era: The National Consumers' League and the American Associa-

tion for Labor Legislation," in *U.S. History as Women's History: New Feminist Essays*, ed. Linda K. Kerber, Alice Kessler-Harris, and Kathryn Kish Sklar (Chapel Hill: University of North Carolina Press, 1995), 36.

7. "You could hardly . . .": "The Reminiscences of Frances Perkins" (1951–1955), 1: 83, CUOHROC.

8. Saul Engelbourg and Leonard Bushkoff, *The Man Who Found the Money: John Stewart Kennedy and the Financing of the Western Railroads* (East Lansing: Michigan State University Press, 1996), 206–15. Many years later, for six-plus years, this author worked in a garret-office in Hamilton Hall researching this book and teaching Columbia's Great Books core curriculum.

9. "the New York X": Charles A. Beard to W. J. Ghent, 29 January 1929?, correspondence file, William James Ghent Papers, Library of Congress. "a group of men . . ." W. J. Ghent to Allan Nevins, September 21, 1926, Allan Nevins Collection, RBML. On the London X Club: Ruth Barton, "'An influential set of chaps': The X-Club and Royal Society Politics, 1864–85," *British Journal for the History of Science* 23, no. 76 (March 1990): 53–81. "Everything . . .": W. J. Ghent to Allan Nevins, 21 September 1926, Allan Nevins Collection. Membership: Morris Hillquit, *Loose Leaves from A Busy Life* (New York: Rand School Press, 1934), 68. Aldine Club: "The Reminiscences of Henry Bruère" (1949), 57, CUOHROC. "Each member . . .": Morris Hillquit, *Loose Leaves*, 68–69. Postal card notification: W. J. Ghent to J. G. Phelps Stokes, 7 November 1906, James Graham Phelps Stokes Manuscript Collection, RBML.

10. The list of New York X Club members is based on later recollections: William H. Allen, "The Reminiscences of Dr. William H. Allen" (1950), 62–63, 69, CUOHROC; W. J. Ghent to Allan Nevins, 21 September 1926, Allan Nevins Collection; Hillquit, *Loose Leaves*, 69. "a sort of personal . . .": Hillquit, *Loose Leaves*, 70.

11. "voluntary group action": Mary Kingsbury Simkhovitch, *Neighborhood: My Story of Greenwich House* (New York: W.W. Norton, 1938), 237. Educational statistics: Snyder, *120 Years of American Education*; Mabel Newcomer, *A Century of Higher Education for American Women* (New York: Harper, 1959), 46. That some women broke free of the traditional bonds of womanhood and began to construct a modern feminism: William Leach, *True Love and Perfect Union: The Feminist Reform of Sex and Society* (New York: Basic Books, 1980); Robyn Muncy, *Creating a Female Dominion in American Reform: 1890–1935* (New York: Oxford University Press, 1991); Rosalind Rosenberg, *Beyond Separate Spheres: Intellectual Roots of Modern Feminism* (New Haven, Conn.: Yale University Press, 1982).

12. Council membership, and "practical handbook": James Bronson Reynolds, ed., *Civic Bibliography for Greater New York* (New York: Russell Sage Foundation, 1911), iv–v.

13. H. G. Wells, *The Future in America* (New York: Harper and Brothers, 1906), 35.

14. "between blocks . . .": Bayrd Still, *Mirror for Gotham: New York as Seen by Contemporaries from Dutch Days to the Present* (New York: New York University Press, 1956), 205. Electrical power: William J. Hausman, "Light and Power," in *The Encyclopedia of New York City*, ed. Kenneth T. Jackson (New Haven, Conn.: Yale University Press, 1995), 673–74.

15. Fifth Avenue: Henry Hope Reed, "A Stroll up the Avenue in 1911," in David G. Lowe, *New York, N.Y.* (New York: American Heritage, 1968), 21. Most crowded neighborhood: Kenneth T. Jackson, "Lower East Side Tenement Museum," in *Encyclopedia of New York City*, 697.

16. On Civil War pensions: Theda Skocpol, *Protecting Soldiers and Mothers: The Political Origins of Social Policy in the United States* (Cambridge, Mass.: Harvard University Press, 1992), 145, passim.

17. Edmund S. Morgan, *Inventing the People: The Rise of Popular Sovereignty in England and America* (New York: W.W. Norton, 1988), 237–306.

18. "Political democracy . . .": James McKeen Cattell, "Paper given by James McKeen Cattell, 17 Feb. 1910," 4, in New York Philosophical Club Minutes 7 February 1900–10 April 1919, box 1, RBML. "the university spirit . . .": *New York Evening Post*, 27 September 1916; also Edwin R. A. Seligman, "The Real University," *Educational Review* (November 1916): 327. "enrollment of . . .": *New York American*, 18 June 1913. "to bring . . .": Paul U. Kellogg, "The Spread of the Survey Idea," *Proceedings of the Academy of Political Science* 2, no. 4 (July 1912): 491.

19. "Because . . .": John Dewey, *John Dewey: The Middle Works, 1899–1924* (Carbondale: Southern Illinois University Press, 1976–1983), 2: 57. "are essentially . . .": John Dewey and James H. Tufts, *Ethics* (New York: Henry Holt, 1908) in Dewey, *The Middle Works*, 5: 423; see the introduction to *Ethics* for Dewey's authorship of the passage. "almost religious faith . . ." "The idea of progress . . ." "Since progress . . .": John Dewey, "Progress," in *A Cyclopedia of Education*, ed. Paul Monroe (New York: Macmillan, 1913), 5: 51–52. Problem-solving, four stages: John Dewey, *How We Think* (Boston: D.C. Heath, 1910).

20. Coining "sociology": Auguste Comte, *Cours de philosophie positive* (Paris: Bachelier, Impremeuv-Libraire, 1839), 4: 252. "to replace . . .": August Comte, *A General View of Positivism* (New York: Robert Speller, 1975), 365. On the beginnings of modern American social science: Dorothy Ross, *The Origins of American Social Science* (New York: Cambridge University Press, 1991), passim.

21. "The order . . .": Mary Kingsbury Simkhovitch, "Friendship and Politics," *Political Science Quarterly* 17, no. 2 (June 1902): 200.

22. On technological and scientific advances: John Louis Recchiuti, "Science and Technology," in *American Decades: 1910–1919*, ed. Vincent Tompkins (Detroit: Gale Research, 1996), 487–522.

23. T. J. Jackson Lears, "Intellectuals and the Intelligentsia," in *Encyclopedia of American Social History*, ed. Mary K. Cayton, Elliott J. Gorn, and Peter Williams (New York: Charles Scribner's Sons, 1993), 3: 2447–63.

Chapter 1. Competing Gospels: "Make Way for Science and for Light!"

1. Johnson's advertisement: "New York, May 31, 1754, Advertisement," in *A History of Columbia University 1754–1904* (New York: Columbia University Press, 1904), 443–44.

2. Columbia's history: David C. Humphrey, *From King's College to Columbia, 1746–1800* (New York: Columbia University Press, 1976), 112–15, 153–54; William B. Hooper, "Columbia Half a Century Ago," *Columbia Alumni News* 6, no. 33 (23 April 1915): 556–59; Robert A. M. Stern, Thomas Mellins, and David Fishman, *New York 1880: Architecture and Urbanism in the Gilded Age* (New York: Monacelli Press, 1999), 142–56; Robert A. McCaughey, *Stand, Columbia: A History of Columbia University in the City of New York, 1754–2004* (New York: Columbia University Press, 2003), 1–48. On the founding of the School of Political Science: "Meeting of the Trustees of Columbia College in the City of New York held at the College on Monday the seventh day of June in the year of our Lord one thousand eight hundred and eighty," typescript, Columbia University Archives, Low Library, 3, 6, 7. "for all . . .": John W. Burgess, *Reminiscences of An American*

Scholar: The Beginnings of Columbia University (New York: Columbia University Press, 1934), 213.

3. Enrollment: "Registration Statistics of Specified Universities on November 1, 1910," *Statistical Abstract of the United States: 1910* (Washington, D.C.: Government Printing Office., 1911), 109. "Columbia Leads in Registration," *New York Times*, 6 October 1914; enrollment that year was 12,509. "science, not theology . . .": Louis Menand, *The Metaphysical Club: A Story of Ideas in America* (New York: Farrar, Straus and Giroux, 2001), 230. "to create . . .": T. J. Jackson Lears, *Fables of Abundance: A Cultural History of Advertising in America* (New York: Basic Books, 1994), 138. European schools as models: Burgess, *Reminiscences of an American Scholar*, 198. From 1865 to 1890 about 6,000 students from the U.S. studied in Germany: Walter P. Metzger, *Academic Freedom: In the Age of the University* (New York: Columbia University Press, 1955), 3–9. International web: Daniel T. Rodgers, *Atlantic Crossings: Social Politics in a Progressive Age* (Cambridge, Mass.: Harvard University Press, 1998), passim.

4. On Du Bois: David Levering Lewis, *W. E. B. Du Bois*, vol. 1, *Biography of a Race, 1868–1919* (New York: Henry Holt, 1993), 131. "yeasty . . ." "a roomier . . .": Mary Kingsbury Simkhovitch, *Here Is God's Plenty: Reflections On American Social Advance* (New York: Harper and Brothers, 1949), 20–21. The "middle way": James T. Kloppenberg, *Uncertain Victory: Social Democracy and Progressivism in European and American Thought, 1870–1920* (New York: Oxford University Press, 1986), passim. German Historical School: Gustav Schmoller, "The Idea of Justice in Political Economy," *Annals of the American Academy of Political and Social Science* (March 1894): 697–737. "convinced of . . .": Schmoller quoted in William D. P. Bliss, *Encyclopedia of Social Reform* (New York: Funk and Wagnalls, 1897), 1277. *Verein*: Eugen von Philippovich, "The Verein fur Sozialpolitik," *Quarterly Journal of Economics* 5 (1891): 222–31.

5. NYU history: Theodore Francis Jones, ed., *New York University, 1832–1932* (New York: New York University Press, 1933), 87, 90, 96. NYU graduate program: "Special Announcement, Supplementary to Page 92 of the University Catalogue," in *New York University, University Catalogue, 1886–1887* (New York, 1886), 4; David M. Potash, *The Graduate School of Arts and Science at New York University a History* (New York: Arts and Science Publications Office of New York University, 1991), 20, passim.

6. City College history: S. Willis Rudy, *The College of the City of New York, 1847–1947* (New York: City College Press, 1949), 288, 362; Stephen Pierce Duggan, "The Spirit of the City College," *The Outlook* 89, no. 9 (27 June 1908): 433–42. "recent arrivals . . .": Stephen Duggan, *A Professor at Large* (New York: Macmillan, 1943), 7. "first and most . . .": Stephen P. Duggan, "The College of the City of New York and Community Service," in *The College and the City*, ed. Edward A. Fitzpatrick (New York: The Committee, 1914?), 49–53.

7. James H. Leuba, *The Belief in God and Immortality* (Chicago: Open Court, 1921), 219–87.

8. W. D. P. Bliss, "The Church and Social Reform Workers," *Outlook*, January 1906, 122–25.

9. "Social science is not . . ." "The Christian pulpit": Rev. James F. Riggs, "Social Science and the Pulpit," *Homiletic Review* 19 (June 1890): 501–2. "The science of . . .": James A. Quarles, "Christian Sociology," *Presbyterian Quarterly* 10, no. 1 (January 1896): 46. "a department . . ." "By adopting . . .": "J. H. W. Stuckenberg, *Christian Sociology* (New York: I.K. Funk, 1880), 26–27. "socioreligious": Ronald C. White, Jr., and Charles Howard Hopkins, *The Social Gospel:*

Religion and Reform in Changing America (Philadelphia: Temple University Press, 1976), 138. "the science of Christian . . .": Connecticut Bible Society, *A Religious Census of Hartford . . . 1889* (Hartford, 1889), 39. "sociology with God . . .": Graham Taylor, "The Church in Social Reforms," in *Proceedings of the Second International Congregational Council* (Boston: n.p., 1900), 45. On Taylor: Charles Howard Hopkins, *The Rise of the Social Gospel in American Protestantism, 1865–1915* (New Haven, Conn.: Yale University Press, 1940), 275–76, passim.

10. "if Jesus alone . . .": Z. Swift Holbrook, "What Is Sociology," *Bibliotheca Sacra: A Religious and Sociological Quarterly* 52 (July 1895): 459; "Christian principles correctly . . .": 460; "I believe Sociology . . .": 469. "As a student of social science . . .": Jeremiah W. Jenks, *The Political and Social Significance of the Life and Teachings of Jesus* (New York: Young Men's Christian Association Press, 1908), vii. "had the scientific insight . . .": Walter Rauschenbusch, *Christianity and the Social Crisis* (New York: Macmillan, 1908), 59; quoted in Richard Wightman Fox, "The Culture of Liberal Protestant Progressivism, 1875–1925," *Journal of Interdisciplinary History* 23, no. 3 (Winter 1993): 652.

11. "the word 'Christian' . . .": in Holbrook, "What Is Sociology," 470; "Sociology is the natural . . .": 466. "Whether we . . .": Franklin Henry Giddings, *The Principles of Sociology* (New York: Macmillan, 1896), 69.

12. Seth Low, "What Facts Have to Do with Faith?" typescript, January 1907, Seth Low Papers, box 24, RBML.

13. John Bates Clark, "The Scholar's Duty to the State," typescript, scrapbook no. 5, box 17, John Bates Clark Papers, RBML. Lester Ward, *Dynamic Sociology* (New York: Appleton, 1883), 21.

14. "There is no science": quoted in William D. P. Bliss, ed., *The Encyclopedia of Social Reform* (New York: Funk and Wagnalls, 1897), 1046. "The term 'scientism' meant originally 'the slavish imitation of the method and language of (natural) science,' especially by social scientists": Karl R. Popper, *Objective Knowledge: An Evolutionary Approach* (New York: Oxford University Press, 1972), 185. On the issue of "nomological knowledge" and social science see Max Weber, "'Objectivity' in Social Science and Science Policy," in *Knowledge and Postmodernism in Historical Perspective*, ed. Joyce Appleby et al. (New York: Routledge, 1996), 241–44; also Richard J. Bernstein, *Beyond Objectivism and Relativism: Science, Hermeneutics, and Praxis* (Philadelphia: University of Pennsylvania Press, 1983), 26–27. "Our modern cities . . ." "The social like . . .": William Howe Tolman, "Scientific Rescue Mission Work," *City Vigilant* 1, no. 3 (March 1894): 44–45. "The survey takes . . .": Paul U. Kellogg, "The Spread of the Survey Idea," in *The Social Survey* (New York: Russell Sage Foundation, 1912), 4. "an attempt to apply . . .": John W. Burgess, *Political Science and Comparative Constitutional Law* (Boston: Ginn, 1891) 1: vi.

15. "Since now scientists . . .": W. E. B. Du Bois, *Some Notes on Negroes in New York City* (Atlanta: Atlanta University Press, 1903), 2; quoted in Adolph L. Reed, Jr., *W. E. B. Du Bois and American Political Thought: Fabianism and the Color Line* (New York: Oxford University Press, 1997), 47. "Political science is to be . . .": Charles Beard, "Political Science in the Crucible," *New Republic*, 17 November, 1917, 6. Walter Lippmann, *Drift and Mastery* (1914; reprint Englewood Cliffs, N.J.: Prentice-Hall, 1961), 61, 155. "careful observation . . ." "laborious watching . . .": James Harvey Robinson and Charles A. Beard, *The Development of Modern Europe: An Introduction to the Study of Current History* (Boston: Ginn, 1907), 405, 421. "the great mass . . .": "Editor's Note," *Cosmopolitan* May 1910, 712; quoted in Marcel C. LaFollette, *Making Science Our Own: Public Images of Science, 1910–1955* (Chicago: University of Chicago Press, 1990), 158.

16. Enrollments and history: *A History of Columbia University 1754–1904*, 270–75. "... and legal questions.": The Constitution of the Academy of Political Science, *Proceedings of the Academy of Political Science in the City of New York* 3, no. 1 (October 1912): 3–6; Herbert B. Adams, *The Study of American Colleges and Universities* (Washington, D.C.: Government Printing Office, 1887), 85–86. "are the methods ...": Munroe Smith, "The Domain of Political Science," *Political Science Quarterly* 1, no. 1 (March 1886): 1, 4.

17. A list of faculty in the School of Political Science can be found in *Studies in History, Economics and Public Law; Columbia University* 5th ser., 43, no. 1 (1911): reverse of title page. "True Civil Service Reform," *Columbia Spectator*, 8 October 1880.

18. "Report on a Department of Social Science at Columbia College," *Charities Review*, April 1894, 288–300. Courses offered in the Department of Social Science: *Courses in the School of Political Science in History, Economics, and Public Law, Under the charge of the University Faculty of Political Science 1894–1895* (New York: Columbia College, 1894).

19. "The city is the natural ..." "the problems of poverty ..." "It would be of immense ..." "a sort of scientific ..." "the simple citizen": "Report on a Department of Social Science," 288, 295, 299.

20. "Report on a Department of Social Science," 289–96. The claim that students were to become expert was repeated in the description for Mayo-Smith's course, "Laboratory Work in Statistics": "in short he [the student] will become an expert in judging of the value of sociological evidence," see: *School of Political Science: Announcement, 1897–1898*, 36.

21. On social welfare, expertise, and democracy: Walter I. Trattner, *Social Welfare or Social Control? Some Historical Reflections on Regulating the Poor* (Knoxville: University of Tennessee Press, 1983), 3–14, passim; Frances F. Piven and Richard A. Cloward, *Regulating the Poor: The Functions of Public Welfare* (New York: Pantheon, 1971), passim; Kloppenberg, *Uncertain Victory*, 267–77.

22. "... alienating in its effect.": Mary Kingsbury Simkhovitch, "Friendship and Politics," *Political Science Quarterly* 17, no. 2 (June 1902): 199. "statistical laboratory" description: "Report on a Department of Social Science," 293.

23. Report's findings: Richmond Mayo-Smith, Franklin H. Giddings, and Frederick W. Holls, "Special Report of the Committee on Statistics," *The C.O.S. 15th Annual Report: From Jan. 1896 to July 1897* (n.p., n.d., 1897?), 33–43, 57–60. On subsequent Columbia-COS joint ventures on unemployment and homelessness: Lilian Brandt, "The Charity Organization Society of The City of New York 1882–1907, History: Account of Present Activities," typescript, 1907?, box 193, Community Service Society Papers, RBML.

24. "the first fruits ...": *Charity Organization Society of The City of New York: 14th Annual Report from January 1, 1895 to July 1st, 1896* (n.p., 1896?), p. 27 in box 192, CSS Papers.

25. Editorial: "University Work," 28 February 1900, scrapbook vol. 3, Edwin Robert Anderson Seligman Papers, RBML. Seligman employed a newspaper clipping service; the clipping is dated, but the name of the newspaper is not recorded. "a 'progressive' ..." "Columbia's influence ...": *New York Tribune*, 19 October 1911.

26. "tall, urbane ..." "very charming": "Reminiscences of Alvin Johnson" (1960), 65, CUOHROC. "Speeding through ...": Burgess, *Reminiscences of an American Scholar*, 23. "ignorant barbarians": John W. Burgess, *Reconstruction and the Constitution, 1866–1876* (New York: Charles Scribner's Sons, 1902), 252; slave

owners, Burgess wrote, saw slavery as, "a grave trust to be faithfully discharged, rather than as an opportunity for exploitation," 3. Failed statecraft and his embrace of Teutonic theory: John W. Burgess, *The Foundations of Political Science* (New York: Columbia University Press, 1933), 40, 139. Study in Europe and early faculty: Burgess, *Reminiscences*, 193.

27. John W. Burgess, "Private Corporations from the Point of View of Political Science," *Political Science Quarterly* 13, no. 2 (June 1898): 201, 210; also, John W. Burgess, *The Reconciliation of Government with Liberty* (New York: Charles Scribner's Sons, 1915), 364–67.

28. "'Professor Burgess, women . . .'" ". . . let them all go there.": Duggan, *Professor at Large*, 6. R. Gordon Hoxie gives 1898 as the earliest date at which women were admitted into the School of Political Science: R. Gordon Hoxie et al., *A History of the Faculty of Political Science, Columbia University* (New York: Columbia University Press, 1955), 67; but Mary Kingsbury Simkhovitch's transcripts in Columbia University's Transcripts Department indicate she studied sociology and statistics in the School of Political Science from 1896 to 1897.

29. John W. Burgess, "What Is Real Political Progress?" 24 October 1912, typescript, box GBI-38, 5–6, 23–24, Nicholas Murray Butler Papers, RBML.

30. "pure investigation . . .": *Popular Science Monthly* 5 (July 1874): 367–68, quoted in Thomas L. Haskell, *The Emergence of Professional Social Science: The American Social Science Association and the Nineteenth Century Crisis of Authority* (Urbana: University of Illinois Press, 1977), 139.

31. "limitations on . . ." "should push . . ." "a stupid and foolish . . .": Nicholas Murray Butler, *What Is Progress in Politics?* (n.p.: An Address Before the Commercial Club, Chicago, Illinois, December 14, 1912), box GBI-27, 10, 20–23, Nicholas Murray Butler Papers. "self-love": Adam Smith, *An Inquiry into the Nature and Causes of the Wealth of Nations* (Chicago: University of Chicago Press, 1976), 1: 18.

32. "the present tendency . . .": Binghamton *Leader*, 20 April 1901. "efforts to reform . . .": Henry Rogers Seager, *Principles of Economics: Being a Revision of Introduction to Economics* (New York: Henry Holt, 1913), 614. "the best interests . . ." James B. Reynolds to Elihu Root, 21 November 1898, quoted in Richard Stephen Skolnik, "The Crystallization of Reform in New York City, 1890–1917" (Ph.D. dissertation, Yale University, 1964), 406.

33. "Modern liberalism . . .": William F. Willoughby, "Presidential Address: The Philosophy of Labor Legislation," *American Labor Legislation Review* 4, no. 1 (March 1914): 39–40. "public opinion . . ." "a condition . . .": E. R. A. Seligman, "The Living Wage," *Gunton Institute Bulletin* 1, no. 17 (26 March 1898): 261, 266. "A kind of . . .": "Reminiscences of Alvin Johnson," 51.

34. Edwin Robert Anderson Seligman was born less than two weeks after the bombardment of Fort Sumter that began the American Civil War; his parents gave him his middle name, Robert Anderson, after the Union commander at Fort Sumter.

35. "merely the night . . ." "more positive . . .": Edwin R. A. Seligman, "The Real University," *Educational Review* (November 1916): 327. "In politics . . .": Edwin R. A. Seligman, "Liberty, Democracy, Productivity and the Closed Shop," *National Civic Federation Monthly Review* (July 1904): 9. "safeguard the . . ." "Recognition by . . ." "certain common . . ." "equality of . . ." "benumbing": Seligman, "The Living Wage," 261, 266.

36. "to apportion . . .": E. R. A. Seligman, *Progressive Taxation in Theory and Practice* (Baltimore: American Economic Association, 1894), 195. Seligman as

"the leading expert" on the income tax: Morton Keller, *Regulating a New Economy: Public Policy and Economic Change in America, 1900–1933* (Cambridge, Mass.: Harvard University Press, 1990), 217. "The College Professor in the Public Service," *South Atlantic Quarterly* (May 1902): 253.

37. Politically conservative trustees: Clyde W. Barrow, *Universities and the Capitalist State: Corporate Liberalism and the Reconstruction of American Higher Education, 1894–1928* (Madison: University of Wisconsin Press, 1990).

38. "knew more . . .": Burgess, *Reminiscences of an American Scholar*, 182. On De Leon: Hoxie, *A History of the Faculty of Political Science*, 30–31.

39. On Ely, Brewster and other cases: Daniel H. Pollitt and Jordan E. Kurland, "Entering the Academic Freedom Arena Running: The AAUP's First Year," *Academe* (July–August 1998): 45–52. "dismissed because . . .": Edwin R. A. Seligman, "The Committee on Academic Freedom of the American Association of University Professors," *Educational Review* 50 (September 1915): 187; "they were . . .": 185–86; "teachers of the political . . .": 185.

40. "the present . . .": Seligman, "The Committee on Academic Freedom," 184; "a large number . . ." and preliminary report: Seligman, "The Committee on Academic Freedom," 184–88..

41. "special dangers to . . .": *American Economic Review* 6, no. 1, suppl. (March 1916): 235; the more than a dozen references: 230–46.

42. "no person . . .": Charles A. Beard, "A Statement by Charles A. Beard," *New Republic*, 29 December 1917, 249. "pointed out . . ." "hauled before . . .": Beard, "A Statement by Charles A. Beard," 250.

43. ". . . with the war.": Beard, "A Statement by Charles A. Beard," 250. "for sundry antiwar . . .": McCaughey, *Stand, Columbia*, 249. "A Program of Radical Democracy" ". . . and the nation.": James McKeen Cattell, "Paper given by James McKeen Cattell, Feb. 17, 1910," New York Philosophical Club Minutes 7 February 1900–10 April 1919, 6–15, box 1, RBML. James McKeen Cattell, *University Control* (New York: Science Press, 1913). On the Columbia cases: Carol S. Gruber, *Mars and Minerva: World War I and the Uses of Higher Learning in America* (Baton Rouge: Louisiana State University Press, 1975), 187–206. On Cattell: McCaughey, *Stand, Columbia*, 242–250.

44. "wander days . . .": Charles A. Beard, "Political Science in the Crucible," typescript, 17 November 1917, 3, Lindsay Rogers Collection, RBML. "When Beard strode . . .": *Current Biography 1941*, 54. "in grave . . .": Richard Hofstadter, *The Progressive Historians: Turner, Beard, Parrington* (New York: Knopf, 1968), 179. Beard's account of his trouble with the trustees: Beard, "A Statement by Charles A. Beard," 249–51. "to generate . . .": McCaughey, *Stand, Columbia*, 252.

45. "it was generally . . ." "'the trustees had learned . . .'": Beard, "A Statement by Charles A. Beard," 249–50. ". . . medieval in religion.": Charles A. Beard to Nicholas Murray Butler, 8 October 1917, *Minutes of the Trustees of Columbia University* 38 (1917–18); 89, Columbia University Archives, Low Library. Student protest: "Columbia Students to Appeal to Butler," *New York Post*, 10 October 1917. "Committee of Nine For Columbia Peace," *New York Times*, 11 October 1917; "Columbia Students Ask Reinstatement of Teacher," *New York Post*, 13 October 1917.

46. "Every liberal . . .": *The New School for Social Research* (n.p., 1968?), 1, pamphlet commemorating the New School's fiftieth anniversary, copy in the New School University Archives.

47. "an Independent School . . ." ". . . laboratory in the world.": *A Proposal for an Independent School of Social Science for Men and Women* (New York: Marchbanks Press, 1918?), 3–10, Archives of the New School University.

48. ". . . from the standpoint of socialism,": William D. P. Bliss, ed., *The New Encyclopedia of Social Reform* (New York: Funk and Wagnalls, 1910), 1049–50. "rally workers . . .": *The Case of the Rand School* (New York: Rand School of Social Science, 1919), 1. History of the Rand School: John L. Recchiuti, "The Rand School of Social Science during the Progressive Era: Will to Power of a Stratum of the American Intellectual Class," *Journal of the History of the Behavioral Sciences* 31 (April 1995): 149–61.

49. "In medicine . . ." ". . . as it is to-day.": Florence Kelley Wischnewetzky, *The Need of Theoretical Preparation for Philanthropic Work. A Paper Presented to the New York Association of Collegiate Alumnae on May 14, 1887* (n.p., 1887), 21–22.

Chapter 2. From Noblesse Oblige to Social Reform in the "New Philanthropy" of "Scientific Charity"

1. William Rhinelander Stewart, *The Philanthropic Work of Josephine Shaw Lowell* (New York: Macmillan, 1911), 1–9.

2. On Lowell: Stewart, *The Philanthropic Work of Josephine Shaw Lowell*, 1–9, 38–61. Joan Waugh, *Unsentimental Reformer: The Life of Josephine Shaw Lowell* (Cambridge, Mass.: Harvard University Press, 1997), 82–85, passim. Robert H. Bremner, *American Philanthropy* (Chicago: University of Chicago Press, 1960), 100–104. On Lowell and the COS and Consumers' League: Lilian Brandt, *The Charity Organization Society of the City of New York, 1882–1907* (New York: P.H. Tyrrel, 1907), 15–17.

3. "the rich . . .": Timothy B. Smith, "Charity and Poor Relief: The Modern Period," in *Encyclopedia of European Social History*, ed. Peter N. Stearns (Detroit: Charles Scribner's Sons, 2001), 3: 456. "I do not agree . . .": Josephine Shaw Lowell, *On the Relation of Employers and Employed*, paper read at the Women's Conference of the Philadelphia Society for Organized Charity, 1 April 1885, pamphlet (Philadelphia?, 1885), 4. "the task . . .": Josephine Shaw Lowell, *Public Relief and Private Charity* (New York: G.P. Putnam's Sons, 1884), i. "It can only . . .": Lowell, *On the Relation of Employers and Employed*, 7.

4. "fearless . . .": Mary Kingsbury Simkhovitch, *Neighborhood: My Story of Greenwich House* (New York: W.W. Norton, 1938), 72. "strong indignation" and "downright plain speaking": Edward T. Devine, *When Social Work Was Young* (New York: Macmillan, 1939), 23.

5. Waugh, *Unsentimental Reformer*, 102, 104, 187–90.

6. "Mrs. Lowell's society": Devine, *When Social Work Was Young*, 23. "promote . . .": Brandt, *The Charity Organization Society*, 306. "investigate thoroughly . . ." ". . . self-dependence": "Constitution," *First Annual Report of the Central Council of the Charity Organization Society of the City of New York, April 1, 1883* (New York: John J. O'Brien Printer, 1883), 20, box 192, CSS Papers.

7. Cooperation of 138 charities: Brandt, *The Charity Organization Society*, 21. Fraudulent case examples: *Second Annual Report of the Central Council of the Charity Organization Society of the City of New York, April 1, 1884* (New York: John J. O'Brien Printer, 1884), 70–75. "it is evident . . .": *Third Annual Report of the Central Council of the Charity Organization Society of the City of New York, April 1, 1885* (New York: Industrial Printing Company, 1885), 16.

8. "No person . . .": Article 2, Section 1 of the Constitution of the Charity Organization Society of the City of New York, *First Annual Report of the Central Council of the Charity Organization Society of the City of New York, April 1, 1883* (New York: John J. O'Brien Printer, 1883), 20, in box 192, CSS papers; also, "Commit-

tee on the Organization of Charities of the City of New York," 22 May 1882, p. 90, box 205, CSS Papers. "This is not to say . . .": Edward Thomas Devine, *The Practice of Charity: Individual, Associated and Organized* (New York: Lentilhon, 1901), 92.

9. "Five Things . . ." "fish is better . . .": *Handbook for Friendly Visitors Among the Poor; Compiled and Arranged by the Charity Organization Society of the City of New York* (New York: G.P. Putnam's Sons, 1883), title page, 23, "Casework (D-R)," box 99, CSS Papers. On 3,400 families: Brandt, *The Charity Organization Society,* 23. On 170,000 files: Edwin G. Burrows and Mike Wallace, *Gotham: A History of New York City to 1898* (New York: Oxford University Press, 1999), 1159. Pre-printed stock cards "Case Files R2-R20," file folder 18, Box 239, CSS Papers. "suitable and adequate . . ." and Lowell's admonition: Brandt, *The Charity Organization Society,* 15, 42. "Directions to Visitors" ". . . broadest charity.": *Handbook for Friendly Visitors,* 11.

10. "may be compelled . . .": E. M. Leonard, *The Early History of English Poor Relief* (Cambridge: Cambridge University Press, 1900), 3–4. "one who . . ." "Idleness is . . .": John Peden Bell, *Christian Sociology* (Aberdeen: George and Robert King, 1853), 192–93. "recipients of alms . . ." "It is the greatest . . .": Lowell, *Public Relief and Private Charity,* 89, 90, 92. "the pressure of . . ." ". . . who suffers.": Josephine Shaw Lowell, "The True Aim of Charity Organization Societies," reprinted from *The Forum,* June 1896, 2, 3; Josephine Shaw Lowell, "Cheap Lodging Houses, Their Influence on City Pauperism," reprint of an address given by Lowell, *New York Evening Post,* 20 February 1897.

For elements in the debate on philanthropy and public policy planning in the late nineteenth and early twentieth centuries, see Judith Sealander, *Private Wealth and Public Life: Foundation Philanthropy and the Reshaping of American Social Policy from the Progressive Era to the New Deal* (Baltimore: Johns Hopkins University Press, 1997); Ellen Lagemann, *The Politics of Knowledge: The Carnegie Corporation, Philanthropy, and Public Policy* (Middletown, Conn.: Wesleyan University Press, 1989); Barry Karl and Stanley Katz, "The American Private Philanthropic Foundation and the Public Sphere, 1890–1930," *Minerva* 19 (1981): 236–70.

11. On the COS's treatment of New York's poor see Michael B. Katz, "Surviving Poverty in Early Twentieth-Century New York City," in *Urban Policy in Twentieth-Century America,* ed. Arnold R. Hirsch and Raymond A. Mohl (New Brunswick, N.J.: Rutgers University Press, 1993), 46–64. "over steaming . . .": Frances A. Kellor, *Out of Work: A Study of Employment Agencies* (New York: G.P. Putnam's Sons, 1904), 162.

12. "a flurry . . ." "give eye-glasses . . ." " 'certainly unnecessary' " "in view of . . ." "supply the needs . . .": Brandt, *The Charity Organization Society,* 22, 51, 106–14. On the distribution of coal to the poor: Jon C. Teaford, *The Unheralded Triumph: City Government in America, 1870–1900* (Baltimore: Johns Hopkins University Press, 1984), 270. On Tammany-connected coal merchants opposition to the proposed COS ban: Burrows and Wallace, *Gotham,* 1160.

13. Perkins, COS, MacManus, and imprisoned young man: George Martin, *Madam Secretary, Frances Perkins* (Boston: Houghton Mifflin, 1976), 82–83.

14. "In how many ways . . ." ". . . and his soul": Lowell, *On the Relation of Employers and Employed,* 3–5.

15. "public opinion . . .": Lowell, *On the Relation of Employers and Employed.* Lowell's support for legislation, arbitration, unions, and workers' cooperatives: Josephine Shaw Lowell, comp., *Industrial Arbitration and Conciliation: Some Chapters from the Industrial History of the Past Thirty Years* (New York: G.P. Putnam's

Sons, 1894), v; Lowell, *On the Relation of Employers and Employed*, 7–8; Waugh, *Unsentimental Reformer*, 183, 191, 193, 197, passim.

16. "the chronically 'homeless . . .'" "a system of public . . .": Josephine Shaw Lowell, *Poverty and Its Relief: The Methods Possible in the City of New York: a paper read before the National Conference of Charities and Corrections at New Haven, Connecticut, May 27, 1895* (Boston: George Ellis, 1895), 5. "an asylum for moral idiots" "workers and not idlers . . .": Lowell, "The True Aim of Charity Organization Societies," 3, 4.

17. "came out for . . ." ". . . uptown friends." Simkhovitch, *Neighborhood*, 72.

18. "determined my . . .": Devine, *When Social Work Was Young*, 10. At Halle, Devine studied with "Professors Conrad, von Loening, and Erdmann": Devine, *When Social Work Was Young*, 12–14. Devine was "often called the 'dean of social welfare'": "E. T. Devine Dies; Welfare Leader," *New York Times*, 28 February 1948. According to the University of Pennsylvania Registrar's records Devine received his doctorate on 16 June 1893. Patten's support for Allen and Perkins: "The Reminiscences of Dr. William H. Allen" (1950), 14, "Reminiscences of Frances Perkins" (1951–1955), 1: 37, CUOHROC. Scott Nearing, the radical economist and another of Patten's students, wrote a book celebrating his teacher's excellence: *Educational Frontiers: A Book About Simon Nelson Patten and Other Teachers* (New York: T. Seltzer, 1925).

19. On Devine's life and aspirations: Edward T. Devine, *When Social Work Was Young*, 6–25. On Devine and the New York School of Philanthropy: Brandt, *The Charity Organization Society*, 44. Overview of Devine's life: William W. Bremer, "Devine, Edward Thomas," in *Biographical Dictionary of Social Welfare in America*, ed. Walter I. Trattner (New York: Greenwood Press, 1986), 228–31.

20. "I can do no work . . .": Lowell to Devine, 9 September 1905, catalogued correspondence, CSS Papers. "There is no charity . . .": Edward T. Devine, "Scientific Charity," reprinted from *Philadelphia Medical Journal*, 24 June 1899, 1–2. On scientific charity: Robert H. Bremner, *From the Depths: The Discovery of Poverty in the United States* (New York: New York University Press, 1956), 135; Michael B. Katz, *In the Shadow of the Poorhouse: The Social History of Welfare in America*, 10th anniversary ed. (New York: Basic Books, 1996), 60–87. "the idea of charity . . .": Devine, *The Practice of Charity*, 7.

21. "Charity reasonably . . .": Devine, *The Practice of Charity*, 12; "In the eighteenth century . . ." ". . . is needed.": *The Practice of Charity*, 67.

22. "The new . . ." ". . . to operate.": Devine, *When Social Work Was Young*, 4.

23. "claims as its . . .": Albert O. Wright, "The New Philanthropy," in *Proceedings of the National Conference of Charities and Corrections, 1896* (Boston: n.p., 1896), 4–5. "makes of charity . . .": Devine, *When Social Work Was Young*, 114. "more attention . . .": Edward T. Devine to Robert W. de Forest, 22 November 1906, "Personalities: Edward T. Devine," box 153, CSS Papers.

24. On COS-Columbia cooperation: Brandt, *The Charity Organization Society*, 15–17; Richmond Mayo-Smith, Franklin H. Giddings, and Frederick W. Holls, "Special Report of the Committee on Statistics," *The C.O.S. 15th Annual Report: From Jan. 1896 to July 1897* (New York, 1897), 33–43. Josephine Shaw Lowell chaired the Society's "District Work": *The Charity Organization Society of the City of New York, Fourteenth Annual Report, From January 1895 to July, 1896* (New York, 1896), 2, 3. On School of Philanthropy 1904 course offerings: "The Winter Course in Philanthropy," *Charities*, 23 April 1904, 415–16. On Chicago, Boston, and elsewhere: Robyn Muncy, *Creating a Female Dominion in American Reform: 1890–1935* (New York: Oxford University Press, 1991), 68.

25. In endowing the School, John S. Kennedy made the following request, agreed to by the COS: "I wish to have Columbia University affiliated with this Committee, as it is with the Society." John S. Kennedy to Robert W. DeForest, president of the Charity Organization Society of the City of New York, 15 November 1904, in *The Charity Organization Society of the City of New York, Twenty-Second Annual Report: From July 1903 to June 1904* (New York, 1904), 23. First summer and "many visitors": "Summer School in Philanthropy," *Annals of the American Academy of Political and Social Science* 12 (September 1898): 319; on expanded School: *Bulletin of the New York School of Philanthropy* 5, no. 1 (September 1911): 16. "ideal.": Devine, *When Social Work Was Young*, 133.

26. Training at the School and "headworkers . . .": Brandt, *The Charity Organization Society*, 135–36.

27. First-summer courses: "Summer School in Philanthropy," *Annals of the American Academy of Political and Social Science* 12 (September 1898): 319–23. In 1899 a "Friendly Visitors Course" on casework was given by Z. D. Smith, who urged case workers to befriend those they counseled; box 99, CSS Papers. On the 18 June to 28 July 1900 summer school program: "Appendix II," in Devine, *The Practice of Charity*, 176–82. Lindsay: *The New York School of Philanthropy: General Announcement, 1914–1915*, 7, no. 2 (March 1914): 19, 23.

Between 1905 and 1911, 128 men completed the year-long program; many more attended classes. In 1904, 159 students enrolled; in 1909, 288 students attended lectures, 34 of them full-time students; by 1910 the School of Philanthropy offered a two-year course: Elizabeth G. Meier, *A History of the New York School of Social Work* (New York: Columbia University Press, 1954), 23.

28. Course offerings: *New York School of Philanthropy, Yearbook, 1906–7* (New York, 1907?), 38–39; *Outline of Courses of Instruction, 1909–1910*, 27–28; *Bulletin* (New York, September 1911): 5–9; *Bulletin* (April 1912): 19. *The New York School of Philanthropy: General Announcement, 1914–1915*, 23–24, 26.

29. "a big red-headed . . ." "scintillating eyes": The Reminiscences of Alvin Johnson, Oral History Research Office, Columbia University, 67. On Giddings: John L. Gillin, "Franklin Henry Giddings," in *American Masters of Social Science*, ed. Howard W. Odum (New York: Henry Holt, 1927), 176, 196–97; Stephen Turner, "The Columbia University Family and Its Connections," in *The Social Survey in Perspective, 1880–1940*, ed. Martin Bulmer (New York: Cambridge University Press, 1991), 269–90.

30. "Shall we . . ." ". . . the inferior.": Franklin H. Giddings, "The Ethics of Social Progress," in *Philanthropy and Social Progress: Seven Essays* (New York: Thomas Y. Crowell, 1893), 232, 246. "America has . . .": *New York World*, 17 October 1906. "His views . . .": William D. P. Bliss, *The New Encyclopedia of Social Reform*, 3rd ed. (New York: Funk and Wagnalls, 1910), 541.

31. Mayo-Smith and COS: *The C.O.S. 15th Annual Report From Jan. 1896 to July 1897*, 3: 33–43; and *The COS 16th Annual Report: From July 1897 to June 1899*, 4: 55. On his life and scholarship: R. Gordon Hoxie et al., *A History of the Faculty of Political Science, Columbia University* (New York: Columbia University Press, 1955), 7, 170–174, 288; Franek Rozwadowski, "From Recitation Room to Research Seminar: Political Economy at Columbia University," in *Breaking the Academic Mould: Economists and American Higher Learning in the Nineteenth Century*, ed. William J. Barber (Middletown, Conn.: Wesleyan University Press, 1988), 194–95. "the burning . . ." ". . . By statistics.": Richmond Mayo Smith, "American Labor Statistics," *Political Science Quarterly* 1, no. 1 (1886): 45, 47. "among children . . .": *University Bulletin. Columbia College in the City of New York* (New York, March 1895), unpaginated.

32. Obituary, "Samuel Lindsay, Educator," *New York Times,* 13 November 1959. Daniel S. Lindsay was his father. *Gopsill's Philadelphia City Directory for 1895* (Philadelphia: James Gopsill's Sons, 1895), 1107, lists both Daniel S. Lindsay and Samuel M. Lindsay, with home address at 3912 Chestnut Street. Head of Civic Club: Samuel McCune Lindsay, "Introduction," to *Civic Club Digest,* compiled by a Committee of the Social Science Section of the Civic Club (Philadelphia: George H. Buchanan, 1895), xii. Executive secretary of NCLC: Edward Devine to Samuel McCune Lindsay, 5 May 1904, Lindsay Papers. From 1895 to 1901, Lindsay edited "Sociology Notes" for the *Annals of the American Academy of Political and Social Science;* he was the Academy's president from 1900 to 1902.

33. "When in search . . .": Florence Kelley to Samuel McCune Lindsay, 23 May 1916, Lindsay Papers. On Anna Robertson Brown Lindsay: "Mrs. S.M. Lindsay," *New York Times,* 1 March 1948.

34. On the Survey: Franz Schneider, Jr., "The Russell Sage Foundation," *Journal of the National Institute of Social Sciences* 1, no. 1 (1915): 128–36; Maurine W. Greenwald and Margo Anderson, eds., *Pittsburgh Surveyed: Social Science and Social Reform in the Early Twentieth Century* (Pittsburgh: University of Pittsburgh Press, 1996), passim. Paul Underwood Kellogg, ed. *The Pittsburgh Survey; Findings in Six Volumes* (New York: Charities Publication Committee, 1909–1914).

35. "decided on . . .": *Proceedings of the Pittsburgh Conference for Good City Government and the Fourteenth Annual Meeting of the National Municipal League* (n.p.: National Municipal League, 1908), 33. On Kellogg: Clarke A. Chambers, *Paul U. Kellogg and the Survey: Voices of Social Welfare and Social Justice* (Minneapolis: University of Minnesota Press, 1971), 16, 25, 18, 42, passim.

36. "microcosm . . .": Edward T. Devine, "The Pittsburgh Survey," 6 March 1909, in *Social Forces* (New York: Charities Publication Committee, 1910), 33, 34 145. On the Survey's origins: Roy Lubove, *Twentieth-Century Pittsburgh* (Pittsburgh: University of Pittsburgh Press, 1995), 1: 6–7. "an attempt . . ." ". . . human life.": Devine, "The Pittsburgh Survey," 145–52; also, Edward T. Devine, "Pittsburgh The Year of the Survey," in *The Pittsburgh District: Civic Frontage, The Pittsburgh Survey,* vol. 5 (New York: Survey Associates, 1914), 3–6. "The Pittsburgh . . .": "Reminiscences of Frances Perkins" (1951–1955) 1: 60, CUOH-ROC. "The sensational . . .": I. M. Rubinow, *The Quest for Security* (New York: Henry Holt, 1934), 338.

37. "normal community" ". . . social control.": Edward T. Devine, *Misery and Its Causes* (New York: Macmillan, 1909), 241.

Chapter 3. Social Settlements as Neighborhood Democracy or Benevolent Paternalism

1. On settlement house movement: Allan F. Davis, *Spearheads for Reform: The Social Settlements and the Progressive Movement, 1890–1914* (New York: Oxford University Press, 1967); Ruth Hutchinson Crocker, *Social Work and Social Order: The Settlement Movement in Two Industrial Cities, 1889–1930* (Urbana: University of Illinois Press, 1992); Mina Carson, *Settlement Folk: Social Thought and the American Settlement Movement: 1885–1930* (Chicago: University of Chicago Press, 1990).

2. Jean Bethke Elshtain describes Hull House as "a site for initiating painstaking social science *and* as a place that accommodated social enthusiasms of all sorts," as well as "a place of interior beauty and grace" where the "teaching of the arts and giving children the opportunity to participate in a variety of artistic activities": Jean Bethke Elshtain, *Jane Addams and the Dream of American Democracy* (New York: Basic Books, 2002), 127.

3. Founding of the Neighborhood Guild: Davis, *Spearheads for Reform*, 8–9; Crocker, *Social Work and Social Order*, 1–6; Michael B. Katz, *In the Shadow of the Poorhouse: The Social History of Welfare in America*, 10th anniversary ed. (New York: Basic Books, 1996), 163–68. "there were no . . .": Helen Moore, "Tenement Neighborhood Idea—University Settlement," in *The Literature of Philanthropy*, ed. Frances A. Goodale (New York: Harper & Brothers, 1893), 45. Ward description: Caroline Williamson Montgomery, ed., *Bibliography of College, Social, University and Church Settlements*, 5th ed. (Chicago: Blakely Press, 1905), 77. "fermenting garbage . . ." ". . . the ward 57,514.": Moore, "Tenement Neighborhood Idea," 36–37, 47–48. "the most . . .": Kenneth T. Jackson, "Lower East Side Tenement Museum," in *The Encyclopedia of New York City*, ed. Kenneth T. Jackson (New Haven, Conn.: Yale University Press, 1995), 697.

4. "homes in . . .": William D. P. Bliss et al., eds., *The New Encyclopedia of Social Reform*, 3rd ed. (New York: Funk and Wagnalls, 1910), 1106. About 60 percent of settlement workers were women, almost 90 percent of settlement residents had attended college, and more than half had studied or were then studying in graduate school: Davis, *Spearheads for Reform*, 33–34. "educated men . . .": Mrs. Vladimir G. Simkhovitch, *Standards and Tests of Efficiency in Settlement Work* (New York: Trow Press, 1911), 2. "It was . . .": "The Reminiscences of Louis H. Pink" (1949), 7, CUOHROC.

5. Eldridge Street facility: Robert A. Woods and Albert J. Kennedy, eds., *Handbook of Settlements* (New York: Charities Publication Committee, 1911), 227–32; Charles Burr Todd, "Social Settlements in New York City," *Gunton's Magazine* 19 (August 1900): 167–68. "was so much . . .": Edwin R.A. Seligman, "Biographical Memoir Richmond Mayo-Smith, 1854–1901," in *Memoirs of the National Academy of Sciences* (Washington, D.C.: Government Printing Office, 1924), 17: 75. Seligman and Duggan's estimates: "A Course in Social Work; New Branch of Instruction Planned by Columbia," *New York Evening Post*, 15 August 1903; Stephen Duggan, *A Professor at Large* (New York: Macmillan, 1943), 11. 1905 and 1911 numbers: Montgomery, *Bibliography of . . . Settlements*, 86; Woods and Kennedy, *Handbook of Settlements*, 230.

6. "full of the thought . . .": Jean Fine Spahr, "College Settlement, 95 Rivington Street," in *Handbook of Sociological Information with Especial Reference to New York City*, ed. William Howe Tolman and William I. Hull (New York: G.P. Putnam's Sons, 1894), 253. "dingy and unattractive": Hester Dorsey Richardson, "The College Settlement," *Lippincott's Monthly Magazine*, June 1891, 785. "with piano . . .": Jane E. Robbins, "The First Year at the College Settlement," *The Survey* 27 (24 February 1912): 1801. Jane Addams' Hull House in Chicago opened within weeks of the College Settlement in New York.

7. The early years: Robbins, "The First Year at the College Settlement," 1800–1802; also, Elizabeth S. Williams, "The New York College Settlement," *Harper's Bazaar*, 19 May 1900, 152–55. "It has seemed . . .": Jane Elizabeth Robbins, "Charity That Helps and Other Charity," *The Forum*, December 1897, 505. On College Settlement: Mary M. Kingsbury, "Women in New York Settlements," *Municipal Affairs* 2 (September 1898): 458–62.

8. Todd, "Social Settlements in New York City," 172–73.

9. "in our rooms . . ." and the clubs: Robbins, "The First Year at the College Settlement," 1801–2. "various of . . .": Jean Fine Spahr and Fannie W. McLean, "Tenement Neighborhood Idea," in *The Literature of Philanthropy*, 29.

10. On the club for married women: Lillian W. Betts, *The Leaven in a Great City* (New York: Dodd, Mead, 1903), 162, 168–71.

11. Isabel Eaton, *Receipts and Expenditures of Certain Wage-Earners in the Garment Trades* (Boston: W.J. Schofield, 1895).

12. Stanton Coit, "University Settlement Society," in *Handbook of Sociological Information*, 256.

13. Stanton Coit, *Neighborhood Guilds: An Instrument of Social Reform* (London: Swan Sonnenschein, 1891), 40, 41, 42–43.

14. "college graduates . . ." ". . . and society.": Joseph B. Gilder, *University Settlement Society of New York* (New York, 1891), 1–2.

15. ". . . of Engineering.": Gilder, *University Settlement Society*, 2.

16. "Unlike the . . ." ". . . mental and moral life.": Coit, *Neighborhood Guilds*, 44, 149–50.

17. Neighborhood Guild events: Coit, "University Settlement Society," 256–57. On ill member, and father killed: Coit, *Neighborhood Guilds*, 43–44.

18. On Social Science Club: Moore, "Tenement Neighborhood Idea," 41–42, 47.

19. On Tenth Ward Social Reform Club: Moore, "Tenement Neighborhood Idea," 41–42.

20. "in our . . .": James Bronson Reynolds, "On Social Workers and Social Work," reprinted from Reynolds's 1899 "Report, as Headworker of the University Settlement," in *James Bronson Reynolds, A Memorial: An Outline of his Public Career, Glimpses of His Inner Self, Eulogies by Friends and Fellow-Workers, and Selections from His Writings* (New York: University Settlement, 1927), 93.

21. On Moskowitz: J. Salwyn Schapiro, "Henry Moskowitz: A Social Reformer in Politics," *The Outlook*, 26 October 1912, 446–49.

22. Its constitution: "University Settlement Society of New York, Constitution," in Gilder, *University Settlement Society*, 1–2, 5. University Settlement work: Todd, "Social Settlements in New York City," 168. Seligman's work on the council: *New York Tribune*, 28 February 1904. "the organization . . .": Gilder, *University Settlement Society*, 3.

23. "to move into . . .": Woods and Kennedy, *Handbook of Settlements*, 205. On Schiff's financing of Wald: Irving Howe, *World of Our Fathers* (New York: Simon and Schuster, 1976), 93. On Wald: R. L. Duffus, *Lillian Wald, Neighbor and Crusader* (New York: Macmillan, 1939), 1–15, passim.

24. "Fresh Air homes": Woods and Kennedy, *Handbook of Settlements*, 205. "colored nurses": Mary White Ovington, "Reminiscences: Chapter III," *The Afro-American*, 1 October 1932, 24.

25. "Lillian Wald was . . ." ". . . that went on.": The Reminiscences of Frances Perkins" (1951–1955) 1: 326–27, CUOHROC. On Harriman: Kristie Miller, "'Eager and Anxious to Work': Daisy Harriman and the Presidential Election of 1912," in *We Have Come to Stay: American Women and Political Parties: 1880–1960*, ed. Malanie Gustafson, Kristie Miller, and Elisabeth I. Perry (Albuquerque: University of New Mexico Press, 1999), 65–75.

26. Settlement cooperative efforts: Woods and Kennedy, *Handbook of Settlements*, 205. On Wald as vice president of the National Institute of Social Sciences: *Journal of the National Institute of Social Sciences* 1, no. 1 (1915): 1. The National Institute of Social Sciences was founded under the charter of the American Social Science Association in 1912. On Wald: Duffus, *Lillian Wald, Neighbor*; Lillian Wald, *The House on Henry Street* (New York: Henry Holt, 1915).

27. Description of neighborhood: Mary Kingsbury Simkhovitch, "Greenwich House, Second Annual Report," quoted in Montgomery, *Bibliography of . . . Settlements*, 77.

28. Records for Mary Melinda Kingsbury (Simkhovitch) in Columbia University Transcripts Department indicate her years of attendance and major subjects studied; apparently, she did not receive a degree. "The settlement is founded . . .": Mary Kingsbury Simkhovitch, "Report of Greenwich House," October, 1902?, quoted in *The New Encyclopedia of Social Reform,* ed. William D. P. Bliss and Rudolph M. Binder, new ed. (New York: Funk and Wagnalls, 1908), 1107.

29. "marked out for . . .": Robert Hunter, "The Relation Between Social Settlements and Charity Organization," *Journal of Political Economy* 11, no. 1 (December 1902): 76. "We knew . . .": Mary Kingsbury Simkhovitch, *Here Is God's Plenty: Reflections on American Social Advance* (New York: Harper, 1949), 174. "a passionate attempt . . .": Mary Kingsbury Simkhovitch, "Community Organization," typescript, 20 May 1915, 13, GHC.

30. "Jewish shopkeepers": Mary Kingsbury Simkhovitch, "Greenwich House, Second Annual Report," quoted in Montgomery, *Bibliography of . . . Settlements,* 77. On moving in at Jones St.: Simkhovitch, *Neighborhood,* 92.

31. "a noisy . . .": Simkhovitch, "Greenwich House, Second Annual Report," 76. "beauty of character" "social pragmatism": Simkhovitch, "Community Organization." Seventeen residents: Montgomery, *Bibliography of . . . Settlements* (1905), 76. By 1911, ten women and five men residents, 28 women and 2 men volunteers: Woods and Kennedy, *Handbook of Settlements,* 200. "a center for . . ." ". . . roll along.": Simkhovitch, "Community Organization," 10. "There were no . . .": Simkhovitch, *Neighborhood,* 171.

32. "A neighbor's child . . .": "Report of the Director [Mary Simkhovitch] November 18, 1903 for preceding month," typescript, 3, GHC. "You cannot imagine . . .": Carmel Pecoraro to Miss Simkhovitch, 12 April 1904, reel 17 "Correspondence," GHC.

33. "primarily an intellectual . . . .": Simkhovitch, *Neighborhood,* 28; "wounded" "under a flag . . ." "anointed with . . .": *Neighborhood,* 17; "if I were willing . . .": *Neighborhood,* 15; on her childhood see also 1–20, 35–40, 171.

34. ". . . jolt.": Simkhovitch, *Here Is God's Plenty,* 9. "colored girls": Simkhovitch, *Neighborhood,* 41. Teaching high school, enrolled at Radcliffe: Simkhovitch, *Neighborhood,* 41; *Here Is God's Plenty,* 13, 95. Reading Kant in the park with Balch: *Neighborhood,* 50. ". . . *Tristan* and beer": *Neighborhood,* 53. Bertrand Russell and Walter Weyl were in her classes: *Neighborhood,* 51. "Here at Columbia . . ." ". . . the City.": Simkhovitch, *Neighborhood,* 58.

35. "like a nun's . . ." Simkhovitch, *Neighborhood,* 72; ". . . our neighbors.": *Neighborhood,* 73.

36. Columbia sociologist Franklin Giddings was the keynote speaker at the Association of Neighborhood Workers' first meeting: Simkhovitch, *Neighborhood,* 86. On Women's Trade Union League: Simkhovitch, *Here Is God's Plenty,* 102; Nancy Shrom Dye, *As Equals and as Sisters: Feminism, Unionism, and the Women's Trade Union League of New York* (Columbia: University of Missouri Press, 1980), 38, 63, 117. On Simkhovitch's service on committee, commission, and league: Simkhovitch, *God's Plenty,* 136–39; Simkhovitch, *Neighborhood,* 173, 189.

37. "Instead of . . ." Davis, *Spearheads for Reform,* 70. Congestion Committee officers: John Martin and Benjamin Marsh to Robert W. Bruere, 25 June 1908, box 18, file folder, "New York Congestion Committee, 1907–1915," CSS Papers. On Moskowitz as a member: Schapiro, "Henry Moskowitz," 447. On exhibit: "A Unique Exhibit; to be held at the American Museum of Natural History beginning on March 9, 1908," (leaflet) box 18, file folder, "New York Congestion

Committee, 1907–1915," CSS Papers; Henry Seager and Jeremiah W. Jenks were among exhibit speakers; "The 22nd meeting of the Committee on Congestion of Population," 10 June 1908 (Mary Simkhovitch, Florence Kelley, and Edwin Seligman attended), box 18, file folder, "New York Congestion Committee, 1907–1915," CSS Papers. Simkhovitch, *Here Is God's Plenty*, 124–25; Davis, *Spearheads for Reform*, 71. The Committee on Congestion sponsored bills in the New York State legislature: "Findings of the New York City Commission on Congestion of Population," 1910? box 18, file "New York Congestion Committee, 1907–1915," CSS Papers. The Committee continued into 1915: "Minutes of the 53rd Meeting of the Executive Board of the New York Congestion Committee," (Mary Simkhovitch, chair; Paul U. Kellogg and Edwin Seligman attended) 15 January 1915, box 18, file "New York Congestion Committee, 1907–1915," CSS Papers.

38. "Has Mrs. Simkhovitch . . .": Nicholas Murray Butler to Franklin H. Giddings 9 February 1907, Lindsay Papers. "in this university . . ." Franklin H. Giddings to Laura Gill [Dean of Barnard College], 10 April 1907, Lindsay Papers. Courses taught: *Barnard College. Columbia University Bulletin of Information, Announcement, 1908–1909* (April 1908), 65–66; *Barnard College. Columbia University Bulletin of Information. Announcement, 1909–1910* (May 1909), 66. Seligman praised her teaching and rapport with students: E. R. A. Seligman to Nicholas Murray Butler, 30 March 1910, "Dean's Office Correspondence," Box 1900–1910, folder no. 25, Barnard College Archives.

39. A settlement's three functions: Mary Kingsbury Simkhovitch quoted in "The Functions of a Social Settlement," *Charities*, 31 May 1902, 481–82.

40. "social impression," "amassing . . .": Simkhovitch, *Standards and Tests*, 2. "has to tell what it finds . . .": Mary Kingsbury Simkhovitch, "The Settlement Movement, Settlement Organization," *Charities and Commons*, 1 September 1906, 568. "on the job . . .": Simkhovitch, *Standards and Tests*, 5.

41. "We went in . . .": Simkhovitch, *Here Is God's Plenty*, 175.

42. "in the old Bleecker . . .": Simkhovitch, *Here Is God's Plenty*, 175. "We have . . .": Simkhovitch, "Community Organization," 12.

43. "much of it . . ." ". . . do people want it": Simkhovitch, "Community Organization," 12.

44. "Our friends at Columbia . . .": Simkhovitch, *Here Is God's Plenty*, 175. "our friends, Henry . . .": Simkhovitch, *Neighborhood*, 151. On Dewey as educational committee head and Seligman as president: 223. "My dear Harry . . .": Mary K. Simkhovitch to Henry Seager, 3 April 1916, reel 18, GHC. Seager replied that he was himself unable to attend the convention, but suggested as possible speakers in his place, "equally interested and equally competent," as he wrote, John Andrews, I. M. Rubinow, and Joseph Chamberlain: Harry Seager to "Dear Mary," 6 April 1916, reel 18, GHC.

45. Committee on Social Studies membership: "Minutes of the Meeting of the Board of Managers of the Co-operative Social Settlement Society, February 15, 1905," "Co-operative Social Settlement Society" folder, box 110, CSS Papers. On membership, also: Franz Boas, "Foreword," in Mary White Ovington, *Half a Man: The Status of the Negro in New York* (New York: Longmans, Green, 1911), ix. Louise Bolard More, *Wage Earners' Budgets* (New York: Henry Holt, 1903).

46. Emily Wayland Dinwiddie, *The Tenant's Manual: A Handbook of Information for Dwellers in Tenement and Apartment Houses and for Settlement and Other Workers* (New York: Greenwich House Publications, 1903). "enlightened" "one more step . . .": Simkhovitch, *Here Is God's Plenty*, 33. Ovington, *Half a Man*. Nassau conducted her research while in residence at Greenwich House in the winter of

1913–14: Mabel Nassau, *Old Age Poverty in Greenwich Village a Neighborhood Study* (New York: F.H. Revell, 1915), ii. Mary Kingsbury Simkhovitch, *The City Worker's World in America* (New York: Macmillan, 1917). The list of members of the New York Research Council appears in James Bronson Reynolds, *Civic Bibliography For Greater New York* (New York: Russell Sage Foundation, 1911), title page. "a practical": Reynolds, *Civic Bibliography*, v. "Public and private . . .": Simkhovitch, *Neighborhood*, 151.

47. "sociological pantheon" ". . . in their neighborhood.": Robert A. Woods, "The University Settlement Idea," in Robert A. Woods, *The Neighborhood in Nation-Building: The Running Comment of Thirty Years at the South End House* (Boston: Houghton Mifflin, 1923), 5, 30, 35. "the most scientific . . .": Herman F. Hegner, "Scientific Value of Social Settlements," *Municipal Affairs* 1, no. 3 (September 1897): 577–78. "social reform centres": "New Social Science Put into Practice," *Harper's Bazaar* 30 (25 December 1897): 1088–89. "carried on for many . . .": Woods and Kennedy, *Handbook of Settlements*, 228. "undertakes through its . . .": quoted in Charles Burr Todd, "Social Settlements in New York City," 166–67. "We must put . . .": James B. Reynolds, "The Need and Value of Settlement Work," *Proceedings of the New York State Conference of Charities and Correction* (Albany, 1900), 49–55. "Only those who . . ." ". . . to benefit.": "Theodore Roosevelt, "Reform Through Social Work," 450–51.

48. "Intimate knowledge . . .": J. Salwyn Schapiro, "Henry Moskowitz," 449. Annual themes: Woods and Kennedy, *Handbook of Settlements*, 228–30.

49. "The many-sideness . . ." ". . . private individuals.": quoted in Montgomery, *Bibliography of . . . Settlements*, 87. "brought about . . ." ". . . and children.": Woods and Kennedy, *Handbook of Settlements*, 229. "consistently labored . . .": Roosevelt, "Reform Through Social Work," 451.

50. Woods and Kennedy, *Handbook of Settlements*, 229. Harry P. Kraus, *The Settlement House Movement in New York City, 1886–1914* (New York: Arno Press, 1980), 65.

51. "We must care enough . . ." ". . . be in vain.": James Bronson Reynolds, "On Social Workers and Social Work," in *James Bronson Reynolds, A Memorial*, 94–95. "worked always . . .": John L. Elliott, "The Settlements of New York and Mr. Reynolds," in *A Memorial*, 54.

52. Reynolds' life: *James Bronson Reynolds, A Memorial*, passim. According to Columbia University Department of Transcripts, Reynolds never took a degree. "Kitchen Cabinet": Reynolds, "Tribute to Theodore Roosevelt on His Death," in *A Memorial*, 151. Investigated Chicago stockyards: *A Memorial*, 15.

53. Coit's hymns: Stanton Coit, *Social Worship: For Use in Families, Schools, and Churches* (New York: Macmillan, 1914), 2: 46, 47, 89.

54. Frances A. Kellor, *Experimental Sociology, Descriptive and Analytical: Delinquents* (New York: Macmillan, 1901).

55. Ellen Fitzpatrick, *Endless Crusade: Women Social Scientists and Progressive Reform* (New York: Oxford University Press, 1990), 17–27.

56. Frances Kellor, *Out of Work: A Study of Unemployment Agencies, Their Treatment of the Unemployed, and Their Influence upon Home and Business* (New York: Putnam Inter-Municipal Committee on Household Research, 1904); Fitzpatrick, *Endless Crusade*, 135. "no previous . . .": C. R. Henderson, review of Kellor's *Out of Work*, *American Journal of Sociology* 10, no. 4 (January 1905): 558. On the treatment of workers: Kellor, *Out of Work*, 8, 17, 64, 74, 92–93, 100.

57. "deeply involved": "The Reminiscences of Frances Perkins," 1: 46. Kellor and Mary Dreier: Fitzpatrick, *Endless Crusade*, 138. Regulation of job placement

industry: Fitzpatrick, *Endless Crusade*, 136. On the Inter-Municipal Committee: Kellor, *Out of Work*, 165–70.

58. Fitzpatrick, *Endless Crusade*, 140–45. John Higham, *Strangers in the Land: Patterns of American Nativism: 1860–1925* (New Brunswick, N.J.: Rutgers University Press, 1992), 239–40. Barbara Sicherman et al., eds., *Notable American Women: The Modern Period* (Cambridge, Mass.: Harvard University Press, 1980), 394.

Chapter 4. "A Science of Municipal Government": "Scientific Training" or "Agents of Wall Street"?

1. "the lowest . . ." "who from their . . .": Jon C. Teaford, *The Unheralded Triumph: City Government in America, 1870–1900* (Baltimore: Johns Hopkins University Press, 1984), 18. "gin-mill keepers" ". . . 3 lawyers.": Teaford, *Unheralded Triumph*, 33–34. "almost hopelessly . . .": John Dewey and James H. Tufts, *Ethics* (1908) in John Dewey, *The Middle Works, 1899–1924* (Carbondale: Southern Illinois University Press, 1976–1983), 5: 423.

2. On Parkhurst: Timothy J. Gilfoyle, *City of Eros: New York City, Prostitution, and the Commercialization of Sex, 1790–1920* (New York: W.W. Norton, 1992), 298–302; Richard L. McCormick, *From Realignment to Reform: Political Change in New York State, 1893–1910* (Ithaca, N.Y.: Cornell University Press, 1981), 47. Union Theological Seminary meeting: William D. P. Bliss, "The Church in Social Reform," *Independent*, 6 June 1907, 1368–69. "we must work out . . .": Walter C. Rauschenbusch, " 'The Christ-Answer to the Cry of the City," *The Survey*, 4 May 1912, 184–85.

3. On City Reform Club: Robert Muccigrosso, "The City Reform Club: a Study in Late Nineteenth-Century Reform," *New-York Historical Society Quarterly* 52 (July 1968): 235–54; Kenneth Fox, *Better City Government: Innovation in American Urban Politics* (Philadelphia: Temple University Press, 1977), 50.

4. "university . . .": Fox, *Better City Government*, 54.

5. "respectables": McCormick, *From Realignment to Reform*, 56; see also 122–23, 185, 210. City's population: Charles A. Beard, *American City Government: A Survey of Newer Tendencies* (New York: Century, 1912), 26. "an interesting . . .": Mary Kingsbury Simkhovitch, "Friendship and Politics," *Political Science Quarterly* 17, no. 2 (June 1902): 197.

6. Kenneth Finegold, "Traditional Reform, Municipal Populism, and Progressivism: Challenges to Machine Politics in Early-Twentieth-Century New York City," *Urban Affairs Review* 31, no. 1 (September 1995): 20–42.

7. "the science of . . .": Frank J. Goodnow, *Municipal Home Rule: A Study in Administration* (New York: Macmillan, 1895), v. "Father of Public Administration": Jane S. Dahlberg, *The New York Bureau of Municipal Research* (New York: New York University Press, 1966), 39. On "the determination . . ." versus "execution" of policy: Frank J. Goodnow, "The Place of the Council and of the Mayor in the Organization of Municipal Government—The Necessity of Distinguishing Legislation from Administration," *Proceedings of the Indianapolis Conference for Good City Government and Fourth Annual Meeting of the National Municipal League* (Philadelphia: National Municipal League, 1898), 71–81. In crafting the politics-administration distinction, Goodnow drew on what had become by the late nineteenth century a familiar mode of business organization in which a board of directors for a corporation delegates to a general manager the day-to-day operation of a business. In China, Goodnow initially promoted a democratic constitution, but as Yuan gathered dictatorial powers, Goodnow backed Yuan's

centralization of authority: Ernest P. Young, *The Presidency of Yuan Shih-k'ai: Liberalism and Dictatorship in Early Republican China* (Ann Arbor: University of Michigan Press, 1977), 175. On Goodnow: Dorothy Ross, *The Origins of American Social Science* (New York: Cambridge University Press, 1991), 274–79, 282–83; Albert Somit and Joseph Tanenhaus, *The Development of American Political Science: From Burgess to Behavioralism* (Boston: Allyn and Bacon, 1967), 49–62.

8. "Mere business . . .": Beard, *American City Government*, 386; "the social and . . .": *American City Government*, ix; "working class . . .": *American City Government*, 8; "From the point . . .": *American City Government*, 13; "The separation . . .": *American City Government*, 7.

9. "Education cannot . . .": Charles A. Beard, "The Study and Teaching of Politics," *Columbia University Quarterly* 12, no. 3 (June 1910): 271. Politics 105: Charles A. Beard, *Party Government, Syllabus* (New York: Columbia University, n.d., 1915?). "burning with . . .": Raymond Moley, *Realities and Illusions, 1886–1931: The Autobiography of Raymond Moley* (New York: Garland, 1980), 81.

10. "laughed aside . . .": C. Vann Woodward, "The Impact was Great," magazine section, *Herald Tribune*, 5 September 1954. On Beard's background: Ellen Nore, *Charles A. Beard: An Intellectual Biography* (Carbondale: Southern Illinois University Press, 1983), 6, passim. "was introduced . . .": Allen F. Davis, *Spearheads for Reform: The Social Settlements and the Progressive Movement, 1890–1914* (1967; New Brunswick, N.J.: Rutgers University Press, 1984), 171. Charles Beard, *The Industrial Revolution* (London: S. Sonnenschein, 1901). Beard's doctorate in Constitutional Law: Columbia University Registrar's Office, Division of Transcripts and Records.

11. On Beard, socialism, and the Rand School: John Louis Recchiuti, "The Rand School of Social Science During the Progressive Era: Will to Power of a Stratum of the American Intellectual Class," *Journal of the History of the Behavioral Sciences* 31 (April 1995): 149–61. "specially low . . .": Rand School of Social Science, *Prospectus* (New York, 15 July 1906). "intelligent interest": Cushing Strout, *The Pragmatic Revolt in American History: Carl Becker and Charles Beard* (New Haven, Conn.: Yale University Press, 1958), 93.

12. "under the guidance . . .": Charles A. Beard, *An Economic Interpretation of the Constitution of the United States* (1913; New York: Macmillan, 1961), 73. Seligman called Marx's work "brilliant and striking" even as he distanced himself from Marx's socialism: Edwin R. A. Seligman, *The Economic Interpretation of History* (New York: Columbia University Press, 1902), 165. "To all appearances": Beard, *American City Government*, 29.

13. "a revolution . . .": quoted in Dahlberg, *New York Bureau*, 39.

14. "substitute . . .": *New York Times*, 1 June 1907.

15. "All of . . .": "Reminiscences of Frances Perkins" (1951–1955) 1: 421, CUOHROC.

16. "a reaction . . .": Frederick A. Cleveland, "Evolution of the Budget Idea in the United States," reprinted from *Annals of the American Academy of Political and Social Science*, publication no. 942 (Philadelphia, November 1915), 21. "To promote . . .": William H. Allen, "Instruction in Public Business" *Political Science Quarterly* 23, no. 4 (1908): 607.

17. On the Bureau: Norman N. Gill, *Municipal Research Bureaus: A Study of the Nation's Leading Citizen-Supported Agencies* (Washington, D.C.: American Council on Public Affairs, 1944), 15; *Purposes and Methods of the Bureau of Municipal Research* (New York: Bureau of Municipal Research, 12 December 1907), 2–4; Henry Bruère, "Government and Publicity," *Independent*, 12 December 1907,

1426; William H. Allen, "Better Business Methods for Cities," *Review of Reviews*, February 1908, 195–200. Lindsay's "New York State Work": *Announcement of the Training School for Public Service, 1917* (New York: Bureau of Municipal Research, 1917?), 2; on Lindsay as secretary: *Ten Years of Municipal Research* (New York: Bureau of Municipal Research, 1916?), 1.

18. On Bruère: *Who's Who in America, 1916–1917*, s.v. "Bruere, Henry"; "Reminiscences of Henry Bruère" (1949), 5–10, CUOHROC. On his move to New York from Chicago: "How New York City's Government was Reorganized," *New York Tribune*, 9 August 1914. Allen studied in Germany under the economist Karl Buecher, and under "Wagner, Schmoller, and Paulson": William H. Allen, "The Reminiscences of Dr. William H. Allen" (1950), 4–22, CUOHROC; Allen's fields of study and doctorate: Records Office, Registrar of the University of Pennsylvania. On Cleveland: A. E. Buck, Henry Bruère, and W. F. Willoughby, *Frederick Albert Cleveland, 1865–1946: A Tribute* (New York: Governmental Research Association, 1946), 2–3, passim; "Reminiscences of William H. Allen," 70, 167.

19. "the voluminous . . .": Robert A. Caro, *The Power Broker: Robert Moses and the Fall of New York* (New York: Knopf, 1974), 65. "whose advice . . .": "Reminiscences of Frances Perkins," 1: 435; "plenty of nerve . . ." and ". . . excellent administrator," "a very tactful . . ." and "the natural qualities": "Reminiscences of Frances Perkins," 2: 292–93. "was very precise . . .": "Reminiscences of Frances Perkins," 1: 421. " 'not a little . . .' ": Caro, *The Power Broker*, 62. "a man of . . .": "Reminiscences of Henry Bruère." "How would I sum . . .": Caro, *The Power Broker*, 63.

20. "not socialistic": "Reminiscences of Dr. William H. Allen," 63. "to socialize capital . . .": William H. Allen, "A National Fund for Efficient Democracy," *Atlantic*, October 1908, 463. "Without intelligent . . .": William Harvey Allen, *Efficient Democracy* (New York: Dodd, Mead, 1907), x. On the New York X Club: "Reminiscences of Dr. William H. Allen," 62–63, 69. "setting new . . ." "illustrations . . .": William H. Allen, *Woman's Part in Government: Whether She Votes or Not* (New York: Dodd, Mead, 1911), 355–58. On Allen teaching at New York University: Charles A. Beard, "New York City as a Political Science Laboratory," in *The College and the City: A Series of Addresses Delivered at the National Conference on Universities and Public Service*, ed. Edward A. Fitzpatrick (New York: The Committee, 1914), 24–25.

21. "only through . . .": Henry Bruère, *The New City Government: A Discussion of Municipal Administration Based on a Survey of Ten Commission Governed Cities*, 2nd ed. (New York: D. Appleton, 1913), 100. "harnessing to . . .": Bruère, *The New City Government*, 2. "the glad hand . . .": Henry Bruère, "Government and Publicity," *Independent*, 12 December 1907: 1423. On Bruère's European travels: "Reminiscences of Henry Bruère," 75, 80–81. "I have not . . .": Henry Bruère to Theodore Roosevelt, 29 July 1912; Bruère to Roosevelt, 3 September 1912, Theodore Roosevelt Papers, Library of Congress. Among Bruère's publications: "Efficiency in City Government," *Annals of the American Academy of Political and Social Science* (May 1912): 3–22.

22. "that the activities . . ." ". . . writings of the past.": Frederick Cleveland, *The Growth of Democracy in the United States* (Chicago: Quadrangle Press, 1898), iii–iv. "the 'poor whites' . . .": *The Growth of Democracy*, 54. "should not the American . . .": F. A. Cleveland, "Municipal Ownership as a Form of Governmental Control," *Annals of the American Academy of Political and Social Science* 28 (November 1906): 370.

23. *How Manhattan Is Governed* (New York: Bureau of City Betterment of the

Citizens Union of the City of New York, 1906). On uncovering graft: Henry Bruère, "Government and Publicity," 1424–26. ". . . Besmirch" and lawsuit: "The Municipal Research Idea," *Municipal Research*, March 1916, 4–5. "official incompetence": "The Municipal Research Idea," 4–5. "in the careful . . .": *The Survey*, 15 January 1910, 519–20.

24. On the Bureau's inquiries and initiatives: the collection of Bureau of Municipal Research pamphlets, leaflets, and broadsides: "Bureau Municipal Research, New York, Efficient Citizenship Series, no. 1–499," held at the New York Public Library; also Cleveland, "Evolution of the Budget Idea," 19; *Analysis of the Salary Expenditure of the Department of Health of the City of New York for the Year 1906* (New York, 1906); *Making a Municipal Budget* (New York: Bureau of Municipal Research, 1907?); *A Bureau of Child Hygiene: Co-Operative Studies and Experiments by the Department of Health of the City of New York and the Bureau of Municipal Research* (New York: Bureau of Municipal Research, 1908).

25. "cleaning up . . ." "We had the police . . .": "Reminiscences of Henry Bruère," 55. On housing inquiries: *Tenement House Administration: Steps Taken to Locate and Solve Problems of Enforcing the Tenement House Law* (New York: Bureau of Municipal Research, 1909). On water system inquiry: H. S. Gilbertson, "Public Administration—A New Profession," *Review of Reviews*, May 1913, 600. On initiatives: Mary R. Cranston, "New York's Civic Search-Light," *Harper's Weekly*, 6 March 1909, 12. *Six Years of Municipal Research for New York City: Record for 1906–1911* (New York: Bureau of Municipal Research, 1911?), 10–11; *Ten Years of Municipal Research* (New York: Bureau of Municipal Research, 1916?), 16.

26. "intelligent popular control" "*facts* . . .": Henry Bruère, "Government and Publicity," 1422. On the Bureau's public exhibits: Jonathan Kahn, "Re-Presenting Government and Representing the People: Budget Reform and Citizenship in New York City, 1908–1911," *Journal of Urban History* 19, no. 3 (May 1993): 84–103. Of coat hooks and erasers: "The Reminiscences of Henry Bruère," 63–64. Bulletins and pamphlets, printed and distributed: *Municipal Research*, March 1916, 83; Dahlberg, *New York Bureau of Municipal Research*, 35–36.

27. On School's founding: William H. Allen, "Training Men and Women for Public Service," *Annals of the American Academy of Political and Social Science: Efficiency in City Government* 41 (May 1912): 311–12. "of executive ability . . ." "lead . . .": *Training School for Public Service, Annual Report, 1912* (New York: Conducted by the Bureau of Municipal Research, 1912?), 4. On the number of women: Mary Ritter Beard, *Woman's Work in Municipalities* (New York: D. Appleton, 1915), 337. On recruitment: George A. Graham, *Education for Public Administration: Graduate Preparation in the Social Sciences at American Universities* (Chicago: Public Administration Service, 1941), 135–41. On placement of School graduates: "Reminiscences of Henry Bruère," 51–52. On Moley: Moley, *Realities and Illusions*, 83–84, 89–90.

28. "That assignment . . .": Dahlberg, *New York Bureau of Municipal Research*, 123–24. On reclaiming $900,000: "How New York City's Government Was Reorganized," *New York Tribune*, 9 August 1914.

29. "a connecting . . .": Beard, *American City Government*, 118–19. "the Training . . ." "spend a portion . . .": "Training School for Public Service Second Annual Report 1913," *Efficient Citizenship: To Promote the Application of Scientific Principles to Government* 670 (18 March 1914): 6–7.

30. "from a practical . . .": *New York Tribune*, 19 October 1911. On Beard and municipal reform: Charles T. Goodsell, "Charles A. Beard, Prophet for Public Administration," *Public Administration Review* 46 (March/April 1986): 105–7;

Luther Gulick, "Beard and Municipal Reform," in *Charles A. Beard: An Appraisal*, ed. Howard K. Beale (Lexington: University of Kentucky Press, 1954), 47–60. Beard was editor of "Events and Personalia," *National Municipal Review* 1, no. 1 (January 1912), for example. On the Wisconsin Idea: Charles McCarthy, *The Wisconsin Idea* (New York: Macmillan, 1912).

31. Conference sponsors: Fitzpatrick, *The College and the City*, title page, 10; "charitable and . . .": *The College and the City*, 15.

32. "closer . . ." "that we have.": John Purroy Mitchel, "The College and the City," in Fitzpatrick, *The College and the City*, 7–9. "practically a virgin . . ." and Duggan's talk: Stephen P. Duggan, "The College of the City of New York and Community Service" in *The College and the City*, 49–53.

33. "presents the greatest laboratory . . .": Charles A. Beard, "New York City as a Political Science Laboratory," in Fitzpatrick, *The College and the City*, 19; "There is not a . . .": Beard, "New York City as . . ." 20; "This term 'laboratory' . . ." ". . . we can use chemistry.": Beard, "New York City as . . ." 23. "a Teeming Sociological Laboratory": Samuel McCune Lindsay, "New York as a Sociological Laboratory," in *The College and the City*, 27; "the highest service . . .": Lindsay, "New York as a Sociological . . .": 30–31.

34. Charles Beard and Frederick Cleveland, "The Constitution and Government of the State of New York," *Municipal Review* 61 (May 1915): 58; Dahlberg, *New York Bureau*, 95–101.

35. "women should be . . .": Henry Rogers Seager, *Introduction to Economics* (New York: Henry Holt, 1904), 412. On Sayles: Mary B. Sayles, "Housing Conditions in Jersey City," *Annals of the American Academy of Political and Social Science* 20 (July 1902): 139–49; John William Leonard, ed., *Woman's Who's Who of America: A Biographical Dictionary of Contemporary Women in the United States and Canada 1914–1915* (New York: American Commonwealth, 1914), s.v. "Sayles, Mary B." Allen, *Woman's Part in Government.* "an important contribution": Elsa Denison, *Helping School Children: Suggestions for Efficient Cooperation with the Public Schools* (New York: Harper and Brothers, 1912), xv.

36. "Women's historic function . . .": Mary Ritter Beard, *Woman's Work in Municipalities* (New York: D. Appleton, 1915), 84.

37. Budget growth: Dahlberg, *New York Bureau*, 22. On the New York Bureau of Municipal Research as the pioneer in the development of the governmental research movement in the U.S., its publications, and on the subsequent growth of similar bureaus: Gustavus A. Weber, *Organized Efforts for the Improvement of Methods of Administration in the United States* (New York: D. Appleton, 1919), 12–13, 173–90, passim.

38. Taft's commission: *Special Message of the President of the United States on The President's Inquiry into Economy and Efficiency* (Washington, D.C.: Government Printing Office, 1911); Dahlberg, *New York Bureau*, 81–91. "to more efficiently . . .": "Municipal Research Plan for Federal Government," *The Survey*, 29 October 1910: 150. "investigation of . . .": *A Compilation of the Messages and Papers of the Presidents*, vol. 17 (New York: Bureau of National Literature, 1897), 7699. Commission plan: "Municipal Research Plan," 150; also, Frederick A. Cleveland, "The Need for Coordinating, Municipal, State and National Activities," *Annals of the American Academy of Political and Social Science: Efficiency in City Government* 41 (May 1912): 23–39. Taft's praise: President William Howard Taft, "Special Message on Economy and Efficiency in Government Service, January 17, 1912" in *A Compilation of the Messages and Papers of the Presidents* 17: 7698–7719.

39. "Vice Mayor": "The Eagle's Hall of Fame: We Nominate Henry Bruère," *Brooklyn Eagle*, 15 February 1915. "He was in everything . . .": "Reminiscences of Frances Perkins," 2: 292. As mayor, Mitchel consulted with Seligman, Cleveland, and Henry Moskowitz, and in February 1915 delivered an address at Columbia's Academy of Political Science at a conference on municipal government: file folder "Desk Diary, 1915," box 45, John Purroy Mitchel Papers, Library of Congress. Bruère's work as chamberlain: "A Servant to Public Servants: Henry Bruère, Appointed to Make New York's Government Efficient," *Independent*, 12 January 1914, 64–65; Henry Bruère, *Administrative Reorganization and Constructive Work in the Government of the City of New York, 1914* (New York: Bureau of City Chamberlain, C.S. Nathan Press, 1915).

40. The Training School for Public Service was allocated $120,000 of this money. On contributions: *Municipal Research*, March 1916, 14. The $2,200,000 estimate is calculated from the consumer price index in conjunction with Scott Derks, ed., *The Value of a Dollar: Prices and Incomes in the United States: 1860–1999* (Lakeville, Conn.: Grey House, 1999), 2.

41. Raymond B. Fosdick, *The Story of the Rockefeller Foundation* (New York: Harper Brothers, 1952); Ellen Condliffe Lagemann, *The Politics of Knowledge: The Carnegie Corporation, Philanthropy, and Public Policy* (Middletown, Conn.: Wesleyan University Press, 1989); Franz Schneider, Jr., "The Russell Sage Foundation," *Journal of the National Institute of Social Sciences* 1, no. 1 (1915): 128–136; Kathleen D. McCarthy, *Noblesse Oblige: Charity and Cultural Philanthropy in Chicago, 1849–1929* (Chicago: University of Chicago Press, 1982), 3, 99.

42. Ida Tarbell, *The History of the Standard Oil Company* (New York: McClure, Phillips, 1904). Lincoln Steffens, another major muckraker, was graduated from the University of California in 1889 and his *The Shame of the Cities* (1904) and *The Struggle for Self-Government* (1906) were important in setting the groundwork for the municipal research and reform movements.

43. "frequently been charged . . .": William H. Allen, *Reasons Why Mr. Allen Believes That Mr. Rockefeller's Conditional Offer of Support to the New York Bureau of Municipal Research Should Not Be Accepted* (privately published, 1914), 14. Future president of the Rockefeller Foundation Raymond B. Fosdick wrote, "Critics have frequently charged that Mr. Rockefeller's benefactions were set up as a shield against public censure, in an attempt to re-establish himself and ward off the abuse to which over many years he was subjected": Fosdick, *The Story of the Rockefeller Foundation*, 4. For critical assessments of modern foundations see Lagemann, *The Politics of Knowledge*, and McCarthy, *Noblesse Oblige*.

44. "go to the root . . ." "of an immediately": Fosdick, *The Story of the Rockefeller Foundation*, 22–23.

45. "the worst . . .": Ron Chernow, *Titan: The Life of John D. Rockefeller, Sr.* (New York: Random House, 1998), 571. "the monster . . .": Chernow, *Titan*, 579. "while this loss . . .": Chernow, *Titan*, 578–79.

46. "things being lauded . . .": "Dr. Allen Would Put Vast Funds in Federal Control; In Recommendations to Industrial Relations Commission He Points Out Insidious Influence of Rich Men's Gifts on Colleges and Even Pulpits of Country," *New York World*, 7 February 1915.

47. The first Rockefeller Foundation trustees were John D. Rockefeller, Sr.; John D. Rockefeller, Jr.; Frederick T. Gates, a former Baptist minister and a principal business and philanthropic advisor to John D. Rockefeller, Sr.; Harry Pratt Judson, president of the University of Chicago; Dr. Simon Flexner, a physician and director of laboratories of the Rockefeller Institute for Medical Research;

Starr J. Murphy, personal counsel to John D. Rockefeller, Sr., in his philanthropies and director of the Colorado Fuel and Iron Company and other Rockefeller interests; Jerome D. Greene; Wickliffe Rose, a former history and philosophy professor at Peabody College in Tennessee; and Charles O. Heydt, Rockefeller's private secretary; after a few months, Harvard president Charles Eliot was added to the board along with A. Barton Hepburn, Chase National Bank president: Fosdick, *The Story of the Rockefeller Foundation*, 21.

48. "you have disagreed . . .": William H. Allen, Director, to Jerome D. Greene, 8 October 1913, folder 147, box 14, series 200, R.G. 1.1, RFA.

49. "The only difference": Jerome D. Greene to Dr. William H. Allen, 9 October 1913, folder 147, box 14, series 200, R.G. 1.1, RFA.

50. "intelligent control . . .": Allen, *Efficient Democracy*, x.

51. "the field of . . .": *Purposes and Methods of the Bureau of Municipal Research*, 28. On objectivity and social science, see Gunnar Myrdal, *Objectivity in Social Research* (1969; Middletown, Conn.: Wesleyan University Press, 1983), 74, 83–85, passim.

52. "one who has . . ." "and entanglements.": "Memorandum Concerning Dr. William H. Allen's Retirement from the Bureau of Municipal Research," 22 June 1915, folder 148, box 14, series 200, record group 1.1., RFA.

53. "Science is a . . .": Frederick A. Cleveland, "The Nomenclature and Phraseology of Municipal Administration and Accounts," *Proceedings of the New York Conference for Good Government and the Eleventh Annual Meeting of the National Municipal League* (Philadelphia: National Municipal League, 1905), 236. "The Bureau originally . . .": F. A. Cleveland, Director, to "Dear Sir" "Copy of letter sent to each member of the Industrial Relations Commission," 2 February 1915, and attachment, "Statement of Facts," folder 148, box 14, series 200, record group 1.1, RFA.

54. "find a basis . . .", narrative attachment to letter, Cleveland to "Dear Sir." "chairman of the . . .": Cleveland to "Dear Sir." "Rift" and "Dr. Cleveland won . . .": "Research Bureau Rift a Real Row," *New York Tribune*, 18 July 1914; "The Reminiscences of Dr. William H. Allen," 244–45; "Cutting Confirms Split in Bureau," *New York Times*, 19 July 1914.

55. In reply, Rockefeller had requested of Cutting information "about certain details of the Bureau practices," and, since Cutting did not apparently possess that information, a luncheon-meeting was set up for the following day between Rockefeller and Bureau director Cleveland (Allen being in Wisconsin on research). Cleveland made a written report of his discussion with Rockefeller to Allen in which he set forth "what questions had been raised and what had been the attitude of Mr. Rockefeller" (Cleveland's report to Allen has apparently not survived): Cleveland to "Dear Sir." See also "Dr. Allen Attacked by Research Chief [Cleveland]," *New York Times*, 4 February 1915.

56. Allen, *Reasons Why Mr. Allen Believes*, 1.

57. "imposing restrictions" "in the hope" "not to surrender": Allen, *Reasons Why Mr. Allen Believes*, 1, 6, 13. "the Right to Impose . . .": William H. Allen, *Modern Philanthropy* (New York: Dodd, Mead, 1912), 393. "Mr. Rockefeller's restrictions . . ." ". . . to spend his own money . . ." ". . . cannot afford to owe . . .": Allen, *Reasons Why Mr. Allen Believes*, 2, 6, 13. "To regard the acceptance . . .": Allen, *Reasons Why Mr. Allen Believes*, 14–15.

58. "voted 'that no subscriptions . . .'" "been lived up to," Allen, *Reasons Why Mr. Allen Believes*, 19–20. "On June 18th I wrote . . .": Allen, *Reasons Why Mr. Allen Believes*, 20.

59. "I can do nothing now but resign . . .": Allen, *Reasons Why Mr. Allen Believes*, 20.

60. "possible influence": "Report of Basil M. Manly," in *Final Report of the Commission on Industrial Relations* (Washington, D.C.: Barnard and Miller, 1915), 123.

61. Allen's subsequent career: "Reminiscences," 1.

62. Greene and Goodnow: *Guide to the Brookings Institution Archives* (Washington, Brookings Institution, 1987), "Governmental Studies," 1.

63. "There can be no doubt . . ." "In earlier times . . ." "The only kind of an expert . . .": Charles A. Beard, "Training for Efficient Public Service," *Annals of the American Association of Political and Social Science* 64 (March 1916): 217.

64. On name change: Gill, *Municipal Research Bureaus*, 19. Beard's posts and resignation: Dahlberg, *New York Bureau*, 25, 30. "emancipated from . . .": *A Proposal for an Independent School of Social Science for Men and Women* (New York, Marchbanks, 1918?), 3–10, Archives of the New School University.

Chapter 5. "To Look at the Nation's Crop of Children"

1. Katherine B. Oettinger, *It's Your Children's Bureau*, Children's Bureau Publication 357 (Washington, D.C.: Government Printing Office, 1962), 2. No primary source has been found to confirm this anecdote. In 1905 Kelley wrote, "if lobsters or young salmon become scarce or are in danger of perishing, the Unites States Fish Commission takes active steps in the matter. But infant mortality continues excessive, from generation to generation . . . yet not one organ of the national government is interested": Florence Kelley, *Some Ethical Gains Through Legislation* (New York: Macmillan, 1905), 101; quoted in Kriste Lindenmeyer, *"A Right to Childhood": The U.S. Children's Bureau and Child Welfare, 1912–1946* (Urbana: University of Illinois Press, 1997), 14–15.

2. "Bully, come down . . .": quoted in Walter I. Trattner, *Crusade for the Children: A History of the National Child Labor Committee and Child Labor Reform in America* (Chicago: Quadrangle Books, 1970), 95–96; also, Lindenmeyer, *"A Right to Childhood"*, 15. On Lindsay's meeting with the President and members of the administration: U.S. Senate Committee on Education and Labor, *Hearings on S. 8323, Establishment of Children's Bureau*, 4 February 1909 (Y4.Ed8/3:C43/2), (Washington, D.C.: Government Printing Office, 1909), 15. Organizational endorsements: Richard A. Meckel, *Save the Babies: American Public Health Reform and the Prevention of Infant Mortality, 1850–1929* (Baltimore: Johns Hopkins University Press, 1990), 108. Kelley, Devine, and Lindsay: *A Federal Children's Bureau: What Is Proposed*, pamphlet 83 (New York: National Child Labor Committee, December 1908), 2.

3. Owen Lovejoy, a minister turned sociologist, had formed a Sociological Club at his church before leaving it in 1904 to become one of two field representatives for the new National Child Labor Committee. He became NCLC president in 1907: "Lovejoy, Owen" in *Who's Who in America: 1912–1913*, and Sandra Opdycke, "Owen Reed Lovejoy," in *American National Biography* 14: 7–8. Lovejoy was American Association of Social Workers' second president in the early 1920s. "the best scientific . . .": U.S. House, House Committee on Expenditures in Interior Department, *Establishment of Children's Bureau in the Interior Department Hearings*, 27 January, 1 February, 1909 (Y4.Ex7/3:C43) (Washington, D.C.: Government Printing Office, 1909), 3–4, 6. "pursue the fullest . . .": U.S. Senate. Committee on Education and Labor, *District of Columbia Child Labor Regulations*

Revision Hearings, 30 April 1906 (Washington, D.C.: Government Printing Office, 1906), 15. "Some Results of the Work of the National Child Labor Committee," *Child Labor Bulletin* 1, no. 4 (February 1913): 96.

4. On two million working children: Steven B. Wood, *Constitutional Politics in the Progressive Era: Child Labor and the Law* (Chicago: University of Chicago Press, 1968), 3–4, 24. "Boys of 10 years . . .": Owen R. Lovejoy, "Child Labor and Health," *Child Labor Bulletin* 1, no. 4 (February 1913): 57. Mill wages: Elizabeth H. Davidson, *Child Labor Legislation in the Southern Textile States* (Chapel Hill: University of North Carolina Press, 1939), 8–17. On 12,000 licensed tenements: Florence Kelley, "Married Women in Industry," *Proceedings of the Academy of Political Science in the City of New York: The Economic Position of Women* (New York: Academy of Political Science, Columbia University, 1910), 95. "Our little kindergarten . . .": Mary Kingsbury Simkhovitch, "Women's Invasion of the Industrial Field," typescript, 31 October 1910, p. 19, GHC.

5. "It might be thought . . .": Henry Rogers Seager, *Introduction to Economics* (New York: Henry Holt, 1904), 412. Homer Folks, *Poverty and Parental Dependence as an Obstacle to Child Labor Reform*, pamphlet 41 (New York: National Child Labor Committee, 1907).

6. "based always upon . . ." "Forty years ago . . .": Julia C. Lathrop, *The Federal Children's Bureau*, Children's Bureau pamphlet 196 (Washington, D.C.: Government Printing Office, 1913), 2–3. Addams and Wald were instrumental in Lathrop's appointment: Lindenmeyer, *"A Right to Childhood"*, 27–29.

7. "No painstaking . . .": Josephine Goldmark, *Impatient Crusader: Florence Kelley's Life Story* (Urbana: University of Illinois Press, 1953), vi. "always . . .": Lathrop quoted in Jane Addams, *My Friend, Julia Lathrop* (New York: Macmillan, 1935), 129. On Kelley: Kathryn Kish Sklar, *Florence Kelley and the Nation's Work: The Rise of Women's Political Culture, 1830–1900* (New Haven, Conn.: Yale University Press, 1995). Florence Kelley, *Some Ethical Gains Through Legislation* (New York: Macmillan, 1905); Florence Kelley, "What Should We Sacrifice to Uniformity?" and "Street Trades," *National Child Labor Committee, Proceedings of the Seventh Annual Conference, Uniform Child Labor Laws* (New York: American Academy of Political and Social Science, 1911), 24–30, 108–11. "resist the inherent . . .": Florence Kelley, *Modern Industry in Relation to the Family, Health, Education, Morality* (New York: Longmans, Green, 1914), 33, 132–39.

8. "the toughest customer . . .": Kathryn Kish Sklar, "Florence Kelley and Women's Activism in the Progressive Era," in *Women's America: Refocusing the Past*, ed. Linda K. Kerber and Jane Sherron De Hart, 5th ed. (New York: Oxford University Press, 2000), 313. "in fear . . .": "Reminiscences of Frances Perkins" (1951–1955), 1: 112–14, 443, CUOHROC.

9. On Kelley: Goldmark, *Impatient Crusader*, 93–104. Sophonisba P. Breckinridge, "Kelley, Florence," in *Dictionary of American Biography*, suppl. 1 (New York: Charles Scribner's Sons, 1954), 462–63. Kathryn Kish Sklar, "Two Political Cultures in the Progressive Era: The National Consumers' League and the American Association for Labor Legislation," in *U.S. History as Women's History: New Feminist Essays*, ed. Linda K. Kerber, Alice Kessler-Harris, and Kathryn Kish Sklar (Chapel Hill: University of North Carolina Press, 1995), 47. "a voice . . ." "robbed the . . ." and childhood experiences: Florence Kelley, *The Autobiography of Florence Kelley* (Chicago: Charles H. Kerr, 1986), 23–24, 26, 30.

10. "college-bred . . ." "fundamental works . . .": Florence Kelley Wischnewetzky, "The Need of Theoretical Preparation for Philanthropic Work: A Paper Presented to the New York Association of Collegiate Alumnae on May 14, 1887,"

16, 22. "hopelessly inadequate": Florence Kelley Wischenewetzky, *Our Toiling Children* (Chicago: Woman's Temperance Publication Association, 1889), 34.

11. On Lowell as founder: Florence Kelley, "Twenty-five Years of the Consumers' League Movement," *The Survey*, 27 November 1915, 214.

12. "What is . . .": *Consumers' League of the City of New York, Room 617, 105 East 22d Street, New York City*, pamphlet (n.p., 1907?), 2. "the interest of . . .": Florence Kelley, "Twenty-Five Years of the Consumers' League Movement," 212, 214. "The Consumers' League is . . .": *State of New York. Preliminary Report of the Factory Investigating Commission 1912* (Albany: Argus, 1912) 2: 310.

13. On label and white list: *Consumers' League of the City of New York*, 2. "the association of cruel . . .": Florence Kelley, *The Responsibility of the Consumer*, pamphlet 81 (New York: National Child Labor Committee, 1908), 5; see also *The Work of the Consumers' League of the City of New York, 1915* (New York: the League, March 1916), 19. On Consumers' League activities: Maud Nathan, *The Story of an Epoch-Making Movement* (New York: Doubleday, 1926), xiii, 15–71, 137, 186–92; *Twenty-Five Years of the Consumers' League of the City of New York* (New York: Consumers' League, 1916), 11–21. "safe or sane . . ." "from a full share . . .": Florence Kelley, "Woman Suffrage: Its Relation to Working Women and Children," *Political Equality Series* (published monthly by the National American Woman Suffrage Association) 4, no. 23 (1908?): 68–71.

14. List of vice presidents: Florence Kelley to Samuel McCune Lindsay, 8 April 1915, Lindsay Papers. Advisory board: *The Work of the Consumers' League*, 24.

15. League committees: *The Work of the Consumers' League*, 25–27. On Brooks: Kelley, "Twenty-Five Years of the Consumers' League Movement," 212. On Baker: "Reminiscences of Frances Perkins," 2: 470–71. *The Work of the Consumers' League*, 14; on Baker's contributions to Kelley's League prior to acceding to the NCL presidency: Kelley, "Twenty-Five Years of the Consumers' League Movement," 212.

16. Committee on Legislation: *Work of the Consumers' League*, 27. On Jackson: "Jackson, Alice Hooker Day," *Woman's Who's Who: 1914–1915*, ed. John W. Leonard (New York: American Commonwealth, 1914). "by means of charts . . .": *Work of the Consumers' League*, 14.

17. On stumping and locals: Louis Lee Athey, "The Consumers' Leagues and Social Reform, 1890–1923" (Ph.D. dissertatin, University of Delaware, 1965), 29; Sklar, "Two Political Cultures," 45, 48. "That no . . .": General Federation of Women's Club's resolution quoted in Homer Folks, "Child Labor and the Law," *Charities*, 1 October 1904, 21. "loving old friend": Florence Kelley to "Dear Mary," 4 October 1912, reel 17, GHC. On attending first international conference: Kelley, "Twenty-Five Years of the Consumers' League Movement," 214. "through the efforts . . .": *Work of the Consumers' League*, 20.

18. "social justice . . .": League motto printed on its early pamphlets: Consumers' League of New York Pamphlet 5307, Kheel Center, School of Industrial and Labor Relations, Cornell University. "the whole crisis . . .": *The Crisis* 3, no. 4 (February 1912): 151.

19. Among the studies Pauline Goldmark directed were *West Side Studies* (New York: Survey Associates, 1914), and Charles B. Barnes, *The Longshoremen* (New York: Survey Associates, 1915). Pauline Goldmark's own research: *Preliminary Report of the Factory Investigating Commission* (Albany: Argus, 1912) 3: 1632–42; her "Preliminary Report on Employment of Women and Children in Mercantile Establishments," in *Second Report of the Factory Investigating Commission* (Albany: J.B. Lyon, 1913); "Child Labor in Canneries," in *Child Employing Industries: Pro-*

ceedings of the Sixth Annual Conference of the National Child Labor Committee (New York: American Academy of Political and Social Science, 1910), 152–54. On Goldmark: "Goldmark, Pauline," in Leonard, *Woman's Who's Who of America*; Irl E. Carter, "Pauline Dorothea Goldmark," *Biographical Dictionary of Social Welfare in America*, ed. Walter I. Trattner (New York: Greenwood Press, 1986), 330–32. "shortening working hours . . .": Pauline Goldmark, Josephine Goldmark, and Florence Kelley, *The Truth About Wage-Earning Women and the State* (Concord, N.H.: Distributed by the Concord Equal Suffrage Association, June 1, 1912), 8.

20. On *Muller*: Alice Kessler-Harris, *Out to Work: A History of Wage-Earning Women in the United States* (New York: Oxford University Press, 1982), 186–87; Judith A. Baer, *The Chains of Protection: The Judicial Response to Women's Labor Legislation* (Westport, Conn.: Greenwood Press, 1978), 57–61; Alice Kessler-Harris, "Affirming the Sexual Division of Labor," in *Days of Destiny: Crossroads in American History*, ed. James M. McPherson, Alan Brinkley, and David Rubel (New York: Dorling Kindersley, 2001), 214–19. Josephine Goldmark, *Child Labor Legislation Handbook* (New York: National Consumers' League, 1907). Josephine Goldmark, *Fatigue and Efficiency: A Study in Industry* (New York: Charities Publications Committee, 1912). Helen Marot, *Handbook of Labor Literature* (Philadelphia: Free Library of Economics and Political Science, 1899).

21. Louis D. Brandeis, assisted by Josephine Goldmark, *Women in Industry . . . Brief for the State of Oregon* (1908; New York: Arno Press, 1969); "The assumption . . .": S. P. Breckinridge, "Legislative Control of Women's Work," *Journal of Political Economy* 14 (1906): 107–9; quoted in *Women in Industry . . . Brief*, 49–50.

22. "there is more water": Havelock Ellis, *Man and Woman: A Study of Human Secondary Sexual Characters* (London: W. Scott, 1894), 156; quoted in Goldmark, *Women in Industry . . . Brief*, 21. "prolonged . . .": Frederick S. Lee, "Fatigue," *Journal of the American Medical Association* (19 May 1906); quoted in . . . *Brief*, 35. "Long hours of labor are . . .": . . . *Brief*, 18. "it cannot be said . . .": . . . *Brief*, 113.

23. "natural . . . delicacy" "unfit for . . .": Ware, *Modern American Women*, 74, 77–78. On the *Muller* debate: Nancy Woloch, *Muller v. Oregon: A Brief History with Documents* (New York: St. Martin's Press, 1996); Kessler-Harris, "Affirming the Sexual Division of Labor," 217–19.

24. "the so-called . . .": "Reminiscences of Frances Perkins," 1: 1; "had a brilliant idea . . .": "Reminiscences," 1: 3; "With a social sense . . .": "Reminiscences," 1: 4; "to New York right from college . . .": "Reminiscences," 1: 4–6.

25. "wrote to anybody . . ." "a league of women's . . .": "Reminiscences of Frances Perkins," 1: 19; "an investigation . . ." "We were to . . .": "Reminiscences," 1: 21.

26. "He took quantities . . ." ". . . and let them stab you.": "Reminiscences of Frances Perkins," 1: 32.

27. "Reminiscences of Frances Perkins," 1: 1, 61–65. On Mary Richmond: "Richmond, Mary," in Leonard, *Woman's Who's Who of America*. "Mary Richmond, *Friendly Visiting Among the Poor* (New York: Macmillan, 1903); *The Good Neighbor in the Modern City* (Philadelphia: Lippincott, 1908).

28. "Reminiscences of Frances Perkins," 1: 42–43, 45. "cash children . . .": Florence Kelley, "Woman Suffrage: Its Relation to Working Women and Children," 68.

29. "Legislation . . .": "Reminiscences of Frances Perkins," 1: 58–59.

30. "To form in every state . . .": *Annals of the American Academy of Political and Social Science* 20, no. 4 (July 1902): 155.

31. On the New York Child Labor Committee: Fred S. Hall, *Forty Years 1902–1942: The Work of the New York Child Labor Committee* (Brattleboro, Vt.: E.L. Hildreth, 1942?). Executive council members of the New York Child Labor Committee were Felix Adler, V. Everit Macy, Lillian D. Wald, William English Walling, Florence Kelley, William H. Baldwin, Jr., and John H. Hammond: Hammond, a member of the American Academy of Political and Social Science, was a wealthy lawyer who had earned his undergraduate degree from Yale's Sheffield Scientific School and his law degree from Columbia.

32. "on behalf of the Charity . . .": Edward T. Devine to Hon. Senator Brackett, Senate Chamber, Capital, Albany, New York, 3 March 1903, box 104, CSS Papers. *The Child Labor Evil in the State of New York*, pamphlet, 1 February 1903, Lillian Wald Papers, box 41, RBML. Carnegie Hall rally and "for preliminary work": "A National Child-Labor Committee: The Announcement of its Organization," *Charities*, 23 April 1904, 409–13.

33. "prominent and wealthy persons . . .": Homer Folks, "Child Labor and the Law," *Charities*, 1 October 1904, 20. On Edgar G. Murphy: "Murphy, Edgar G.," *Who's Who in American: 1912–1913.* "It should be . . .": Samuel Gompers, *Organized Labor's Attitude Toward Child Labor*, pamphlet 31 (New York: National Child Labor Committee, 1906?), 1.

34. "at least two . . .": "The Child Labor . . .": E. T. Devine to S. M. Lindsay, 5 May 1904, Lindsay Papers. "the rights, awareness . . .": Owen R. Lovejoy, "Child Labor and Health," *Child Labor Bulletin* 1, no. 4 (February 1913): 58. "investigation, and then . . .": quoted in Folks, "Child Labor and the Law," 21. "to awaken . . .": Lovejoy, "Child Labor and Health." "scientific research and . . .": Edward F. Brown, "Child Labor in New York Canning Factories," *Child Labor Bulletin* 1, no. 4 (February 1913): 12. Brown was a special agent for the NCLC.

35. On Murphy, Lindsay, and state versus federal child labor law: Trattner, *Crusade*, 90–93.

36. "exhibits of photographs . . .": "Some Results of the Work of the National Child Labor Committee," *Child Labor Bulletin* 1, no. 4 (February 1913): 96; "What the National Child Labor Committee Is Doing to Combat Abusive Child Labor," *Child Labor Bulletin* 1, no. 2 (August 1912): 127. "be of practical . . .": William F. Ogburn, *Progress and Uniformity in Child-Labor Legislation: A Study in Statistical Measurement* (New York: Columbia University, Longmans, Green, 1912), 18. "It is expected . . .": Ogburn, *Progress and Uniformity*, 20. "awaken from the lethargy . . .": John Dewey, "Some Dangers in the Present Movement for Industrial Education," *Child Labor Bulletin* 1, no. 4 (February 1913): 69. The eighty-page "Summary of State Laws" published in *Child Labor Bulletin* 1, no. 2 (August 1912) is an example of the NCLC's research and legislative effort. At the NCLC's ninth annual conference in Jacksonville, Florida, Florence Kelley, Samuel McCune Lindsay, John B. Andrews, and Owen Lovejoy delivered papers or led discussion groups: "Program, Ninth Annual Conference on Child Labor," *Child Labor Bulletin* 1, no. 4 (February 1913): 1–4.

37. On incremental successes: Lovejoy, "Child Labor and Health."

38. "I contend . . .": Jean M. Gordon, "Symposium: Unreasonable Industrial Burdens on Women and Children:—Effect on Education," *Child Labor Bulletin* 1, no. 1 (June 1912): 181. "Public aid would . . ." "care of families.": Simkhovitch, "Women's Invasion of the Industrial Field." On Civil War pensions: Theda Skocpol, *Protecting Soldiers and Mothers: The Political Origins of Social Policy in the United States* (Cambridge, Mass.: Harvard University Press, 1992), 2, 65, 110, 132, pas-

sim; Robert H. Bremner, *The Public Good: Philanthropy and Welfare in the Civil War Era* (New York: Knopf, 1980), 144; I. M. Rubinow, *The Quest for Security* (New York: Henry Holt, 1934), 236–37.

39. "the advisability . . .": *Third New York City Conference of Charities and Correction: "Report of Committee on Governmental Aid to Dependent Families,"* (Albany, J.B. Lyon, 1912), 3. Copy in box 19, Lillian D. Wald Papers. "the prevailing . . .": *Third New York City Conference: "Report of Committee on Governmental Aid to Dependent Families"*, 10. On Devine's belief that private charity organizations were often a better venue for aid to children and women: Rubinow, *The Quest for Security*, 487–88.

40. "lift the burden . . .": Florence Kelley, "Symposium: Unreasonable Industrial Burdens," 161. On early history of mothers' pensions: Rubinow, *The Quest for Security*, 477–96; Lindenmeyer, *"A Right to Childhood"*, 153–54. On expanding mothers' pensions: Muriel W. Pumphrey and Ralph E. Pumphrey, "The Widow's Pension Movement, 1900–1930: Prevention Child-Saving or Social Control?" in *Social Welfare or Social Control? Some Historical Reflections on Regulating the Poor*, ed. Walter I. Trattner (Knoxville: University of Tennessee Press, 1983), 51–66; Michael B. Katz, *Improving Poor People: The Welfare State, The "Underclass," and Urban Schools as History* (Princeton, N.J.: Princeton University Press, 1995), 43–44.

41. Moral standards: Judith Sealander, *Private Wealth and Public Life: Foundation Philanthropy and the Reshaping of American Social Policy from the Progressive Era to the New Deal* (Baltimore: Johns Hopkins University Press, 1997), 104. African American recipients, payment levels: *Private Wealth and Public Life*, 101, 114. Women's marginalization: Skocpol, *Protecting Soldiers and Mothers*, 476; Sealander, *Private Wealth and Public Life*, 113–16. Richmond's proposal: *Private Wealth and Public Life*, 117.

42. "it is the earnest hope . . .": *Supporters of the Keating-Owen Bill* (New York: National Child Labor Committee, 1916), 3; also, John Golden, "Children in the Textile Industry," *Child Employing Industries: Proceedings of the Sixth Annual Conference of the National Child Labor Committee* (New York: American Academy of Political and Social Science, 1910), 42–46. "No particular hardship . . .": *Supporters of the Keating-Owen Bill*, 2. "if there is any matter . . .": *Hammer v. Dagenhart*, 247 U.S. 251 (1918).

43. *Bailey v. Drexel Furniture Co.*, 259 U.S. 20 (1922).

Chapter 6. "Self-Constituted Leaders or 'Teachers' Whose Principal Aim Is Domination"? Social Science, Organized Labor, and Social Insurance Legislation

1. "Among those . . ." "are certain . . ." "professional social . . ." "disinterested third . . .": Samuel Gompers, "Editorials: Labor Must Decide Its Own Course," *American Federationist* 22, no. 6 (June 1915): 430–32.

2. "scientific . . .": Samuel Gompers to Dr. John B. Andrews, 15 May 1915 reprinted in *American Federationist* 22, no. 6 (June 1915): 432. The Andrews-Gompers dispute: Gompers, "Labor Must Decide Its Own Course," 431–32.

3. "With insistence . . ." ". . . aim is domination.": Gompers, "Labor Must Decide Its Own Course," 430–32.

4. "studied industrial . . .": Gompers, "Labor Must Decide Its Own Course," 430–31. "dilettantes" "In all of the . . .": Samuel Gompers to John B. Andrews, January 8, 1913, reel 8, Papers of the American Association for Labor Legislation 1905–1943 (Glen Rock, N.J.: Microfilming Corporation of America, 1974).

5. "barnacles": Samuel Gompers, "Labor vs. Its Barnacles," *American Federationist* 23 (April 1916): 268. Gompers, " 'Intellectuals,' Please Note," *American Federationist* 23 (March 1916): 198. "enthusiasm for . . ." "inauguration of . . .": Samuel Gompers, "Not Even Compulsory Benevolence Will Do," *American Federationist* 24 (January 1917): 48. See also Gompers's testimony before the "Commission to Study Social Insurance and Unemployment," *Hearings Before the Committee on Labor*, U.S. Congress, House of Representatives, 64th Cong., 1st sess., 6, 11 April 1916 (Washington, D.C.: Government Printing Office, 1916), 185. "under the domination . . .": Gompers, "Labor Must Decide Its Own Course," 432.

6. On voluntarism: George Cotkin, "The Spencerian and Comptean Nexus in Gompers' Labor Philosophy: The Impact of Non-Marxian Evolutionary Thought," *Labor History* 20 (1979): 514. Theda Skocpol, *Protecting Soldiers and Mothers: The Political Origins of Social Policy in the United States* (Cambridge, Mass.: Harvard University Press, 1992), 205–47. Roy Lubove, *The Struggle for Social Security: 1900–1935* (Cambridge, Mass.: Harvard University Press, 1968), 15–16.

7. "friendly societies" "tenement-house production" "harassed the . . .": Samuel Gompers, *Seventy Years of Life and Labor: An Autobiography* (New York: E.P. Dutton, 1925) 1: 190–93, 197. Insurance companies and other private organizations who opposed government-run social insurance often quoted Gompers's anti-legislative philosophy of voluntarism: Lubove, *The Struggle for Social Security*, 15.

8. "a young man . . .": Mary Kingsbury Simkhovitch, *Here Is God's Plenty: Reflections on American Social Advance* (New York: Harper, 1949), 33. "to sell" "They were as near ugly . . .": "Reminiscences of Frances Perkins" (1951–1955) 1: 59,CUOHROC "I do differentiate . . .": "Reminiscences of Frances Perkins," 1: 315–16.

9. On AFL political activism: Morton Keller, *Regulating a New Economy: Public Policy and Economic Change in America, 1900–1933* (Cambridge, Mass.: Harvard University Press, 1990), 134–35. Defeat of Massachusetts and Rhode Island bills: Irene Osgood Andrews, *Review of Labor Legislation of 1910* (Princeton, N.J.: Princeton University Press, August 1910), 6–7. "both hands . . .": Andrews, *Review of Labor Legislation*, 9. Divisions within AFL and "prolonged . . .": Robert F. Wesser, "Conflict and Compromise: The Workmen's Compensation Movement in New York, 1890s-1913," *Labor History* 12 (1971): 345–72, quote 348. In New York, organized labor broke ranks with the national position of the AFL and sponsored health insurance legislation for all workers: Irwin Yellowitz, *Labor and the Progressive Movement in New York State, 1897–1916* (Ithaca, N.Y.: Cornell University Press, 1965). On the UMW's backing of government ownership of industries: Keller, *Regulating a New Economy*, 116. "The American Federation of Labor, as in the past . . .": *Proceedings* of the A.F. of L. convention for 1914, 421–44, quoted in Henry R. Seager, *Labor and other Economic Essays* (New York: Harper and Brothers, 1931), 282–83.

10. "an army . . .": Alexander Johnson, ed., *Proceedings of the National Conference of Charities and Corrections at the Thirty-Ninth Annual Session, Held in Cleveland, Ohio, June 12–19 1912* (Fort Wayne, Ind.: Fort Wayne Printing Company, 1912), 384.

11. "economic science": Edwin R. A. Seligman *Economics and Social Progress* (New York: Macmillan for American Economic Association, 1902), 1. "The revolt . . .": Seager, *Labor and Other Economic Essays*, 227. Seager is quoting *The Survey*, 2 August 1913. On the German studies of 1885: Young-Sun Hong, *Welfare,*

Modernity, and the Weimar State, 1919–1933 (Princeton, N.J.: Princeton University Press, 1998), 23–25. As Hong notes, German social insurance programs had been crafted by Bismarck's administration in an effort to subvert the growth of socialist sympathies among the more skilled German workers, and in consequence the benefits of these programs initially covered skilled, unionized, male workers in Germany almost exclusively. Disability pensions, for example, were only adequate to support better-paid workers, while low-paid workers had to continue to depend on traditional poor relief when they were injured.

12. Old age security in Denmark and other countries: I. M. Rubinow, *The Quest for Security* (New York: Henry Holt, 1934), 254. The most frequently imitated system of unemployment insurance was the so-called Ghent system, which began in Belgium in 1901. The Ghent system combined municipal government payments with (when present) existing union unemployment benefits to offer unemployed workers modest cash payments. On the Ghent system: Frances A. Kellor, *Out of Work: A Study of Unemployment*, rev. ed. (New York: G.P. Putnam, 1915), 444–84. Nationally funded unemployment insurance programs were begun in England in 1920 and in Germany in 1927: Rubinow, *Quest for Social Security*, 392–416.

13. "the most democratically . . .": Gompers, "Labor Must Decide Its Own Course," 432.

14. "I say here . . .": Samuel Gompers, *The Samuel Gompers Papers*, ed. Stuart Bruce Kaufman (Urbana: University of Illinois Press, 1986), 2: 401. "I want to tell you . . .": Gompers, *Seventy Years of Life and Labor*, 1: 397. "as working men . . ." and "abandoned . . .": Gompers quoted in Bernard Mandel, "Samuel Gompers and the Negro Workers, 1886–1914," in *Black Workers and Organized Labor*, ed. John H. Bracey, August Meier, and Elliott Rudwick (Belmont, Calif.: Wadsworth, 1971), 27, 35.

15. On Seager: Samuel McCune Lindsay, "Henry Rogers Seager," *Columbia University Quarterly* 22, no. 4 (December 1930): 428–31; Samuel McCune Lindsay, H. E. Hoagland, and Charles A. Gulick, Jr., "Henry Rogers Seager," *American Economic Review* 20, no. 4 (December 1930): 794–97. On 1910 union membership: Leo Troy, *Trade Union Membership, 1897–1962* (New York: National Bureau of Economic Research, 1965), 2. "reactionary": "American Labor Legislation" (Seager's presidential address before the American Association for Labor Legislation in joint session with the American Political Science Association in Washington, 28 December 1915), reprinted in Seager, *Labor and Other Economic Essays*, 277; "takes no . . .": Seager, "American Labor Legislation," 285. On the AALL and AFL see also *American Labor Legislation Review* 1, no.1 (1911): 118–19.

16. "American socialists . . .": Rubinow, *Quest for Security*, 82. "our American universities . . .": John Kirby to William Howard Taft, 6 September 1912, William Howard Taft Papers, Library of Congress. Kirby's letter to Taft contains an eleven-page attachment that describes in detail "on behalf of the National Association of Manufacturers and some three hundred commercial and industrial organizations throughout the country" the NAM nominations of candidates for the then-forming U.S. Commission on Industrial Relations, the quotation "our American . . ." is on page 10 of Kirby's attachment.

17. On the executive council, along with Kelley and Addams, were Richard T. Ely, the Wisconsin economist (president of the AALL that year); Devine, Lindsay, and Seager of Columbia; Henry Farnam of Yale, Charles P. Neill; and Adna Weber: "Meeting of the Council, April 16, 1907 Room 306 United Charities Building, New York City," reel 61, AALL Papers. "We have much to learn . . .":

Proceedings of the Second Annual Meeting, American Association for Labor Legislation (Princeton, N.J.: Princeton University Press, 1909), 9–10. The meeting was held at Atlantic City, 29–30 December 1908. In 1908 the AALL Committee of the International Association members included Jane Addams, Felix Adler, John R. Commons, Richard T. Ely, Ernst Freund (the Chicago economist), John Mitchell, Charles P. Neill, Henry R. Seager, and John Graham Brooks, president of the National Consumers' League and sometime lecturer in economics: *Proceedings of the Second Annual Meeting*, 13. Florence Kelley also served on the AALL New York State Constitutional Committee in 1915: *Constitutional Amendments Relating to Labor Legislation and Brief in Their Defense* (New York: American Association for Labor Legislation, 1915), 2. "strictly scientific . . .": Andrews, *Review of Labor Legislation*, 25.

18. On early meetings: "Meeting of Executive Committee, March 16, 1906," which Henry Rogers Seager chaired, was held in the United Charities Building, as was the "Meeting of the Council, April 16, 1907 Room 306 United Charities Building," reel 61, AALL Papers. On recruitment of social scientists from other organizations: Samuel McCune Lindsay to Dr. Adna F. Weber, 15 March 1906, reel 1, AALL Papers. Throughout the Progressive Era the AALL meetings were held in conjunction with one or another of the social science professional associations' annual meetings.

19. "Bureaus of Labor . . .": *Proceedings of the Second Annual Meeting*, 10–11. Membership: Lloyd F. Pierce, "The Activities of the American Association for Labor Legislation in Behalf of Social Security and Protective Labor Legislation" (Ph.D. dissertation, University of Wisconsin, 1953), 19. AALL membership fees were $1, $3, or $5 annually: Andrews, *Review of Labor Legislation*, 25.

20. On AALL officers, executive committee members, and advisory council members: Henry R. Seager President to Hon Charles F. Brown, 14 March 1911, on "New York Association for Labor Legislation (Branch of American Association)," reel 5, AALL Papers. Other members of the executive committee, but not social scientists, were John Martin, an aging coal mine owner turned philanthropist, John Martin Philemon Tecumseh Sherman (son of the Civil War general), earlier commissioner of labor for New York State, Leo Arnstein, F. S. Tomlin, John Williams, and Lindon Bates, Jr. Those on the advisory council who were not social scientists included Adler, John M. Glenn, Albert Shaw, and Henry L. Stimson. On Woershoffer: Henry Rogers Seager to Samuel McCune Lindsay, 4 August 1911, Lindsay Papers. On Woershoffer's work and life: Vladimir G. Simkhovitch, "Carola Woerishoffer in Memoriam," *The Survey*, 30 September 1911, 2–4.

21. Mary K. Simkhovitch, "Isabel Dillingham," typescript, 6 February 1914, Greenwich House Papers, Tamiment Library, New York University.

22. On Andrews: Gerald D. Nash, "Andrews, John B.," *Dictionary of American Biography*, suppl. 3, 18–19; Andrews was also a member of the President's Unemployment Conference 1921 and a member of the New York Commission on Workmen's Compensation in 1932. On Osgood: *Portrait and Biographical Album of Mecosta County, Michigan* (Chicago: Chapman Brothers, 1883), 230; *Who's Who in America, 1916–1917*, 57. Born in 1879 in Michigan, Osgood was also a member of the American Political Science Association. She gave addresses before the AALL on "Irregular Employment and the Living Wage," and the annual report on the Woman's Work Committee: *Final Programs, Eighth Annual Meeting American Association for Labor Legislation and Second National Conference on Unemployment . . . December 28–29, 1914* (n.p., 1915?), 3–4; copy, Organizational Materials,

AALL Papers. Irene Osgood Andrews, *Minimum Wage Legislation*, (Albany, N.Y.: J.B. Lyon for the Factory Investigating Commission, 1914); *Review of Labor Legislation of 1909* (Madison, Wis.: Parsons Printery, 1909). On Lucius L. Osgood, her father: obituary, *Big Rapids Pioneer*, 21 April 1908.

23. On various members: *Meeting for the Purpose of Organizing a New York Branch of the American Association for Labor Legislation, Friday, February 19, 1909* (n.p., c. 1909), 1; at this meeting, Seligman spoke on "An Economist's Interpretation of Modern Labor Legislation," copy of in AALL Papers. The Third Annual Meeting was held 28–30 December 1909 in the Horace Mann Auditorium, Columbia University, and at AALL headquarters in the Metropolitan Building in Manhattan. On Van Kleeck: Jan L. Hagen, "Mary Abby Van Kleeck," *Biographical Dictionary of Social Welfare in America*, ed. Walter Trattner (New York: Greenwood Press, 1986), 725–28. On Perkins's membership: "Perkins, Frances," in John W. Leonard, ed., *Woman's Who's Who: 1914–1915* (New York: American Commonwealth, 1914). On Haynes's membership: membership renewal letter (1912?), Papers of George Edmund Haynes, Fiske University, Nashville, Tennessee. For a list of AALL members in 1909: "Membership List, American Association for Labor Legislation, New York State. Jan. '09," reel 5, AALL Papers.

24. "a scientific . . .": John B. Andrews to Laura A. Hughes, 12 October 1910, AALL Papers. "protective labour laws . . .": Seager, *Introduction to Economics*, 412–13. Seager's agenda: Henry R. Seager, "Outline of a Program of Social Legislation with Special Reference to Wage-Earners," *Proceedings of the First Annual Meeting; American Association for Labor Legislation; Madison, Wis., December 30–31, 1907* (Princeton, N.J.: Princeton University Press, April 1908), 85–103. "means for . . .": Henry R. Seager, "Program for Social Reform," *The Survey*, 2 April 1910, 25–31.

25. "We have again and again . . .": William F. Willoughby, "The Philosophy of Labor Legislation," *American Labor Legislation Review* 4, no. 1 (March 1914): 36–46.

26. Publication figures: John B. Andrews, "Report of Work for 1910," *American Labor Legislation Review* 1 (January 1911): 101.

27. On Seligman's involvement: Nicholas Murray Butler to Seligman, 8 April 1911; Joseph P. Chamberlain to Butler, 27 April 1911; and Thomas I. Parkinson to John Bassett Moore, 19 May 1914, Legislative Drafting Research Bureau Archives (LDRB), Columbia University Law School. On Lindsay's involvement: "A Laboratory of Legislation and Administration," typescript, 1912?, no author given, p. 2, LDRB Archives.

On LDRB formation: "Certificate of Incorporation of Legislative Drafting Association," 29 April 1910, LDRB archives; also: T. I. Parkinson to John M. Avery, 27 May 1913, LDRB Archives. On Parkinson in LDRB: Thomas I. Parkinson, "Legislation and Efficiency in Government," offprint, paper presented before the Second Pan American Scientific Congress, Washington, D.C., 27 December 1915–8 January 1916, 1–5, LDRB Archives.

The founders of the LDRB at Columbia were building on the example of the Legislative Reference Library at the University of Wisconsin, which, around 1903, had begun drafting progressive legislation in that state through the work of political scientist Charles McCarthy, economist John R. Commons, and others at the University of Wisconsin who worked with Wisconsin's progressive governor, Robert M. La Follette in Madison; the university's Madison campus was only a mile from the state capitol: Edward A. Fitzpatrick, *McCarthy of Wisconsin* (New York: Columbia University Press, 1944), 111–12.

28. "modest, retiring . . .": Stephen Duggan, *A Professor at Large* (New York: Macmillan, 1943), 14. Chamberlain's contribution to the LDRB for $100,000: typescript beginning, "I give and transfer to Thomas I. Parkinson . . . for the following purpose . . ." 1 July 1916, signed by Chamberlain, Thomas I. Parkinson Papers, American Heritage Center, University of Wyoming (Parkinson Papers).

29. On Chamberlain and Parkinson talks: *Program, American Association for Labor Legislation, Seventh Annual Meeting . . . December 30–31, 1913* (n.p., c. 1914), 2–3. On Parkinson's work with the Bureau: Parkinson to Henry Bruère, 8 March 1909; Parkinson to Dr. William H. Allen, 1 September 1909, Parkinson Papers. Parkinson's obituary: *New York Times*, 18 June 1958, 31: 2. "a laboratory . . .": "A Laboratory of Legislation and Administration," manuscript copy, 1912? LDBR Archives. "through careful . . .": Thomas I. Parkinson to R. Fulton Cutting, 24 September 1913, Parkinson Papers. "bill drafting . . .": "Reminiscences of Frances Perkins," 2: 77. "seen the vision . . .": Samuel McCune Lindsay, *How to Make Child Labor Legislation More Effective*, pamphlet 197 (New York: National Child Labor Committee, 1913), 7. "administration . . .": Thomas I. Parkinson to R. Fulton Cutting, September 24, 1913, Parkinson Papers.

30. "a departure . . ." *U.S. v. Darby* 1941, 312 U.S. 100.

31. "greater . . .": Andrews, "Report of Work: 1909," *The Third Annual Meeting of the AALL, December, 28–30, 1909*, 10. "by scientific . . .": Thomas I. Parkinson, "Problems and Progress of Workmen's Compensation Legislation," *American Labor Legislation Review* 1, no. 3 (1911): 55–71. On Kent Hall on Columbia's campus as a meeting place: Samuel McCune Lindsay to John B. Andrews, 9 September 1913, reel 10, AALL Papers.

32. *The Legislative Drafting Research Fund of Columbia University in the City of New York, 1911–1971; A Brief History of the First Sixty Years* (New York: the Fund, 1972), 13; copy in LDRB Archives; also, Samuel McCune Lindsay to John B. Andrews, 9 September 1913, Lindsay Papers. Thomas I. Parkinson, *Precedents for Federal Child Labor Legislation*, pamphlet 250 (New York: National Child Labor Committee, January 1916), 3–12.

33. Overview of phosphorus poisoning: John B. Andrews, "Phosphorous Poisoning: History, Statistics and Prevention," in *Industrial Health*, ed. George M. Kober and Emery R. Hayhurst (Philadelphia:. Blakiston's, 1924), 526–30; also David A. Moss, "Kindling a Flame Under Federalism: Progressive Reformers, Corporate Elites, and the Phosphorous Match Campaign of 1909–1912," *Business History Review* 68, no. 2 (1994): 244–75.

34. Andrews' report: John B. Andrews, *Phosphorous Poisoning in the Match Industry in the United States*, in U.S. Bureau of Labor Bulletin 86 (Washington, D.C., 1910), 40–47; John B. Andrews, Ph.D., Lead Poisoning in New York: Deaths from Industrial Lead Poisoning (Actually Reported) in New York State in 1909 and 1910, in Bulletin of the Bureau of Labor 95, July 1911 (Washington, D.C., 1911), 260–82. The AALL as well as organizations in England and other European countries had collected convincing evidence of the "phossy jaw" disfigurements the chemical caused in workers: Seager to Frederick L. Hoffman, 3 January 1912, Frederick Hoffman, Correspondence with the American Association for Labor Legislation, New York City, 1908–1913, Hagley Museum and Archives, Wilmington, Delaware.

35. "zealous advocacy": Mary Ritter Beard, *Woman's Work in Municipalities* (New York: D. Appleton, 1915), 50. On Farnam and Taft: Moss, "Kindling a Flame Under Federalism," 244–75; John B. Andrews to Dr. Hill, 31 March 1911, reel 5, AALL Papers. On 1912 Congressional Act: Andrews, "Phosphorous Poisoning: History, Statistics and Prevention," 526–30.

36. State structures that would limit management's share of liability were embraced by the National Association of Manufacturers: Lubove, *Struggle*, 55–56; also, Gabriel Kolko, *The Triumph of Conservatism* (New York: Free Press, 1963).

On workers' compensation: Michael B. Katz, *In the Shadow of the Poorhouse: The Social History of Welfare in America*, 10th anniversary ed. (New York: Basic Books, 1996), 197–212; Randy Bergstrom, *Courting Danger: Injury and Law in New York City, 1870–1910* (Ithaca, N.Y.: Cornell University Press, 1992); David Moss, *Socializing Social Security: Progressive-Era Economists and the Origins of American Social Policy* (Cambridge, Mass.: Harvard University Press, 1996).

37. On Wainwright Commission: State Senator Jonathan Mayhew Wainwright chaired the commission; along with Eastman and Seager, the governor's commission appointees included John Mitchell of the United Mine Workers, George W. Smith of the Lacawanna Steel Company; Otto M. Eidlitz, a governor of the Building Trades Employers Association of the City of New York, and Philip Titus, president of the Railway Trainmen's Association. *Report to the Legislature of the State of New York, by the Commissioner appointed Under Chapter 518 of the Laws of 1909 to inquire into the question of employer's liability and other matters* (Albany, N.Y.: J.B. Lyons, 1910), 1; also, *The Third Annual Meeting of the AALL, December 28–30, 1909*, 29–31. On the AALL lobbying efforts on the bill's behalf: Crystal Eastman, *Second Annual Report of the Executive Committee, New York Branch, AALL* (New York, 1910?), 3.

38. On Eastman as a founding member and first secretary of the AALL New York Branch: "American Association for Labor Legislation, New York State Branch, Oct. 23rd, 1909," reel 5, AALL Papers; also, *Meeting for the Purpose of Organizing a New York Branch of the American Association for Labor Legislation, Friday, February 19, 1909* (c. 1909) 2. Eastman's work with the AALL went back to 1908: *Proceedings of the Second Annual Meeting*, 2; also Eastman, secretary of the New York Branch of the American Association for Labor Legislation, to Samuel McCune Lindsay, 25 November 1910, Lindsay Papers. Crystal Eastman, *Employers' Liability: A Criticism Based on Facts*, publication 1 (New York: American Association for Labor Legislation, New York Branch; 1910?). Crystal Eastman, *Work-Accidents and the Law: Findings in Six Volumes, Pittsburgh Survey*, vol. 2 (New York: Charities Publication Committee, 1910).

39. "confidently expecting . . ." "feminist faith": Crystal Eastman, "Mother Worship," *The Nation*, 16 March 1927, 284. On Eastman: Blanche Wiesen Cook, "The Radical Women of Greenwich Village: From Crystal Eastman to Eleanor Roosevelt," in *Greenwich Village: Culture and Counterculture* , ed. Rick Beard and Leslie Cohen Berlowitz (New Brunswick, N.J.: Rutgers University Press, 1993), 243–51; Sylvia A. Law, "Eastman, Crystal," in *American National Biography*, ed. John A. Garraty and Mark C. Carnes (New York: Oxford University Press, 1999), 7: 245–46.

40. On Wainwright Commission findings: Eastman, *Work-Accidents and the Law*, 271, 283. "that the present . . .": Eastman, *Work-Accidents and the Law*, appendix 4, "Quotations from First Report of New York State Employers' Liability Commission," 269. "If there was little . . ." "pride in the enactment of this law.": John B. Andrews, Secretary of the AALL, "To the New York Members of the American Association of Labor Legislation," 17 December 1913; Andrews's letter in *New York State Federation of Labor, Proceedings for 1914* (unnumbered pages).

41. "Reminiscences of Frances Perkins," 1: 125.

42. On the Factory Investigating Commission: "State Factory Commission Bills," attached to the unsigned letter to Mr. Frederick Howe, 9 January 1913, box 83, file "New York State Factory Investigating Commission," Wald Papers. On Dreier: Marilyn Elizabeth Perry, "Dreier, Margaret," in *American National Biography*, 6: 895–97.

43. Testimony: *State of New York. Preliminary Report of the Factory Investigating Commission 1912* (Albany, N.Y.: Argus, 1912), Seager, 2: 422–26, 1: 754–58; "a student . . .": 3: 1722, "if there was . . .": 3: 1725; "Lindsay's testimony, 3: 1721–30; Moskowitz, 2: 99–132; Perkins's testimony, 2: 310–31; Pratt, 1: 25, 3: 1692–99; "employment of experts . . .": 2: 661, Irene Osgood Andrews, 2: 660–62. John Andrews, 2: 642–48; Josephine Goldmark, 3:1604–9; "what is . . ." and "we should . . .": 3: 1641, Pauline Goldmark, 3: 1632–42; Bruère, 3: 1968–78; Wald, 3: 1730–48. See also Abram I. Elkus to John B. Andrews on New York State Factory Investigating Commission stationery, letter of 15 September 1913; reel 10, AALL Papers; "N.Y. Industrial Disease Committee [of the AALL] March 18, 1912," reel 61, AALL Papers; "State Factory Commission Bills," attached to unsigned letter to Mr. Frederick Howe, 9 January 1913, box 83, file "New York State Factory Investigating Commission," Wald Papers.

44. "too hot about . . .": "Reminiscences of Frances Perkins," 2: 217. Lindsay and Wald quoted: Thomas Jefferson Kerr, "New York Factory Investigating Commission and the Progressives" (Ph.D. dissertation, Syracuse University, 1965), 223.

45. Elisabeth I. Perry, *Belle Moskowitz: Feminine Politics and the Exercise of Power in the Age of Alfred E. Smith* (New York: Routledge, 1992).

46. On the minimum wage: Henry R. Seager, *The Theory of the Minimum Wage* (Princeton, N.J.: Princeton University Press, 1912); Henry R. Seager, "The Minimum Wage as a Part of a Program for Social Reform," *Annals of the American Academy of Political and Social Science* 48 (July 1913): 3–12; Henry Rogers Seager, "The Theory of the Minimum Wage," *American Labor Legislation Review* 3 (February 1913): 81–91; Florence Kelley, "Minimum Wage Laws," *Journal of Political Economy* 20 (December 1912), 999–1010; Samuel McCune Lindsay, "Minimum Wage as a Legislative Proposal in the United States," *Annals of the American Academy of Political and Social Science* 48 (July 1913): 45–53; John Bates Clark, "The Minimum Wage," *Atlantic Monthly*, September 1913, 289–97. On Woolston and Van Kleeck: "New York State Factory Investigating Commission," *The Survey*, 21 March 1914, 183–84. John R. Commons and John B. Andrews, *Principles of Labor Legislation* (New York: Harper, 1916), 170–71. John R. Commons and John B. Andrews, eds., vols. 9 and 10, *A Documentary History of American Industrial Society: Labor Movement 1860–1880* (Cleveland: Arthur H. Clark, 1911).

47. Factory Investigating Commission testimony: *State of New York. Fourth Report of the Factory Investigating Commission*, 5 vols. (Albany, N.Y. : J.B Lyon, 1915), 4: 412–15, 592–921.

48. Three months before the Chicago conference, a conference had been held at New York's City Club: "Minutes of the Conference on Social Insurance, Held at the City Club, March 17 [1913]," reel 18, Greenwich House Collection, Tamiment Library, New York University. On the AALL Chicago conference: "Second Quarterly Report, 1913, American Association for Labor Legislation," typescript, reel 61, AALL Papers. The National Conference of Charities and Correction had for many years entertained papers and discussions on many aspects of social reform, but, as historian Roy Lubove has noted: "before the establishment of the American Association for Labor Legislation in 1906, social insur-

ance was not a serious subject of debate in the United States": Lubove, *The Struggle for Social Security*, 25. On the AALL and social and labor legislation, also see Skocpol, *Protecting Soldiers and Mothers*, 160–204, 248–310.

49. Broad-coverage insurance: Henry R. Seager, "Old Age Pensions," *Charities and the Commons*, 3 October 1908, 150. "be considered . . .": Rubinow, *The Quest for Security*, 237. Even while the programs and policies they promoted in the U.S. were homegrown and articulated with American accents, social scientists drew on European labor and social welfare policy and policies developed in the British Commonwealth countries of New Zealand and Australia: Peter Flora and Jens Alber, "Modernization, Democratization, and the Development of Welfare States in Western Europe," in *The Development of Welfare States in Europe and America* ed.,Peter Flora and Arnold J. Heidenheimer (New Brunswick, N.J.: Transaction Books, 1984): 37–80; Daniel T. Rogers, *Atlantic Crossings: Social Politics in a Progressive Age* (Cambridge, Mass.: Harvard University Press, 1998).

50. "noncontributory old-age pensions . . .": Skocpol, *Protecting Soldiers and Mothers*, 217.

51. On AALL and unemployment: Rubinow, *Quest for Security*, 428, 434–40. "We are beginning to . . .": John B. Andrews, "A Practical Program for the Prevention of Unemployment in America," *American Labor Legislation Review* 5 (June 1915): 173–92, cited in Lubove, *Struggle*, 147. "governmental machinery": U.S. House Committee on Labor, *National Employment Bureau . . . A Bill to Establish in the Department of Labor a Bureau to be Known as the Bureau of Employment, and for Other Purposes* Hearings, 5 June 1914 (Y4.L11:Em7/1–1) (Washington, D.C.: Government Printing Office, 1914), quote 39; see also, 10–19, 36–50. AFL reversal: Rubinow, *Quest for Security*, 432.

52. "was initiated . . ." "When . . .": Rubinow, *Quest for Security*, 207–8. On Rubinow: "vita" facing p. 2376 of his dissertation: *Studies in Workmen's Insurance: Italy, Russia, Spain; A Dissertation, submitted in partial fulfillment of the requirements for the degree of doctor of philosophy in the Faculty of Political Science, Columbia University* (New York, 1911); also "Rubinow, Isaac," *Who's Who in America: 1936–1937*. Columbia University Transcript Department records indicate Rubinow was awarded the doctorate in economics in June 1914.

53. "all coming . . .": I. M. Rubinow, *Social Insurance: With Special Reference to American Conditions* (New York: Henry Holt, 1913), iii–iv. "the standard of living . . .": Rubinow, *Social Insurance*, 490–91.

54. "Health Insurance . . .": Rubinow, *Quest for Security*, 208–9. Also on health insurance initiative: "Minutes, Committee on Social Insurance, American Association for Labor Legislation, October 14, 1915"; AALL pamphlet, *Report of Work for 1915* (c. 1915), 1, AALL Papers. "Some Activities of the American Association for Labor Legislation, for the first Quarter, 1916," notes that the AALL Health Insurance Bill was introduced in the New York and Massachusetts legislatures, and that the first legislative hearings on health insurance in the U.S. were initiated by the AALL. "Minutes of Social Insurance Committee, January 3, 1916, Faculty Club, Columbia University," for discussion of AALL support for a "cash maternity benefit" for poor women. AALL Papers.

55. "Night after night . . .": John B. Andrews, "To the Members of the Social Insurance Committee," 3 November 1916; reel 61, AALL Papers; see also "Health Insurance for Working People in New York State": *The American Association for Labor Legislation appeals to all those forward-looking patriots who have the industrial welfare of our nation at heart to support and work for the Nicoll Bill (Senate Print No. 692)*, box 82, file folder "AALL 1915–1916," Wald Papers. "aroused . . .":

Rubinow, *Quest for Security*, 213; "The opposition . . .": Rubinow, *Quest for Security*, 209. See also Skocpol, *Protecting Soldiers and Mothers*, 198–203.

56. "social insurance generally": U.S. House Committee on Labor, *Commission to Study Social Insurance and Unemployment . . . Resolution for the Appointment of a Commission to Prepare and Recommend a Plan for the Establishment of a National Insurance Fund and For the Mitigation of the Evil of Unemployment* Hearings, 6 and 11 April 1916 (Y4.L11:In7/2) (Washington, D.C.: Government Printing Office, 1916) , quote 33; also, 16–17, 32–45; John B. Andrews, "Labor Laws in the Crucible," *Journal of the National Institute of Social Sciences* 4 (1 April 1918): 81–88.

57. AFL and NAM opposition: Lloyd F. Pierce, "The Activities of the American Association for Labor Legislation," 403–4.

Chapter 7. Social Science and "the Negro Problem": From "Nordic Myth" to the NAACP and National Urban League

1. On Aryanism and Anglo-Saxonism: Reginald Horsman, *Race and Manifest Destiny: The Origins of American Racial Anglo-Saxonism* (Cambridge, Mass.: Harvard University Press, 1981), 11–15, 27–29, passim. "the Pilgrim . . .": Herbert Baxter Adams, *The Germanic Origin of New England Towns. Read Before the Harvard Historical Society, May 9, 1881,* Johns Hopkins University Studies, Historical and Political Science 1, ser. 1 (Baltimore: Johns Hopkins University, 1883), 23. "the Village Community . . .": Adams, *The Germanic Origin*, 21.

2. On eugenics and Galton: Daniel J. Kevles, *In the Name of Eugenics: Genetics and the Uses of Human Heredity* (Berkeley: University of California Press, 1985), ix, 3–19, passim. Morton's view: Samuel George Morton, *Catalogue of Skulls of Man and the Inferior Animals*, 3rd ed, (Philadelphia: Merrihew and Thompson, 1849).

3. "The national state" "Teutonic political genius": John W. Burgess, *Political Science and Comparative Constitutional Law* (Boston: Ginn, 1891), 1: 44–45. "was infected by . . .": Stephen Duggan, *A Professor at Large* (New York: Macmillan, 1943), 6. "only Nordics could . . .": "Reminiscences of Alvin Johnson" (1960), 46, CUOHROC.

4. "ignorant barbarians" "blunder-crime": John W. Burgess, *Reconstruction and the Constitution, 1866–1876* (New York: Charles Scribner's Sons, 1902), 252. "credulity . . ." "exercised an influence . . .": William Archibald Dunning, *Essays on the Civil War and Reconstruction* (New York: Macmillan, 1897), 354, 372. "there is much of this eugenics . . .": Edward T. Devine, *The Family and Social Work* (New York: Association Press, 1912), 44–45. "deprived of the support . . ." "The Negro . . .": Franklin H. Giddings, *The Principles of Sociology: An Analysis of the Phenomena of Association and Social Organization* (New York: Macmillan, 1902), 328–29. See also George M. Fredrickson, *The Black Image in the White Mind: The Debate on Afro-American Character and Destiny, 1817–1914* (1971; Middletown, Conn.: Wesleyan University Press, 1987), 314, 316. Fredrickson points out that Giddings' "consciousness of kind" theory was no clear argument against racism and segregation: "presented as the manifestation of an inescapable law of human association, it became the perfect basis for a sophisticated defense of racial segregation."

5. "anglo Saxon . . .": Charles A. Beard, "The Story of a Race," *DePauw Palladium, 18 April 1898*, quoted in Ellen Nore, *Charles A. Beard: An Intellectual Biography* (Carbondale: Southern Illinois University Press), 9–10. "slaves torn from African wilds . . ." "No fair-minded . . .": Beard, *American City Government* (New York: Century, 1912), 13, 25. "Dago" was used to refer to darker skinned peo-

ples such as Italians, Spaniards, and Portuguese; for example, *Harper's Weekly*, January 1897, 90: "Our townfolk call every black-haired, swarthy-skinned foreigner (except the Chinese) all 'dagoes.' "

6. "the prime mover in the American Eugenics Society": Kevles, *In the Name of Eugenics*, 60. "The most vital problem . . ." "the movements for . . .": Irving Fisher, "The Menace of Racial Deterioration," *Journal of the National Institute of Social Sciences* 1, no. 1 (1915): 37–38.

7. "Aryan descent will . . ." "The lower races . . .": Frederick L. Hoffman, *Race Traits and Tendencies of the American Negro* (New York: Macmillan, 1896), 326, 328.

8. On Kellogg's Race Betterment Foundation and other proponents of eugenics mentioned here: Edwin Black, *War Against the Weak: Eugenics and America's Campaign to Create a Master Race* (New York: Four Walls Eight Windows, 2003), 40–44, 87–89. "Degenerate offspring . . .": Edward T. Devine, *Misery and Its Causes* (New York: Macmillan, 1909), 241–42. "permanent . . ." "become apparent.": Devine, *The Family and Social Work*, 44–45. "normal community": Devine, *Misery and Its Causes*, 241. "normal family life": Devine, *The Family and Social Work*, 69. "direction . . .": Edward T. Devine, *"Pauperism: An Analysis,"* A Paper submitted in Section VII, Public Health and Medical Science, of the Second Pan-American Scientific Congress: Washington, December, 1915 (New York: New York School of Philanthropy, 1916), 5.

9. "charity of itself . . .": Edward T. Devine, *Organized Charity and Industry: A Chapter from the History of the Charity Organization Society of the City of New York* (New York: New York School of Philanthropy, 1915), 3–4. "a moderate exercise . . .": Devine, *Misery and Its Causes*, 241. COS committees: *The COS 16th Annual Report: From July 1897 to June 1899* (New York, 1899), 55, CSS Papers. Edward T. Devine, *Social Forces* (New York: Charities Publication Committee, 1910). Lilian Brandt, *Five Hundred and Seventy-Four Deserters and Their Families: A Descriptive Study of Their Characteristics and Circumstances* (New York: Charity Organization Society, 1905).

10. "his idea was . . .": "Reminiscences of Alvin Johnson," 46–47, CUOH-ROC. "convinced that nobody . . .": "Reminiscences of Alvin Johnson," 54. "had real anti-semitism . . .": "Reminiscences of Alvin Johnson," 67. "used his veto . . .": "Reminiscences of Alvin Johnson," 69. ". . . was a Jew.": "Reminiscences of Alvin Johnson," 69.

11. "natural communities" "savage, barbarian": Franklin Giddings, "What Is Sociology," *Bibliotheca Sacra: A Religious and Sociological Quarterly* 52 (July 1895): 466, 469–70. His first use of the term "consciousness of kind" occurred in his "Utility, Economics and Sociology," *Annals of the American Academy of Political and Social Science* 5 (November 1894): 298–404. See also Walter P. Metzger, "College Professors and Big Business Men: A Study of American Ideologies 1880–1915" (Ph.D. dissertation, State University of Iowa, 1950), 378; Giddings obituary: "Professor F. H. Giddings, Sociologist," *New York Times*, 12 June 1931. On Giddings's 1898 view on the discipline of sociology: Samuel McCune Lindsay, "The Study and Teaching of Sociology," *Annals of the American Academy of Political and Social Science,* 12 (July 1898): 1–48.

12. "The ultimate aim . . .": Franklin H. Giddings and Alvan A. Tenney, "Sociology," in *A Cyclopedia of Education*, ed. Paul Monroe (New York: Macmillan, 1913) 5: 356. "The key . . .": Franklin Giddings, "The Ethics of Social Progress," *International Journal of Ethics* (January 1893): 243–44. "If then . . .": 1908 lecture quoted in "Prof. F. H. Giddings, Sociologist," *New York Times*, 12 June 1931. "Dr. Giddings held that . . .": "Dr. F. H. Giddings: Forum Speaker, Believes

Progress Depends on Thinkers," *Bennington (Vermont) Banner*, 6 January 1922, copy in Franklin H. Giddings file, Columbia University Archives.

13. "A good part of. . . . cancer of the cheek": "Reminiscences of Alvin Johnson," 70; on the rumored duel: Louis Menand, *The Metaphysical Club: A Story of Ideas in America* (New York: Farrar, Straus, Giroux, 2001), 383. "inferior ability": Franz Boas, "The Negro and the Demands of Modern Life: Ethnic and Anatomical Considerations," *Charities*, 7 October 1905, 85. "The biological evidence . . .": Franz Boas, "The Real Race Problem," *The Crisis* 1, no. 2 (December 1910): 23. Boas's talk was first delivered at the Second National Negro Conference in May, 1910. On Boas: Melville J. Herskovits, *Franz Boas: The Science of Man in the Making* (New York: Scribner's Sons, 1953); in 1883 Boas traveled to Canada's Baffin Island where he studied Eskimos; after teaching geography at the University of Berlin briefly, he returned to Canada in 1886 to study the Bella Coola Indians in the Pacific Northwest; Herskovits, *Franz Boas*, 1, 11–12, 21, passim. Boas was on the faculty at Columbia until his retirement in 1937.

14. "how far we are justified . . ." "anatomical. . . .": Franz Boas, *The Mind of Primitive Man* (New York: Macmillan, 1911), 5, 29. I have reversed the word order of the sentence beginning "anatomical. . . ." "The old idea of . . ." ". . .types over others.": Franz Boas, "Instability of Human Types," in *Papers on Inter-Racial Problems Communicated to the First Universal Races Congress*, ed. G. Spiller (London: P.S. King, 1911), 99–103. "words quietly spoken . . .": W.E. Burghardt Du Bois, "The First Universal Races Congress," *Independent*, 24 August 1911, 401.

15. "leading anthropologists . . ." "in the light of science . . .": W. E. B. Du Bois, "The Races Congress," *The Crisis* 2, no. 5 (September, 1911): 200.

16. "There are some signs . . .": W. E. B. Du Bois, "The Negro Race in the United States of America," in Spiller, *Papers on Inter-Racial Problems*, 348–64. "a distinct feeling . . ." : Du Bois, "The Races Congress," 202. "described conditions . . .": Du Bois, "The Races Congress," 208.

17. "There was one . . .": Du Bois, "The First Universal Races Congress," 401. "unscientific to assert . . .": Du Bois, "The First Universal Races Congress," 401–3.

18. "great majority . . .": Thomas G. Dyer, *Theodore Roosevelt and the Idea of Race* (Baton Rouge: Louisiana State University Press, 1980), 109. "I would say that . . .": Woodrow Wilson to Reverend H. A. Bridgman, *Congregationalist*, 8 September 1913, quoted in Arthur S. Link, *Woodrow Wilson and the Progressive Era: 1910–1917* (New York: Harper and Row, 1954), 66.

19. New York City race riot: *New York Daily Tribune*, 26 August 1900.

20. "The riot was . . .": W. E. B. Du Bois to Miss Ovington, 28 September 1906, box 1, file folder 34, Mary White Ovington Papers, Archives of Labor History and Urban Affairs, Wayne State University. On the riot: Charles Crowe, "Racial Massacre in Atlanta, Sept. 22, 1906," *Journal of Negro History* 54 (April 1969): 150–73; also Charles Crowe, "Racial Violence and Social Reform: Origins of the Atlanta Riot of 1906," *Journal of Negro History* 53 (July 1968): 234–56.

21. Haynes obituary, *New York Times*, 10 January 1960, 87.

22. On Du Bois: David Levering Lewis, *W. E. B. Du Bois: Biography of a Race, 1868–1919* (New York, Henry Holt, 1993).

23. On Haynes at Yale Divinity School and work with the YMCA: *Eighth General Catalogue of the Yale Divinity School, Centennial Issue, 1822–1922* (New Haven, Conn.: Published by the University, 1922), 424. Courses taken at the University of Chicago: University Registrar's Records, Office of the Registrar, University of

Chicago. Columbia University Registrar records indicate that George Edmund Haynes graduated from Columbia on 5 June 1912 with a Ph.D. in Social Economy. On Haynes: Iris Carlton, "A Pioneer Social Work Educator: George Edmund Haynes" (Ph.D. dissertation, University of Maryland, 1982), 35–36, passim; Daniel Perlman, "Stirring the White Conscience: The Life of George Edmund Haynes" (Ph.D. dissertation, New York University, 1972), 16–17, 46, passim; Jesse Thomas Moore, Jr., *A Search for Equality: The National Urban League, 1910–1961* (University Park: Pennsylvania State University Press, 1981), 42–44; Haynes obituary, *New York Times*, 10 January 1960, 87; "Tribute to George E. Haynes," *New York Times*, 16 January 1960, 20; "Haynes, George Edmund," in *Who's Who in America: 1948–1949.*

24. "My plan . . .": W. E. B. Du Bois to Samuel McCune Lindsay, 10 July 1896, Lindsay Papers. On Du Bois's coming to Philadelphia: W. E. B. Du Bois to Dr. S.M. Lindsay, 20 May 1896. See also Du Bois to Lindsay, 12 October 1896; Du Bois to Lindsay, 20 October 1896; Du Bois to Lindsay, undated, ca. November 1896; Du Bois to Lindsay, 15 November, 1896, Lindsay Papers. "for aid . . .": W. E. B. Du Bois, *The Philadelphia Negro: A Social Study* (Philadelphia: Published for the University of Pennsylvania, 1899), iii. "If Lindsay . . .": quoted from Du Bois's *Autobiography* in Lewis, *W. E. B. Dubois*, 179. "delicacy of . . .": Du Bois, *The Philadelphia Negro*, xiv.

25. "interest, advice . . .": George Edmund Haynes, *The Negro at Work in New York City: A Study in Economic Progress*, Columbia University Faculty of Political Science Studies in History, Economics, and Public Law 49, 3, no. 124 (New York: Longmans, Green, 1912), 7.

26. "the function . . .", "pauperism . . .", "Negro suffrage", "final word", "the duty . . .": Du Bois, *The Philadelphia Negro*, xvii–xx; "That the Negro . . .": 389; "It is right and proper . . .": 390; "a delicate avoidance . . .", and "a generous granting": 397.

27. "The Negro problem was in my mind . . .": W. E. Du Bois, *Dusk of Dawn: An Essay Toward an Autobiography of a Race Concept* (New York: Harcourt, Brace, 1940), 58. "had something of . . .": Lewis, *W. E. B. Dubois*, 193. "More than any other . . .": Lewis, *W. E. B. Dubois*, 202. "an unambiguously . . .": Adolph L. Reed, Jr., *W. E. B. Du Bois and American Political Thought: Fabianism and the Color Line* (New York: Oxford University Press, 1997), 46.

28. "*Sociology* is the science that . . .": W. E. B. Du Bois, "A Program for Social Betterment," four-page pamphlet (1898?) in *Pamphlets and Leaflets by W. E. B. Du Bois*, ed. Herbert Aptheker (New York: Kraus-Thomson, 1986.), 9–10. A paragraph introduces the text as follows: "Abstract of paper read before the First Sociological Society of Atlanta, Georgia, by W. E. B. Du Bois, Ph.D., professor of Economics and History in Atlanta University."

29. On Du Bois and his views on government: Francis L. Broderick, *W. E. B. Du Bois: Negro Leader in a Time of Crisis* (Stanford, Calif.: Stanford University Press, 1954), 35; Thomas C. Holt, "The Political Uses of Alienation: W. E. B. Du Bois on Politics, Race, and Culture, 1903–1940," in *Intellectuals and Public Life: Between Radicalism and Reform*, ed. Leon Fink, Stephen T. Leonard, and Donald M. Reid (Ithaca, N.Y.: Cornell University Press, 1996), 236–56.

30. "I could not lull . . .": Du Bois, *Dusk of Dawn*, 51; quoted in Reed, *Du Bois and American Political Thought*, 45.

31. "Testimony of Prof. W. E. Burghardt Du Bois, University of Atlanta," in *Reports of the Industrial Commission on Immigration, and on Education* (Washington, D.C.: Government Printing Office, 1901), 5: 159, 175. "from private . . .": "The

Training of Negroes for Social Power," originally published in *The Outlook*, 17 October 1903; reproduced in *The Oxford W. E. B. Du Bois Reader*, ed. Eric J. Sundquist (New York: Oxford University Press, 1996), 357.

32. "an expert in . . .": Samuel McCune Lindsay to W. E. B. Du Bois, May 1907, reel 2, image 383, Du Bois Papers, Fisk University, Nashville, Tenneses. "I was amazed . . .": *The Correspondence of W. E. B. Du Bois*, vol. 1, *Selections, 1877–1934*, ed. Herbert Aptheker (Amherst: University of Massachusetts Press, 1973), 1: 123.

33. "good books . . .": Du Bois, *The Horizon: A Journal of the Color Line* 1 (June 1907): 14. "supplied intellectual . . .": Lewis, *W. E. B. Du Bois*, 352.

34. "I would . . .": Du Bois to Isaac Max Rubinow, 17 November 1904, in *The Correspondence of W. E. B. Du Bois*, 1: 82. "a well-mannered . . .": Lewis, *W. E. B. Du Bois*, 347. In 1912 W. E. B. Du Bois was a member of the Socialist Party. He carried a card in that year (affixed with membership dues stamps for the year): "Socialist Party Card of Membership . . . New York Local," box 2, file folder "Correspondence 1893–1906," Du Bois Papers.

35. "talented tenth" "thinking classes": W. E. B. Du Bois, *The Souls of Black Folk* (1903; Boston: Bedford Books, 1997), 70, 100. See also W. E. B. Du Bois, "The Training of Negroes for Social Power," *Outlook*, 17 October 1903.

36. "The problem of social . . .": George Edmund Haynes, "Co-Operation with Colleges in Securing and Training Negro Social Workers for Urban Conditions," *Proceedings of the National Conference of Charities and Corrections*, June 1911 (Fort Wayne, Ind.: Press of Fort Wayne, 1911), 385; quoted in Carlton, "A Pioneer Social Work Educator," 104. Fellow at the Bureau: Perlman, "Stirring the White Conscience," 53.

37. "for more grounding . . ." "as a basis . . .": George Edmund Haynes, "The Birth and Childhood of the National Urban League" twelve typescript pages (1960), 4, ser. 5, box 25, file folder, "George Edmund Haynes," National Urban League Papers, Library of Congress.

38. "Why not . . .": Guichard Parris and Lester Brooks, *Blacks in the City: A History of the National Urban League* (Boston: Little Brown, 1971), 26. On Haynes and Devine, Seligman, and Lindsay: A. R. Schorer to George Edmund Haynes, 13 January 1910 (in which Schorer notifies Haynes that Devine has appointed Haynes to membership on the board of the Negro Fresh Air Conference), box 3, file folder 8, Haynes Papers, Fisk University. Seligman to Haynes, 3 June 1912, and Seligman to Haynes 31 May 1912, box 3, file folder 8; Haynes to Lindsay, 13 May 1912, also Lindsay to Haynes, 31 January 1916, box 2 file folder 12, Haynes Papers.

39. Obituary of Mrs. G. E. Haynes, *New York Times*, 27 October 1953; obituary of George Edmund Haynes, *New York Herald Tribune*, 10 January 1960.

40. "Negro men and women" and "economics, sociology . . .": "Minutes of the First Meeting of the Committee on Urban Conditions Among Negroes Held at the School of Philanthropy, September 29, 1910," 2, Minutes of the Executive Board 1910–1960, National Urban League Papers, Library of Congress.

41. Haynes explained the new program he was establishing at the 1911 National Charities and Correction annual conference: George Edmund Haynes, "Cooperation with Colleges in Securing and Training Negro Social Workers for Urban Conditions," *Proceedings of the National Conference of Charities and Correction*, 384–87. At Fisk, his course, "History of the Negro in America," assigned Benjamin Brawley's *Short History of the American Negro* (New York: Macmillan, 1913), Du Bois's *Suppression of the African Slave-Trade to the United States of America, 1638–*

1870 (New York: Longmans, Green, , 1896), and for his course, "The Negro Problem," he assigned his own *The Negro at Work in New York City* and Du Bois's *Philadelphia Negro*. Lecture notes for some of Haynes's classes can be found in box 4, file folder 7, Haynes Papers. For required texts: Fisk, *Bulletin* (1912), 49; Fisk, *Bulletin* (1913), 49, Fisk University Archives.

42. "economic and social justice . . .": George Edmund Haynes, "The Basis of Race Adjustment," *The Survey*, 1 February 1913, 569.

43. "permanent progress . . .": Haynes, "The Basis of Race Adjustment," 569–70.

44. "Competition . . .": Haynes, "The Basis of Race Adjustment," 569.

45. "my childhood's . . .": quoted in Gilbert Osofsky, "Progressivism and the Negro: New York 1900–1915," *American Quarterly* 16, no. 2, pt. 1 (Summer 1964): 160. "impartial history . . .": quoted in Carolyn Wedin, *Inheritors of the Spirit: Mary White Ovington and the Founding of the NAACP* (New York: John Wiley, 1998), 27.

46. "saw the struggle . . .": Mary White Ovington, *The Walls Came Tumbling Down* (New York: Harcourt, Brace, 1947), 10; Wedin, *Inheritors*, 45. See also Mary White Ovington, "Reminiscences," *Afro-American*, 24 September 1932, 24.

47. "to be of some . . ." ". . . nothing about the people you want to work with,'": Ovington, *The Walls Came Tumbling Down*, 13; Ovington, "Reminiscences," *Afro-American*, 1 October 1932, 24. On Ovington's work as a fellow at Greenwich House: "Report of Director Feb. 15, [1905] For Preceding Month," in "Cooperative Social Settlement Society," folder, Box 110, CSS Papers.

48. "genuinely sympathetic . . .": Ovington, *The Walls Came Tumbling Down*, 13; Wedin, *Inheritors*, 57. The list of members of the Greenwich House Committee on Social Investigation appears in *Charities*, 16 July 1904, 740–41.

49. "a refutation of . . .": Mary White Ovington, *Half a Man: The Status of the Negro in New York* (New York: Longmans, Green, 1911), vii. As Boas put it in the foreword, "Miss Ovington's description of the status of the Negro in New York City is based on a most painstaking inquiry into his social and economic conditions, and brings out in the most forceful way the difficulties under which the race is laboring, even in the large cosmopolitan population of New York."

50. "Du Bois enthusiast": Ovington, "Reminiscences," *The Afro-American*, 1 October 1932, 24. "the economic opportunities . . .": Ovington to Du Bois, 10 June 1904, in *The Correspondence of W. E. B. Du Bois*, 1:76.

51. "I am sorry . . .": Du Bois to Ovington, 8 November 1904, box 1, file folder 34, Ovington Papers. Du Bois wrote Ovington on the stationery of the "Ninth Annual Conference, 1904, on the Negro." "I believe in Liberty . . .": *Independent*, October 1904.

52. Wedin, *Inheritors*, 59–62.

53. "where John Brown . . .": Mary White Ovington, "Reminiscences," *Afro-American*, 8 October 1932, 24.

54. On race riot: "Atlanta Outdone," *Independent*, 20 August 1908, 442–43; Lewis, *W. E. B. Du Bois*, 388. On Walling: Mary White Ovington, "William English Walling," *The Crisis* 43 (Nov. 1936): 335; "Walling, William English," *Who's Who in America: 1926–1927*, "race hatred . . .": William English Walling, "Race War in the North," *Independent*, 3 September 1908, 530. "Within the hour": Ovington, *The Walls Came Tumbling Down*, 102; "in a New York Negro tenement . . .": Ovington's, six-page unpaginated pamphlet, *How the National Association for the Advancement of Colored People Began* (New York: National Association for the Advancement of Colored People, 1914), 1. On Ovington, White, and Moskowitz's meeting: Lewis, *W. E. B. Du Bois*, 389; Ovington, *How the National Association*

. . . *Began*, 2. Ovington's account of the founding of the NAACP is reprinted in *The Crisis* 8, no. 4 (August 1914): 184–88. Ovington held a variety of leading positions in the Association for almost four decades, serving as NAACP chair from 1919 to 1932 and as treasurer from 1932 to 1947. Allen Davis notes that Ovington, Moskowitz, and Walling were all associated with the settlement house movement: Davis, *Spearheads for Reform*, 101–2. On Moskowitz's education: J. Salwyn Schapiro, "Henry Moskowitz: A Social Reformer in Politics," *The Outlook*, 26 October 1912, 446–47.

55. "a call for . . .": Ovington, *How the National Association . . . Began*, 2–3.

56. "The celebration of the . . .": Charles Flint Kellogg, *NAACP: A History of the National Association for the Advancement of Colored People*, (Baltimore: Johns Hopkins University Press, 1967), 1: 297–99; this copy of the "Call" is from the Oswald Garrison Villard Papers, Houghton Library, Harvard University. Mary White Ovington's copy of the Call, *How the National Association for the Advancement of Colored People Began* varies slightly, and lists fifty-three signers, instead of sixty.

57. *Charities*, 7 October 1905, 11–88.

58. "National Negro Committee, 500 Fifth Avenue, New York," undated, printed sheet, part 1, reel 1, microfilm, Papers of the NAACP (Frederick, Md.: University Publications of America, 1982). On activism of Dewey, Seligman, and James B. Reynolds: "Visitors to the Conference on the Status of the Negro, May 30, 1909," file "NAACP," box 27, Wald Papers.

59. On Ovington's personal connections: Wedin, *Inheritors of the Spirit*, 107.

60. Du Bois's count: W. E. Burghardt Du Bois, "National Committee on the Negro," *The Survey*, 12 June 1909, 408. "a visible bursting . . .": W. E. Burghardt Du Bois, "National Committee on the Negro," *The Survey*, 12 June 1909, 407. "the white people": Ovington, *How the National Association . . . Began*, 5. On the meeting and public forum: Du Bois, "National Committee on the Negro," 407–9. On Lincoln's 1860 address at Cooper Union: Lincoln, *Collected Works of Abraham Lincoln*, ed. Roy P. Basler (New Brunswick, N.J.: Rutgers University Press, 1953–1955), 3: 522–50.

61. "emphasizing . . .": Du Bois, "National Committee on the Negro," 407. On conference speakers: *Proceedings of the National Negro Conference 1909: New York, May 31 and June 1* (reprint New York: Arno Press, 1969), 22–66. "'the term . . .'" ". . . races exist." *Proceedings of the National Negro Conference 1909*, 14, 21.

62. "The more scientific . . .": "Address of Edwin R. A. Seligman, Professor of Political Economy at Columbia University," in *Proceedings of the National Negro Conference 1909*, 68. ". . . good fight." *Proceedings of the National Negro Conference 1909*, 69–70. "in the matter of this scientific . . .": "Address of John Dewey, Professor of Philosophy, Columbia University," *Proceedings of the National Negro Conference 1909*, 71–72.

63. On conference speakers: *Proceedings of the National Negro Conference 1909*, 74–210.

64. *New York Sun, Brooklyn Eagle*, and *Washington Post*, 31 May 1909, 1 June 1909. Copies in scrapbook 4, Edwin R.A. Seligman Papers, RBML.

65. "great central committee . . ." ". . . no color line.": Du Bois, "National Committee on the Negro," 408–9.

66. Second conference: E. R. A. Seligman to Jacob H. Hollander on 28 February 1910 on "National Negro Committee: Sub-Committee on Plans and Organization" letterhead, Jacob H. Hollander Papers, Johns Hopkins University. Franz Boas, "The Real Race Problem," *The Crisis* 1, no. 2 (December 1910). "Report

of the Preliminary Committee on Permanent Organization," 1910? part 1, reel 1, Papers of the NAACP. In 1908 Russell published *Why I Am a Socialist.* He ran for governor of New York in 1910 and 1912 on the Socialist party ticket, in 1913 for mayor of New York, and in 1914 for U.S. Senate. John E. Milholland was also union representative at the *New York Tribune.* He led the effort to investigate the events that led to the dismissal of the black soldiers at Brownsville, Texas, in 1907. Membership in the "General Committee": *The Crisis* 1, no. 1 (November 1910): 12–13.

67. "N.A.A.C.P. Lecture Recital": *The Crisis* 1, no. 2 (December 1910), 25. "voice of surpassing . . ." *Chicago Defender,* 21 October 1911, quoted in Lisa Pertillar Brevard, *A Biography of E. Azalia Smith Hackley, 1867–1922: African American Singer and Social Activist* (New York: Edwin Mellen Press, 2001), 60. Mary Simkhovitch subsequently served on the National Urban League executive board: Minutes of the Executive Board 1910–1960, Minutes of the National Urban League for 17 June, 1919, and 4 February 1920, National Urban League Papers.

68. "What is . . .": "What is the National Association for the Advancement of Colored People?" *The Crisis* 1, no. 2 (December 1910): 16.

69. "in the opinion of . . .": *The Crisis* 4, no. 3 (July 1912): 119–20.

70. On the League: Parris and Brooks, *Blacks in the City,* 7.

71. "the born criminal . . ." ". . . until 10 o'clock": Frances A. Kellor, *Experimental Sociology, Descriptive and Analytical: Delinquents* (New York: Macmillan, 1901), 3, 257–58. See also Kellor, "The Criminal Negro: A Sociological Study," *Arena* 25, 1–5 (January–May 1901): 59–68, 190–97, 308–16, 419–28, 510–20, in which she argued that "the domestic life and the training surrounding the child" was the key to unlocking the motive toward crime. Though treated barbarically during slavery and in the thirty years since emancipation, blacks had, in Kellor's view, escaped barbarism, but barely: "there is no race outside of barbarism where there is so low a grade of domestic life, and where the child receives so little training, as among the negroes." Casare Lombroso, *L'homme criminel: Atlas* (Rome: Bocca Frères, 1888).

For an alternative reading of Kellor's work on "The Criminal Negro": Elizabeth Lasch-Quinn, *Black Neighbors: Race and the Limits of Reform in the American Settlement House Movement, 1890–1945* (Chapel Hill: University of North Carolina Press, 1993), 17–19. On Kellor: Ellen Fitzpatrick, *Endless Crusade: Women Social Scientists and Progressive Reform* (New York: Oxford University Press, 1990), 130–65, passim.

72. On League activities: "Report of the National League for the Protection of Colored Women—September 1912," box 4, file folder 20, Haynes Papers; also S. W. Layten, "The Servant Problem," *Colored American* 12 (January 1907): 13–17. "the Negro women . . .": *Bulletin of the Inter-Municipal Committee on Household Research* (March 1906): 3–4. Commission reprimands and activities: National League for the Protection of Colored Women, *Annual Report* (November 1910), cited in Parris and Brooks, *Blacks in the City,* 8–10.

73. "a square deal . . .": quoted in Osofsky, "Progressivism and the Negro: New York 1900–1915," 166. On social centers, trade schools, employment locator service: *Charities and Commons,* 23 June 1906, 378.

74. On Bulkley: Parris and Brooks, *Blacks in the City,* 11; *Annual Catalog of Wesleyan University, 1886–87* (Middletown, Conn.: Pelton and King, 1886), 10; *Alumni Record of Wesleyan University* (Middletown, Conn.: Pelton and King, 1931), 341.

75. "responded favorably to my . . .": George Edmund Haynes, "The Birth

and Childhood of the National Urban League," 6–7. Splitting his time: "Minutes of the First Meeting of the Committee on Urban Conditions Among Negroes Held at the School of Philanthropy, September 29, 1910." Minutes of the Executive Board 1910–1960, 2–3, National Urban League Papers.

76. Work of the Urban League: Parris and Brooks, *Blacks in the City*, 40–41, 71, 88.

77. "a long stride . . .": Haynes, "The Basis of Race Adjustment," 569. "making every effort . . .": "National League On Urban Conditions Among Negroes Report of the Director [George E. Haynes] for June, July, August and to 22 September 1913, ser. 5, file folder "George Edmund Haynes," box 25, National Urban League Papers.

78. "Meeting of the Executive Committee of the Committee on Urban Conditions Among Negroes, Friday 31 March 1911, at New York School of Philanthropy," box 4, file folder 18, Haynes Papers.

79. "the State Department . . .": Nancy J. Weiss, *The National Urban League: 1910–1940* (New York: Oxford University Press, 1974), 67.

80. "to promote . . .": "Constitution, National League on Urban Conditions Among Negroes" (n.d.), National Urban League Papers; quoted in Weiss, *National Urban League*, 71. On tenements, playgrounds, housing, and businesses: Parris and Brooks, *Blacks in the City*, 65, 131.

Chapter 8. "Our Ideas Will Become Common Currency": Social Science Political Engagement in the Election of 1912 and Its Aftermath

1. "The product of . . .": "Addressed the Ladies: Miss Frances Kellor Spoke on Woman's Suffrage Last Sunday," *Coldwater (Michigan) Daily Courier,* 13 August 1912. My thanks to Ellen Fitzpatrick for helping me tracking down this source; see also Ellen Fitzpatrick, *Endless Crusade: Women Social Scientists and Progressive Reform* (New York: Oxford University Press, 1990), 147. "our little committee . . .": Samuel McCune Lindsay to Oscar S. Straus, 13 November 1912, Lindsay Papers. "The men and women . . .": *The Survey,* 24 August 1912, 668. "our ideas will . . .": Henry Moskowitz to Lillian Wald, August 2, 1912, Wald Papers; quoted in Allen F. Davis, "The Social Workers and the Progressive Party, 1912–1916" *American Historical Review* 69, no. 3 (1964): 678; see also Walter I. Trattner, "Theodore Roosevelt, Social Workers, and the Election of 1912: A Note," *Mid-America: An Historical Quarterly* 50, no. 1 (January 1968): 65.

2. "Perhaps we felt . . .": Jane Addams, *The Second Twenty Years at Hull-House* (New York: Macmillan, 1930), 31. "The libraries . . .": Samuel John Duncan-Clark, *The Progressive Movement: Its Principles and Its Programme,* intro. Theodore Roosevelt (Boston: Small, Maynard, 1913), xii, 296.

3. "I am of course . . .": James Bronson Reynolds to Theodore Roosevelt, 29 June 1912, Theodore Roosevelt Papers, Library of Congress (hereafter TRLC). The two-page typed letter discusses details of "our new party." "I have not . . .": Henry Bruère to Theodore Roosevelt, 29 July 1912; Bruère to Roosevelt, 3 September 1912, TRLC. On several occasions, William Allen also wrote to Roosevelt expressing his support. "I thought that you . . .": E. R. A. Seligman to Theodore Roosevelt, 28 July 1912, TRLC. See also John Allen Gable, *The Bull Moose Years: Theodore Roosevelt and the Progressive Party* (New York: Kennikat Press, 1978), 166–67; John Allen Gable, "The Bull Moose Years: Theodore Roosevelt and the Progressive Party, 1912–1916" (Ph.D. dissertation, Brown University, 1972), 1: 136. "If there is . . .": Mary Simkhovitch to Theodore Roosevelt, 15 August 1912,

TRLC. Roosevelt replied with a short note: "I appreciate your letter so much that I must send you a line of personal acknowledgement." Theodore Roosevelt to Mrs. V. G. Simkhovitch, 21 August 1912, TRLC. "my husband . . .": Mary Kingsbury Simkhovitch to Roosevelt, 28 May 1913, TRLC.

4. *Proceedings of the National Conference of Charities and Correction at the Thirty-Sixth Annual Session Held in the City of Buffalo, New York, June 9th to 16th, 1909* (Fort Wayne, Ind.: Press of Fort Wayne, 1909), 118, 163, 138, 193–98, 213–25.

5. Lindsay, Seager, and Devine articles: *Proceedings of the Academy of Political Science in the City of New York* 2, no. 2 (January 1912): 149–52, 173–79, 87–89. Clark and Seager articles: *Proceedings of the Academy of Political Science in the City of New York* 2, no. 4 (July 1912): 71–74, 75–78.

6. On the platform and its various names: Davis, "The Social Workers and the Progressive Party," 674; Allen F. Davis, *Spearheads for Reform: The Social Settlements and the Progressive Movement, 1890–1914* (1967; New Brunswick, N.J.: Rutgers University Press, 1984), 194–217. "The Progressive Party . . . devoted": "A Comparison of the Platforms of the Progressive Party and of the Social Scientists—as to Social and Industrial Justice," printed pamphlet (n.p., 1912?), 1, Theodore Roosevelt Collection, Houghton Library, Harvard University (hereafter TRC, Harvard). "Having read the . . .": "A Comparison of the Platforms," 4. Lindsay as delegate: New York Board of Elections certificate for the 19th Assembly District, County of New York, certifying Lindsay's election as a Progressive Party delegate, Lindsay Papers, box 112. On Kirchwey's taking copies to the party: Paul U. Kellogg, "The Industrial Platform of the New Party," *The Survey*, 24 August 1912, 668–70.

7. Lindsay was a member of the National Conference of Charities and Corrections (NCCC) executive committee that year, and, although not formally listed as a member of the Standards of Living and Labor committee was nevertheless an active member. As he recalled, "I helped draft the so-called Cleveland declaration, presented at the Cleveland (Ohio) NCCC meeting. It asked all political parties and platforms that year to take a definite stand on social questions, such as child labor, workmen's compensation, and social welfare." Samuel McCune Lindsay, "Recollections of Theodore Roosevelt" (April 1955), 45, CUOHROC.

8. For lists of the members of the Standards of Living and Labor Committee for 1912 see NCCC *National Bulletin* 57, March, 1912, 20; "A Comparison of the Platforms," 1. Also see "Social Standards for Industry: A Platform," by "The Committee on Standards of Living and Labor," offprint in John A. Kingsbury Papers, box A34, file folder "Progressive Party," Library of Congress. On Andrews's presence at the conference see John B. Andrews to Prof. Henry R. Seager, 21 June 1912, reel 7, AALL Papers. As Andrews said at the NCCC convention, "there is no greater problem before us in this country today than the promotion of the comfort, health and safety of those who labor in factory, workshop and mine.": John B. Andrews, "The Industrial Disease Problem," *Proceedings of the National Conference of Charities and Correction at the Thirty-Ninth Annual Session Held in Cleveland, Ohio, 12–19 June 1912* (Fort Wayne, Ind.: Press of Fort Wayne, 1912), 424–29. On Frankel's membership in the AALL: "American Association for Labor Legislation, New York State Branch, Oct. 23rd, 1909," reel 61, AALL Papers. On Cohen: Jameson W. Doig, "Creating a New Institution: Julius Henry Cohen and the Public Authority Movement," *Portfolio: Port Authority, New York and New Jersey* 1, no. 4 (Winter 1988): 36. Among other activities, Cohen had worked closely with Louis Brandeis on the "Protocol of Peace" for the garment

workers in 1910: Doig, "Creating a New Institution," 38. On Margaret Dreier Robins's work with Frances Kellor: Fitzpatrick, *Endless Crusade,* 138. On Robins's enthusiastic support for Roosevelt and the new party—she was elected to the executive board of the Illinois state Progressive party—see Mary E. Dreier, *Margaret Dreier Robins* (New York: Island Press, 1950), 88–90; Floyd Dell, *Women as World Builders: Studies in Modern Feminism* (Chicago: Forbes, 1913), 65–75. V. Everit Macy's fortune derived in part from holdings in Rockefeller oil; he was not part of the R.H. Macy family that owned Macy's Department Store.

Otey, after attending Bryn Mawr College and a year's graduate training at the University of Chicago, had gone on to three years of social science graduate study at the University of Berlin, and earned her Ph.D. there in 1907; in Otey's view, safe and healthy working conditions, along with workmen's compensation, "are things which concern the welfare of society as a whole, and should be under the direct supervision of the State": *Bulletin of the U.S. Bureau of Labor Statistics* (Washington, D.C.: Government Printing Office, 15 May 1913), 76.

9. "The welfare of society": "Social Science Platform" reproduced in "A Comparison of the Platforms," 2.

10. Kirk H. Porter and Donald Bruce Johnson, *National Party Platforms: 1840–1968* (Urbana: University of Illinois Press, 1970), 175–82.

11. Porter and Johnson, *National Party Platforms,* 175–79.

12. Porter and Johnson, *National Party Platforms,* 175–79. President Roosevelt asked Seligman to serve on a presidential committee on statistical work in the federal government: Roosevelt to Seligman, 4 December 1908, TRLC; see also Seligman to Roosevelt, 24 February 1911; and Roosevelt to Seligman, 28 February 1911, TRLC.

13. Porter and Johnson, *National Party Platforms,* 175–82. The party's stance on immigration was drawn straight from the New York Committee on Congestion, founded five years earlier; the Committee had called for the easing of tensions in urban living caused by overcrowding in immigrant ghettos by disbursing the immigrant population into the countryside. Mary Simkhovitch, Florence Kelley, and Benjamin Marsh had organized and promoted the Committee on Congestion's agenda.

14. Porter and Johnson, *National Party Platforms,* 175–81.

15. "To me,": J. Salwyn Schapiro, "Henry Moskowitz: A Social Reformer in Politics," *The Outlook,* 26 October 1912, 449.

16. "much the most . . .": Theodore Roosevelt to the Progressive National Committee, dated at Oyster Bay, (22) June 1916, quoted in Lindsay, "Recollections of Theodore Roosevelt," 48–49.

17. "Dear Mr. President . . .": Samuel McCune Lindsay to Theodore Roosevelt, 17 August 1908, Lindsay Papers. "the best people . . .": Theodore Roosevelt to Samuel McCune Lindsay, 18 August 1908, Lindsay Papers.

18. "conferred freely": John A. Kingsbury, "Does Roosevelt Know What Social and Industrial Justice Means?" Draft of an Article for *Progress,* 14 October 1912, 4, Kingsbury Papers, box A34, file folder "Progressive Party." "what he proposed . . .": Kingsbury, "Does Roosevelt Know?" 10. "small company . . .": Paul U. Kellogg, "The Bull Moose Leader," *The Survey,* 18 January 1919, 528–29. "This report . . .": Addams, *The Second Twenty Years at Hull-House,* 27.

19. On Roosevelt's classes at Harvard: Theodore Roosevelt, *The Letters of Theodore Roosevelt,* ed. Elting E. Morison (Cambridge, Mass.: Harvard University Press, 1951), 1: 25–26. "all of the courses . . .": John W. Burgess, *Reminiscences of an American Scholar* (New York: Columbia University Press, 1934), 213. "work of

sociological . . .": Theodore Roosevelt, "Reform Through Social Work—Some Forces That Tell for Decency in New York City," *McClure's*, March 1901, 450–51.

20. "a government for . . .": Herbert Croly, *The Promise of American Life* (1909; New York: Macmillan, 1914), 170, 265–88. On Croly: David W. Levy, *Herbert Croly of the New Republic: The Life and Thought of an American Progressive* (Princeton, N.J.: Princeton University Press, 1985), 74–75, passim. "I do not know . . .": Theodore Roosevelt, *The New Nationalism* (1910; Englewood Cliffs, N.J.: Prentice-Hall, 1961), 11. "social workers . . .": *The Outlook*, October 1912, 294–95.

21. "wise and moderate . . .": Theodore Roosevelt, "What a Progressive Is," Address at Louisville, Kentucky, 3 April 1912, in Theodore Roosevelt, *Progressive Principles* (London: Effingham Wilson, 1913), 11. "Our purposes are . . .": preface to Duncan-Clark, *The Progressive Movement*, xiii. "All we wish . . .": Roosevelt, *The New Nationalism*, 54. "All that I ask . . .": *The New Nationalism*, 57; praise of trade unions: 99; "a rate of wages . . .": *The New Nationalism*, 107.

22. "The Progressive party recognizes . . .": David Levering Lewis, *W. E. B. Du Bois: Biography of a Race, 1868–1919* (New York: Henry Holt, 1993), 422.

23. Spingarn's presentation of Du Bois's plank: "Roosevelt in Huff over Party Snarls," *New York Times*, 6 August 1912. "heartily indorsed": "Roosevelt in Huff over Party Snarls"; see also Lewis, *W. E. B. Du Bois*, 422–23.

24. Dueling delegations: *The Letters of Theodore Roosevelt*, vol. 7, *The Days of Armageddon: 1909–1914* (Cambridge, Mass.: Harvard University Press, 1954), 584, n. 1.

25. "represent absolutely . . .": Theodore Roosevelt to Julian La Rose Harris, 1 August 1912, *The Letters of Theodore Roosevelt*, 7: 588; "In this country . . ." "essential that . . ." "I believe . . .": Roosevelt to Harris, 1 August 1912, 7: 585.

26. "Our objective . . ." "to speak only . . .": Roosevelt to Harris, 1 August 1912, *The Letters of Theodore Roosevelt* 7: 586. "We are now . . .": Roosevelt to Harris, 1 August 1912, 7: 587.

27. "When told that . . ." "Chairman of the negro . . ." "lifted her voice . . .": "Roosevelt in Huff over Party Snarls." "several others, who . . .": Jane Addams, "The Progressive Party and the Negro," *The Crisis* 5 (November 1912): 30–31; "Roosevelt in Huff over Party Snarls."

28. "I asked myself most . . .": Addams, "The Progressive Party and the Negro."

29. "The charge of . . .": *Attitude of the Progressive Party Toward the Colored Race: Colonel Roosevelt's Reply to a Query at the Progressive National Convention; His Letter to Julian Harris, of Atlanta, and the Statement of All the Negro Delegates in the Convention* (New York: Stoddard-Sutherland Press, 1912), 15. The pamphlet's claim "All the Negro Delegates in the Convention" was technically true, but it masked the fact that those delegates who had disagreed with Roosevelt's exclusion of black delegates from the South had walked out of the convention.

30. "We've been with . . .": "Roosevelt in Huff over Party Snarls." "No definite conclusion . . .": "Minutes of Meeting of the Council of Chairmen, April 21, 1913," 3, which notes: "Mr. Kellogg then precipitated a good deal of discussion by laying before the Council the suggestion of Professor Spingarn that some Department of the Progressive national Service should occupy itself with the consideration of the negro problem," Lindsay Papers; "possibility of an . . .": Lewis, *W. E. B. Du Bois*, 421.

31. "stirred by . . .": "Speech of Jane Addams Seconding the Nomination of Theodore Roosevelt," TRC, Harvard..

32. "I prized your action . . .": Theodore Roosevelt to Jane Addams, 8 August 1912, TRC, Harvard.

33. "those humanitarian measures . . .": "To the Women Voters of the United States from the Women in Political Bondage: Vote the Progressive Ticket to Make Us Free," TRC, Harvard.

34. "in every district . . .": Frances A. Kellor, "What Women Can Do for the Progressive Cause—Why They Should Do It," *The Progressive Bulletin*, September 1912, 7.

35. "I presume . . .": Henry R. Seager to John B. Andrews, 18 August 1912, reel 7, AALL Papers. On Wilson and Brandeis as AALL vice presidents: *American Labor Legislation Review* 1, no. 1 (1911): frontispiece; also, Henry R. Seager President to Hon. Charles F. Brown, 14 March 1911, on AALL letterhead that lists Wilson and Brandeis as vice presidents: reel 5, AALL papers. On Wilson as governor: Frederick Austin Ogg, *National Progress, 1907–1917* (New York: Harper and Brothers, 1918), 204–5, 210. "not only . . .": *The Outlook*, 5 November 1910, 521. "truly a progressive" "a man of progressive views": *The Outlook*, 19 November 1910, 607–8.

36. "it was clear to us . . .": Oscar King Davis, *Released for Publication: Some Inside Political History of Theodore Roosevelt and His Times, 1898–1918* (Boston: Houghton Mifflin, 1925), 318.

37. On Wilson: Arthur S. Link, *Woodrow Wilson and the Progressive Era, 1910–1917* (New York: Harper and Brothers, 1954), 8–9, passim. On Wilson's attacks against Roosevelt: Link, *Woodrow Wilson*, 20–24. Democratic platform: Porter and Johnson, *National Party Platforms*, 168–75. "rural toryism": George E. Mowry, *Theodore Roosevelt and the Progressive Movement* (1946; New York: Hill and Wang, 1960), 277.

38. "The history of liberty . . .": Mowry, *Theodore Roosevelt*, 277. "that every law . . .": *New York Sun*, 16 September 1912, quoted in Mowry, *Theodore Roosevelt*, 277. "We are for liberty. . . ." *New York Times*, 31 October 1912, quoted in Mowry, *Theodore Roosevelt*, 278.

39. On Debs: Nick Salvatore, *Eugene V. Debs: Citizen and Socialist* (Urbana: University of Illinois Press, 1982), 149–50, passim. "utterly incapable . . .": Porter and Johnson, *National Party Platforms*, 188–90.

40. On the activism of Dewey and others in 1913: The pamphlet "Progressive Service of the National Progressive Party" (January 1913) lists Dewey as a member of the Bureau of Education, Lindsay Papers, box 112. Dewey's codirector was Philadelphia-based educationalist A. Duncan Yocum. The typescript of "A Meeting of the Educational Committee of the National Progressive Party," held 3 April 1913, notes on p. 7, "Resolved that Professors Yocum and Dewey be designated as a special committee to consider and undertake the organization of a Division of Public Education under the Bureau of Education." That same month, the "Report of the Director of the Bureau of Education. April, 1913," 16, noted that the division "under the direction of Professors John Dewey and A. Duncan Yocum, has assumed an importance scarcely expected a month ago." On Dewey's vote for Debs see Robert B. Westbrook, *John Dewey and American Democracy* (Ithaca, N.Y.: Cornell University Press, 1991), 194.

41. On Wald's support for Roosevelt: "Reminiscences of Eugene Meyer" (1961), 72.CUOHROC.

42. "the so called . . .": John W. Burgess, "What is Real Political Progress?" 24 October 1912, typescript, 5, Nicholas Murray Butler Papers, box GBI-38, Columbia University.

43. "should push forward along . . .": Nicholas Murray Butler, *What Is Progress in Politics?* (An Address Before the Commercial Club, Chicago, Illinois, December 14, 1912), 10, 22, Nicholas Murray Butler Papers, box GBI-27.

44. "the sufferings of . . . ." "That was why . . .": "Reminiscences of Frances Perkins," 2: 187–88. George Perkins, the leading financial backer of the Progressive party reportedly contributed $262,500 to the party; Frank Munsey, owner of a string of newspapers, contributed $229,250: "Survey of the World," *Independent*, 5 December 1912, 1276.

45. "Proposed Platform of the National Progressive Party of the State of New York," typescript, Lindsay Papers, folder "Progressive Party." On Seligman's handwritten comments (with Lindsay's penciled-in comment "From Prof. E. R. A. Seligman"): Lindsay Papers, box 112. On the final state platform: *Annotated Edition of the Platform of the National Progressive Party of the State of New York* (Adopted by the State Convention, Syracuse, N.Y., September 5, 1912), 4, 32, 42; see also *National Progressive Party of the State of New York, State Platform, Adopted by the State Convention, Syracuse, N.Y., Sept. 5, 1912* (n.p., n.d.).

Lindsay's draft of the state platform included planks on "Industry and Labor"; Moskowitz emphasized direct primaries, the need for a State Constitutional convention, home rule for cities, and woman suffrage; Folks's draft emphasized social welfare. Lindsay, "Tentative Draft of a Platform for the National Progressive Party in the State of New York," typescript initialed "S. M. L."; Henry Moskowitz, "Proposed Platform of the National Progressive Party of the State of New York," typescript, "Moskowitz 1st draft," both in Lindsay Papers, box 112..

46. *Annotated Platform*, 10–11, 13, 32, 33, 35–36, 39–40, 48.

47. "I have tried to get you . . .": William H. Hotchkiss to Dr. Henry Moskowitz, August 28, 1912. See also, Hotchkiss to Dr. Henry Moskowitz, 18 August 1912, on "your proposed draft of the platform . . ."; Moskowitz to Hotchkiss, August 24, 1912, in Lindsay Papers Box 112.

48. "We are not opposed . . .": "Progressives are Gathering for Convention," *Troy Times*, 3 September: Scrapbooks, vol. 6, E. R. A. Seligman Papers, RBML; see also Seligman's "Address on Moving the Resolution for Acceptance of the Platform," Scrapbooks, vol. 6.

49. On Goodnow and the party: "Progressive Party" folder, box 24, Frank J. Goodnow Papers, Johns Hopkins University. On Goodnow as one of fourteen members of the party's Legislative Committee: *Statement as to the Official Proposal of the National Progressive Party in the State of New York for a Minimum Wage Act* (n.p.: Legislative Committee of the National Progressive Party in the State of New York, April 1913), 16.

Henry Bruère to Theodore Roosevelt, 29 July 1912, TRLC. Bruère also wrote Roosevelt, 3 September 1912, on Bureau of Municipal Research stationery, "I should very much like to have you interested in the work of the Bureau of Municipal Research," and enclosed a copy of his book *The New City Government*, TRLC. William Allen also wrote to Roosevelt expressing his support: William H. Allen to Theodore Roosevelt, 16 December 1912; William H. Allen to Theodore Roosevelt, 23 December 1912, in which he noted he was sending Roosevelt a copy of his *Modern Philanthropy*. Roosevelt responded with a note on 27 December 1912: "I look forward to receiving that copy of 'Modern Philanthropy.' I certainly shall agree with it in all essentials." TRLC.

50. "intellectual polish,": "Reminiscences of Frances Perkins," 2: 257; "with fire . . .": Mary Kingsbury Simkhovitch, *Neighborhood: My Story of Greenwich House* (New York: W.W. Norton, 1938), 77. On Moskowitz: J. Salwyn Schapiro, "Henry Moskowitz: A Social Reformer in Politics," *The Outlook*, 26 October 1912, 446–47. On Moskowitz on New York State platform subcommittee: *Annotated Edition*

of the Platform of the National Progressive Party, 2. "'industry wears out . . .'": Schapiro, "Henry Moskowitz: A Social Reformer," 447–48. Moskowitz received 2,602 votes, third behind Democrat Henry M. Goldfogle (4,592 votes), and Socialist Meyer London (3,646 votes), but ahead of Republican Alexander Wolf (839 votes): Edgar L. Murin, *The New York Red Book, an Illustrated Legislative Manual* (Albany: J.B. Lyon, 1913), 672.

51. "One of the finest . . .": Theodore Roosevelt to Mary Dreier, 4 February 1913, Mary E. Dreier Papers, box 9, folder 143, Radcliffe College; quoted in Fitzpatrick, *Endless Crusade*, 146.

52. On Kellor as the person who submitted a plan for the new committee and as its first "executive head": Addams, *Second Twenty Years at Hull-House*, 40–41. Progressive Party pamphlet, *The Progressive National Service: A Department of the Progressive Party: What It Is; What It Does; What It Means to You* (n.p., n.d.), 8. In 1913 the Progressive party could count only one governor (Hiram Johnson of California), two senators, sixteen representatives, and 250 local elected officials; in 1914 all the important Progressive party candidates (except Hiram Johnson) were defeated.

53. On membership on the "Council of Chairmen": "Minutes of Meeting of the Council of Chairmen, April 21, 1913," 1; letterhead titled "Progressive National Committee, Office of Progressive Service, Forty-Second Street Building," dated 24 May 1913; Lindsay Papers, box 112. On the committee membership: *Statement as to the Official Proposal of the National Progressive Party*, 16. Walter F. Willcox had earned the Ph.D. at Columbia in 1891 and was professor of economics and statistics at Cornell: *Who's Who in America: 1926–1927*, 2039. On Kirchwey: "National Child Life Committee, Progressive National Service, REPORT, From Dec. First, to June First [1913]"; "Minutes of Meeting of the Council of Chairmen," 2.

54. On Lindsay's initiatives and activism: *Annotated Edition of the Platform of the National Progressive Party*, 2; also, "Minutes of Progressive Service Committee. Held on Monday, September 22, 1913"; pamphlet: "The Progressive National Lyceum Service, Offers Speakers of Renown on the Social, Political and Economic Problems of the Day" (n.p., c. 1913), which lists Lindsay as a member of the Platform Committee of the Progressive National Convention; also, "The Progressive Service of the National Progressive Party," pamphlet, January, 1913, 2. During the summer of 1913, "demands made upon the Service for bills and information concerning the labor planks in the platform led the Service to place $2500 at the disposal of Prof. Lindsay for the purpose of preparing the fall program"; Frances Kellor to Lindsay, 17 September 1913, in which Kellor enclosed a copy of a report of the organization and administration of the Service: "The Progressive Service of the National Progressive Party, Jan.–Aug. 31, 1913," typescript, Lindsay Papers, box 112.

55. "keep the promises . . .": "The Progressive Service of the National Progressive Party, Jan.–Aug. 31, 1913," 2. "defined by scientific . . .": Fitzpatrick, *Endless Crusade*, 152. Progressive Service activities in pamphlet "The Progressive National Lyceum Service: Offers Speakers of Renown"; "The Progressive Service of the National Progressive Party," pamphlet, January 1913, Lindsay Papers, box 112. See also Fitzpatrick, *Endless Crusade*, 153.

56. "We have in four years . . . : "The Field of Politics," *The Outlook*, 13 September 1916, 61.

57. "So long as . . .": Walter Johnson, *William Allen White's America* (New York: Henry Holt, 1947), 218.

58. "The Bull Moose party . . .": William Allen White, *Autobiography of William Allen White* (New York: Macmillan, 1946), 512.

59. "spent a quarter . . ." "A Comparison of the Platforms of the Progressive Party and of the Social Scientists," 1.

Epilogue

1. John W. Burgess, "Private Corporations from the Point of View of Political Science," *Political Science Quarterly* 13, no. 2 (June 1898): 201.

2. "the best interests . . .": James B. Reynolds to Elihu Root, 21 November 1898, quoted in Richard Stephen Skolnik, "The Crystallization of Reform in New York City, 1890–1917" (Ph.D. dissertation, Yale University, 1964), 406.

3. "the word 'Christian' prefixed . . .": Z. Swift Holbrook, "What Is Sociology," *Bibliotheca Sacra: A Religious and Sociological Quarterly* 52 (July 1895): 470.

4. "to bring the knowledge . . .": Paul U. Kellogg, "The Spread of the Survey Idea," *Proceedings of the Academy of Political Science* 2, no. 4 (July 1912): 491.

5. "a passionate attempt to realize democracy.": Mary Kingsbury Simkhovitch, "Community Organization," typescript, 20 May 1915, 13, Greenwich House Collection, Tamiment Library, New York University.

6. "the greatest . . .": "New York . . .": *A Proposal for an Independent School of Social Science for Men and Women* (New York: Marchbanks, 1918?), 10, Archives of the New School for Social Research.

Index

Acknowledgments

In writing this book I have been assisted by the suggestions, criticisms, and encouragements of many people. A book about scholar-activists, it is the product of a community of scholarship. My chief intellectual debt is to Eric Foner who followed the evolution of this project from its beginnings. I first met Foner a quarter century ago when, as Pitt Professor of American History at Cambridge University, he delivered a lecture at E. P. Thompson's Centre for the Study of Social History at Warwick University in Coventry, England where I was studying for a master's degree. "The people's Eric," as we fondly came to call him during my years of study and teaching at Columbia University, has been an inspiration, not only in his published work and in his life of scholarly activism, but also in his many careful readings of my work and his encouragements across the years. Foner pointed me to my editor, Jeannette Hopkins. Hopkins is a superb editor, brilliant, generous, learned, incisive, precise, and demanding. We first met on a bitterly cold afternoon in the warmth of her fine eighteenth-century house by the bay in Portsmouth, New Hampshire—on New Year's Day, 2001. She has taught me much about the craft of writing since, improved this book's every page, and been a gracious—and invariably correct—guide on a multitude of issues. I owe her a debt of deepest gratitude. In turn, Hopkins introduced me to my agent, William Goodman, whose wise counsel, good cheer, and commitment to this book has been enormously important. I thank Peter Agree, social sciences editor at The University of Pennsylvania Press, for his enthusiasm, professional, and his supportive stewardship of the manuscript into press.

My interest in the matters taken up in this book date to my undergraduate and graduate years. After all this time it is a pleasure to thank Henry Abelove and Richard Ohmann of Wesleyan University; Royden Harrison and James Hinton of Warwick University; Elizabeth Blackmar, Kenneth Jackson, Alden Vaughan, and the late James Shenton of Columbia University for their instruction and encouragement.

Several scholars took the time to read and comment on all or portions of various drafts of the manuscript. I am particularly grateful to Thomas Bender, Ruth Crocker, Allen Davis, Andrew Feffer, Leon Fink, Ellen Fitzpatrick, Steve Fuller, Michael Kazin, William Keith, Jackson Lears, Dorothy Ross, Richard Rorty, Richard Cándida Smith, and Stephen Turner for their suggestions and trenchant criticisms. Kathrine Kish Sklar pointed me in the right direction at a crucial juncture. Earlier versions of various chapters benefited by readings before the Intellectual History Group at the University of Michigan, and before the Philosophy of Social Science Roundtable in St. Louis, organized by James Bohman, Paul Roth, and Alison Wylie. The summertime National Endowment for the Humanities institute, "The Idea of a Social Science," directed by Bohman and Roth, afforded me an opportunity to learn from Robert Brandom, Clifford Geertz, Thomas McCarthy, Richard Rorty, Alexander Rosenberg, Charles Taylor, Stephen Turner and a wonderful group of scholar participants.

My intellectual debt to Darren Staloff and Michael Sugrue is enormous. I not only had the good fortune to study alongside them in Columbia University's graduate history program but also to learn a great deal from each of them during the years we taught sections of Columbia's famous core curriculum in the history of ideas, "Contemporary Civilization." Together, from their different perspectives, they awakened me from my dogmatic slumbers. Early discussions with Sugrue were formative in shaping this study. Staloff has offered more than one detailed and searching reading of the manuscript and discussed its ideas with me at length every step of the way; I am ever in his debt. Peter Field, our fellow graduate student and common friend, read portions of the manuscript and offered insightful comments. James Shankland, my dear friend, discussed ideas with me in the course of pleasant spring-time hikes through California's deserts and in the hills outside Berkeley. The intellectual community afforded by Steve Deyle, Randy Bergstrom, Tim Gilfoyle, and Betty Dessants across the years deserves special thanks.

I wish to thank The Center for the Study of Philanthropy at The Graduate Center, City University of New York for its financial assistance early on, and especially The Gilder Lehrman Institute of American History for generous financial support that allowed me to complete research for the book. A year's visiting fellowship with the Humanities Research Group, University of Windsor, Ontario, Canada, offered me a welcome opportunity to revise an earlier version of the manuscript. Summertime grants from Mount Union College aided my research.

I wish to sincerely thank the staffs of the following libraries: The Bobst and Tamiment Libraries, New York University; The University Archives and Columbiana Library, The Diamond Law Library, The Rare Books and Manuscript Division, and The Oral History Research Office Collection, Columbia University; Archives and Special Collections, The City College, City University of New York; Fisk University Library, Fisk University;

Fogelman Library, New School University; The Houghton and Widener libraries, Harvard University; Special Collections, Manuscript Division, The Library of Congress; The Municipal Archives and Research Center, New York City; The New York Public Library; The Walter P. Reuther Library, Wayne State University; Rockefeller Archive Center, Pocantico Hills, North Tarrytown, New York; the Rutgers University Libraries; the Schomburg Center for Research in Black Culture, the New York Public Library; Special Collections, Sheridan Libraries, The Johns Hopkins University. Librarians at each of these libraries were invariably gracious in helping me locate materials on my visits to their collections. Robert Garland, director of the libraries at Mount Union College, a gifted librarian with a delightful knack for turning up difficult to locate sources, graciously came to my aid more than once, and I thank him and his wonderful staff for their professionalism and for the generosity of their time. My thanks, too, to Alison Anderson, Laura Giuliani, Laura Young, and the many others at Penn Press, as well as copyeditor Ellen Young and indexer Maria DenBoer, who worked in important ways to bring this book into print.

My wife, Amy Recchiuti, and our children, Jack and Elizabeth, have made my life come true, and to them I dedicate this book. (Our last name is pronounced Re-cute-tee; we are forever having to explain this, as it is an uncommon and somewhat confusing surname.)